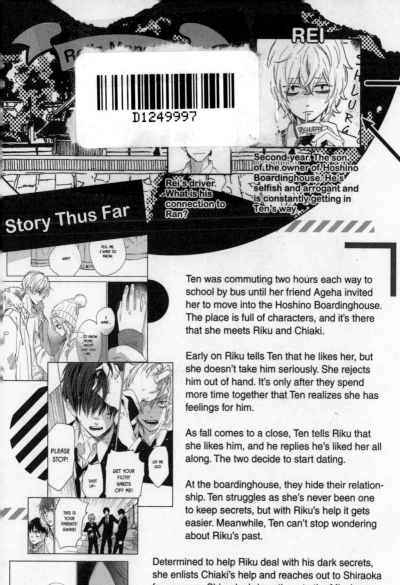

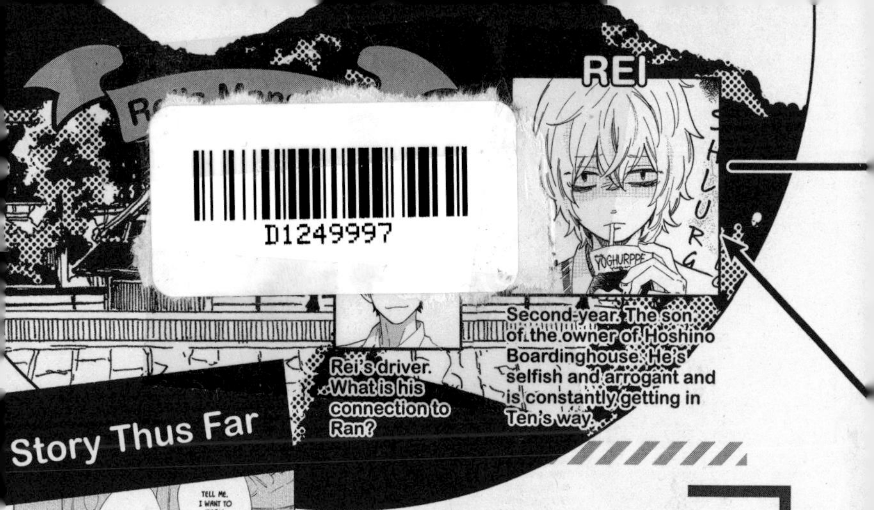
REI
SHLURG
YOGHURPPE
Second-year. The son of the owner of Hoshino Boardinghouse. He's selfish and arrogant and is constantly getting in Ten's way.
Rei's driver. What is his connection to Ran?

Story Thus Far

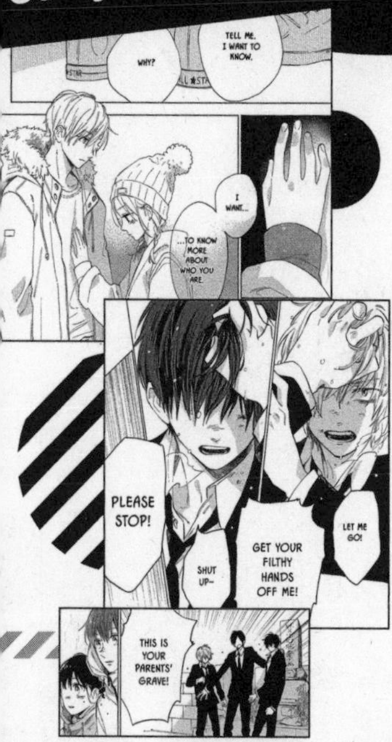
TELL ME. I WANT TO KNOW.
WHY?
I WANT...
...TO KNOW MORE ABOUT WHO YOU ARE.
LET ME GO!
PLEASE STOP!
GET YOUR FILTHY HANDS OFF ME!
SHUT UP—
THIS IS YOUR PARENTS' GRAVE!

Ten was commuting two hours each way to school by bus until her friend Ageha invited her to move into the Hoshino Boardinghouse. The place is full of characters, and it's there that she meets Riku and Chiaki.

Early on Riku tells Ten that he likes her, but she doesn't take him seriously. She rejects him out of hand. It's only after they spend more time together that Ten realizes she has feelings for him.

As fall comes to a close, Ten tells Riku that she likes him, and he replies he's liked her all along. The two decide to start dating.

At the boardinghouse, they hide their relationship. Ten struggles as she's never been one to keep secrets, but with Riku's help it gets easier. Meanwhile, Ten can't stop wondering about Riku's past.

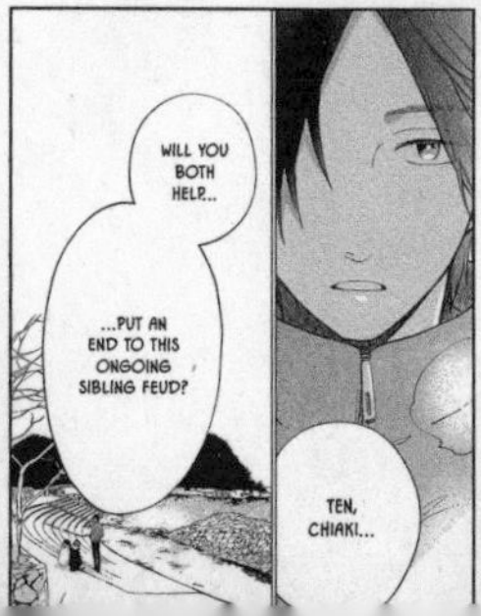
TEN, CHIAKI...
WILL YOU BOTH HELP...
...PUT AN END TO THIS ONGOING SIBLING FEUD?

Determined to help Riku deal with his dark secrets, she enlists Chiaki's help and reaches out to Shiraoka for answers. Shiraoka brings them to the Mizuhara family grave, and they witness Riku and the insolent Rei in a fistfight.

Shiraoka tells them that Riku and Rei are brothers, though not by blood. He then asks Chiaki and Ten to help put an end to their ongoing sibling feud.

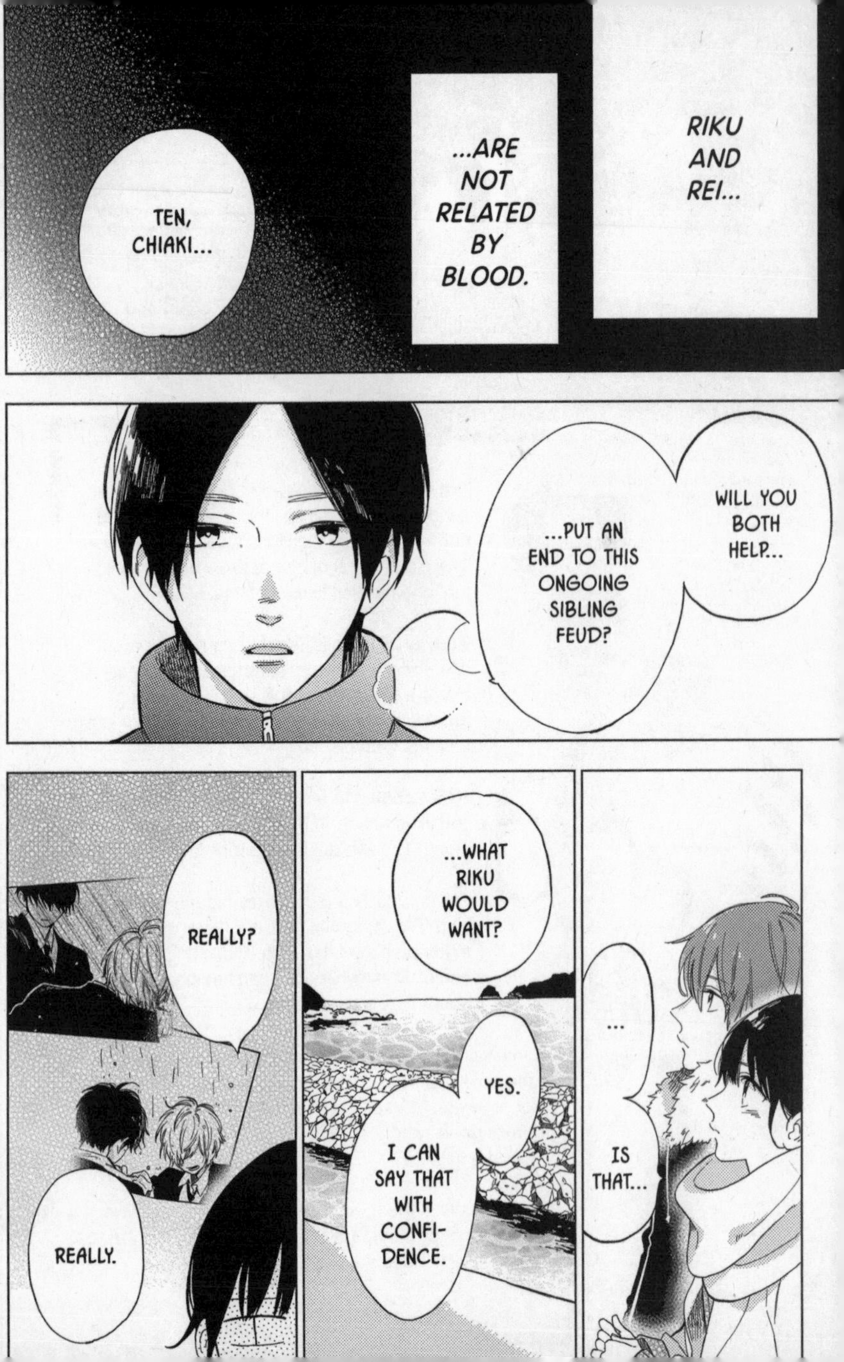
RIKU AND REI...
...ARE NOT RELATED BY BLOOD.
TEN, CHIAKI...
WILL YOU BOTH HELP...
...PUT AN END TO THIS ONGOING SIBLING FEUD?
...
IS THAT...
...WHAT RIKU WOULD WANT?
YES.
I CAN SAY THAT WITH CONFI-DENCE.
REALLY?
REALLY.

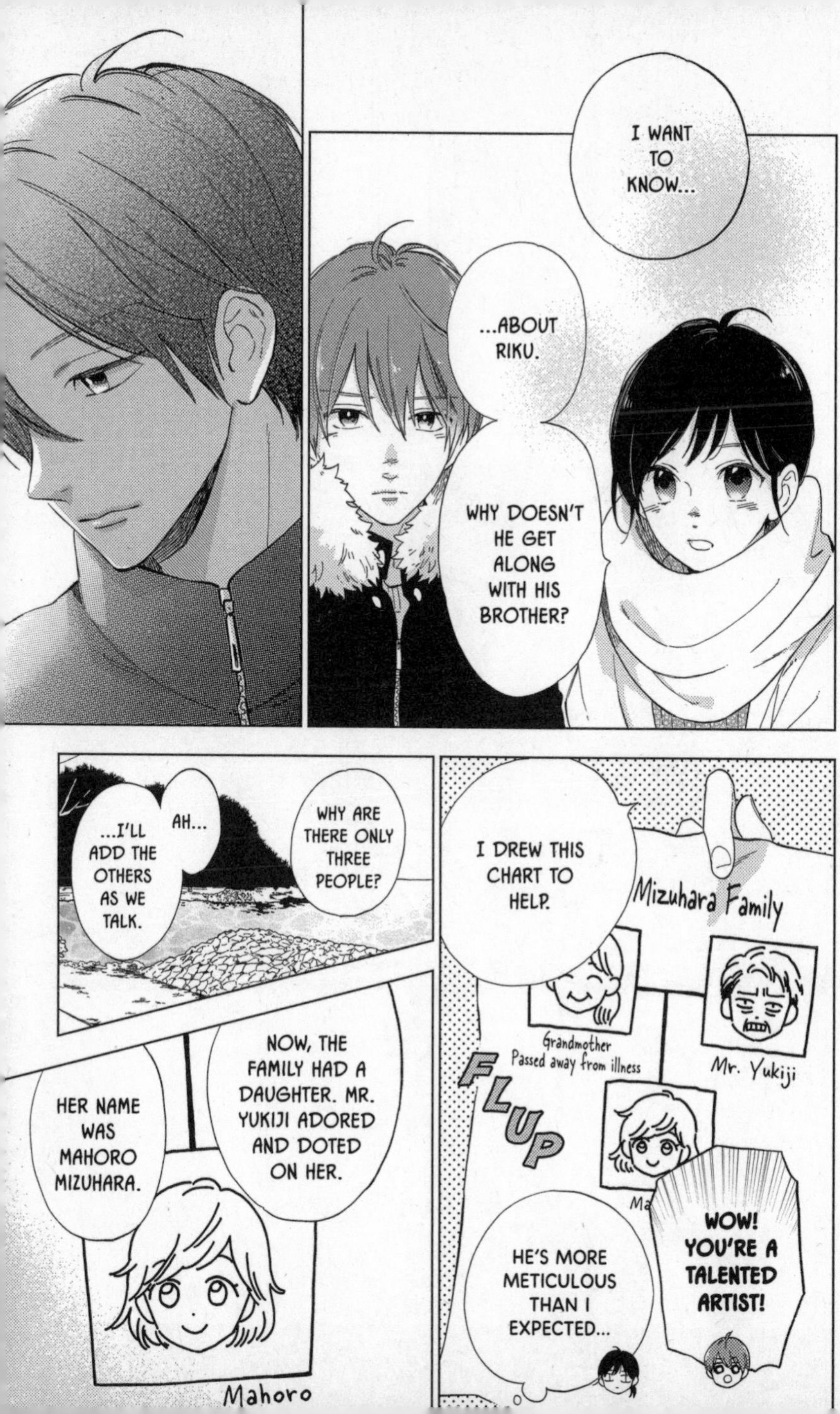
I WANT TO KNOW...
...ABOUT RIKU.
WHY DOESN'T HE GET ALONG WITH HIS BROTHER?
I DREW THIS CHART TO HELP.
Mizuhara Family
Grandmother
Passed away from illness
Mr. Yukiji
FLUP
WOW! YOU'RE A TALENTED ARTIST!
HE'S MORE METICULOUS THAN I EXPECTED...
WHY ARE THERE ONLY THREE PEOPLE?
AH...
...I'LL ADD THE OTHERS AS WE TALK.
NOW, THE FAMILY HAD A DAUGHTER. MR. YUKIJI ADORED AND DOTED ON HER.
HER NAME WAS MAHORO MIZUHARA.
Mahoro

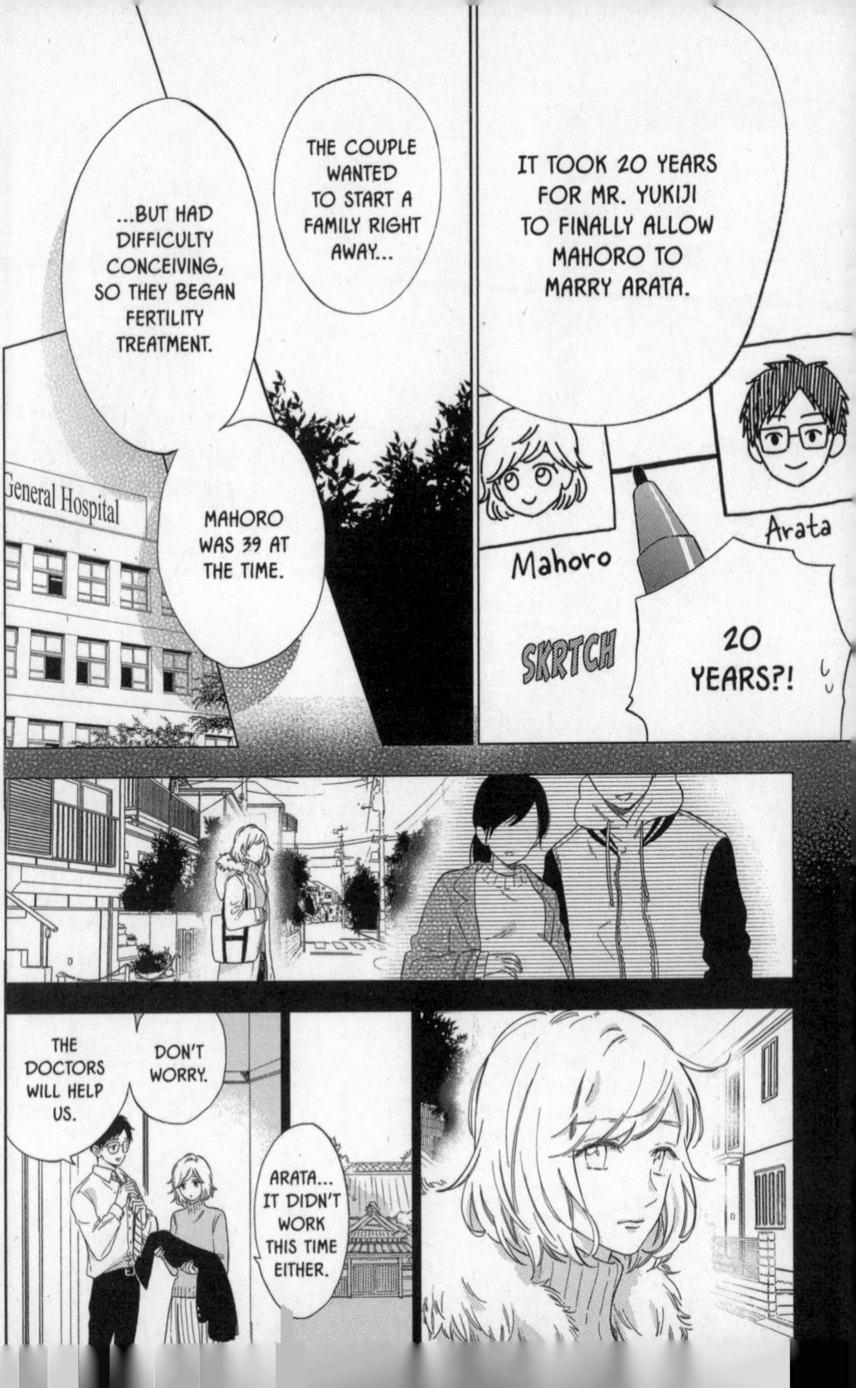
IT TOOK 20 YEARS FOR MR. YUKIJI TO FINALLY ALLOW MAHORO TO MARRY ARATA.
Arata
Mahoro
SKRTCH
20 YEARS?!
THE COUPLE WANTED TO START A FAMILY RIGHT AWAY...
...BUT HAD DIFFICULTY CONCEIVING, SO THEY BEGAN FERTILITY TREATMENT.
General Hospital
MAHORO WAS 39 AT THE TIME.
ARATA... IT DIDN'T WORK THIS TIME EITHER.
DON'T WORRY.
THE DOCTORS WILL HELP US.

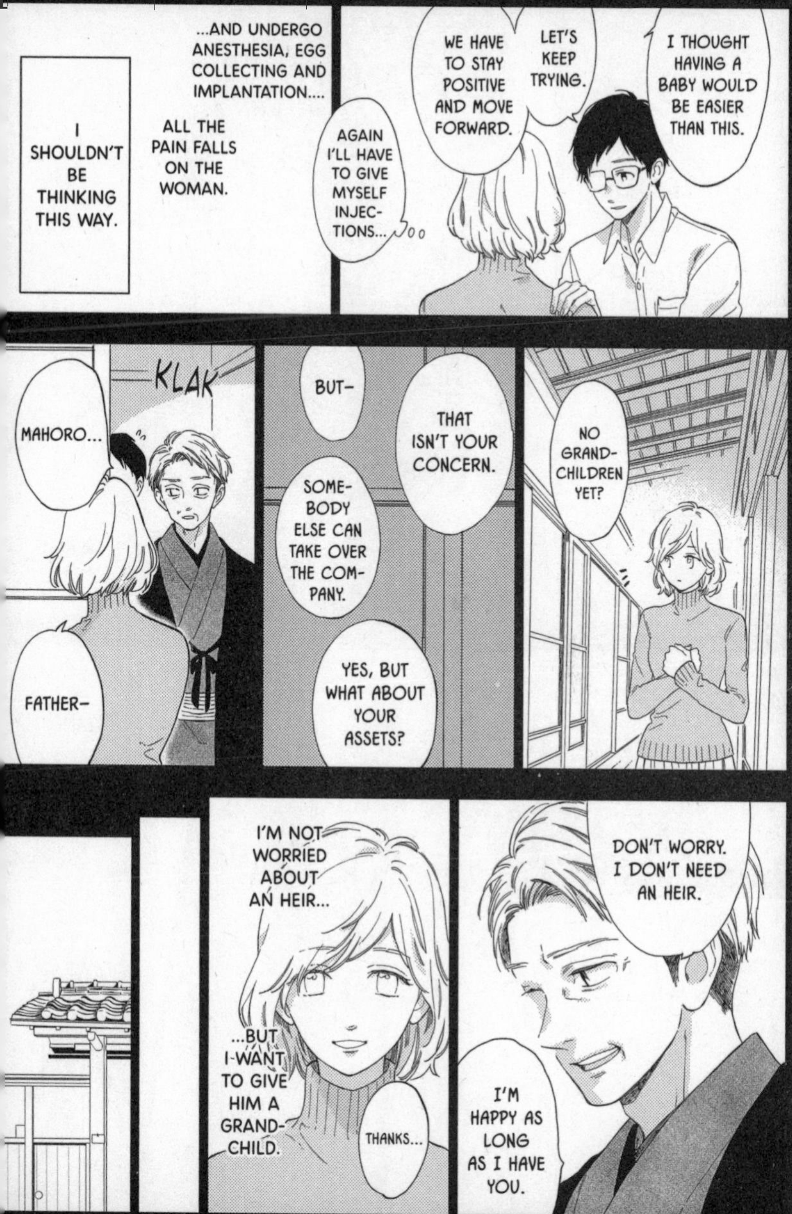
I THOUGHT HAVING A BABY WOULD BE EASIER THAN THIS.
LET'S KEEP TRYING.
WE HAVE TO STAY POSITIVE AND MOVE FORWARD.
AGAIN I'LL HAVE TO GIVE MYSELF INJECTIONS...
...AND UNDERGO ANESTHESIA, EGG COLLECTING AND IMPLANTATION....
ALL THE PAIN FALLS ON THE WOMAN.
I SHOULDN'T BE THINKING THIS WAY.
NO GRANDCHILDREN YET?
THAT ISN'T YOUR CONCERN.
BUT—
SOMEBODY ELSE CAN TAKE OVER THE COMPANY.
YES, BUT WHAT ABOUT YOUR ASSETS?
KLAK
MAHORO...
FATHER—
DON'T WORRY. I DON'T NEED AN HEIR.
I'M HAPPY AS LONG AS I HAVE YOU.
I'M NOT WORRIED ABOUT AN HEIR...
...BUT I WANT TO GIVE HIM A GRANDCHILD.
THANKS...

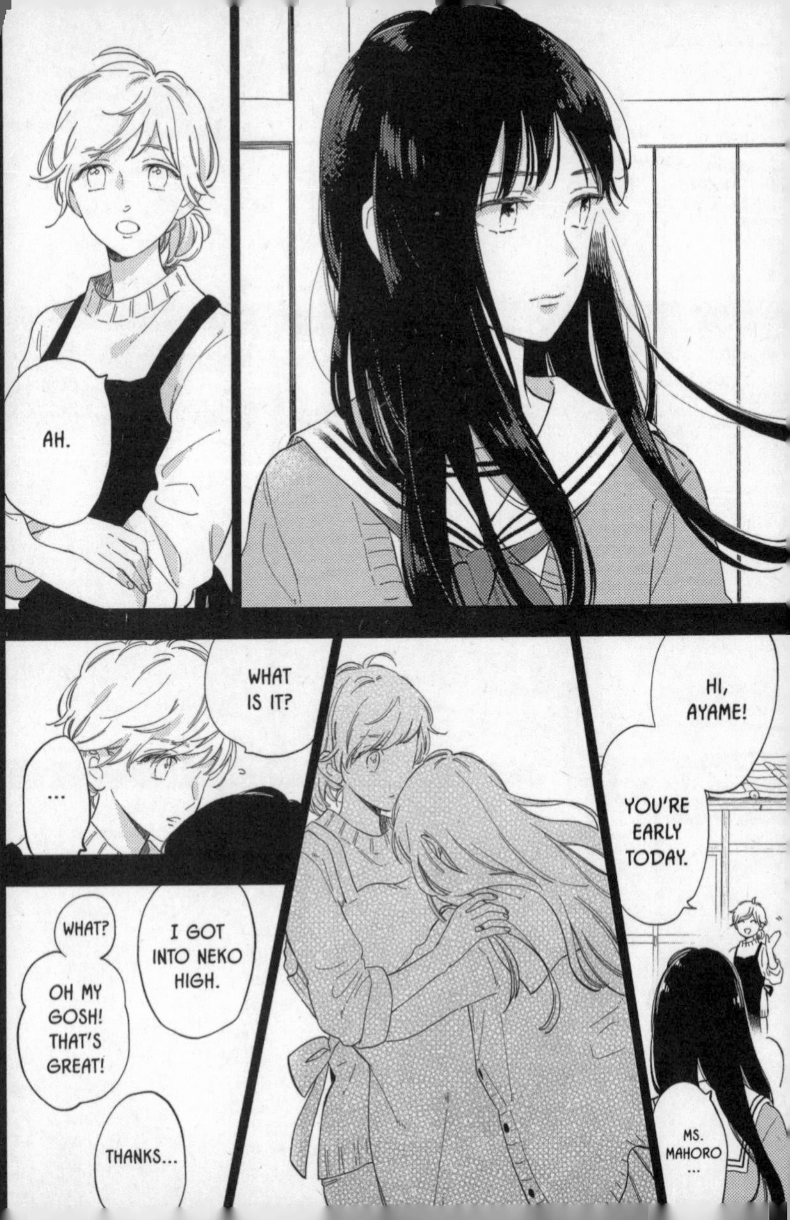
AH.
HI, AYAME!
YOU'RE EARLY TODAY.
MS. MAHORO...
WHAT IS IT?
...
I GOT INTO NEKO HIGH.
WHAT?
OH MY GOSH! THAT'S GREAT!
THANKS...

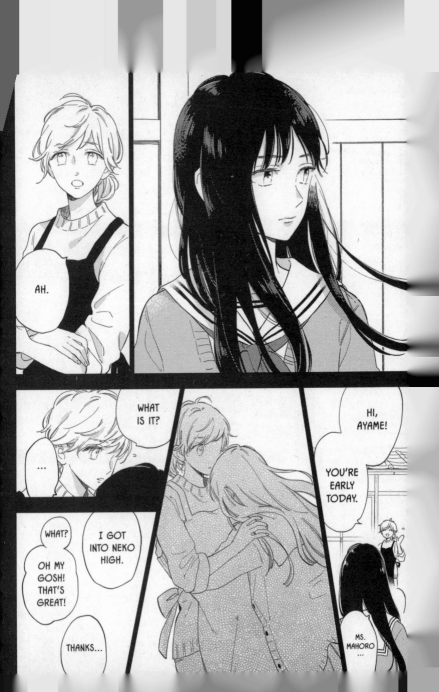

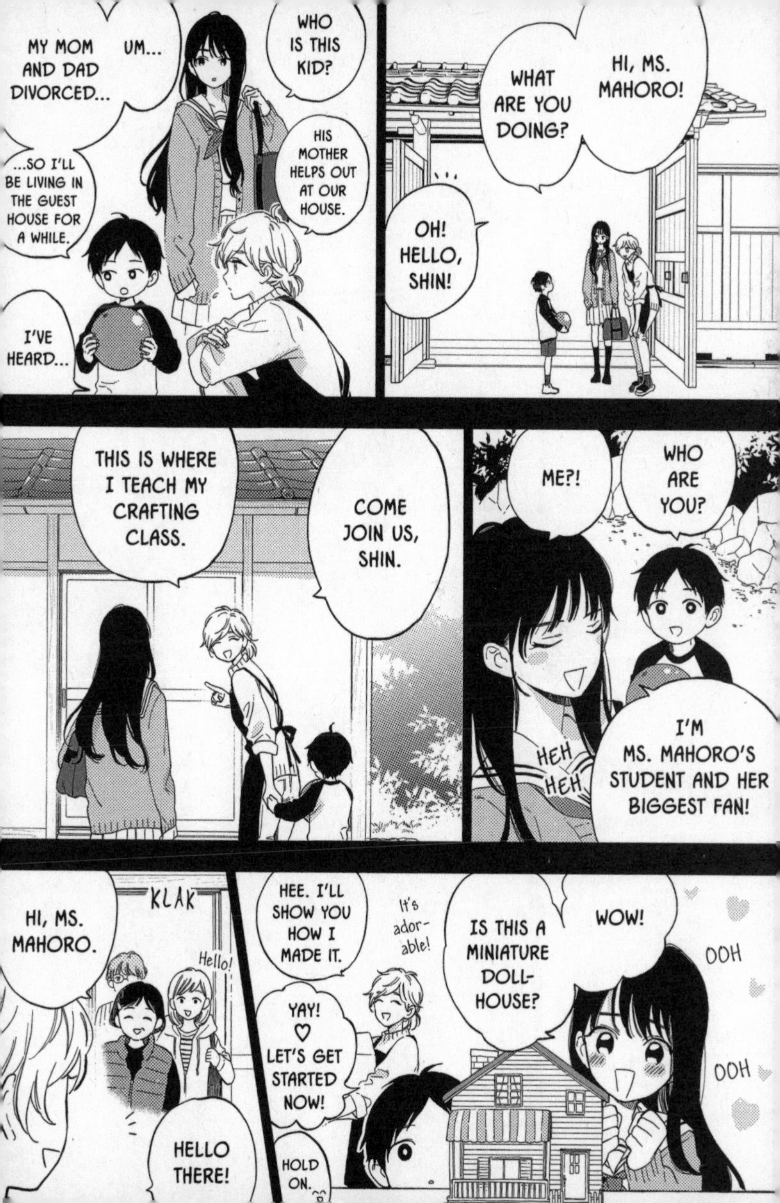
HI, MS. MAHORO!
WHAT ARE YOU DOING?
OH! HELLO, SHIN!
WHO IS THIS KID?
HIS MOTHER HELPS OUT AT OUR HOUSE.
UM...
MY MOM AND DAD DIVORCED...
...SO I'LL BE LIVING IN THE GUEST HOUSE FOR A WHILE.
I'VE HEARD...
WHO ARE YOU?
ME?!
HEH HEH
I'M MS. MAHORO'S STUDENT AND HER BIGGEST FAN!
COME JOIN US, SHIN.
THIS IS WHERE I TEACH MY CRAFTING CLASS.
WOW!
OOH
OOH
IS THIS A MINIATURE DOLL-HOUSE?
It's adorable!
HEE. I'LL SHOW YOU HOW I MADE IT.
YAY! ♡ LET'S GET STARTED NOW!
HOLD ON.
KLAK
HI, MS. MAHORO.
Hello!
HELLO THERE!

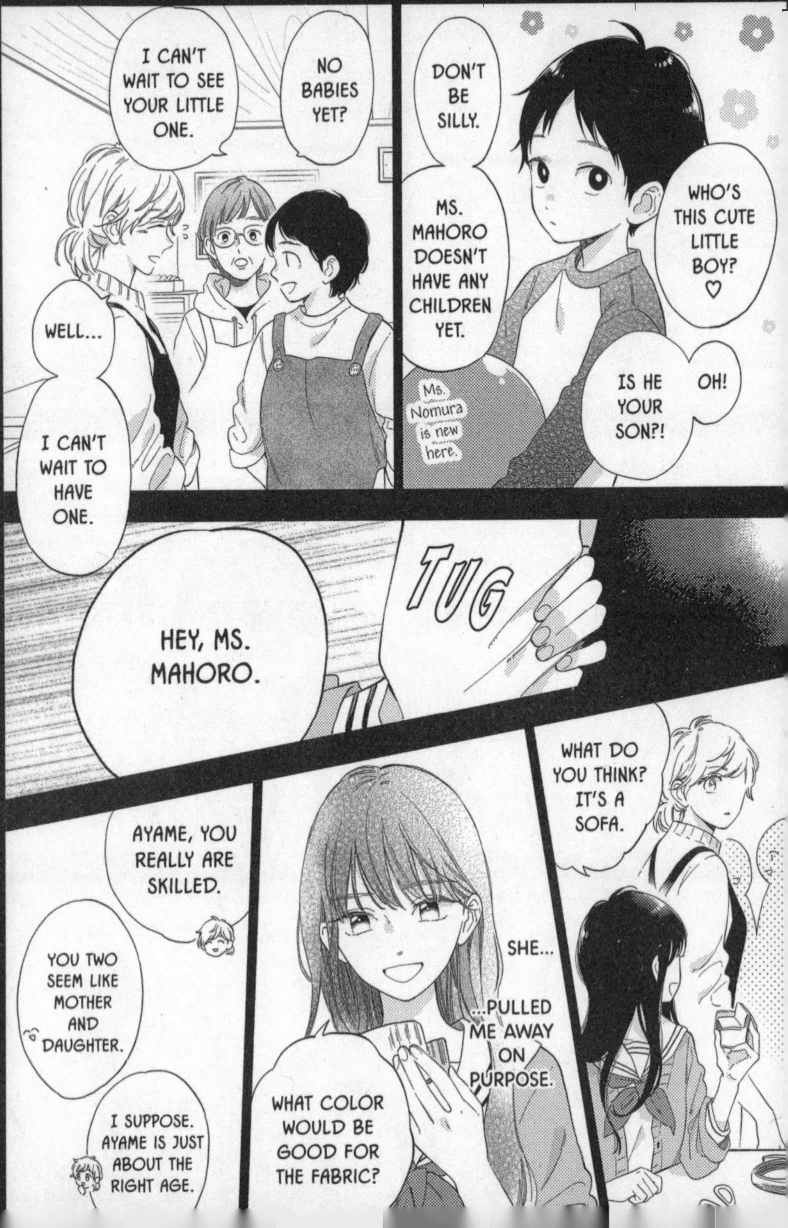
WHO'S THIS CUTE LITTLE BOY? ♡
OH!
IS HE YOUR SON?!
DON'T BE SILLY.
MS. MAHORO DOESN'T HAVE ANY CHILDREN YET.
Ms. Nomura is new here.
NO BABIES YET?
I CAN'T WAIT TO SEE YOUR LITTLE ONE.
WELL...
I CAN'T WAIT TO HAVE ONE.
TUG
HEY, MS. MAHORO.
WHAT DO YOU THINK? IT'S A SOFA.
SHE...
...PULLED ME AWAY ON PURPOSE.
WHAT COLOR WOULD BE GOOD FOR THE FABRIC?
AYAME, YOU REALLY ARE SKILLED.
YOU TWO SEEM LIKE MOTHER AND DAUGHTER.
I SUPPOSE. AYAME IS JUST ABOUT THE RIGHT AGE.

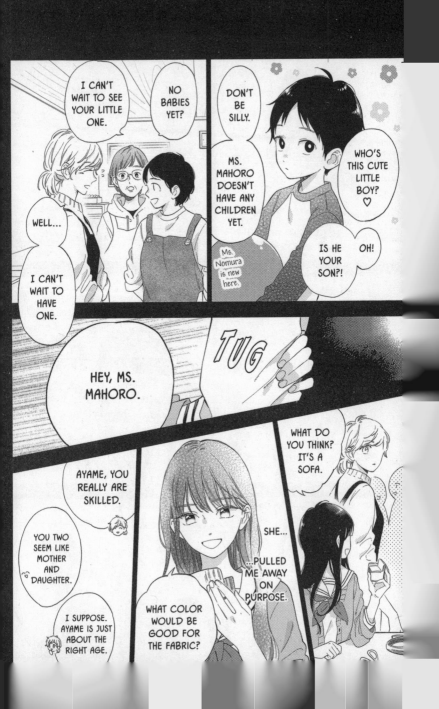

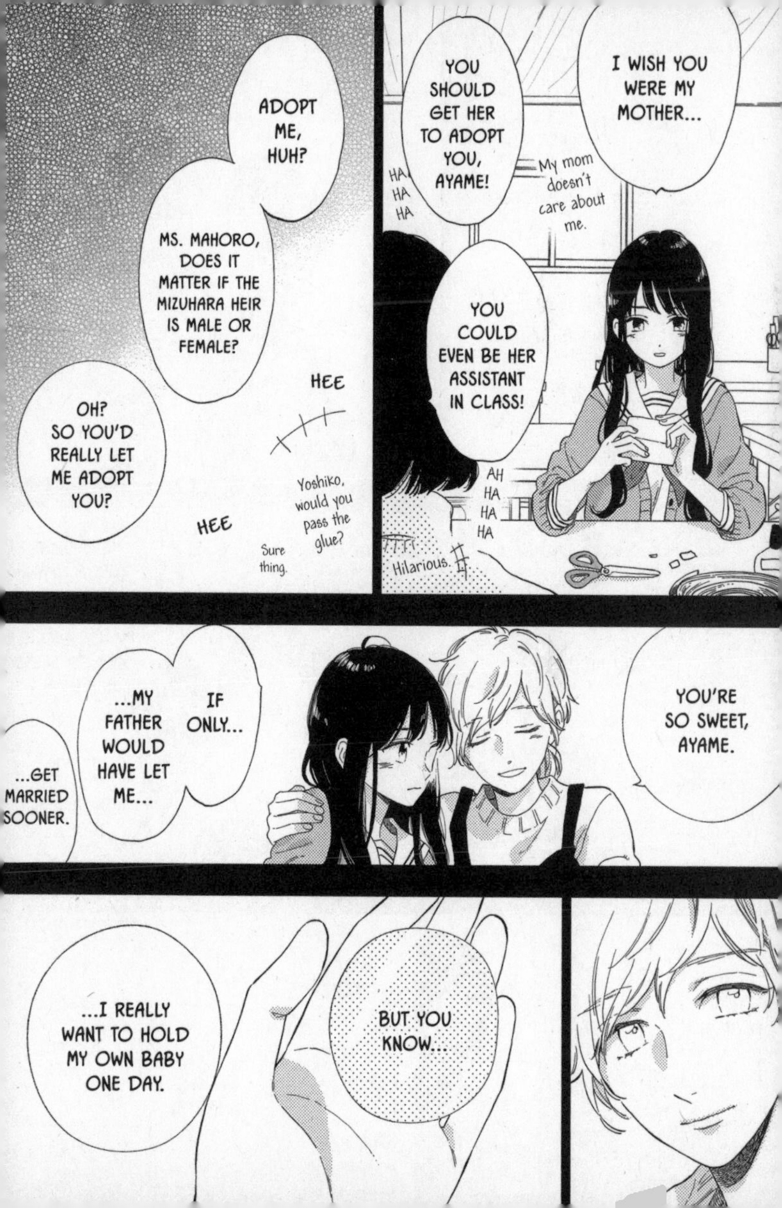
I WISH YOU WERE MY MOTHER...
My mom doesn't care about me.
YOU SHOULD GET HER TO ADOPT YOU, AYAME!
HA HA HA
YOU COULD EVEN BE HER ASSISTANT IN CLASS!
AH HA HA HA
Hilarious.
ADOPT ME, HUH?
MS. MAHORO, DOES IT MATTER IF THE MIZUHARA HEIR IS MALE OR FEMALE?
HEE
Yoshiko, would you pass the glue?
HEE
Sure thing.
OH? SO YOU'D REALLY LET ME ADOPT YOU?
YOU'RE SO SWEET, AYAME.
IF ONLY...
...MY FATHER WOULD HAVE LET ME...
...GET MARRIED SOONER.
BUT YOU KNOW...
...I REALLY WANT TO HOLD MY OWN BABY ONE DAY.

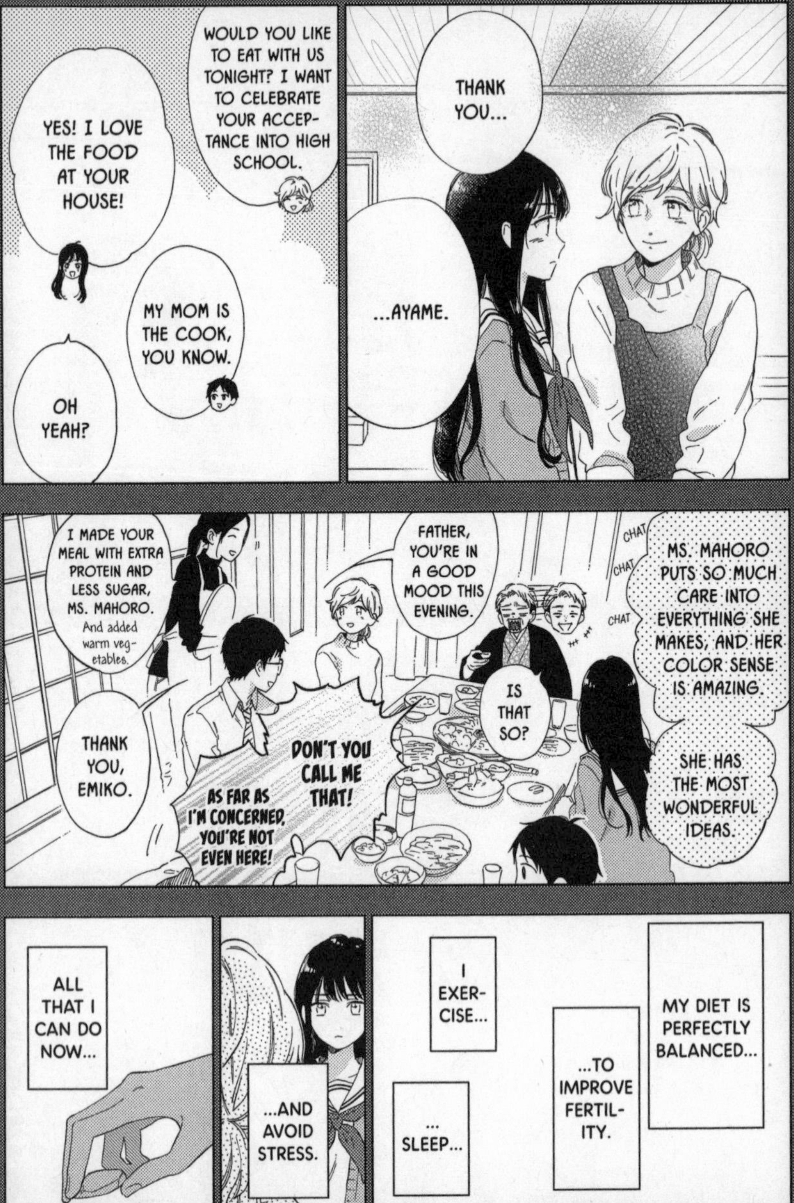
THANK YOU...
...AYAME.
WOULD YOU LIKE TO EAT WITH US TONIGHT? I WANT TO CELEBRATE YOUR ACCEPTANCE INTO HIGH SCHOOL.
YES! I LOVE THE FOOD AT YOUR HOUSE!
MY MOM IS THE COOK, YOU KNOW.
OH YEAH?
CHAT CHAT CHAT
MS. MAHORO PUTS SO MUCH CARE INTO EVERYTHING SHE MAKES, AND HER COLOR SENSE IS AMAZING.
SHE HAS THE MOST WONDERFUL IDEAS.
IS THAT SO?
FATHER, YOU'RE IN A GOOD MOOD THIS EVENING.
DON'T YOU CALL ME THAT!
AS FAR AS I'M CONCERNED, YOU'RE NOT EVEN HERE!
I MADE YOUR MEAL WITH EXTRA PROTEIN AND LESS SUGAR, MS. MAHORO. And added warm vegetables.
THANK YOU, EMIKO.
MY DIET IS PERFECTLY BALANCED...
I EXERCISE...
...SLEEP...
...TO IMPROVE FERTILITY.
...AND AVOID STRESS.
ALL THAT I CAN DO NOW...

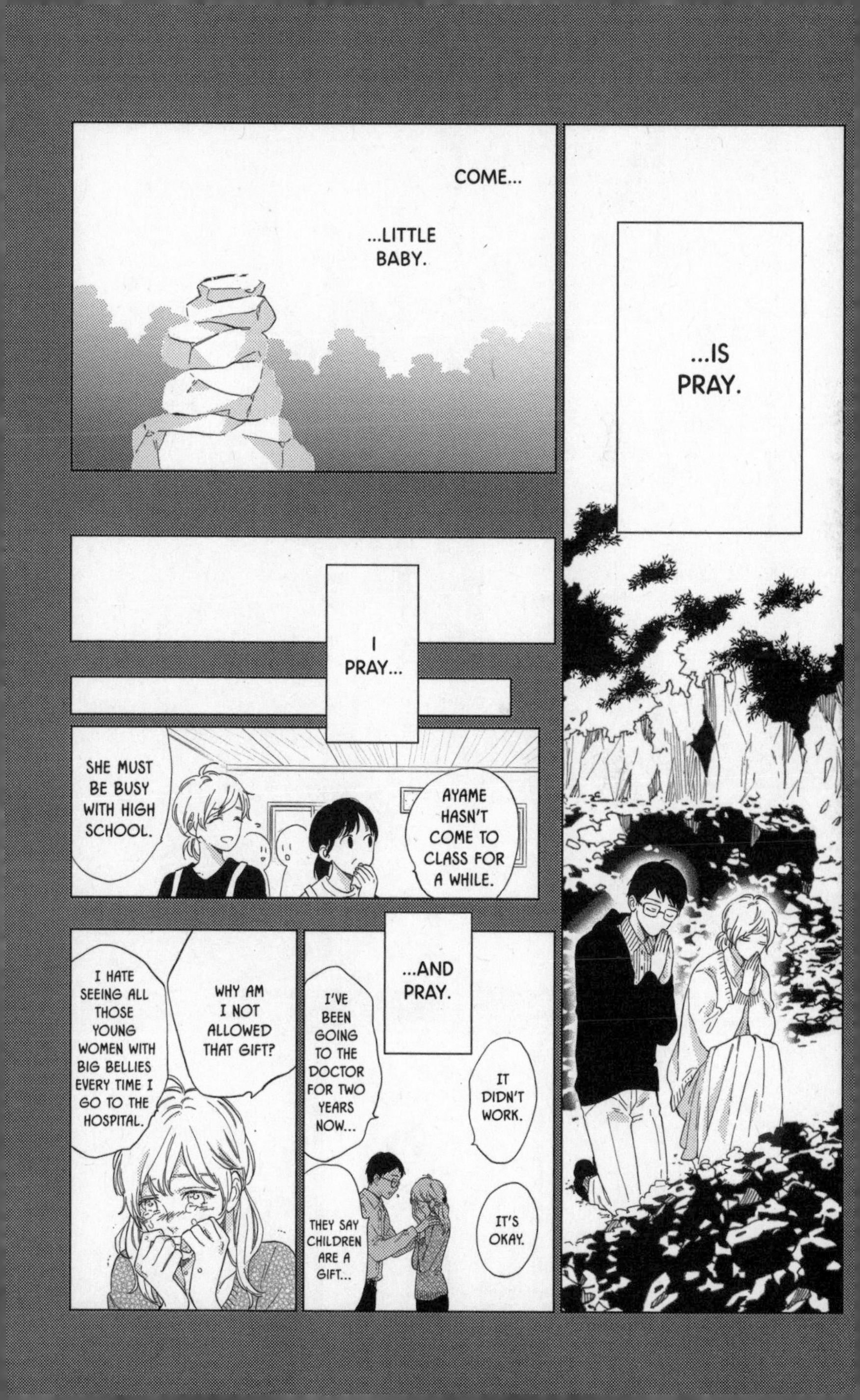
...IS PRAY.
COME...
...LITTLE BABY.
I PRAY...
AYAME HASN'T COME TO CLASS FOR A WHILE.
SHE MUST BE BUSY WITH HIGH SCHOOL.
...AND PRAY.
IT DIDN'T WORK.
I'VE BEEN GOING TO THE DOCTOR FOR TWO YEARS NOW...
IT'S OKAY.
THEY SAY CHILDREN ARE A GIFT...
WHY AM I NOT ALLOWED THAT GIFT?
I HATE SEEING ALL THOSE YOUNG WOMEN WITH BIG BELLIES EVERY TIME I GO TO THE HOSPITAL.

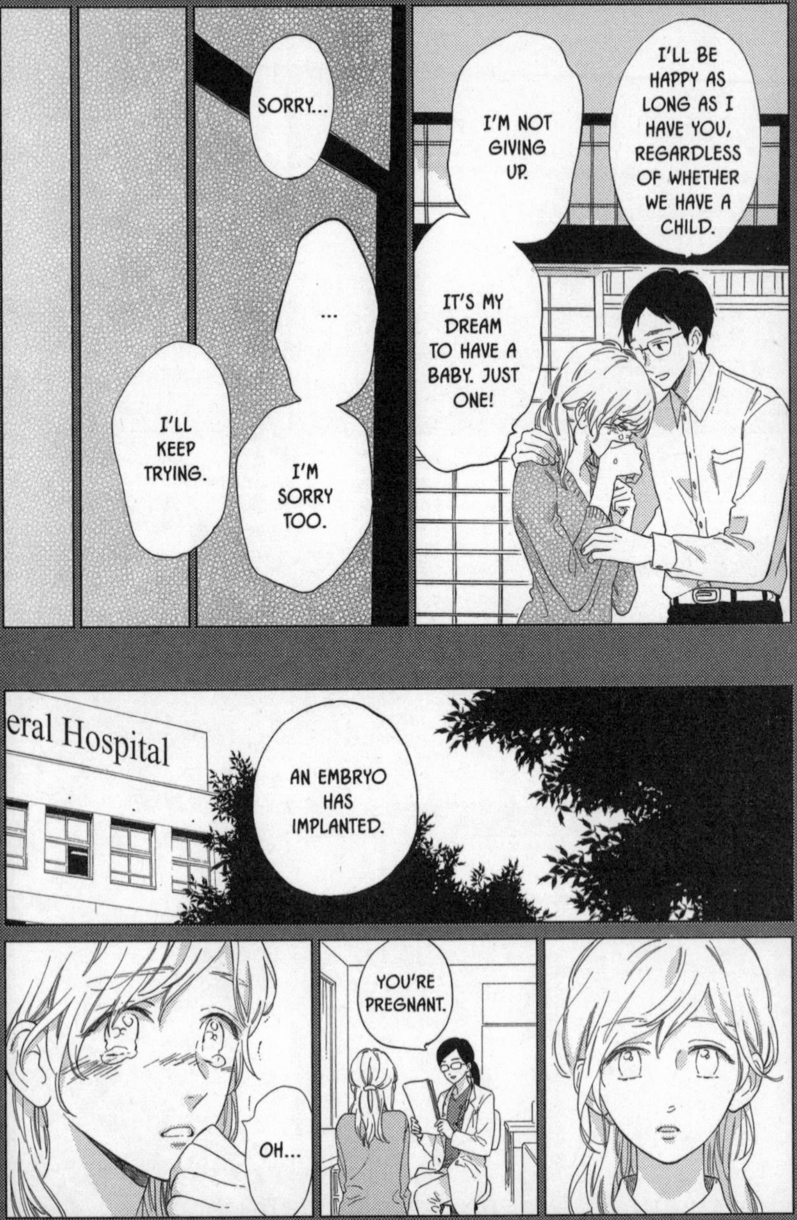
I'LL BE HAPPY AS LONG AS I HAVE YOU, REGARDLESS OF WHETHER WE HAVE A CHILD.
I'M NOT GIVING UP.
IT'S MY DREAM TO HAVE A BABY. JUST ONE!
SORRY...
...
I'M SORRY TOO.
I'LL KEEP TRYING.
eral Hospital
AN EMBRYO HAS IMPLANTED.
YOU'RE PREGNANT.
OH...

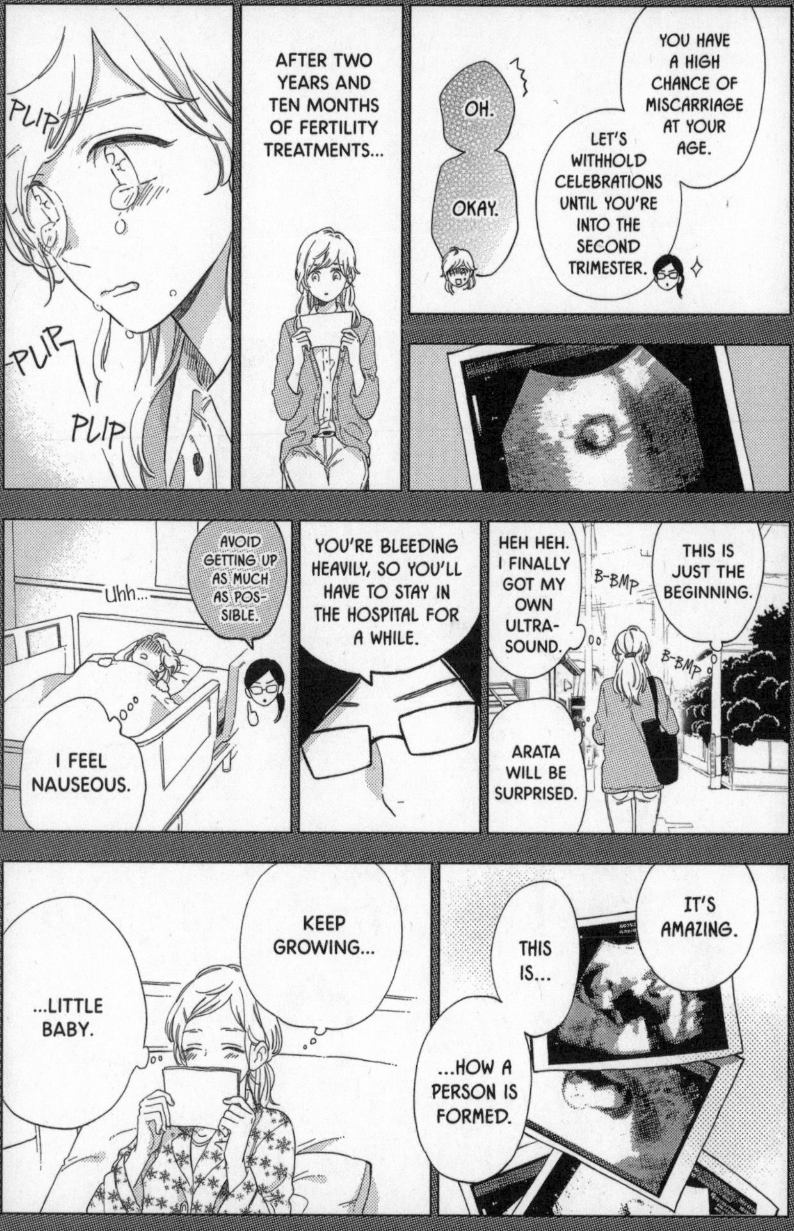
YOU HAVE A HIGH CHANCE OF MISCARRIAGE AT YOUR AGE.
LET'S WITHHOLD CELEBRATIONS UNTIL YOU'RE INTO THE SECOND TRIMESTER.
OH.
OKAY.
AFTER TWO YEARS AND TEN MONTHS OF FERTILITY TREATMENTS...
PLIP
PLIP
PLIP
THIS IS JUST THE BEGINNING.
B-BMP
HEH HEH. I FINALLY GOT MY OWN ULTRASOUND.
B-BMP
ARATA WILL BE SURPRISED.
YOU'RE BLEEDING HEAVILY, SO YOU'LL HAVE TO STAY IN THE HOSPITAL FOR A WHILE.
AVOID GETTING UP AS MUCH AS POS-SIBLE.
Uhh...
I FEEL NAUSEOUS.
IT'S AMAZING.
THIS IS...
...HOW A PERSON IS FORMED.
KEEP GROWING...
...LITTLE BABY.

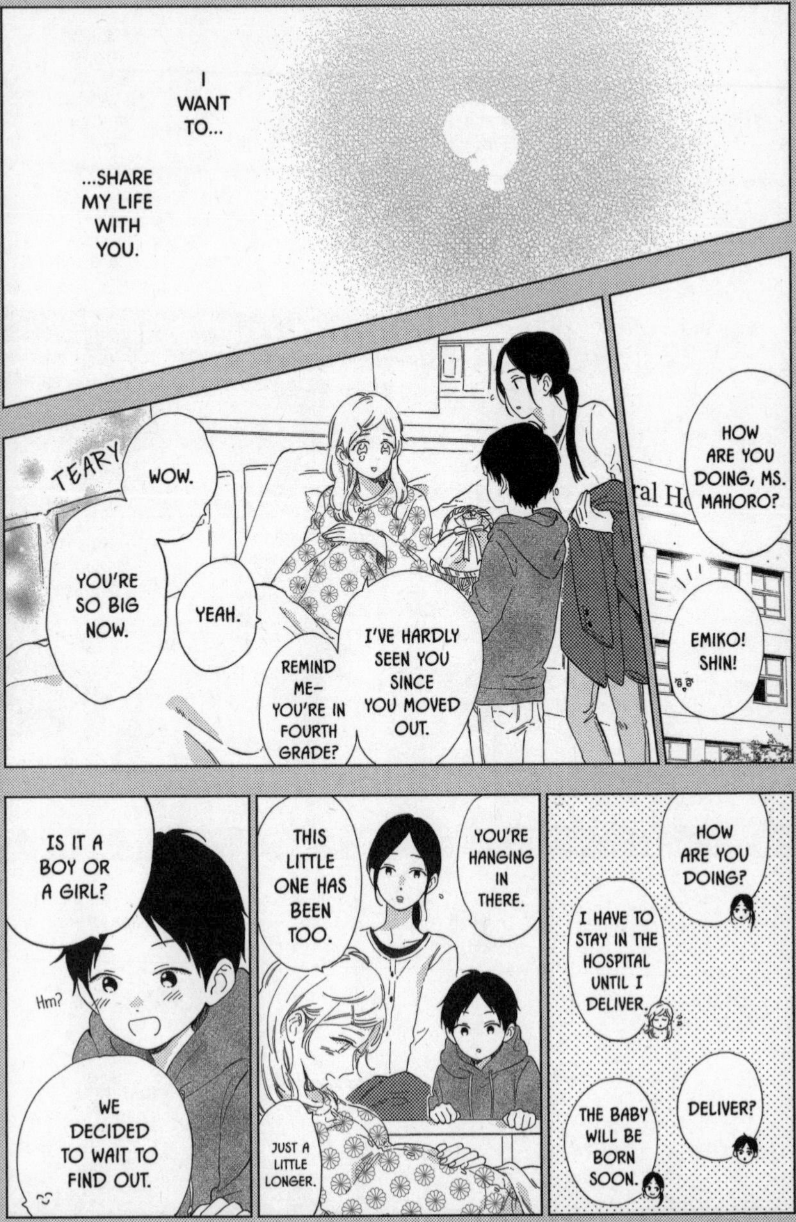
I WANT TO...
...SHARE MY LIFE WITH YOU.
HOW ARE YOU DOING, MS. MAHORO?
EMIKO! SHIN!
TEARY
WOW.
YOU'RE SO BIG NOW.
YEAH.
I'VE HARDLY SEEN YOU SINCE YOU MOVED OUT.
REMIND ME— YOU'RE IN FOURTH GRADE?
HOW ARE YOU DOING?
I HAVE TO STAY IN THE HOSPITAL UNTIL I DELIVER.
DELIVER?
THE BABY WILL BE BORN SOON.
YOU'RE HANGING IN THERE.
THIS LITTLE ONE HAS BEEN TOO.
JUST A LITTLE LONGER.
IS IT A BOY OR A GIRL?
Hm?
WE DECIDED TO WAIT TO FIND OUT.

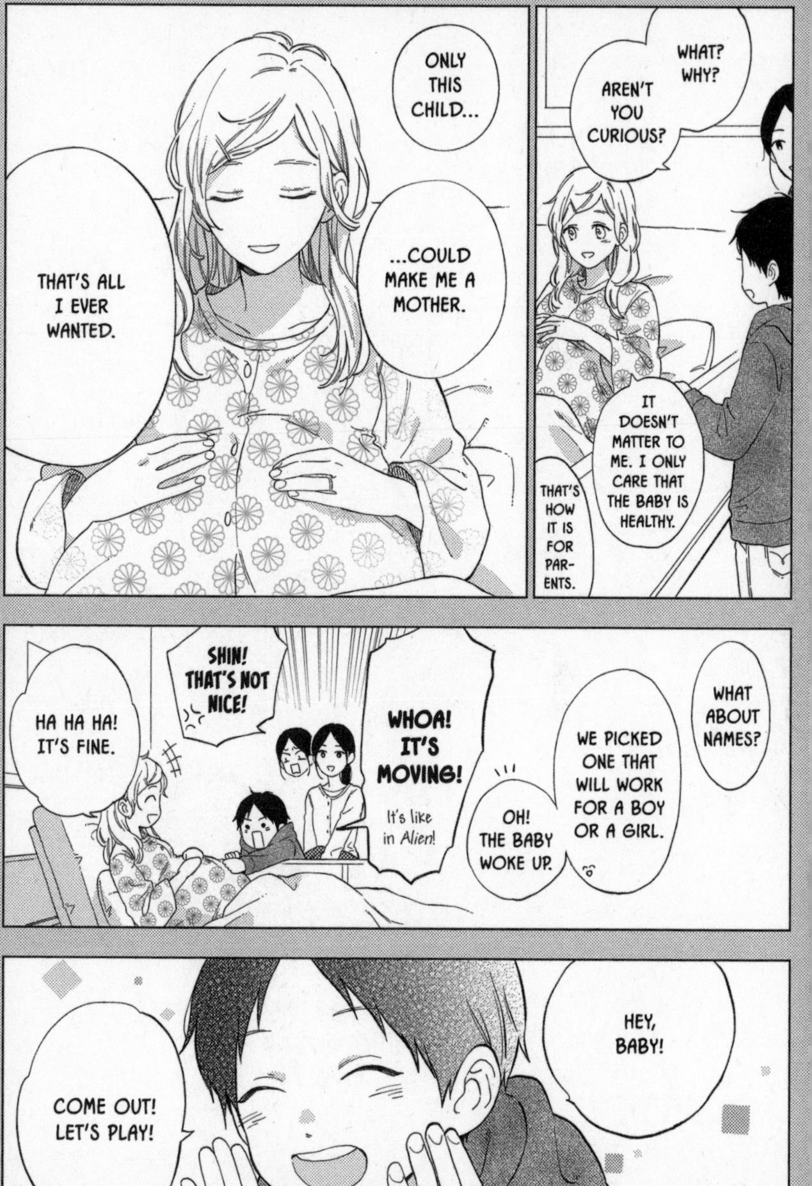
WHAT? WHY?
AREN'T YOU CURIOUS?
IT DOESN'T MATTER TO ME. I ONLY CARE THAT THE BABY IS HEALTHY.
THAT'S HOW IT IS FOR PAR-ENTS.
ONLY THIS CHILD...
...COULD MAKE ME A MOTHER.
THAT'S ALL I EVER WANTED.
WHAT ABOUT NAMES?
WE PICKED ONE THAT WILL WORK FOR A BOY OR A GIRL.
OH! THE BABY WOKE UP.
WHOA! IT'S MOVING!
It's like in *Alien*!
SHIN! THAT'S NOT NICE!
HA HA HA! IT'S FINE.
HEY, BABY!
COME OUT! LET'S PLAY!

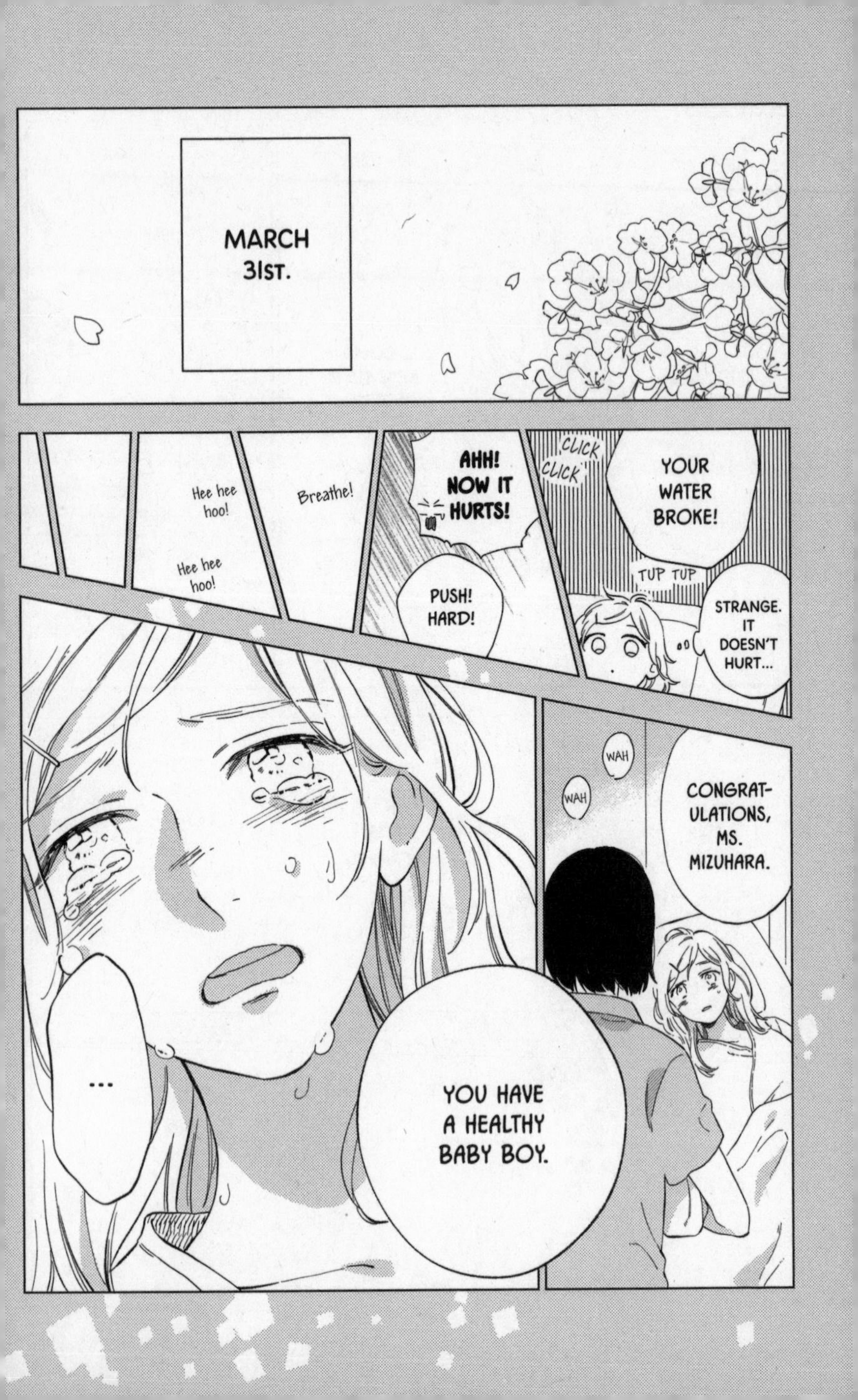
MARCH 31ST.
CLICK
CLICK
YOUR WATER BROKE!
TUP TUP
STRANGE. IT DOESN'T HURT...
AHH! NOW IT HURTS!
PUSH! HARD!
Breathe!
Hee hee hoo!
Hee hee hoo!
WAH
WAH
CONGRAT-ULATIONS, MS. MIZUHARA.
YOU HAVE A HEALTHY BABY BOY.
...

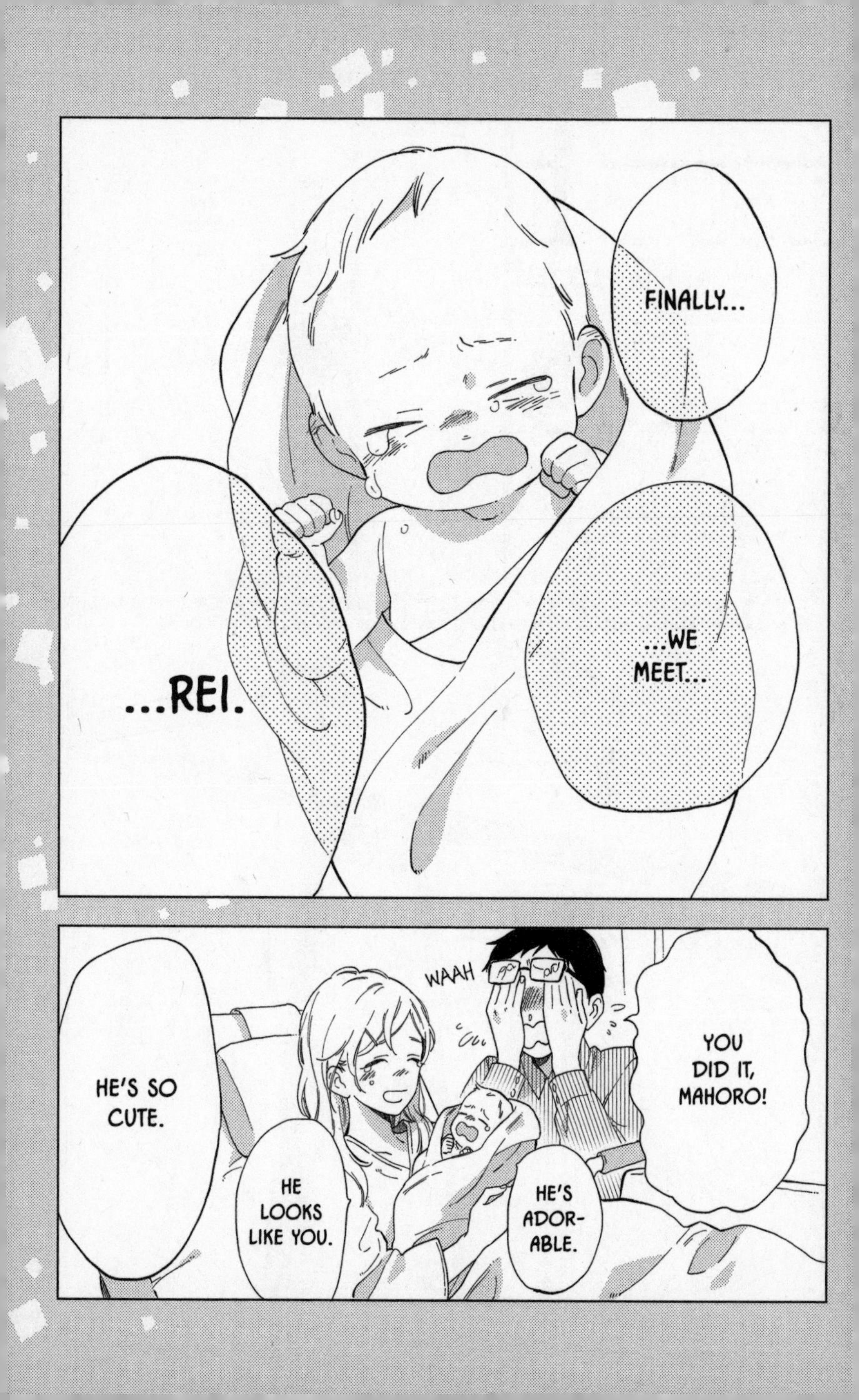
FINALLY...
...WE MEET...
...REI.
YOU DID IT, MAHORO!
WAAH
HE'S ADORABLE.
HE LOOKS LIKE YOU.
HE'S SO CUTE.

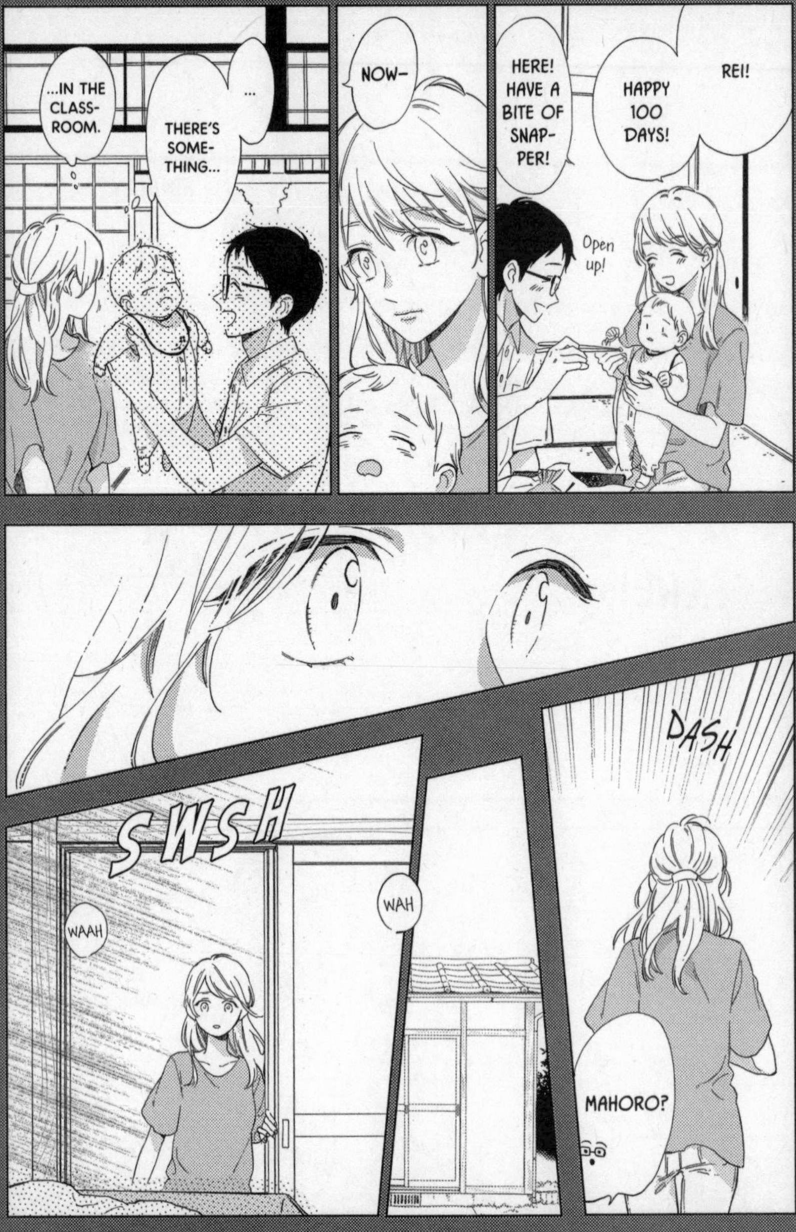
REI!
HAPPY 100 DAYS!
HERE! HAVE A BITE OF SNAPPER!
Open up!
NOW-
...
THERE'S SOMETHING...
...IN THE CLASSROOM.
DASH
MAHORO?
WAH
SWSH
WAAH

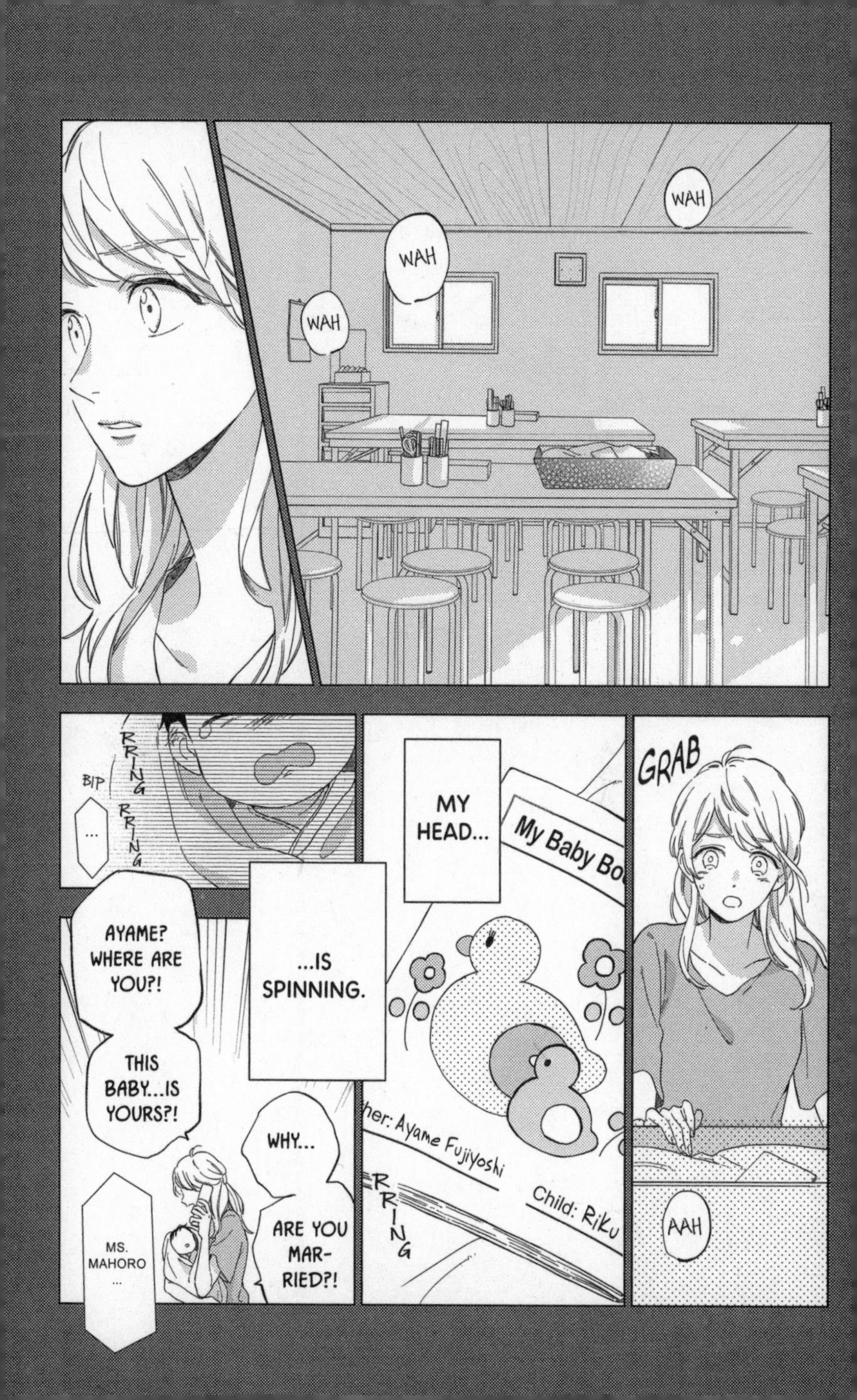
WAH
WAH
WAH
GRAB
AAH
My Baby Bo
her: Ayame Fujiyoshi
Child: Riku
RRING
MY HEAD...
...IS SPINNING.
RRING
RRING
BIP
...
AYAME? WHERE ARE YOU?!
THIS BABY...IS YOURS?!
WHY...
ARE YOU MAR-RIED?!
MS. MAHORO ...

WHY IS IT THAT...
...PEOPLE WHO WANT BABIES CAN'T HAVE THEM...
SNIFF
...AND PEOPLE WHO DON'T WANT THEM CAN?

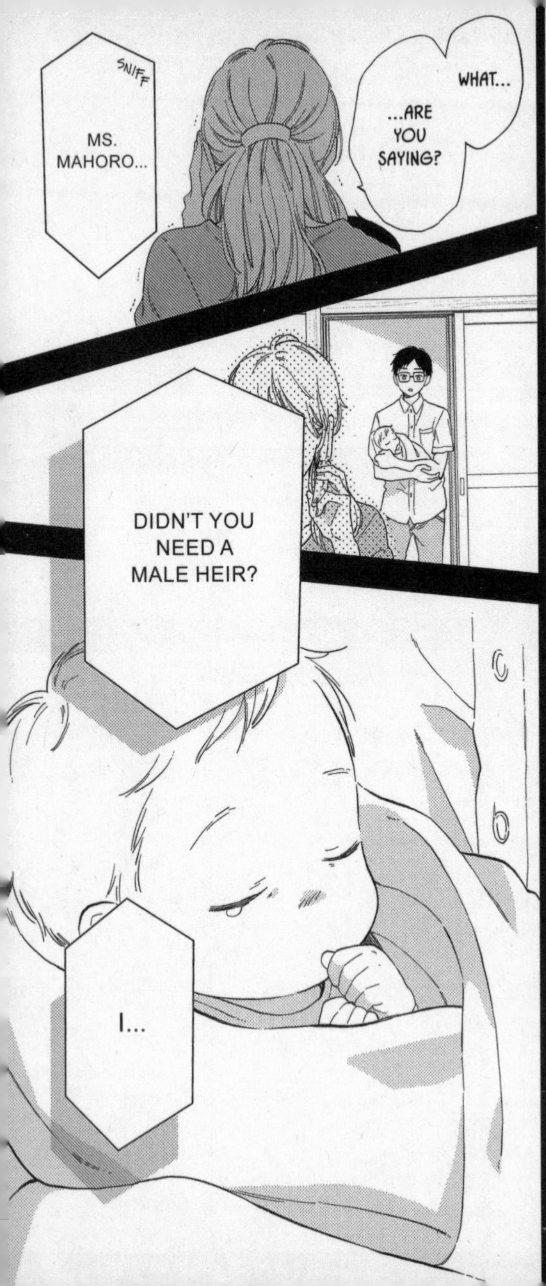
WHAT...
...ARE YOU SAYING?
SNIFF
MS. MAHORO...
DIDN'T YOU NEED A MALE HEIR?
I...

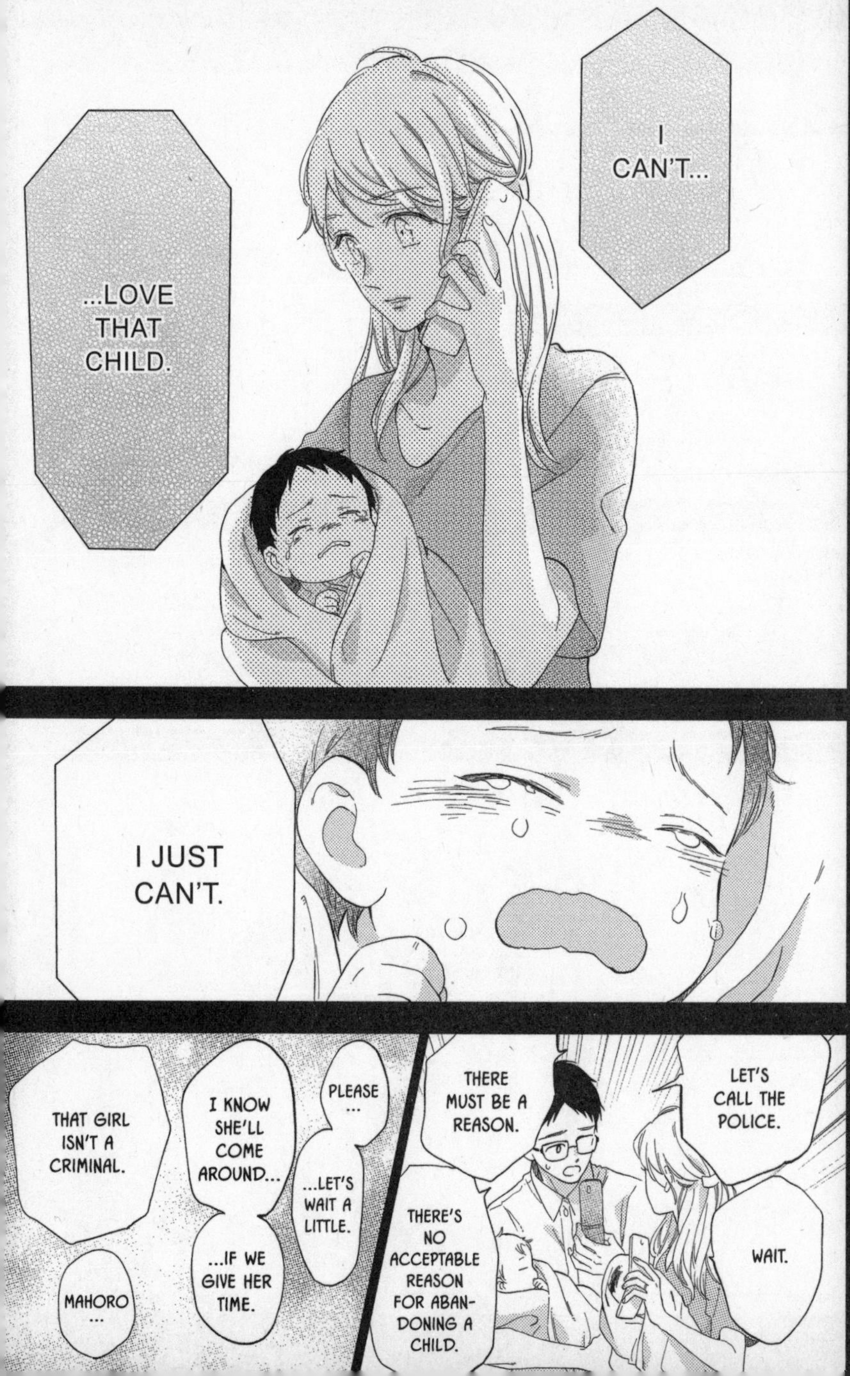
I CAN'T...
...LOVE THAT CHILD.
I JUST CAN'T.
LET'S CALL THE POLICE.
THERE MUST BE A REASON.
WAIT.
THERE'S NO ACCEPTABLE REASON FOR ABAN-DONING A CHILD.
PLEASE...
...LET'S WAIT A LITTLE.
I KNOW SHE'LL COME AROUND...
...IF WE GIVE HER TIME.
THAT GIRL ISN'T A CRIMINAL.
MAHORO...

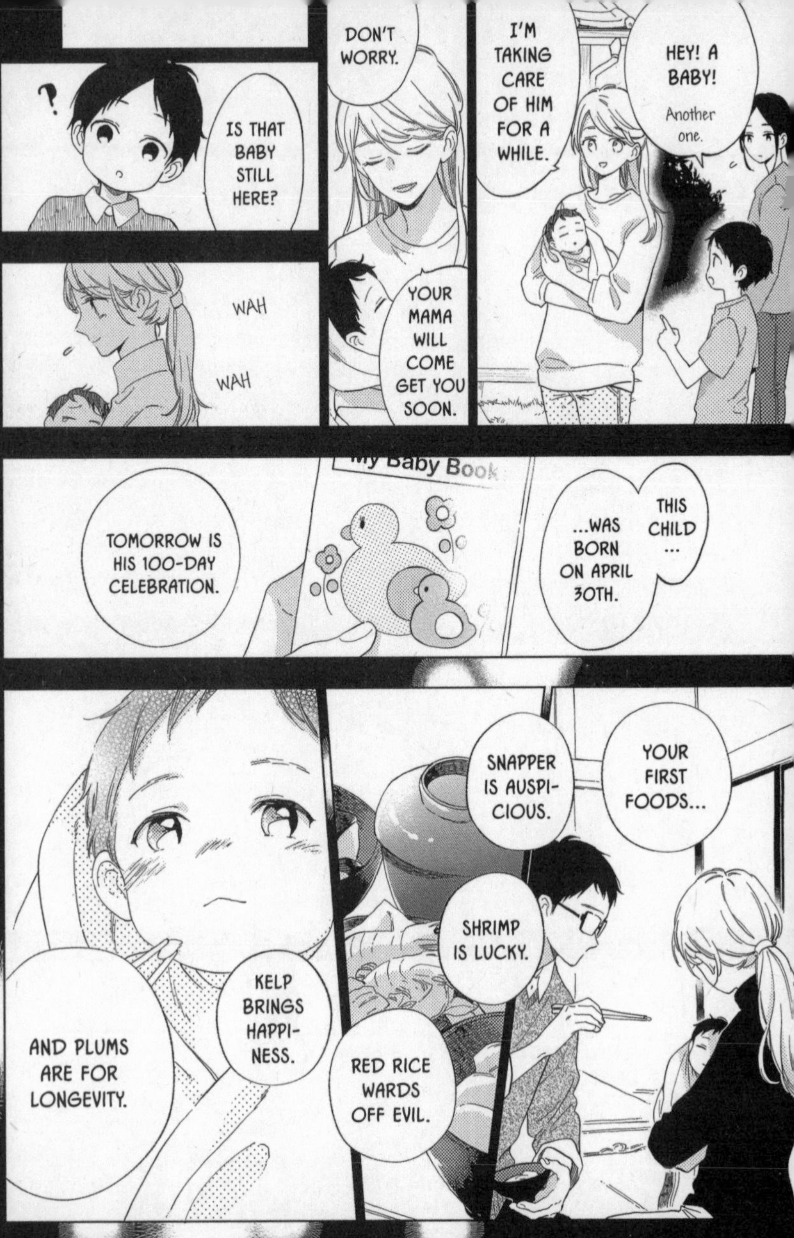
HEY! A BABY!
Another one.
I'M TAKING CARE OF HIM FOR A WHILE.
DON'T WORRY.
YOUR MAMA WILL COME GET YOU SOON.
IS THAT BABY STILL HERE?
WAH
WAH
My Baby Book
THIS CHILD...
...WAS BORN ON APRIL 30TH.
TOMORROW IS HIS 100-DAY CELEBRATION.
YOUR FIRST FOODS...
SNAPPER IS AUSPICIOUS.
SHRIMP IS LUCKY.
RED RICE WARDS OFF EVIL.
KELP BRINGS HAPPINESS.
AND PLUMS ARE FOR LONGEVITY.

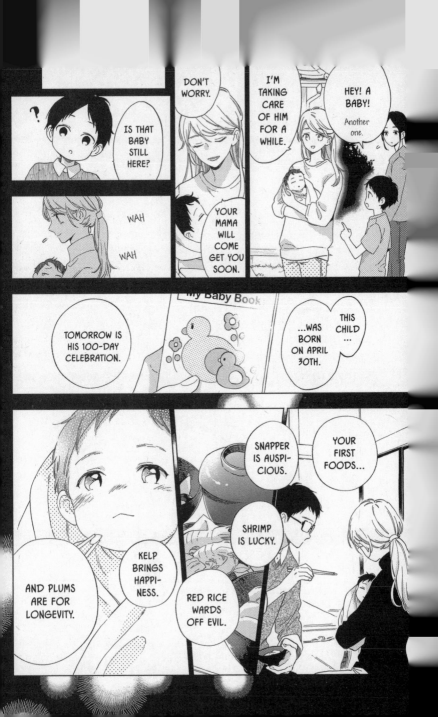

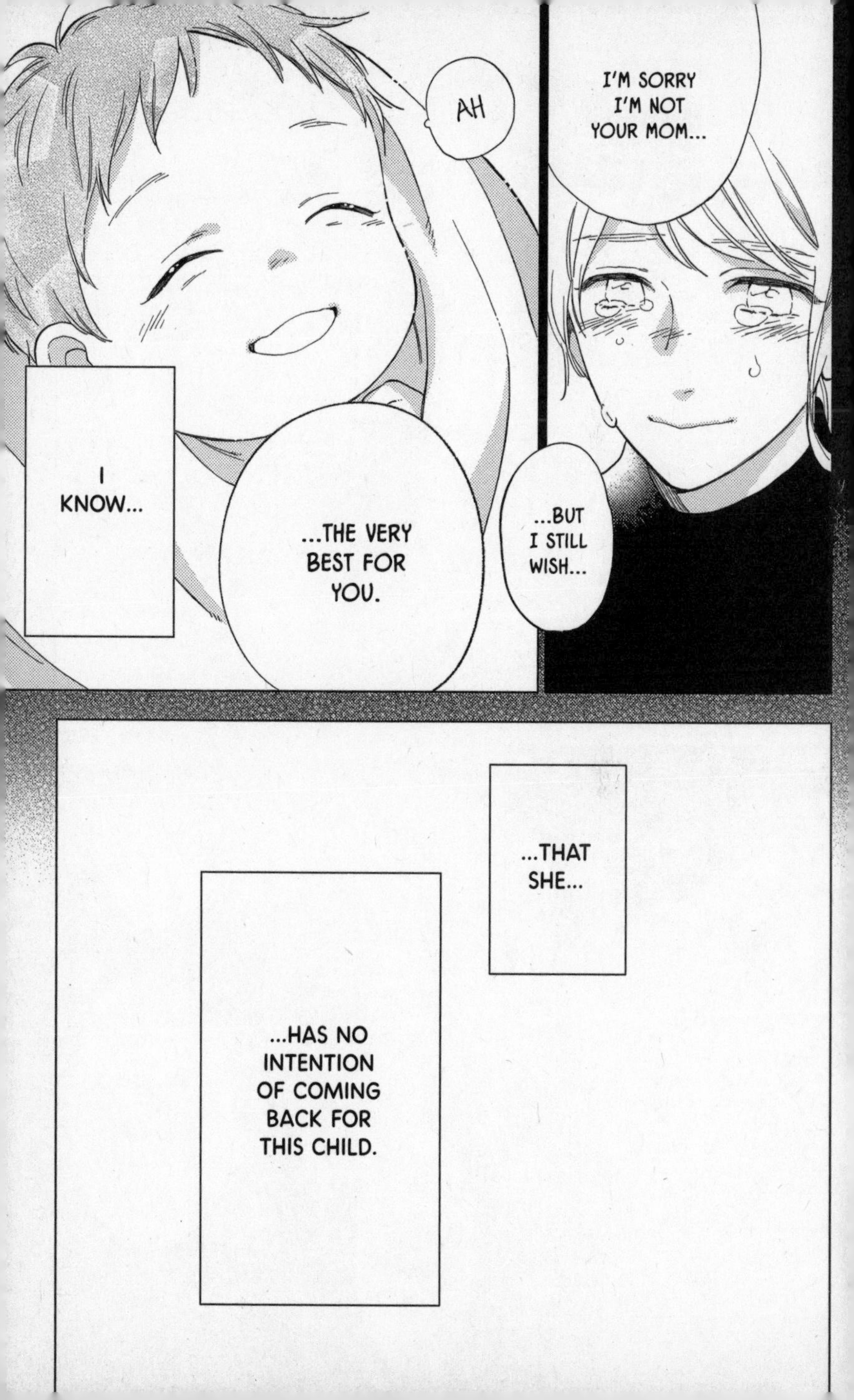
I'M SORRY I'M NOT YOUR MOM...
...BUT I STILL WISH...
AH
...THE VERY BEST FOR YOU.
I KNOW...
...THAT SHE...
...HAS NO INTENTION OF COMING BACK FOR THIS CHILD.

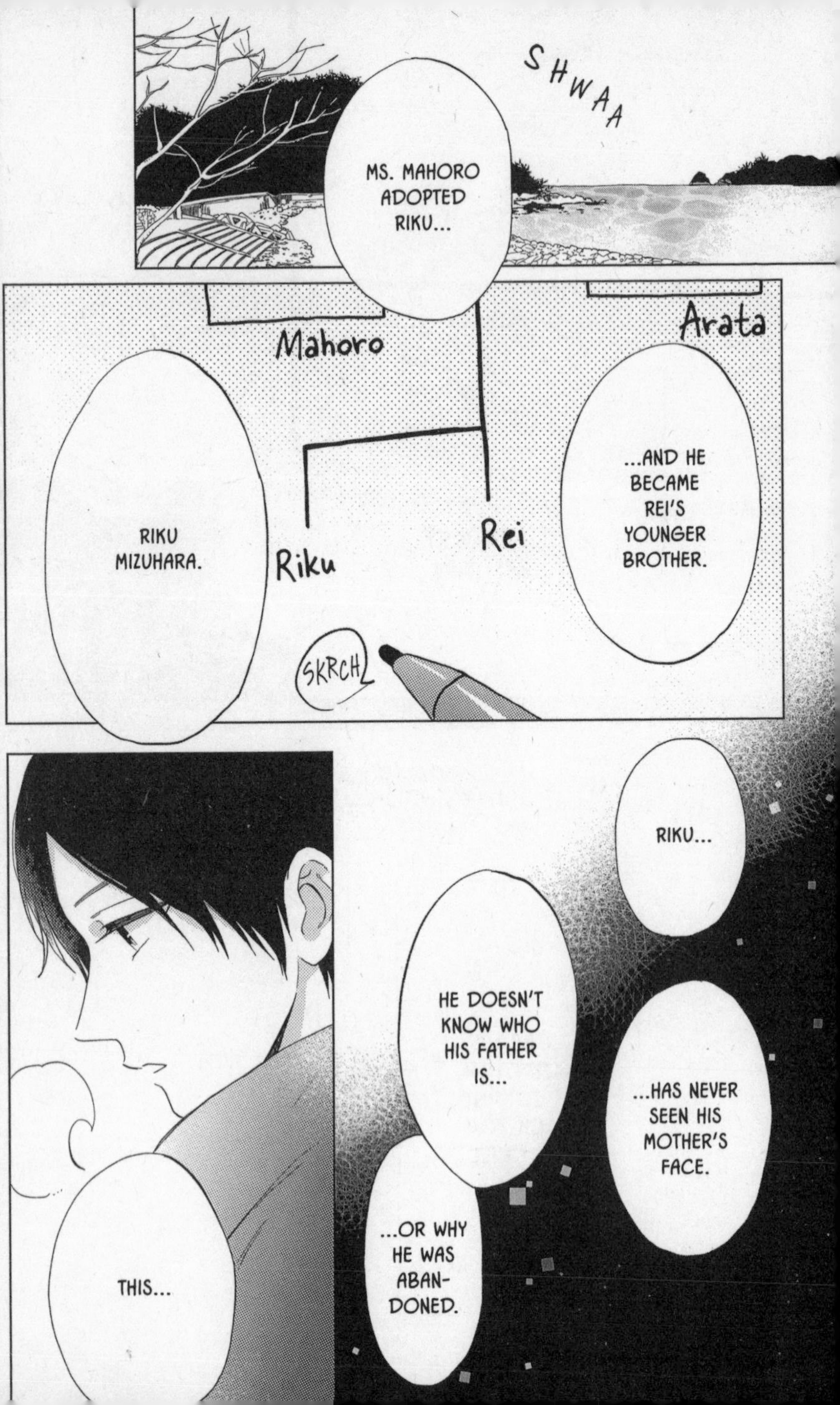
SHWAA
MS. MAHORO ADOPTED RIKU...
Arata
Mahoro
Rei
Riku
...AND HE BECAME REI'S YOUNGER BROTHER.
SKRCH
RIKU MIZUHARA.
RIKU...
...HAS NEVER SEEN HIS MOTHER'S FACE.
HE DOESN'T KNOW WHO HIS FATHER IS...
...OR WHY HE WAS ABAN-DONED.
THIS...

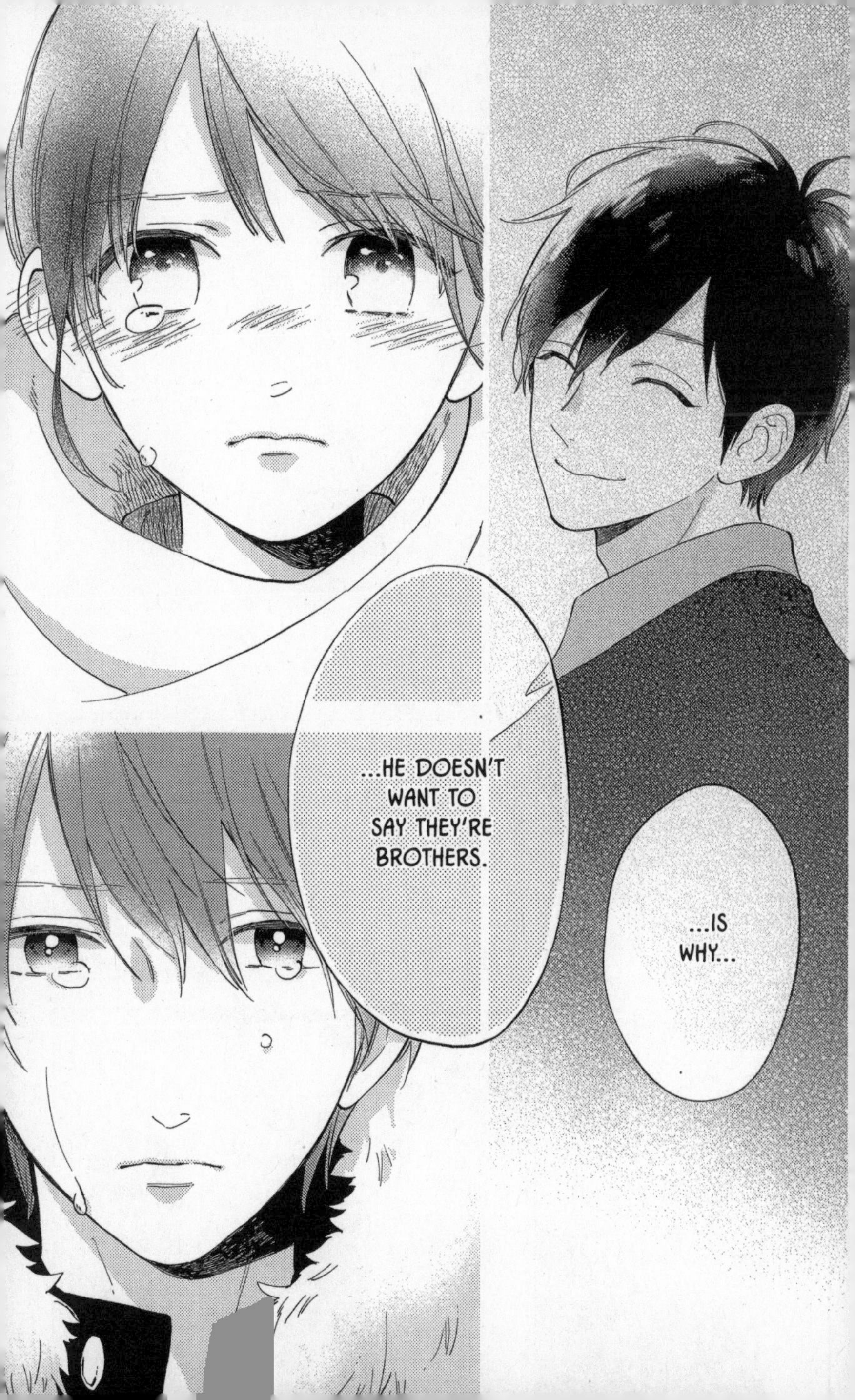
...IS WHY...
...HE DOESN'T WANT TO SAY THEY'RE BROTHERS.

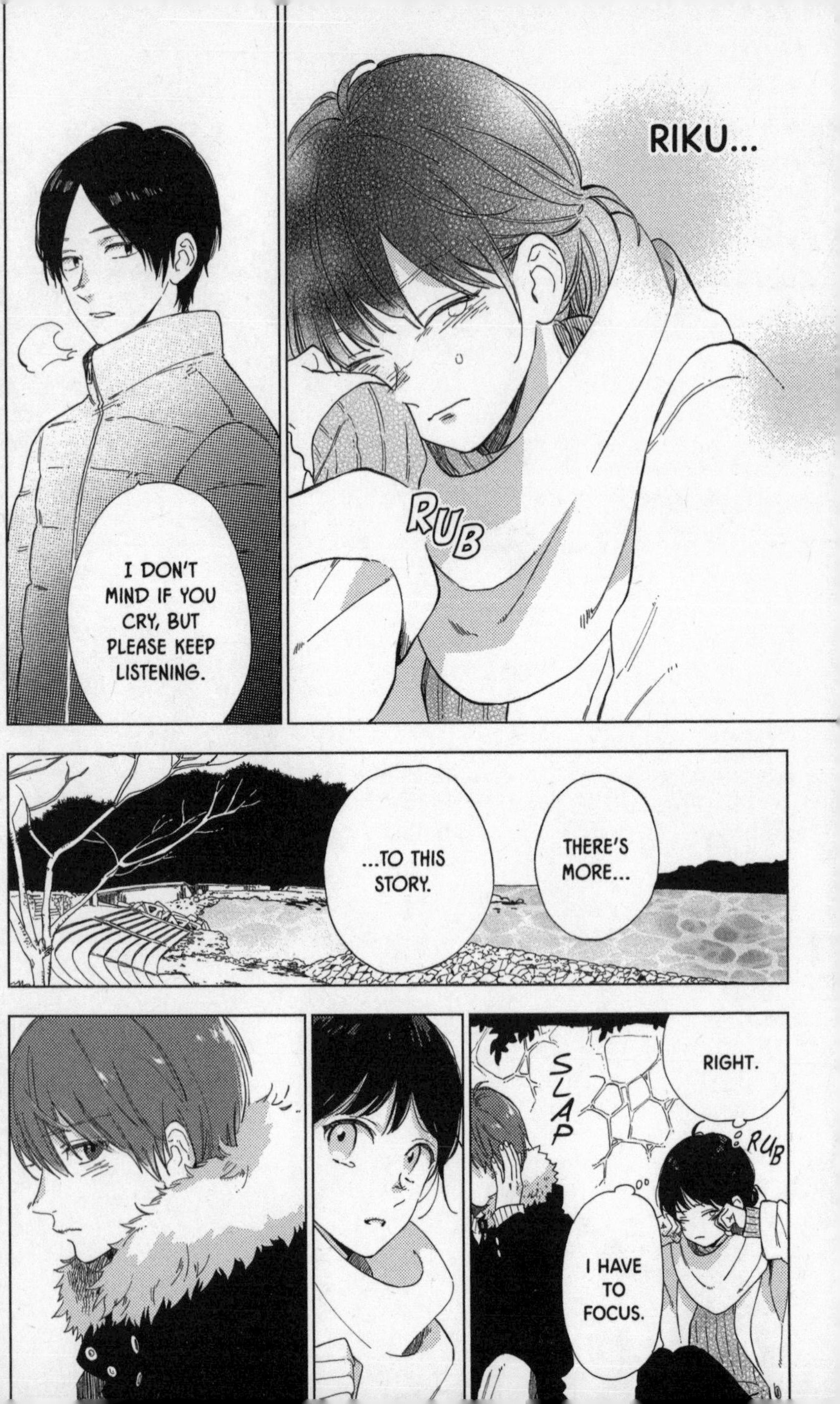
RIKU...
RUB
I DON'T MIND IF YOU CRY, BUT PLEASE KEEP LISTENING.
THERE'S MORE...
...TO THIS STORY.
RIGHT.
SLAP
RUB
I HAVE TO FOCUS.

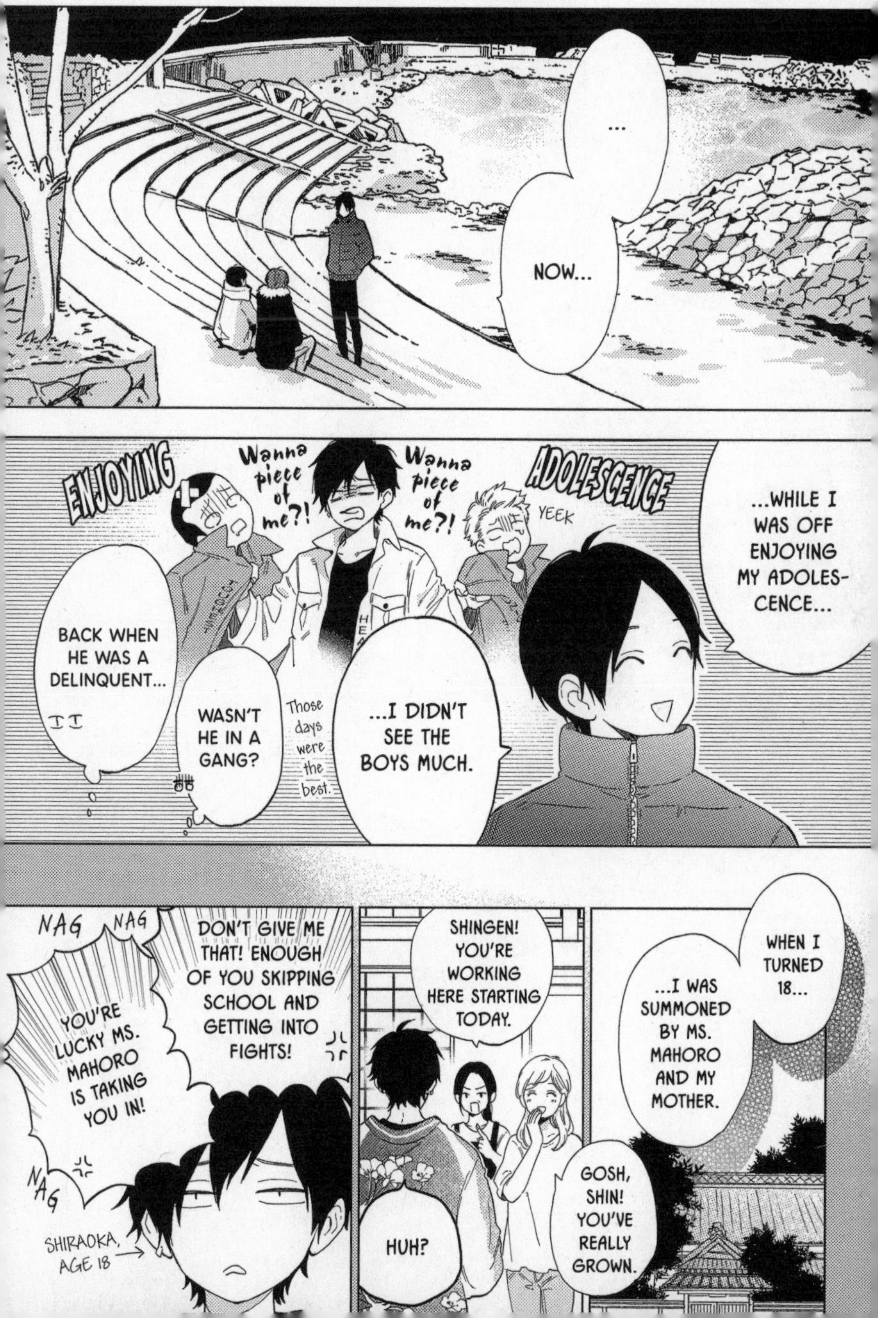
...
NOW...
...WHILE I WAS OFF ENJOYING MY ADOLESCENCE...
ADOLESCENCE
YEEK
Wanna piece of me?!
Wanna piece of me?!
ENJOYING
...I DIDN'T SEE THE BOYS MUCH.
Those days were the best.
WASN'T HE IN A GANG?
BACK WHEN HE WAS A DELINQUENT...
WHEN I TURNED 18...
...I WAS SUMMONED BY MS. MAHORO AND MY MOTHER.
SHINGEN! YOU'RE WORKING HERE STARTING TODAY.
GOSH, SHIN! YOU'VE REALLY GROWN.
HUH?
DON'T GIVE ME THAT! ENOUGH OF YOU SKIPPING SCHOOL AND GETTING INTO FIGHTS!
NAG NAG
YOU'RE LUCKY MS. MAHORO IS TAKING YOU IN!
NAG
SHIRAOKA, AGE 18

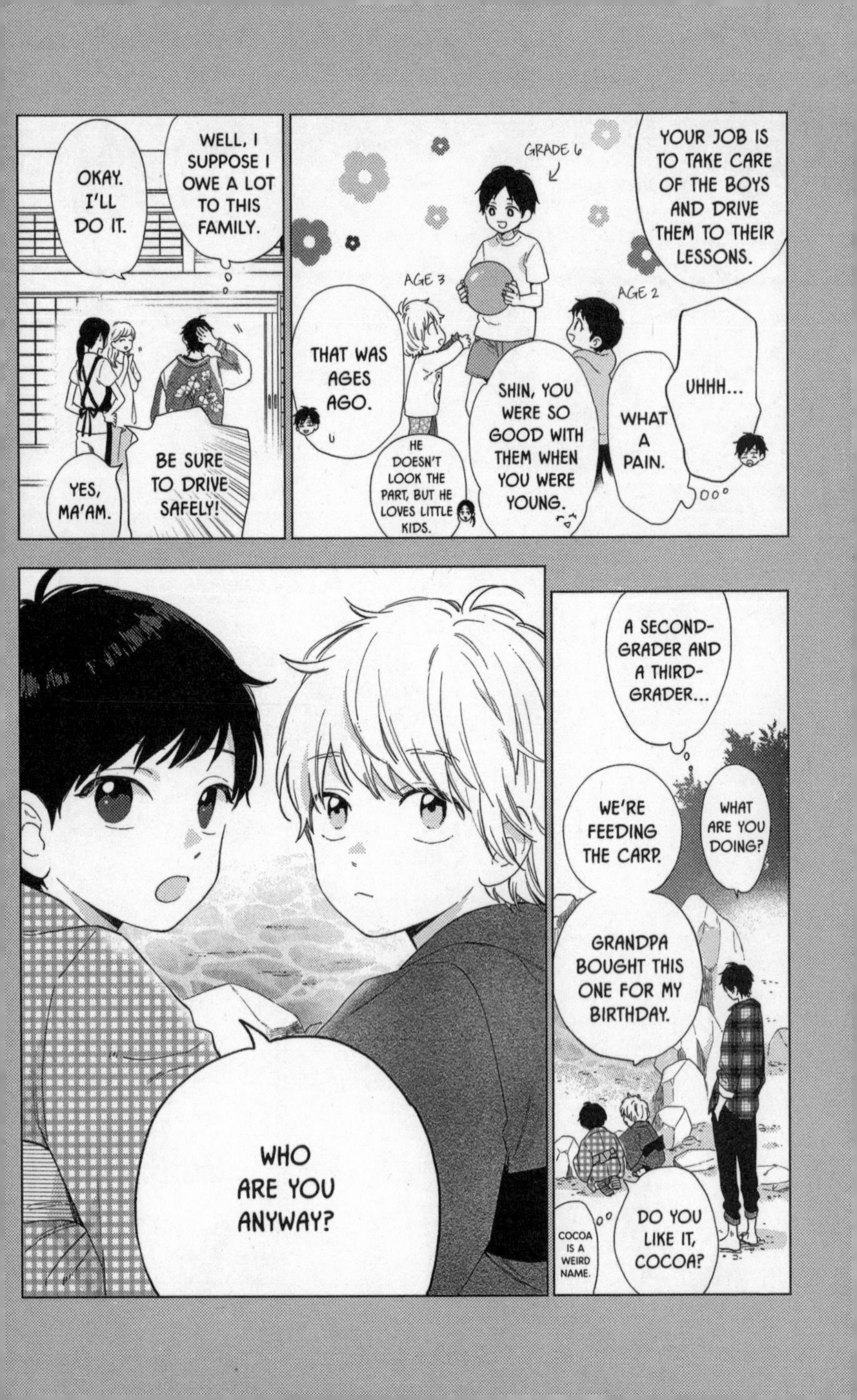
YOUR JOB IS TO TAKE CARE OF THE BOYS AND DRIVE THEM TO THEIR LESSONS.
GRADE 6
AGE 2
AGE 3
UHHH...
WHAT A PAIN.
SHIN, YOU WERE SO GOOD WITH THEM WHEN YOU WERE YOUNG.
HE DOESN'T LOOK THE PART, BUT HE LOVES LITTLE KIDS.
THAT WAS AGES AGO.
WELL, I SUPPOSE I OWE A LOT TO THIS FAMILY.
OKAY. I'LL DO IT.
BE SURE TO DRIVE SAFELY!
YES, MA'AM.
A SECOND-GRADER AND A THIRD-GRADER...
WHAT ARE YOU DOING?
WE'RE FEEDING THE CARP.
GRANDPA BOUGHT THIS ONE FOR MY BIRTHDAY.
DO YOU LIKE IT, COCOA?
COCOA IS A WEIRD NAME.
WHO ARE YOU ANYWAY?

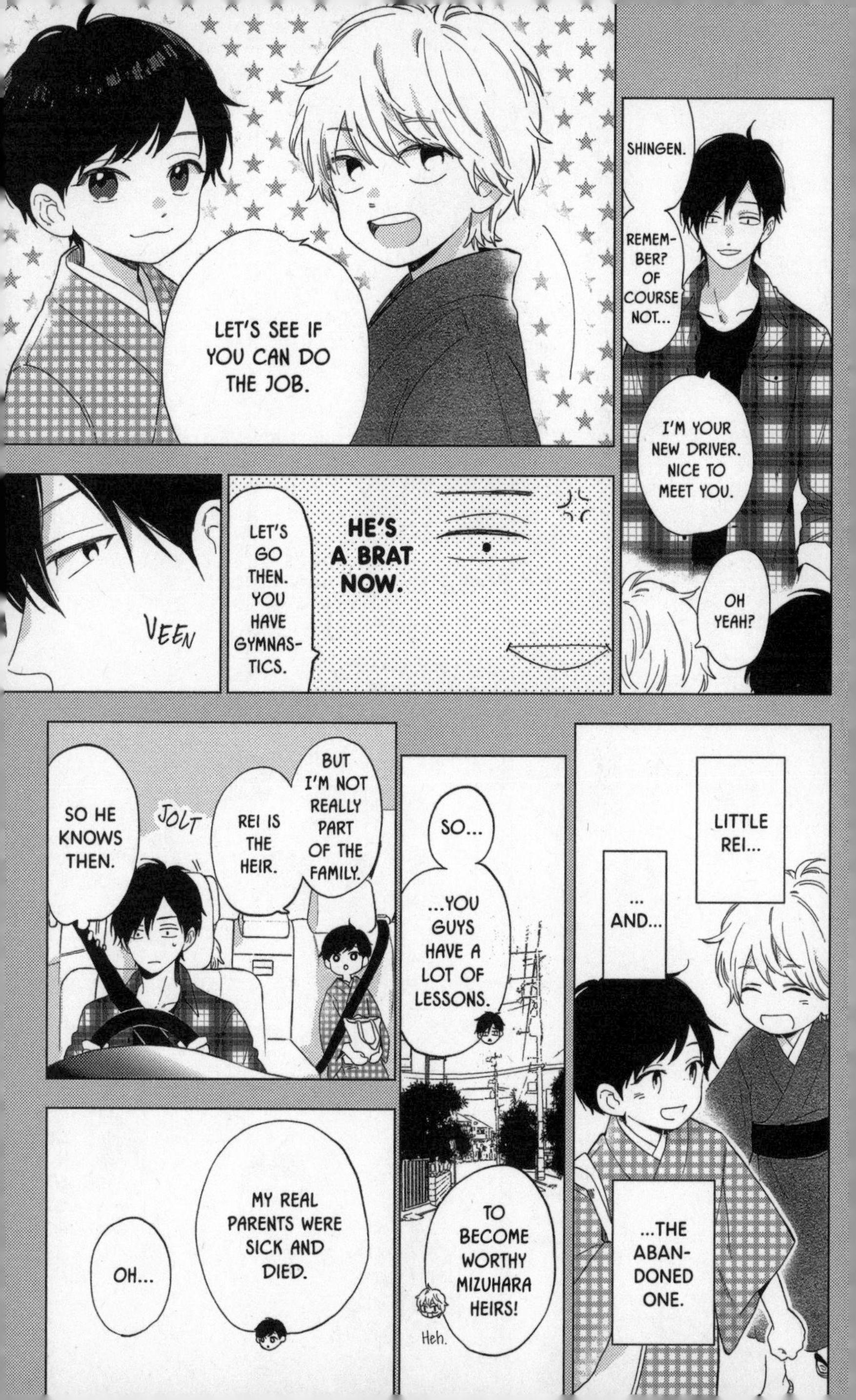
SHINGEN.
REMEMBER? OF COURSE NOT...
I'M YOUR NEW DRIVER. NICE TO MEET YOU.
OH YEAH?
LET'S SEE IF YOU CAN DO THE JOB.
HE'S A BRAT NOW.
LET'S GO THEN. YOU HAVE GYMNASTICS.
VEEN
LITTLE REI...
...AND...
...THE ABANDONED ONE.
SO...
...YOU GUYS HAVE A LOT OF LESSONS.
TO BECOME WORTHY MIZUHARA HEIRS!
Heh.
REI IS THE HEIR.
BUT I'M NOT REALLY PART OF THE FAMILY.
JOLT
SO HE KNOWS THEN.
MY REAL PARENTS WERE SICK AND DIED.
OH...

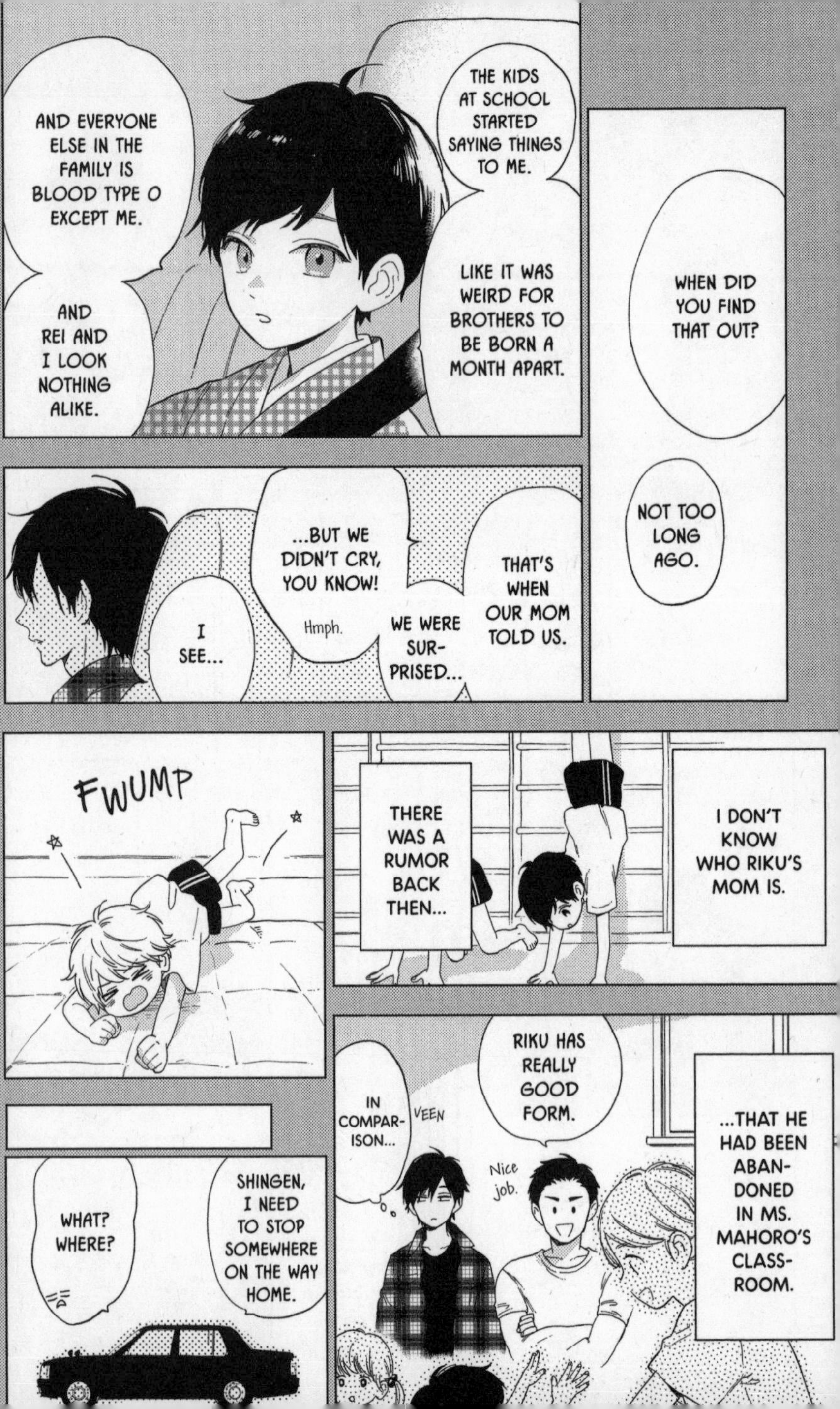
WHEN DID YOU FIND THAT OUT?
NOT TOO LONG AGO.
THE KIDS AT SCHOOL STARTED SAYING THINGS TO ME.
LIKE IT WAS WEIRD FOR BROTHERS TO BE BORN A MONTH APART.
AND EVERYONE ELSE IN THE FAMILY IS BLOOD TYPE O EXCEPT ME.
AND REI AND I LOOK NOTHING ALIKE.
THAT'S WHEN OUR MOM TOLD US.
...BUT WE DIDN'T CRY, YOU KNOW!
WE WERE SUR-PRISED...
Hmph.
I SEE...
I DON'T KNOW WHO RIKU'S MOM IS.
THERE WAS A RUMOR BACK THEN...
FWUMP
...THAT HE HAD BEEN ABAN-DONED IN MS. MAHORO'S CLASS-ROOM.
RIKU HAS REALLY GOOD FORM.
Nice job.
VEEN
IN COMPAR-ISON...
SHINGEN, I NEED TO STOP SOMEWHERE ON THE WAY HOME.
WHAT? WHERE?

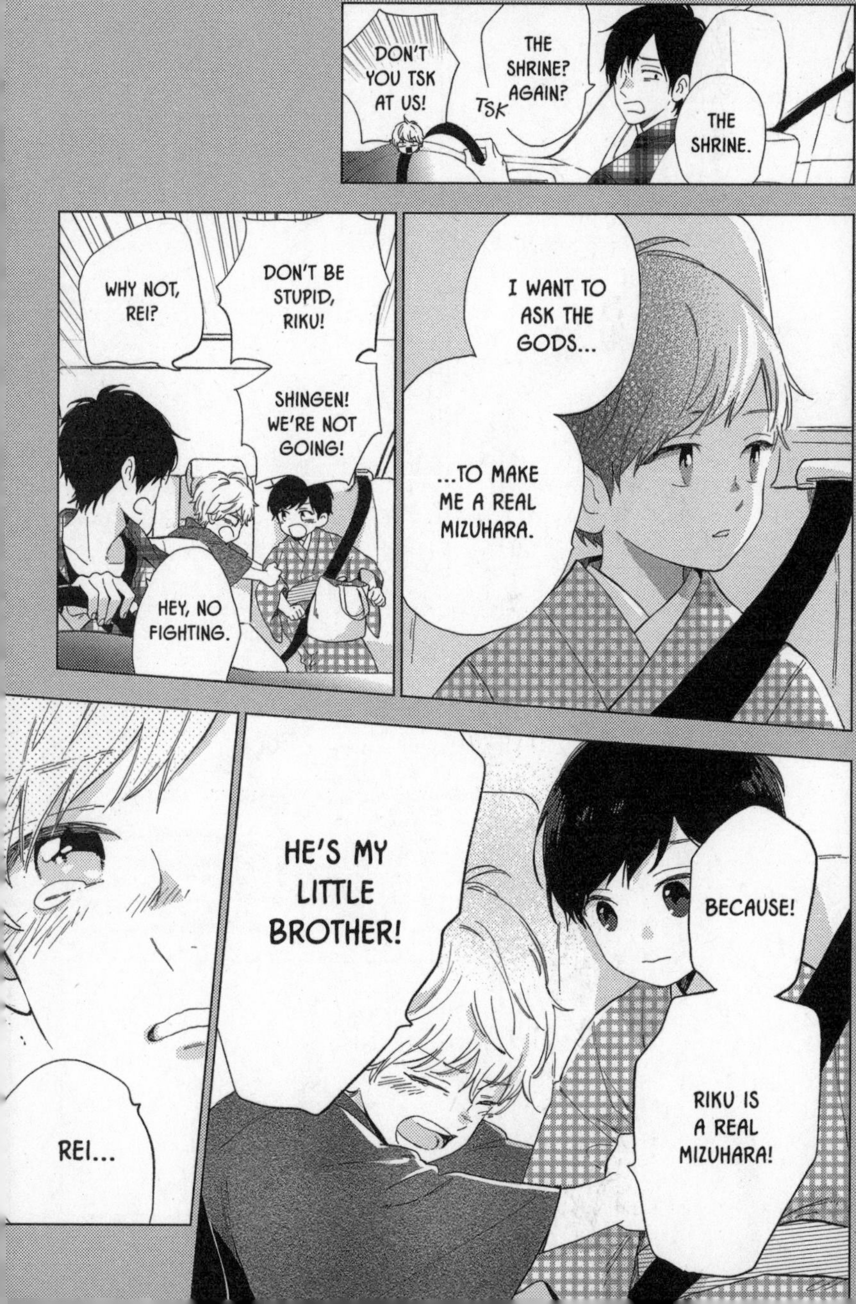
THE SHRINE.
THE SHRINE? AGAIN?
TSK
DON'T YOU TSK AT US!
I WANT TO ASK THE GODS...
...TO MAKE ME A REAL MIZUHARA.
DON'T BE STUPID, RIKU!
WHY NOT, REI?
SHINGEN! WE'RE NOT GOING!
HEY, NO FIGHTING.
BECAUSE!
RIKU IS A REAL MIZUHARA!
HE'S MY LITTLE BROTHER!
REI...

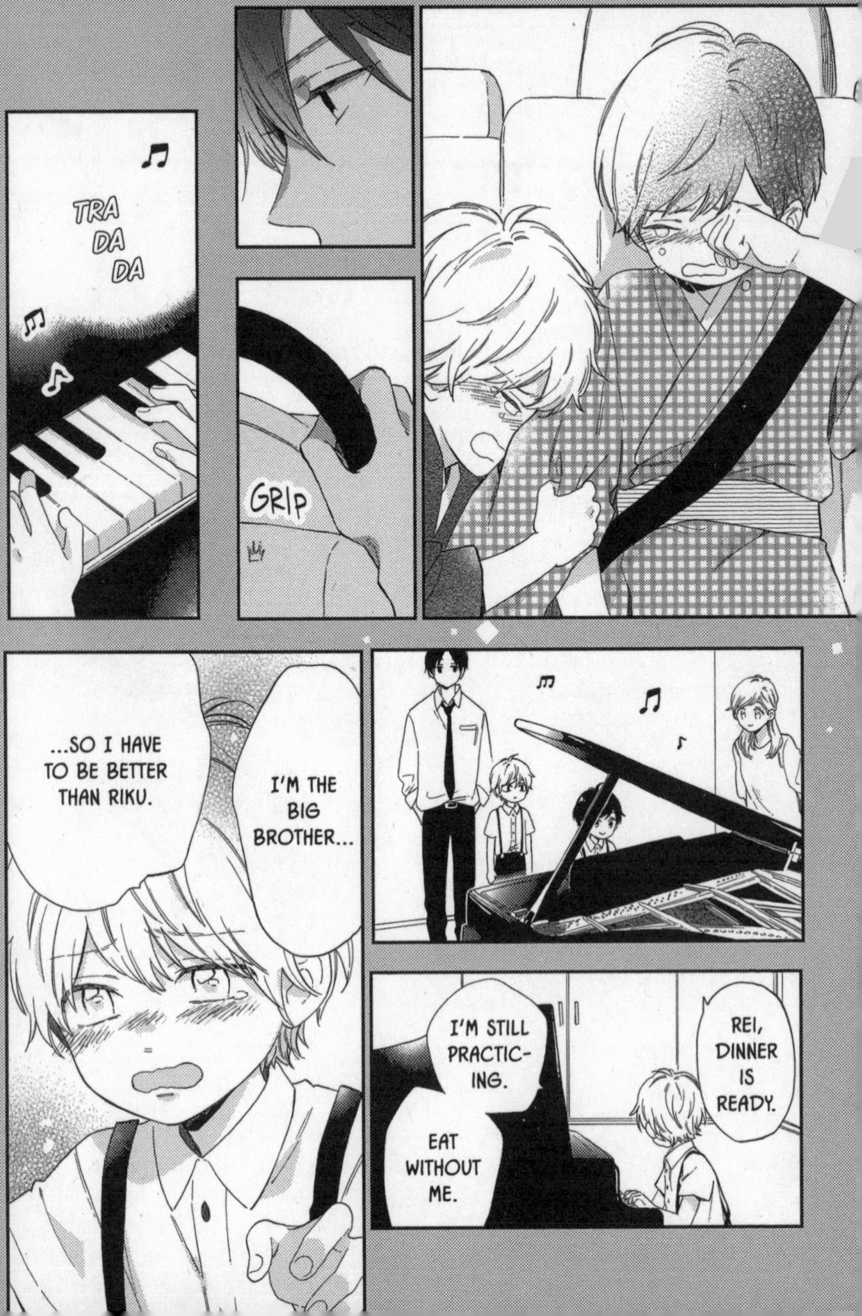
GRIP
TRA
DA
DA
REI, DINNER IS READY.
I'M STILL PRACTICING.
EAT WITHOUT ME.
I'M THE BIG BROTHER...
...SO I HAVE TO BE BETTER THAN RIKU.

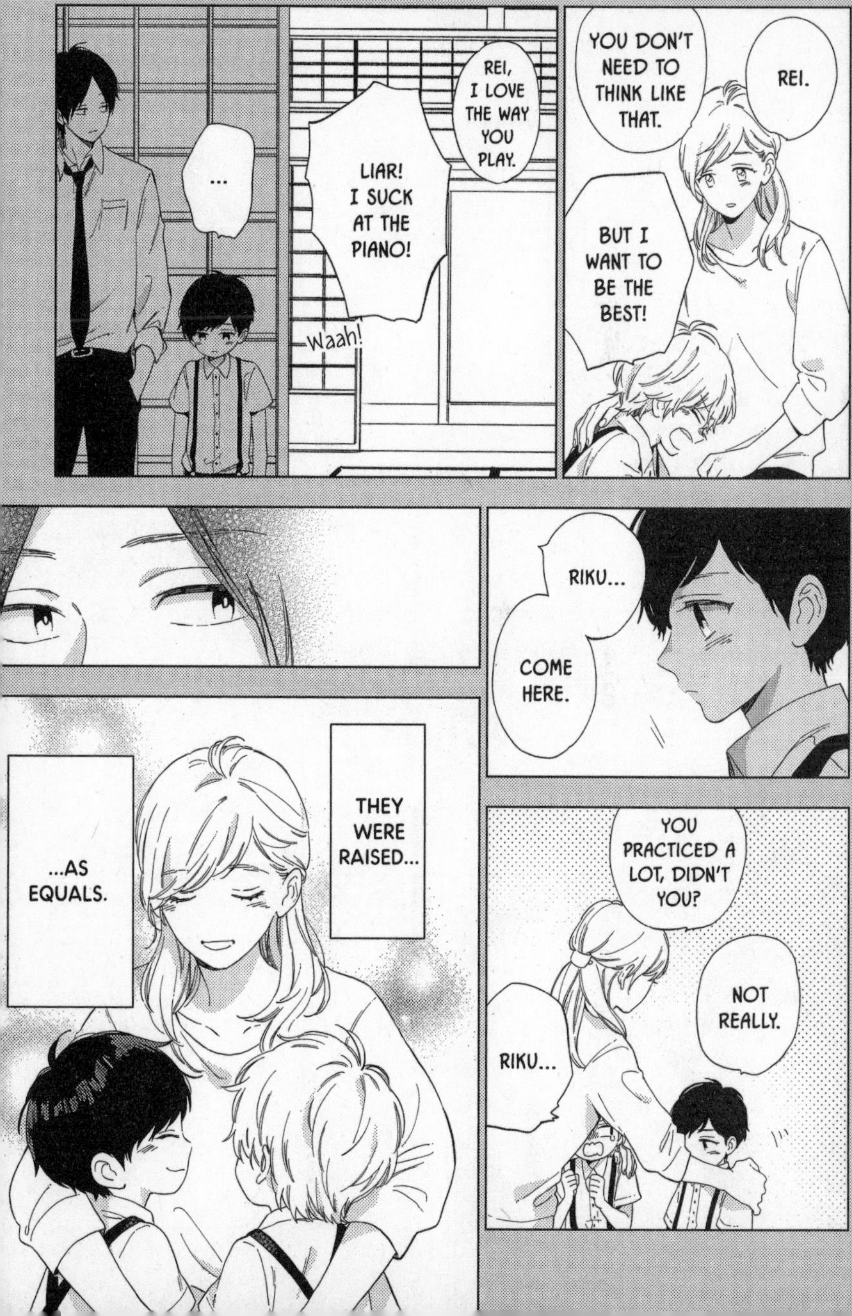
REI.
YOU DON'T NEED TO THINK LIKE THAT.
BUT I WANT TO BE THE BEST!
REI, I LOVE THE WAY YOU PLAY.
LIAR! I SUCK AT THE PIANO!
Waah!
...
RIKU...
COME HERE.
YOU PRACTICED A LOT, DIDN'T YOU?
NOT REALLY.
RIKU...
THEY WERE RAISED...
...AS EQUALS.

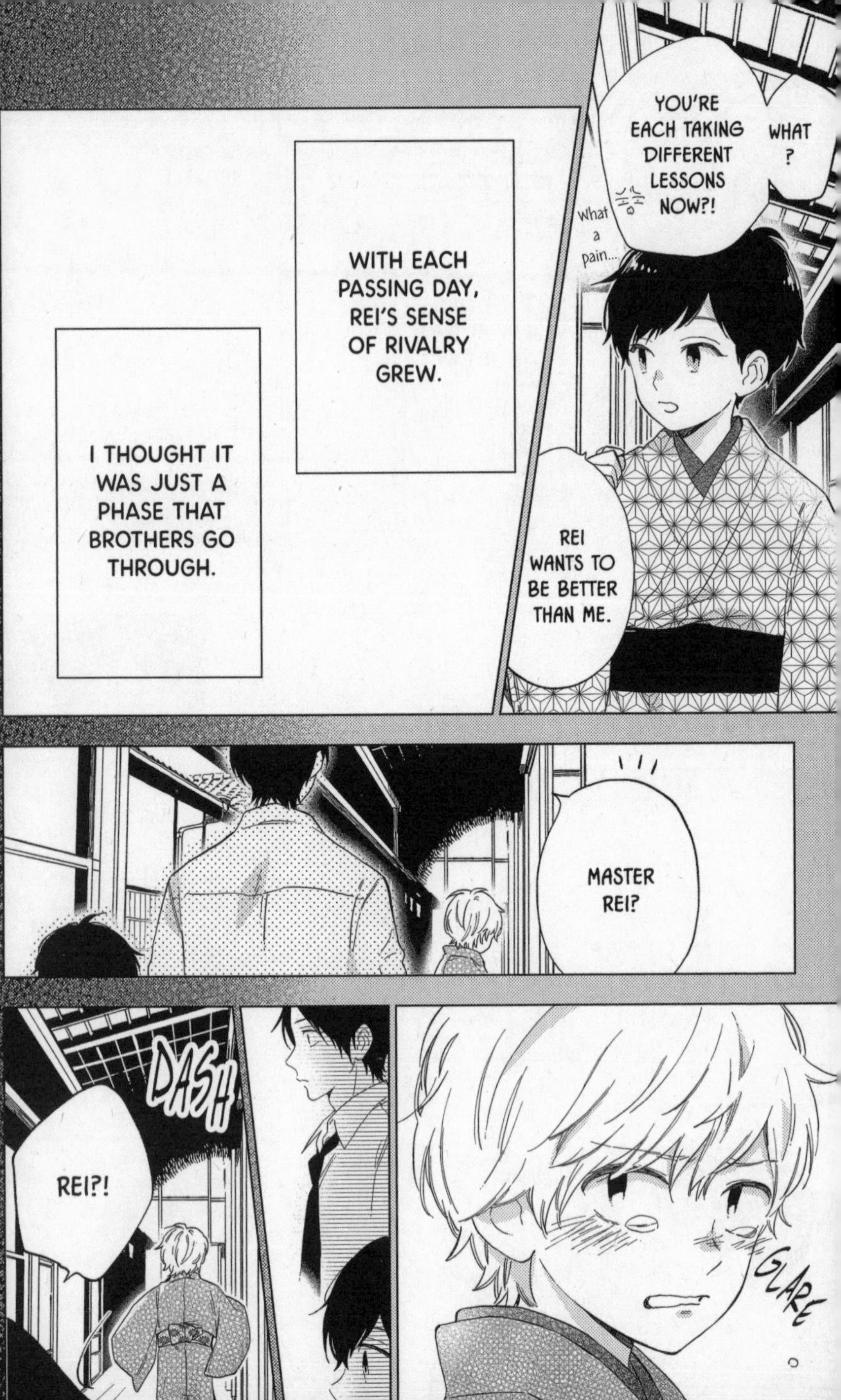
YOU'RE EACH TAKING DIFFERENT LESSONS NOW?!
WHAT?
What a pain...
REI WANTS TO BE BETTER THAN ME.
WITH EACH PASSING DAY, REI'S SENSE OF RIVALRY GREW.
I THOUGHT IT WAS JUST A PHASE THAT BROTHERS GO THROUGH.
MASTER REI?
GLARE
DASH
REI?!

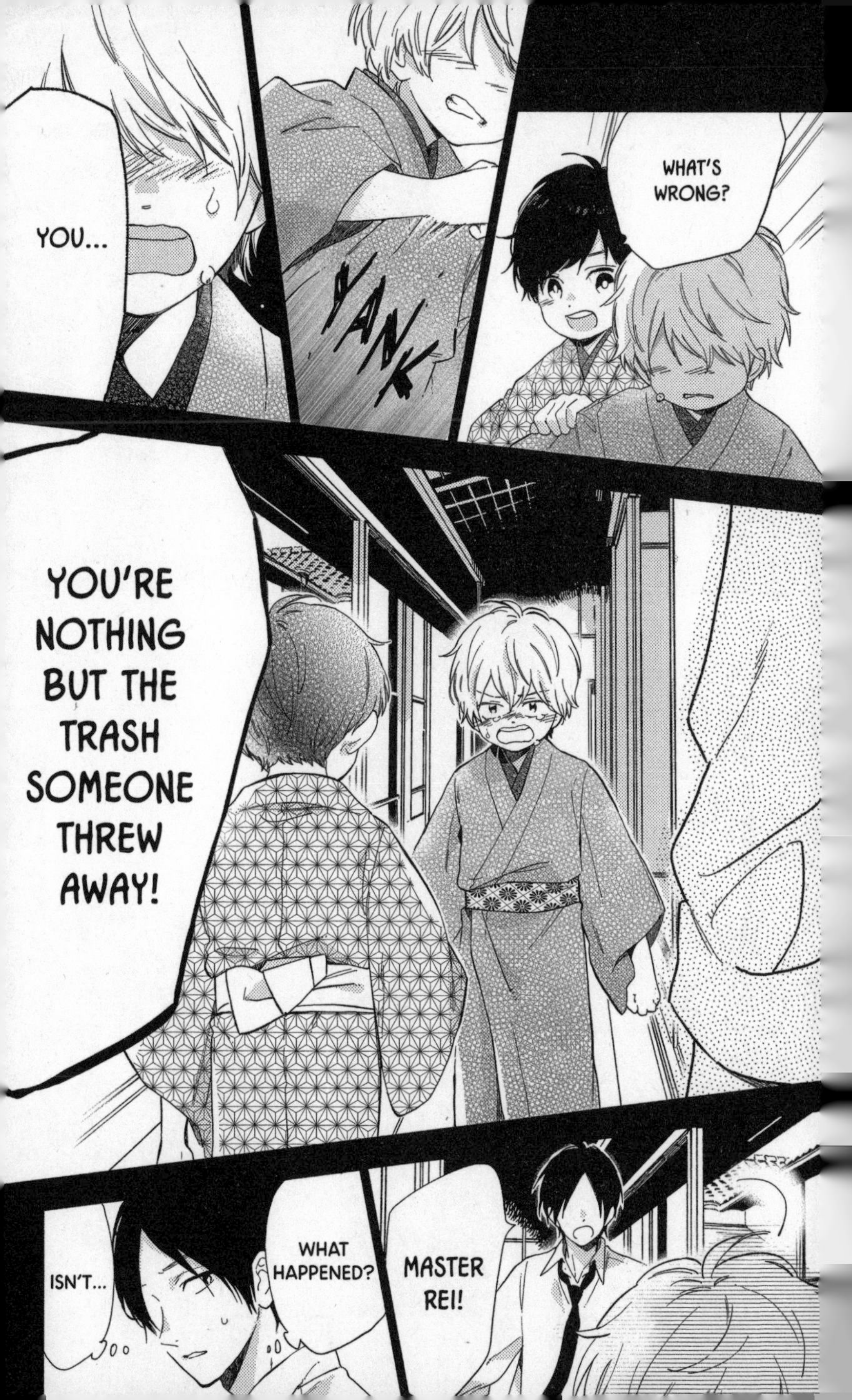
WHAT'S WRONG?
YANK
YOU...
YOU'RE NOTHING BUT THE TRASH SOMEONE THREW AWAY!
MASTER REI!
WHAT HAPPENED?
ISN'T...

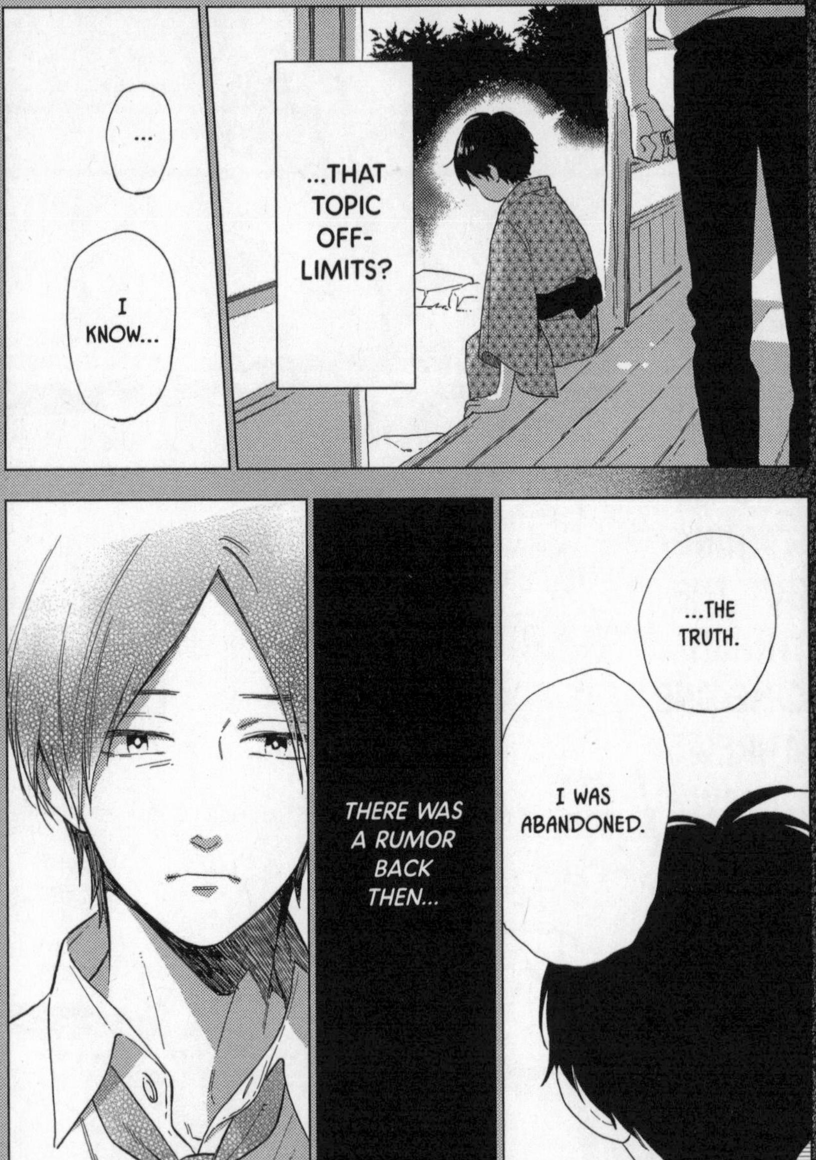
...THAT TOPIC OFF-LIMITS?
...
I KNOW...
...THE TRUTH.
I WAS ABANDONED.
THERE WAS A RUMOR BACK THEN...

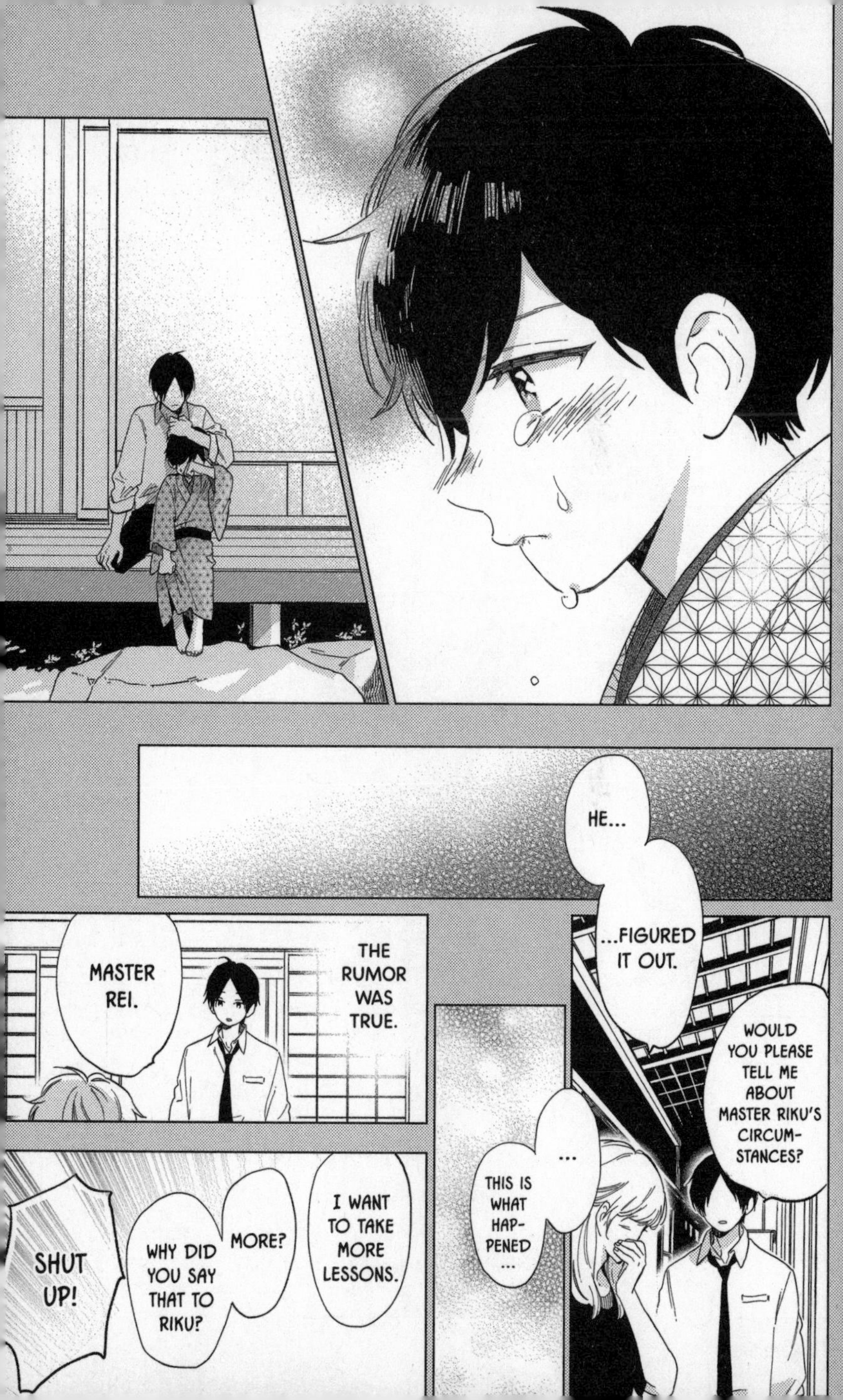
HE...
...FIGURED IT OUT.
WOULD YOU PLEASE TELL ME ABOUT MASTER RIKU'S CIRCUM-STANCES?
...
THIS IS WHAT HAP-PENED...
THE RUMOR WAS TRUE.
MASTER REI.
I WANT TO TAKE MORE LESSONS.
MORE?
WHY DID YOU SAY THAT TO RIKU?
SHUT UP!

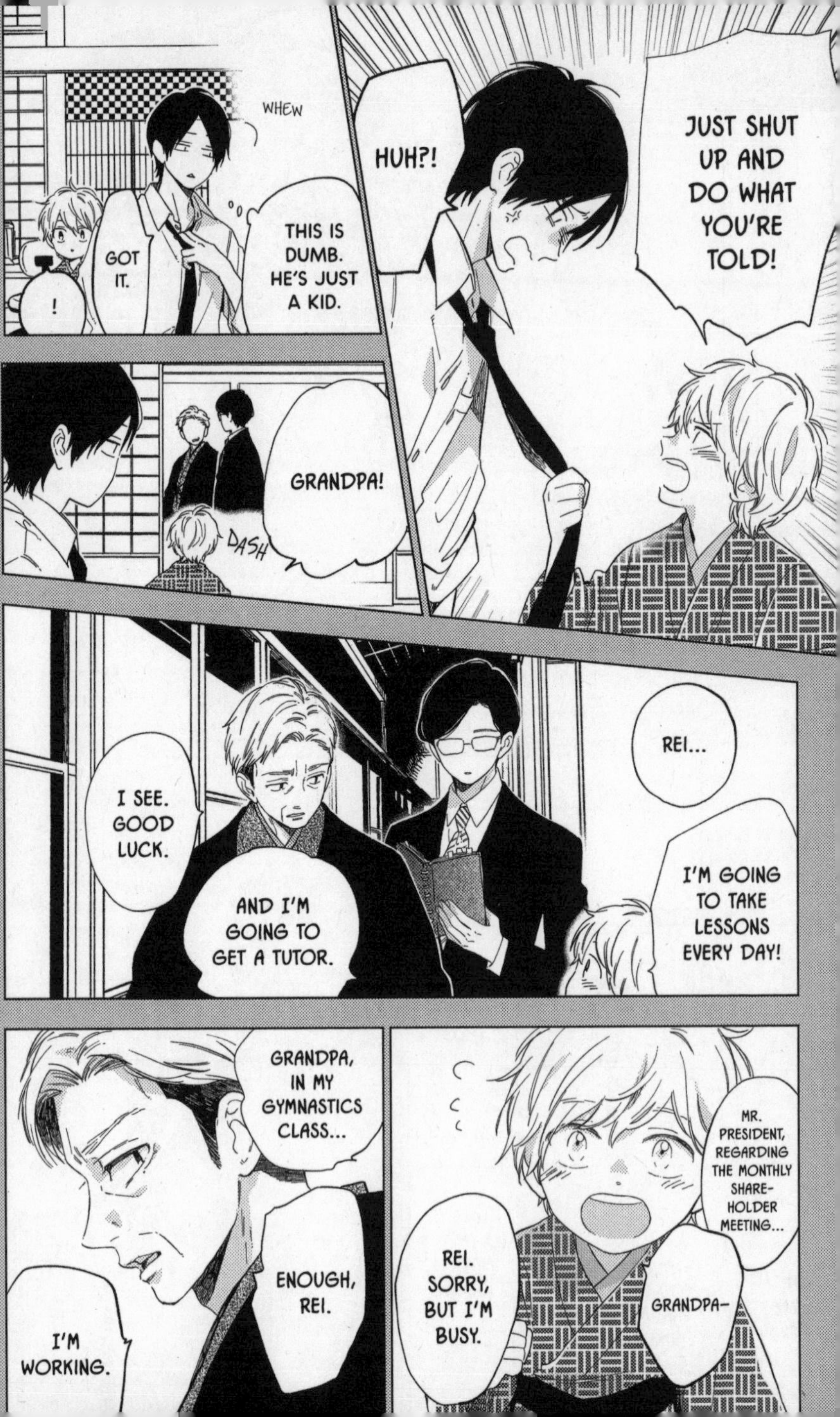
JUST SHUT UP AND DO WHAT YOU'RE TOLD!
HUH?!
WHEW
THIS IS DUMB. HE'S JUST A KID.
GOT IT.
!
GRANDPA!
DASH
REI...
I'M GOING TO TAKE LESSONS EVERY DAY!
AND I'M GOING TO GET A TUTOR.
I SEE. GOOD LUCK.
MR. PRESIDENT, REGARDING THE MONTHLY SHARE-HOLDER MEETING...
GRANDPA—
REI. SORRY, BUT I'M BUSY.
GRANDPA, IN MY GYMNASTICS CLASS...
ENOUGH, REI.
I'M WORKING.

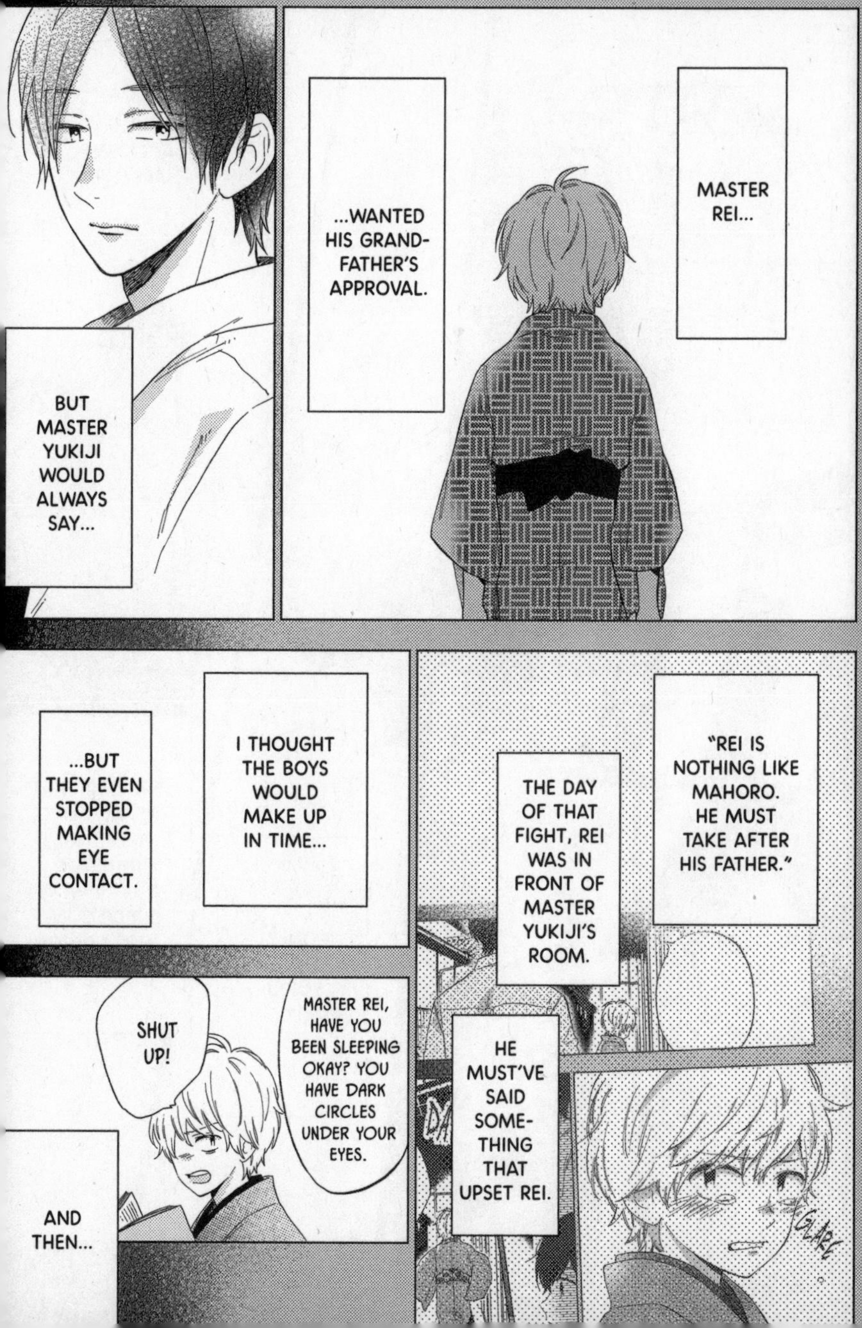
MASTER REI...
...WANTED HIS GRAND-FATHER'S APPROVAL.
BUT MASTER YUKIJI WOULD ALWAYS SAY...
"REI IS NOTHING LIKE MAHORO. HE MUST TAKE AFTER HIS FATHER."
THE DAY OF THAT FIGHT, REI WAS IN FRONT OF MASTER YUKIJI'S ROOM.
HE MUST'VE SAID SOME-THING THAT UPSET REI.
GLARE
I THOUGHT THE BOYS WOULD MAKE UP IN TIME...
...BUT THEY EVEN STOPPED MAKING EYE CONTACT.
MASTER REI, HAVE YOU BEEN SLEEPING OKAY? YOU HAVE DARK CIRCLES UNDER YOUR EYES.
SHUT UP!
AND THEN...

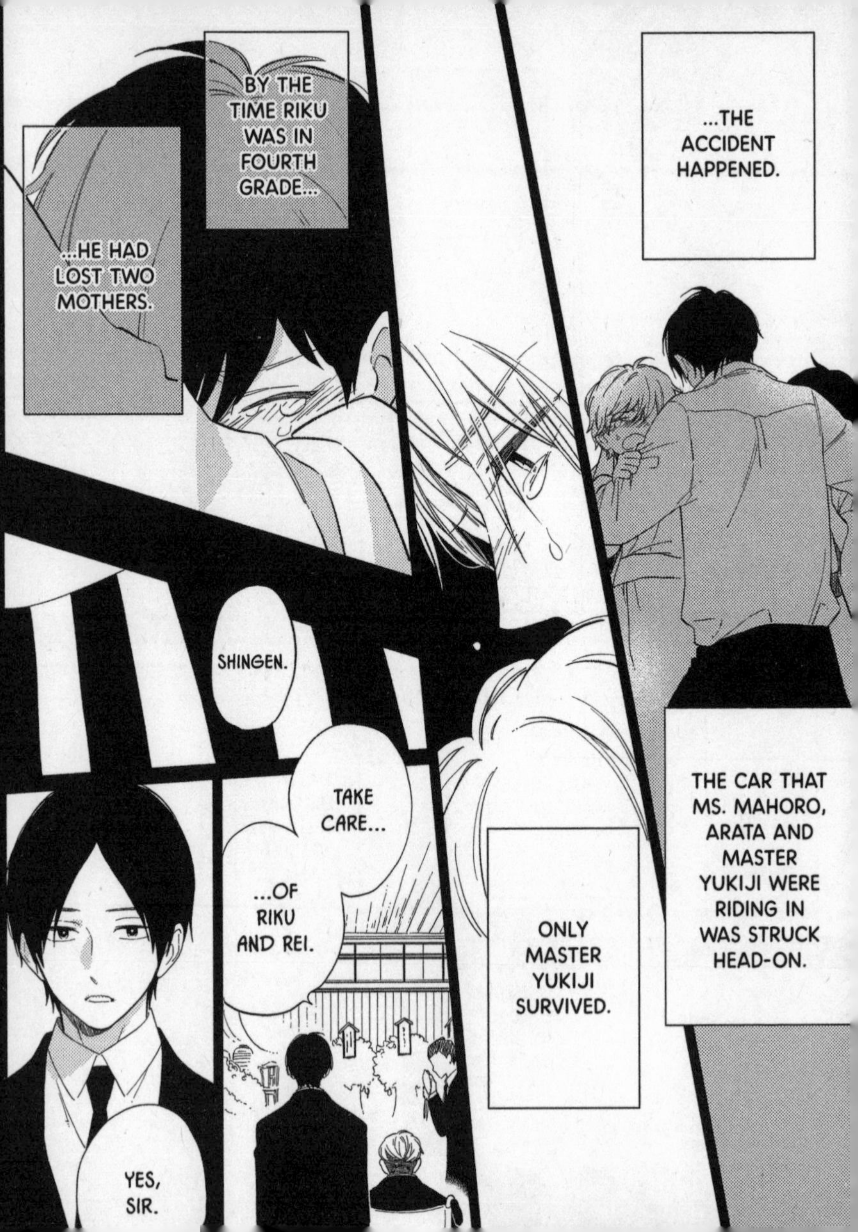
...THE ACCIDENT HAPPENED.
THE CAR THAT MS. MAHORO, ARATA AND MASTER YUKIJI WERE RIDING IN WAS STRUCK HEAD-ON.
ONLY MASTER YUKIJI SURVIVED.
BY THE TIME RIKU WAS IN FOURTH GRADE...
...HE HAD LOST TWO MOTHERS.
SHINGEN.
TAKE CARE...
...OF RIKU AND REI.
YES, SIR.

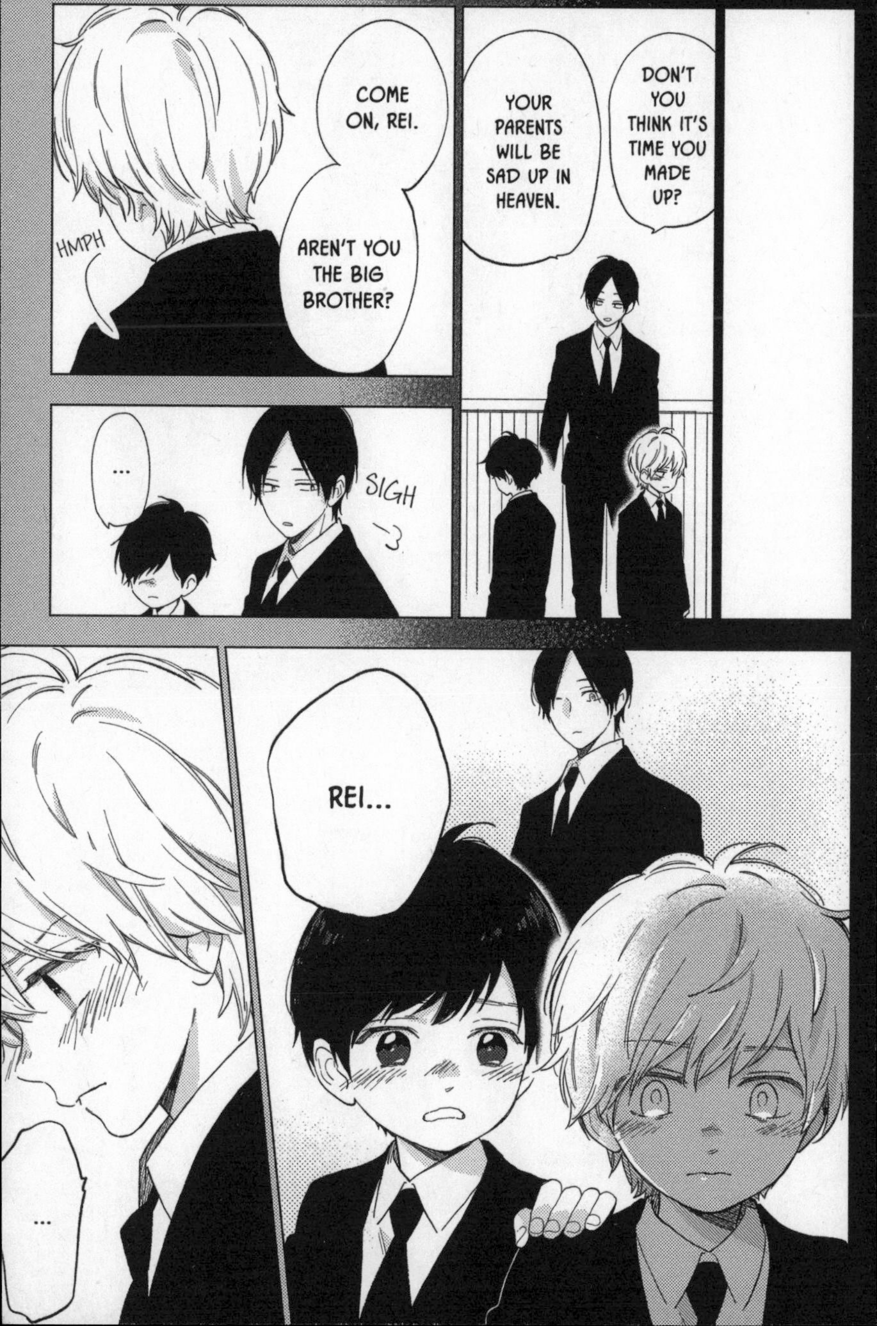
DON'T YOU THINK IT'S TIME YOU MADE UP?
YOUR PARENTS WILL BE SAD UP IN HEAVEN.
COME ON, REI.
AREN'T YOU THE BIG BROTHER?
HMPH
SIGH
...
REI...
...

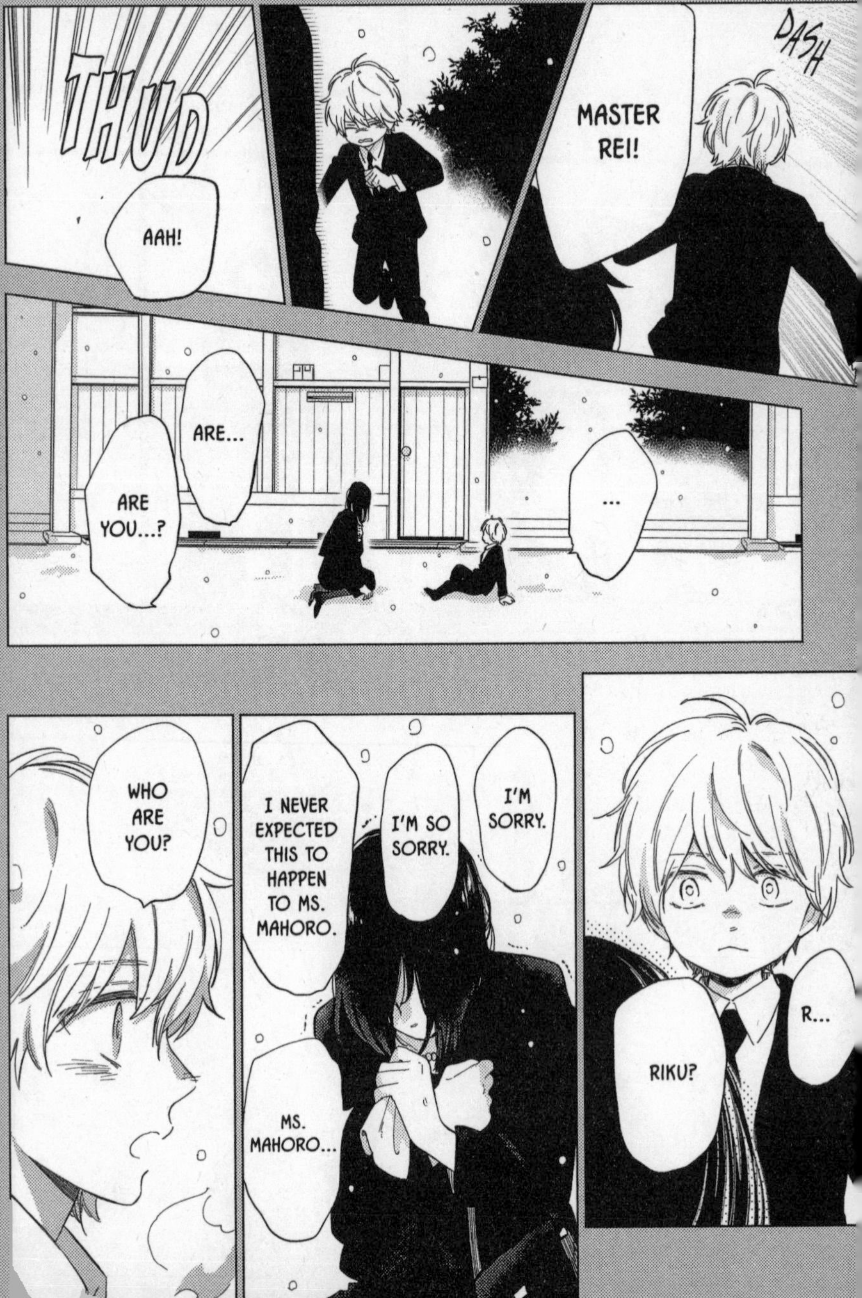
DASH
MASTER REI!
THUD
AAH!
...
ARE...
ARE YOU...?
R...
RIKU?
I'M SORRY.
I'M SO SORRY.
I NEVER EXPECTED THIS TO HAPPEN TO MS. MAHORO.
MS. MAHORO...
WHO ARE YOU?

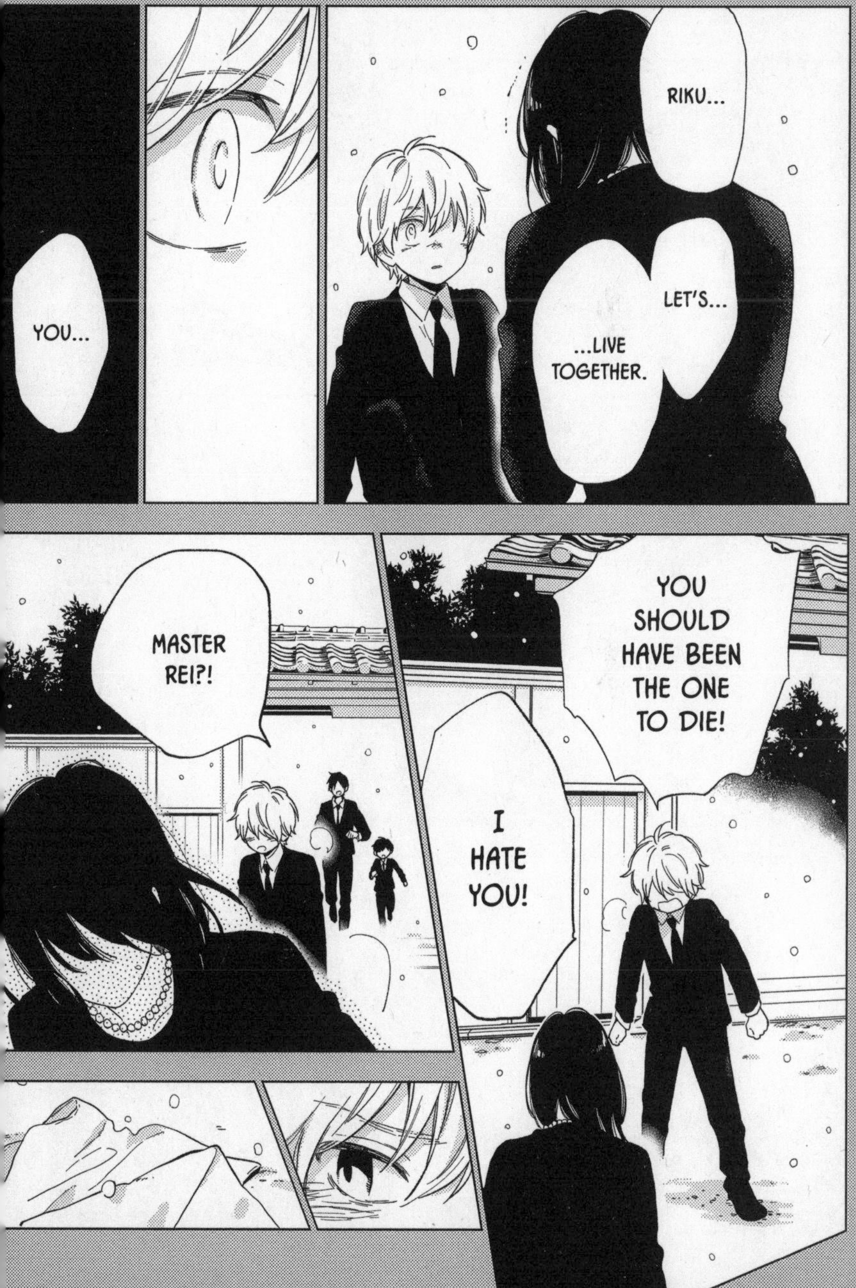
RIKU...
LET'S...
...LIVE TOGETHER.
YOU...
YOU SHOULD HAVE BEEN THE ONE TO DIE!
I HATE YOU!
MASTER REI?!

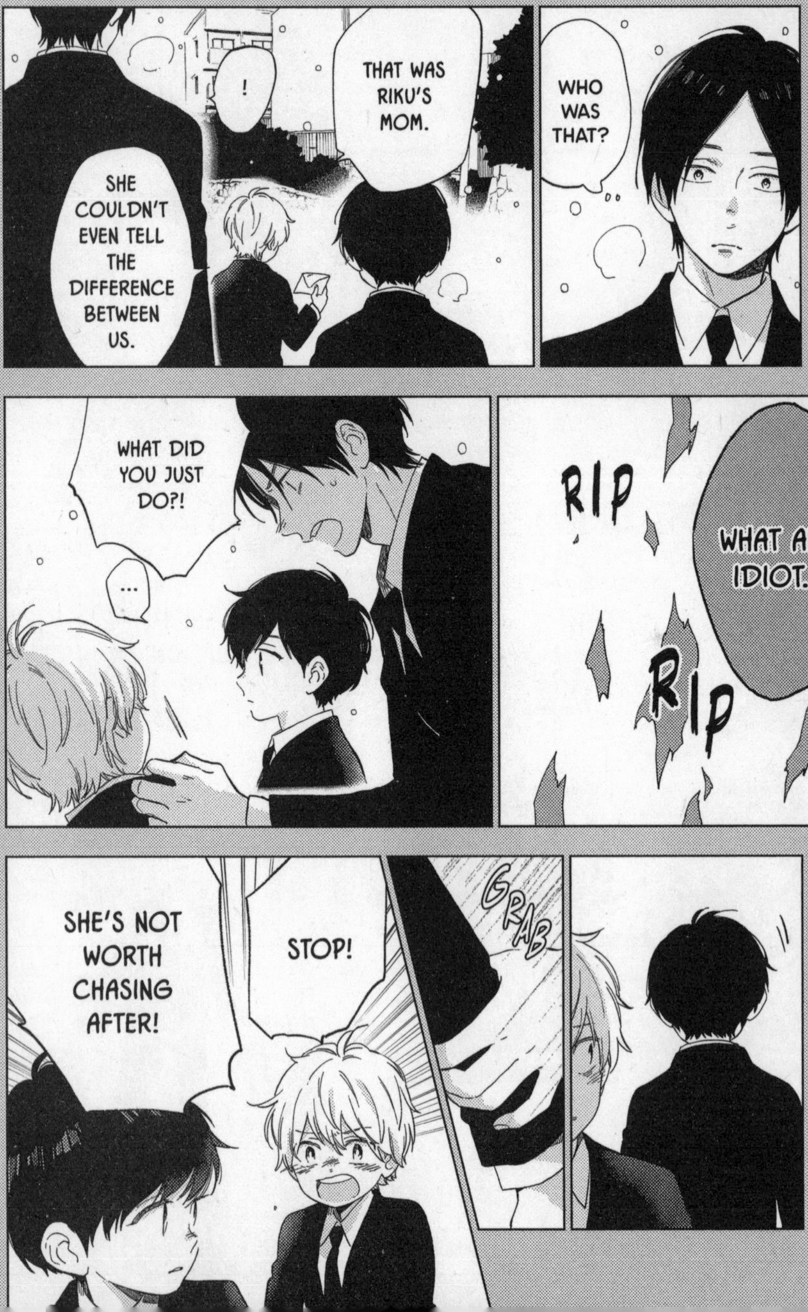
WHO WAS THAT?
THAT WAS RIKU'S MOM.
!
SHE COULDN'T EVEN TELL THE DIFFERENCE BETWEEN US.
WHAT AN IDIOT.
RIP
RIP
WHAT DID YOU JUST DO?!
...
GRAB
STOP!
SHE'S NOT WORTH CHASING AFTER!

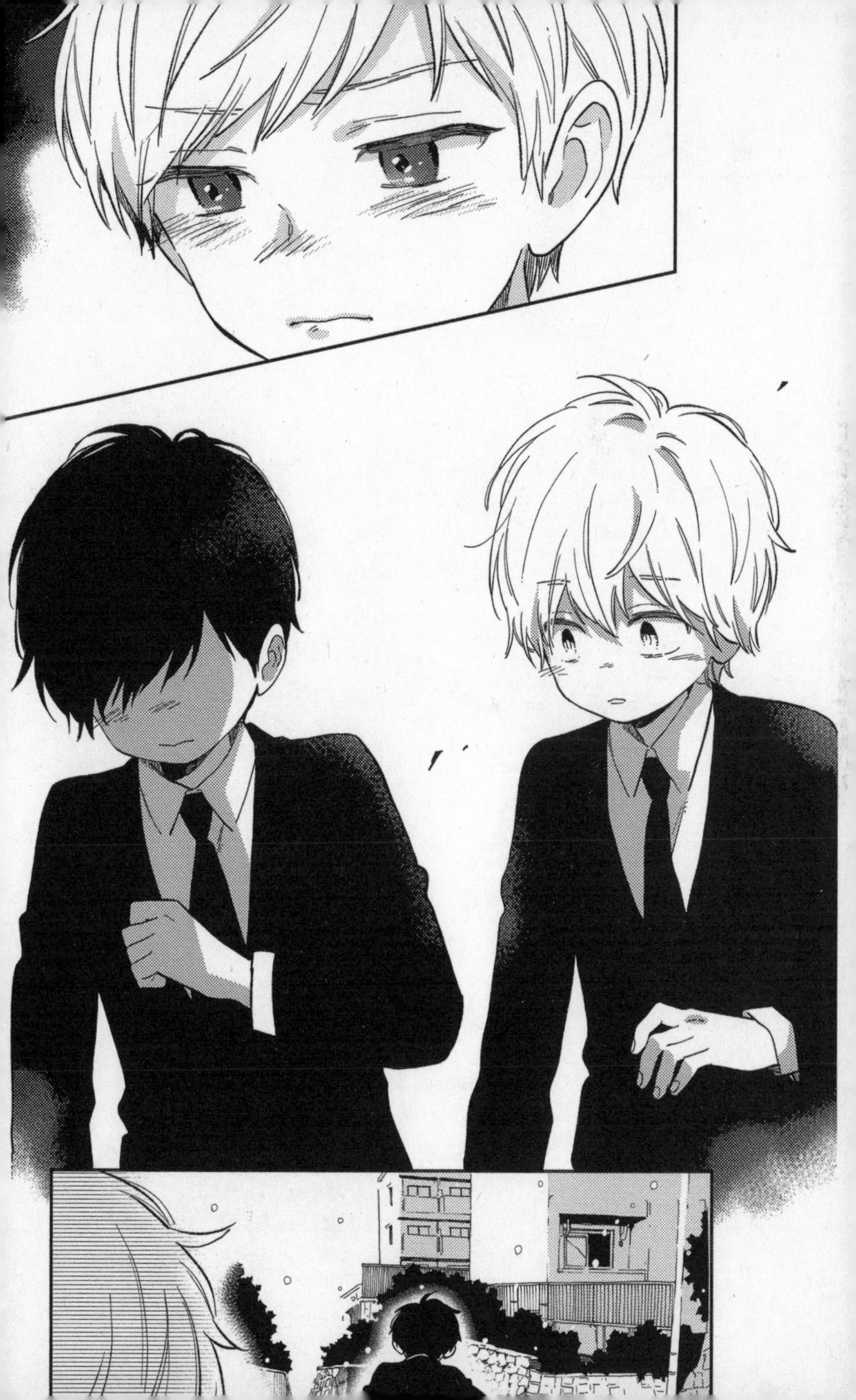

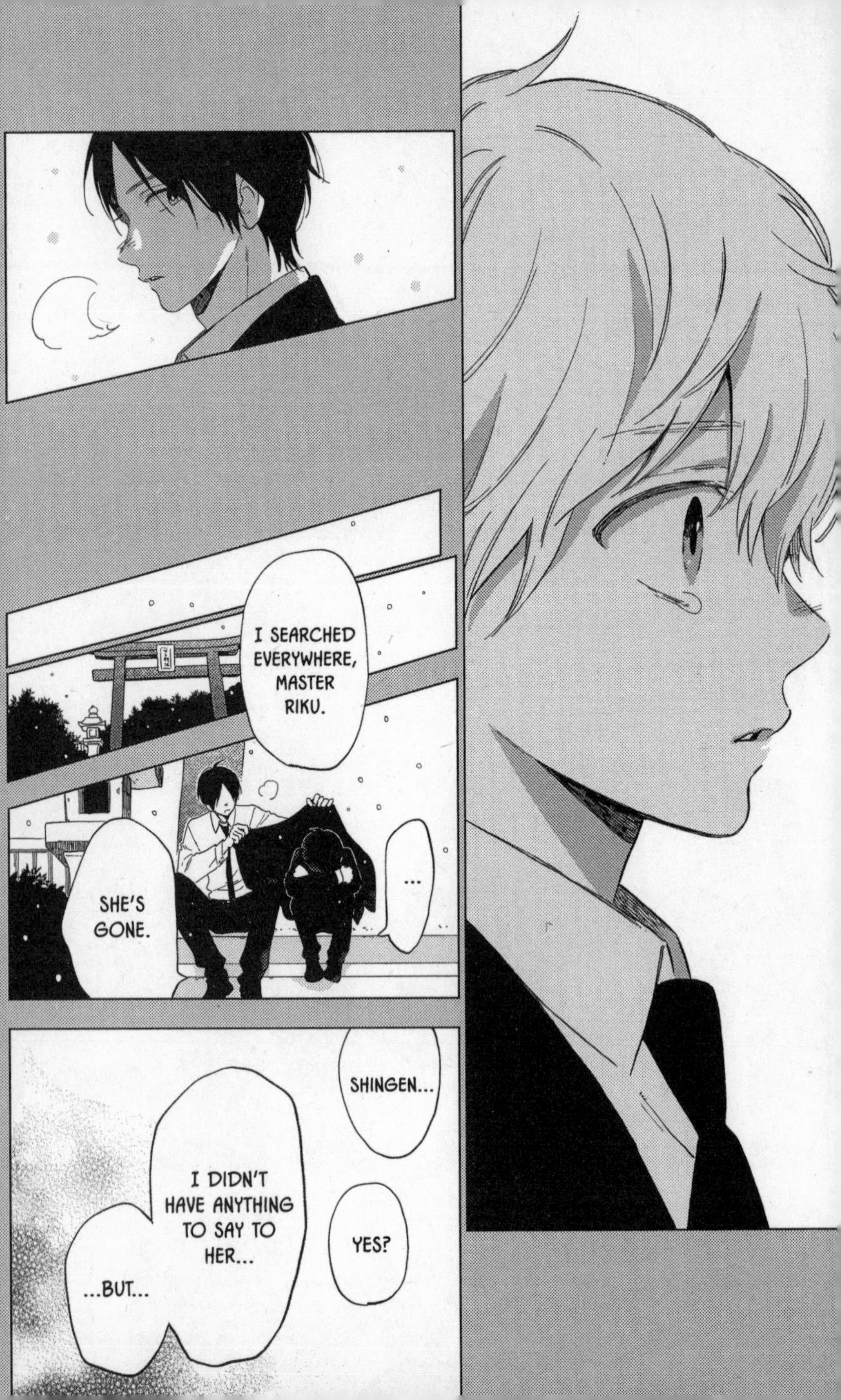
I SEARCHED EVERYWHERE, MASTER RIKU.
...
SHE'S GONE.
SHINGEN...
YES?
I DIDN'T HAVE ANYTHING TO SAY TO HER...
...BUT...

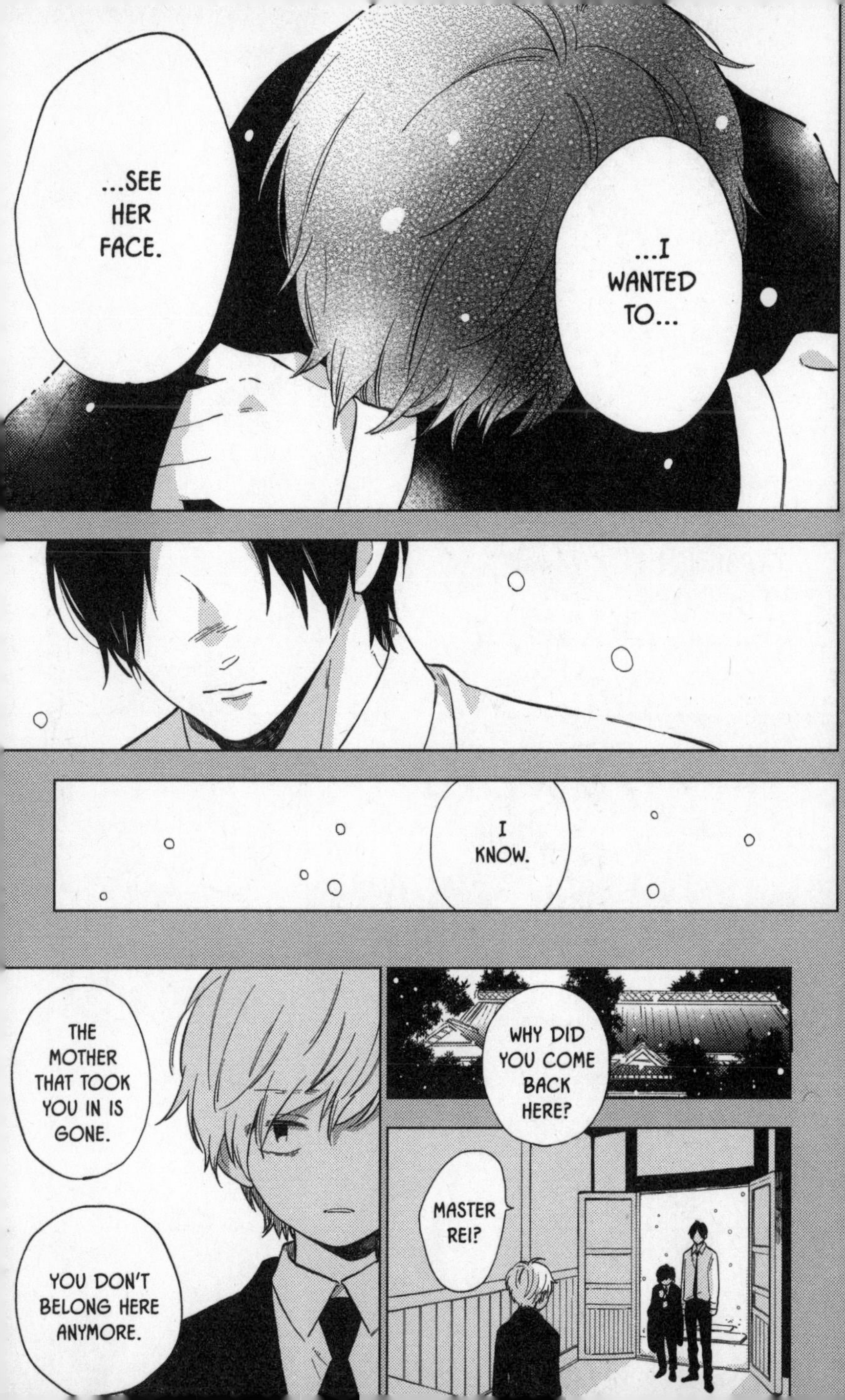
...I WANTED TO...
...SEE HER FACE.
I KNOW.
WHY DID YOU COME BACK HERE?
MASTER REI?
THE MOTHER THAT TOOK YOU IN IS GONE.
YOU DON'T BELONG HERE ANYMORE.

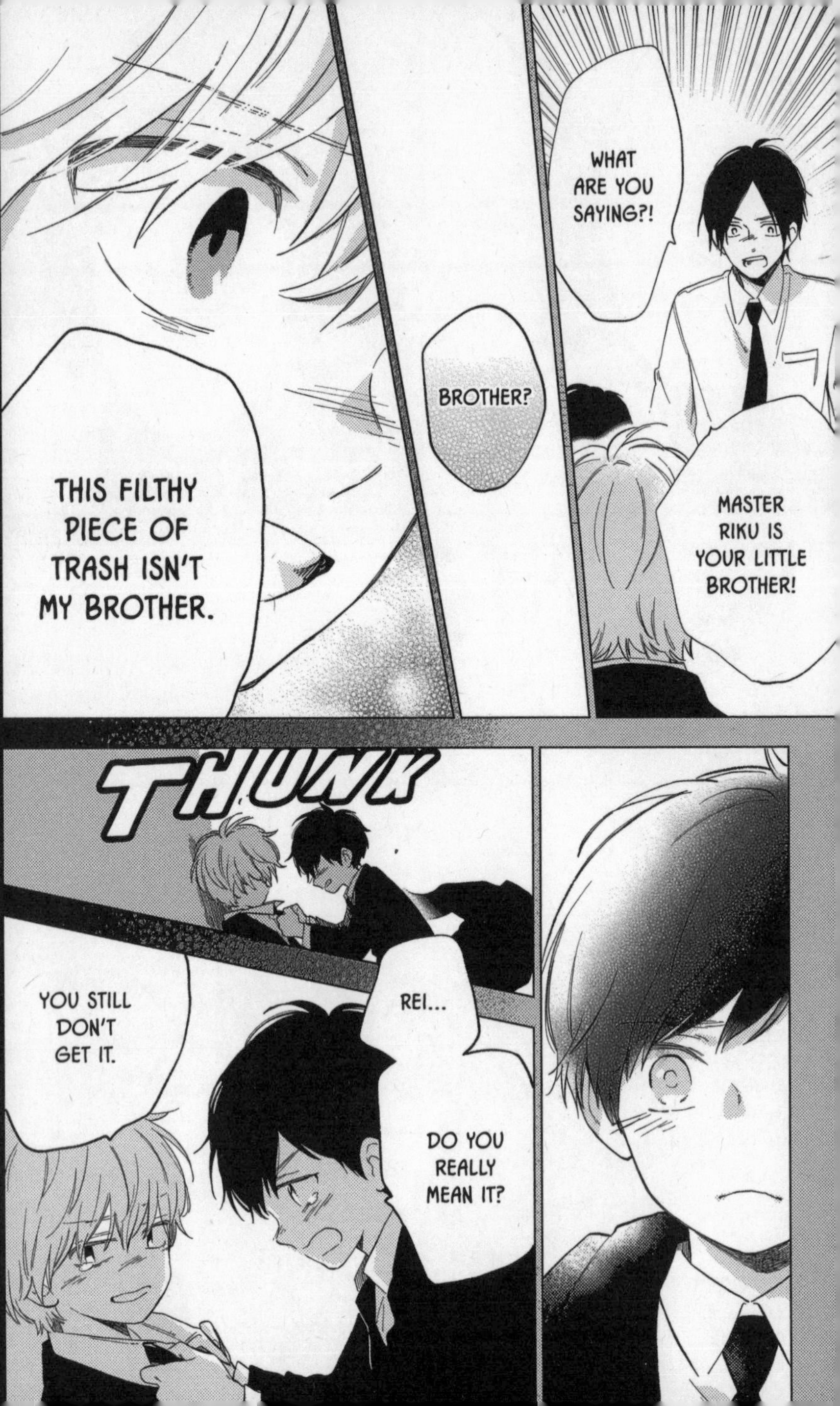
WHAT ARE YOU SAYING?!
MASTER RIKU IS YOUR LITTLE BROTHER!
BROTHER?
THIS FILTHY PIECE OF TRASH ISN'T MY BROTHER.
THUNK
REI...
DO YOU REALLY MEAN IT?
YOU STILL DON'T GET IT.

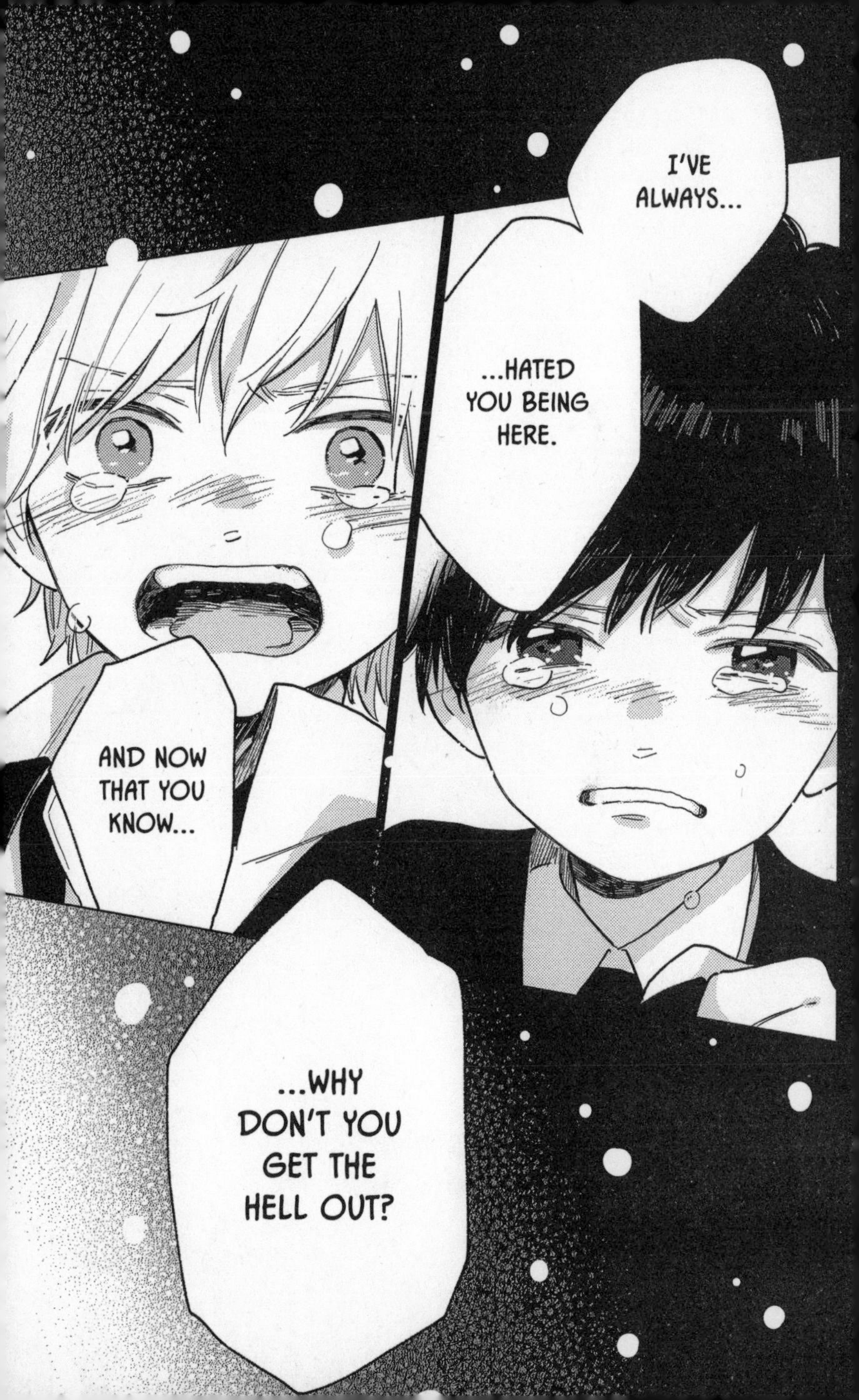
I'VE ALWAYS...
...HATED YOU BEING HERE.
AND NOW THAT YOU KNOW...
...WHY DON'T YOU GET THE HELL OUT?

SHORTCAKE
CAKE

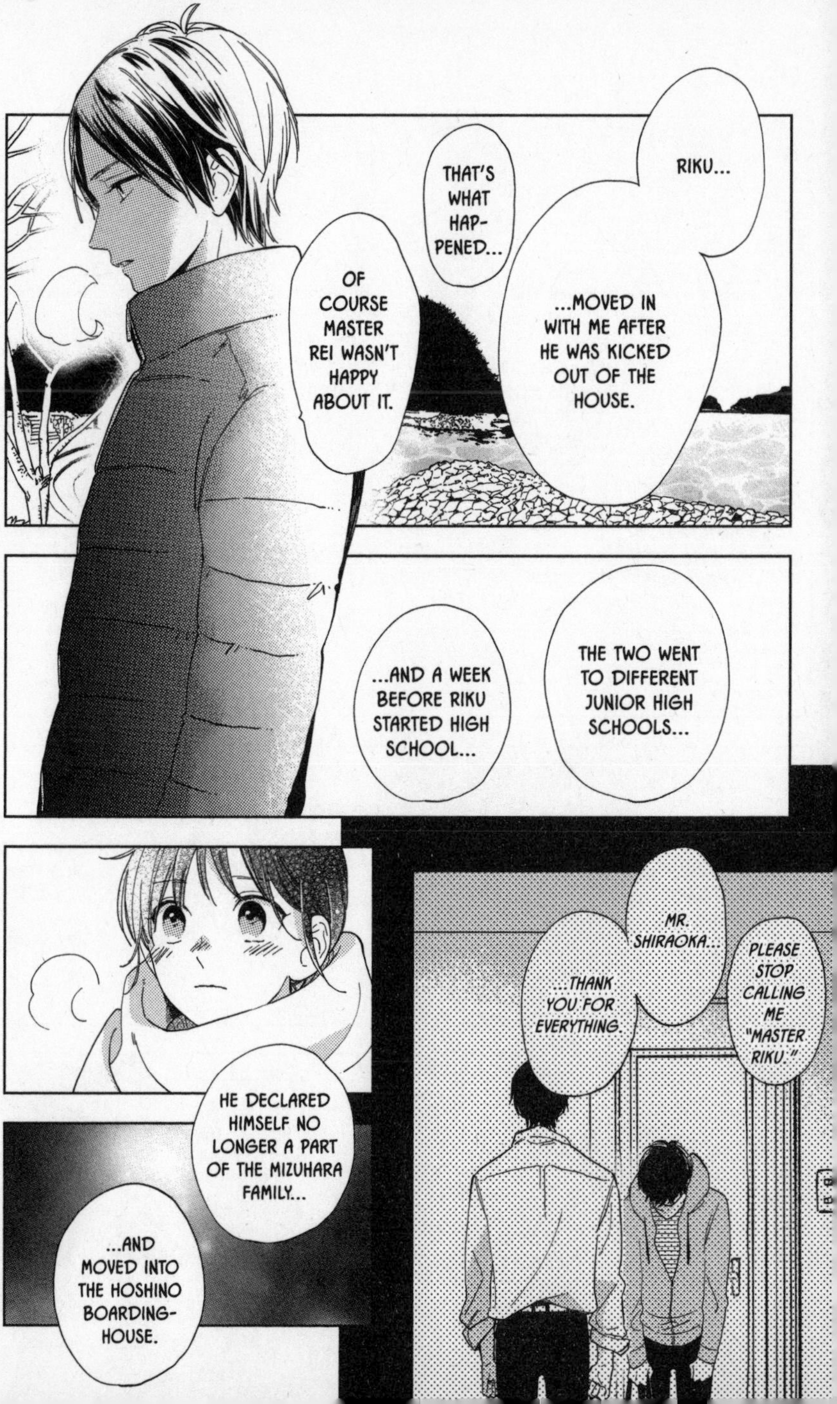
RIKU...
...MOVED IN WITH ME AFTER HE WAS KICKED OUT OF THE HOUSE.
THAT'S WHAT HAP-PENED...
OF COURSE MASTER REI WASN'T HAPPY ABOUT IT.
THE TWO WENT TO DIFFERENT JUNIOR HIGH SCHOOLS...
...AND A WEEK BEFORE RIKU STARTED HIGH SCHOOL...
MR. SHIRAOKA...
PLEASE STOP CALLING ME "MASTER RIKU."
...THANK YOU FOR EVERYTHING.
HE DECLARED HIMSELF NO LONGER A PART OF THE MIZUHARA FAMILY...
...AND MOVED INTO THE HOSHINO BOARDING-HOUSE.

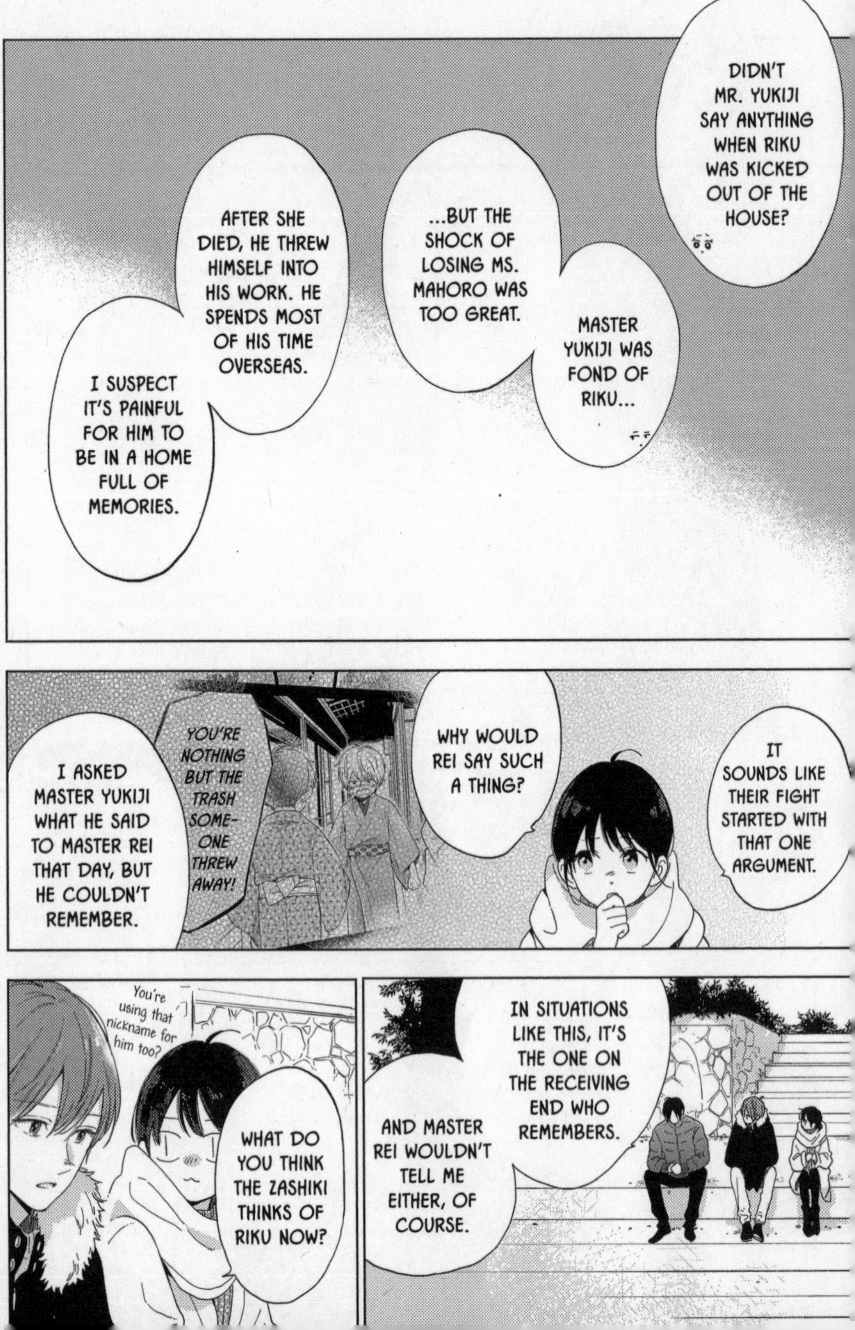
DIDN'T MR. YUKIJI SAY ANYTHING WHEN RIKU WAS KICKED OUT OF THE HOUSE?
MASTER YUKIJI WAS FOND OF RIKU...
...BUT THE SHOCK OF LOSING MS. MAHORO WAS TOO GREAT.
AFTER SHE DIED, HE THREW HIMSELF INTO HIS WORK. HE SPENDS MOST OF HIS TIME OVERSEAS.
I SUSPECT IT'S PAINFUL FOR HIM TO BE IN A HOME FULL OF MEMORIES.
IT SOUNDS LIKE THEIR FIGHT STARTED WITH THAT ONE ARGUMENT.
WHY WOULD REI SAY SUCH A THING?
YOU'RE NOTHING BUT THE TRASH SOME-ONE THREW AWAY!
I ASKED MASTER YUKIJI WHAT HE SAID TO MASTER REI THAT DAY, BUT HE COULDN'T REMEMBER.
IN SITUATIONS LIKE THIS, IT'S THE ONE ON THE RECEIVING END WHO REMEMBERS.
AND MASTER REI WOULDN'T TELL ME EITHER, OF COURSE.
WHAT DO YOU THINK THE ZASHIKI THINKS OF RIKU NOW?
You're using that nickname for him too?

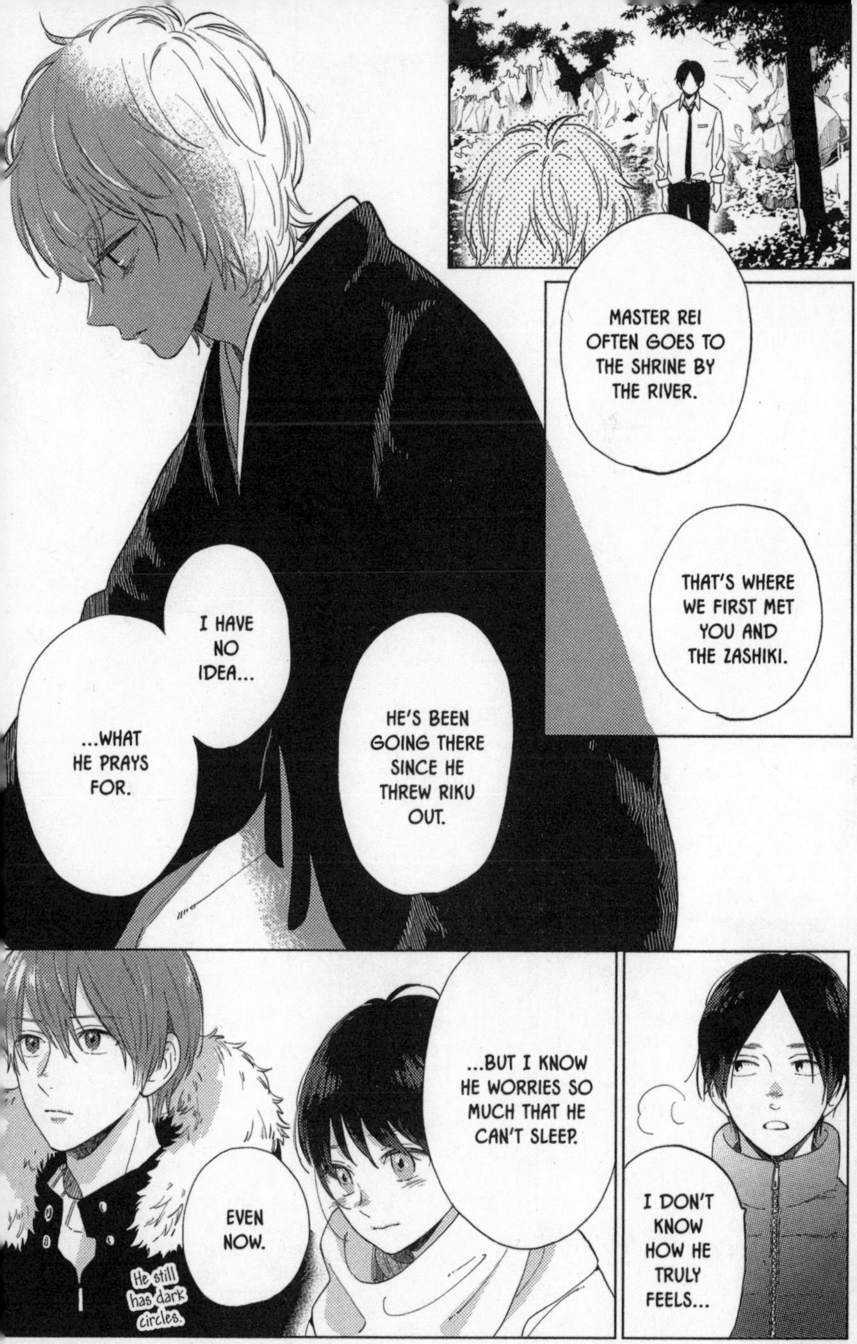
MASTER REI OFTEN GOES TO THE SHRINE BY THE RIVER.
THAT'S WHERE WE FIRST MET YOU AND THE ZASHIKI.
HE'S BEEN GOING THERE SINCE HE THREW RIKU OUT.
I HAVE NO IDEA...
...WHAT HE PRAYS FOR.
I DON'T KNOW HOW HE TRULY FEELS...
...BUT I KNOW HE WORRIES SO MUCH THAT HE CAN'T SLEEP.
EVEN NOW.
He still has dark circles.

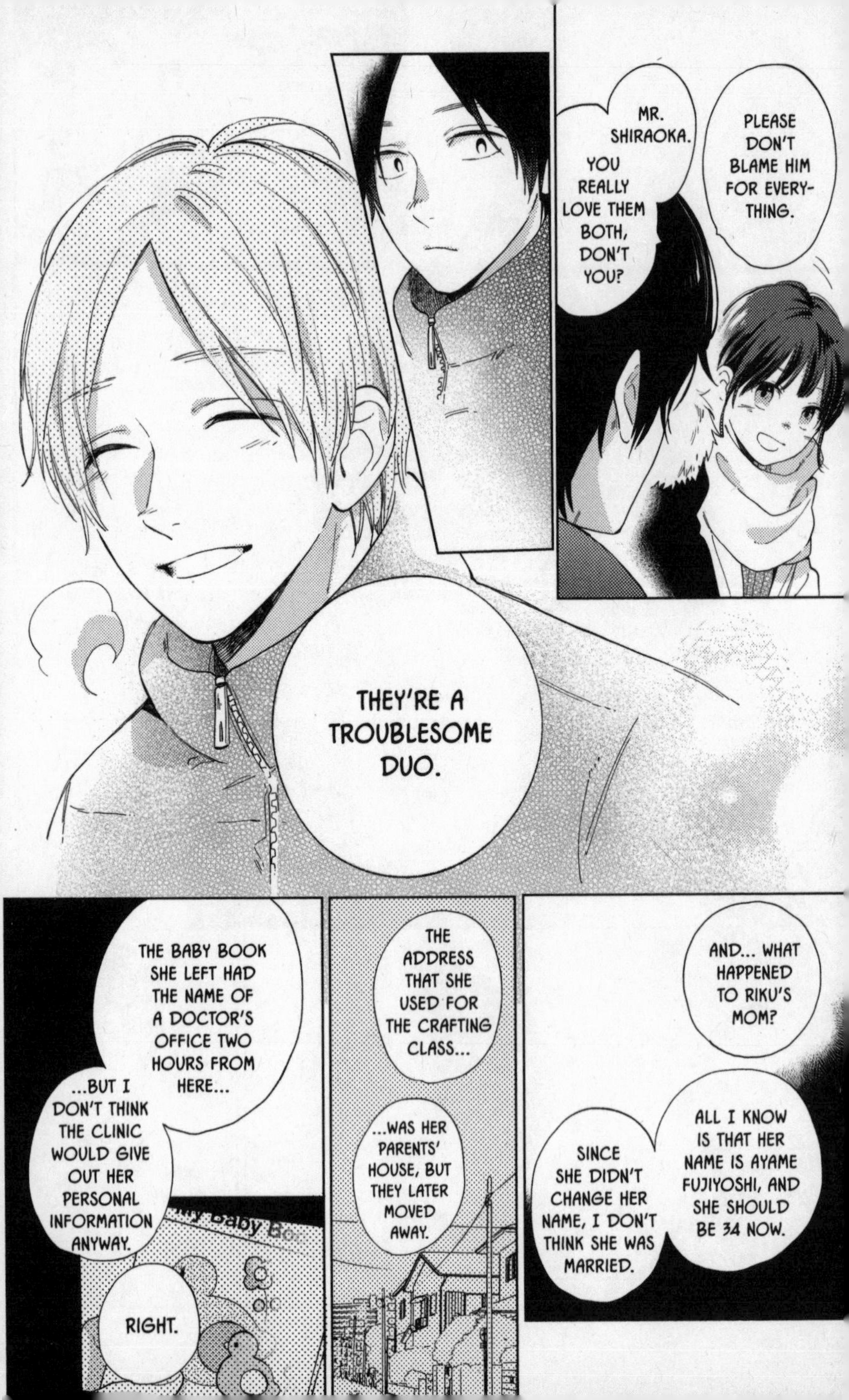
PLEASE DON'T BLAME HIM FOR EVERY-THING.
MR. SHIRAOKA. YOU REALLY LOVE THEM BOTH, DON'T YOU?
THEY'RE A TROUBLESOME DUO.
AND... WHAT HAPPENED TO RIKU'S MOM?
ALL I KNOW IS THAT HER NAME IS AYAME FUJIYOSHI, AND SHE SHOULD BE 34 NOW.
SINCE SHE DIDN'T CHANGE HER NAME, I DON'T THINK SHE WAS MARRIED.
THE ADDRESS THAT SHE USED FOR THE CRAFTING CLASS...
...WAS HER PARENTS' HOUSE, BUT THEY LATER MOVED AWAY.
THE BABY BOOK SHE LEFT HAD THE NAME OF A DOCTOR'S OFFICE TWO HOURS FROM HERE...
...BUT I DON'T THINK THE CLINIC WOULD GIVE OUT HER PERSONAL INFORMATION ANYWAY.
RIGHT.

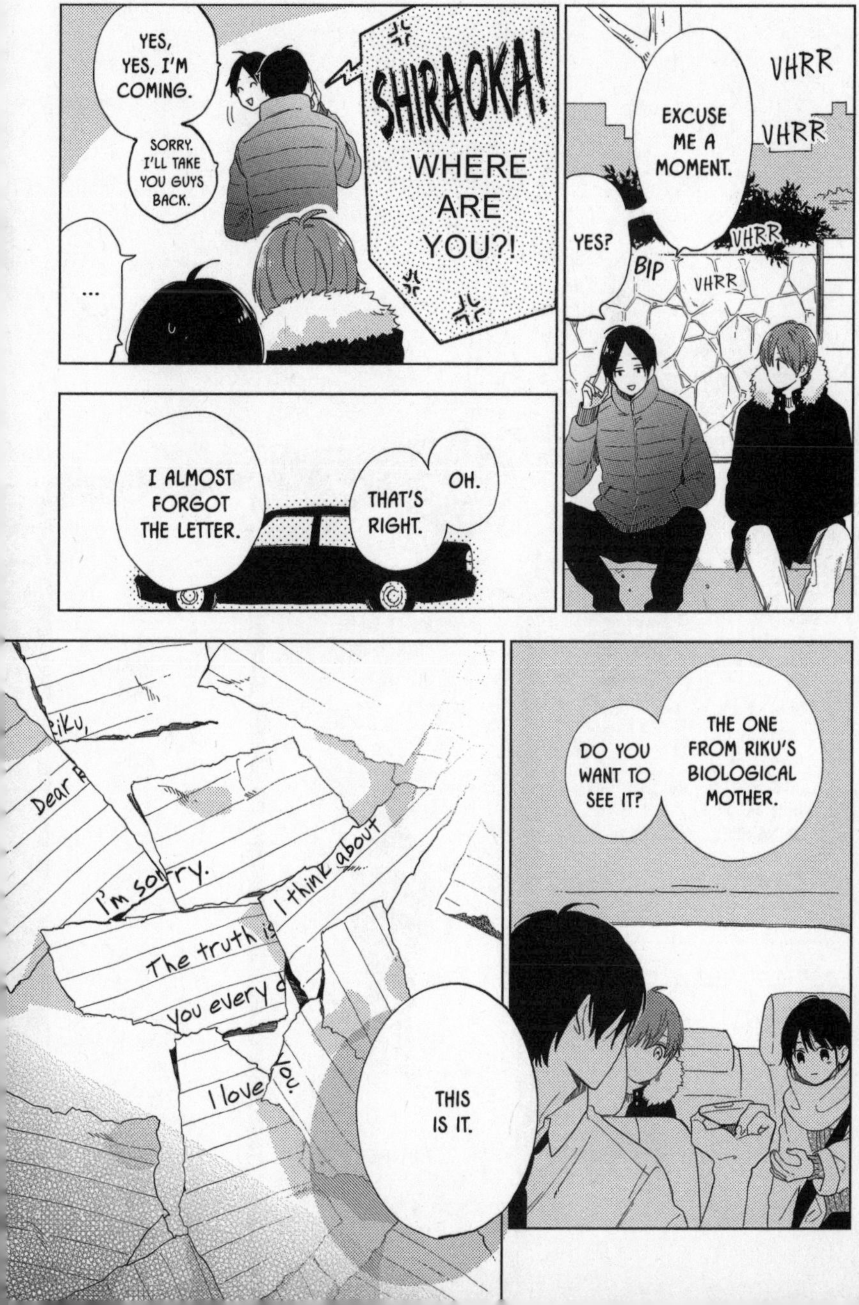
VHRR
VHRR
EXCUSE ME A MOMENT.
VHRR
BIP
VHRR
YES?
SHIRAOKA! WHERE ARE YOU?!
YES, YES, I'M COMING.
SORRY. I'LL TAKE YOU GUYS BACK.
...
OH.
THAT'S RIGHT.
I ALMOST FORGOT THE LETTER.
THE ONE FROM RIKU'S BIOLOGICAL MOTHER.
DO YOU WANT TO SEE IT?
THIS IS IT.
Riku,
Dear R
I'm sorry.
I think about
The truth is
you every d
I love you.

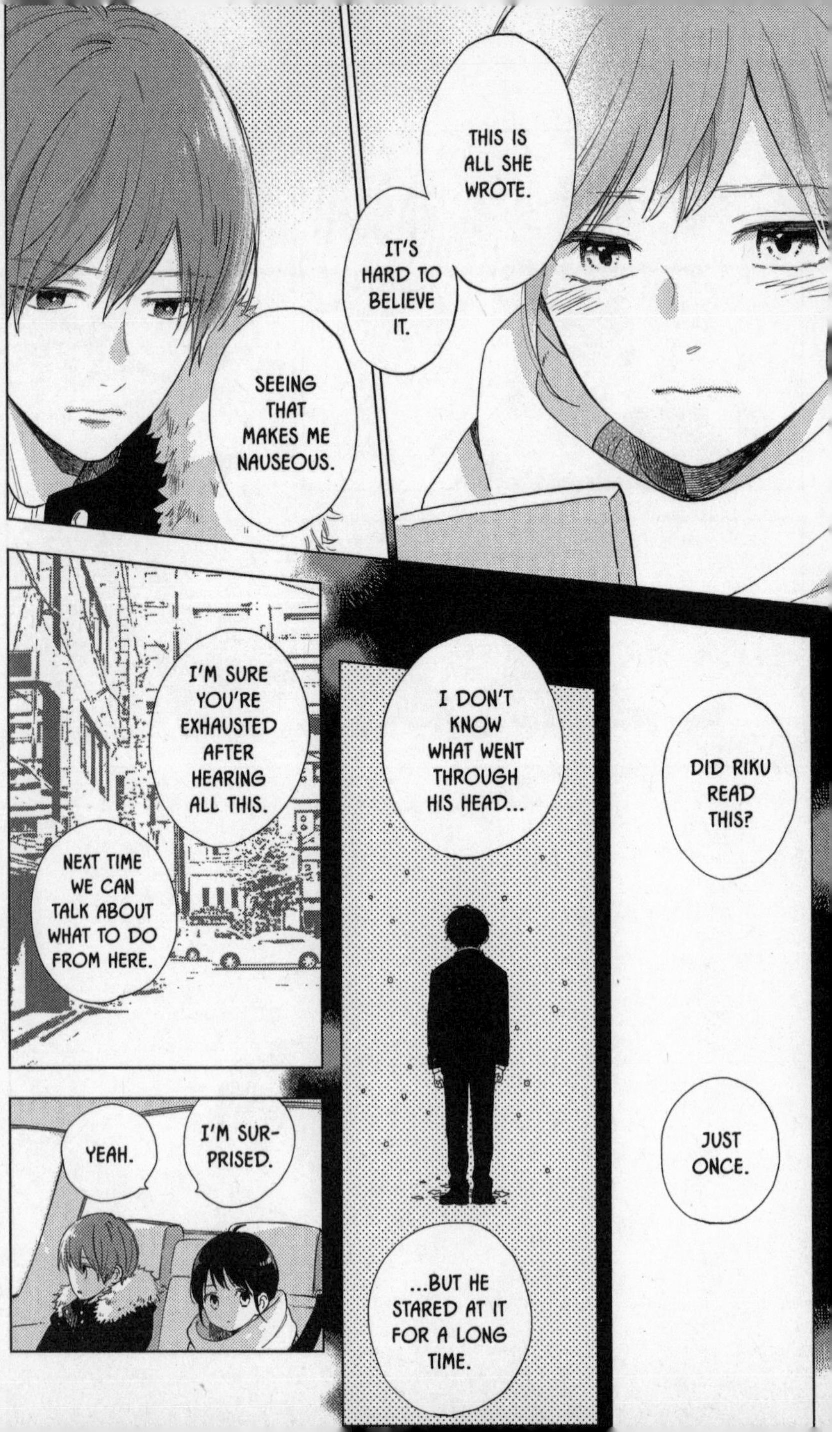
THIS IS ALL SHE WROTE.
IT'S HARD TO BELIEVE IT.
SEEING THAT MAKES ME NAUSEOUS.
DID RIKU READ THIS?
JUST ONCE.
I DON'T KNOW WHAT WENT THROUGH HIS HEAD...
...BUT HE STARED AT IT FOR A LONG TIME.
I'M SURE YOU'RE EXHAUSTED AFTER HEARING ALL THIS.
NEXT TIME WE CAN TALK ABOUT WHAT TO DO FROM HERE.
I'M SUR-PRISED.
YEAH.

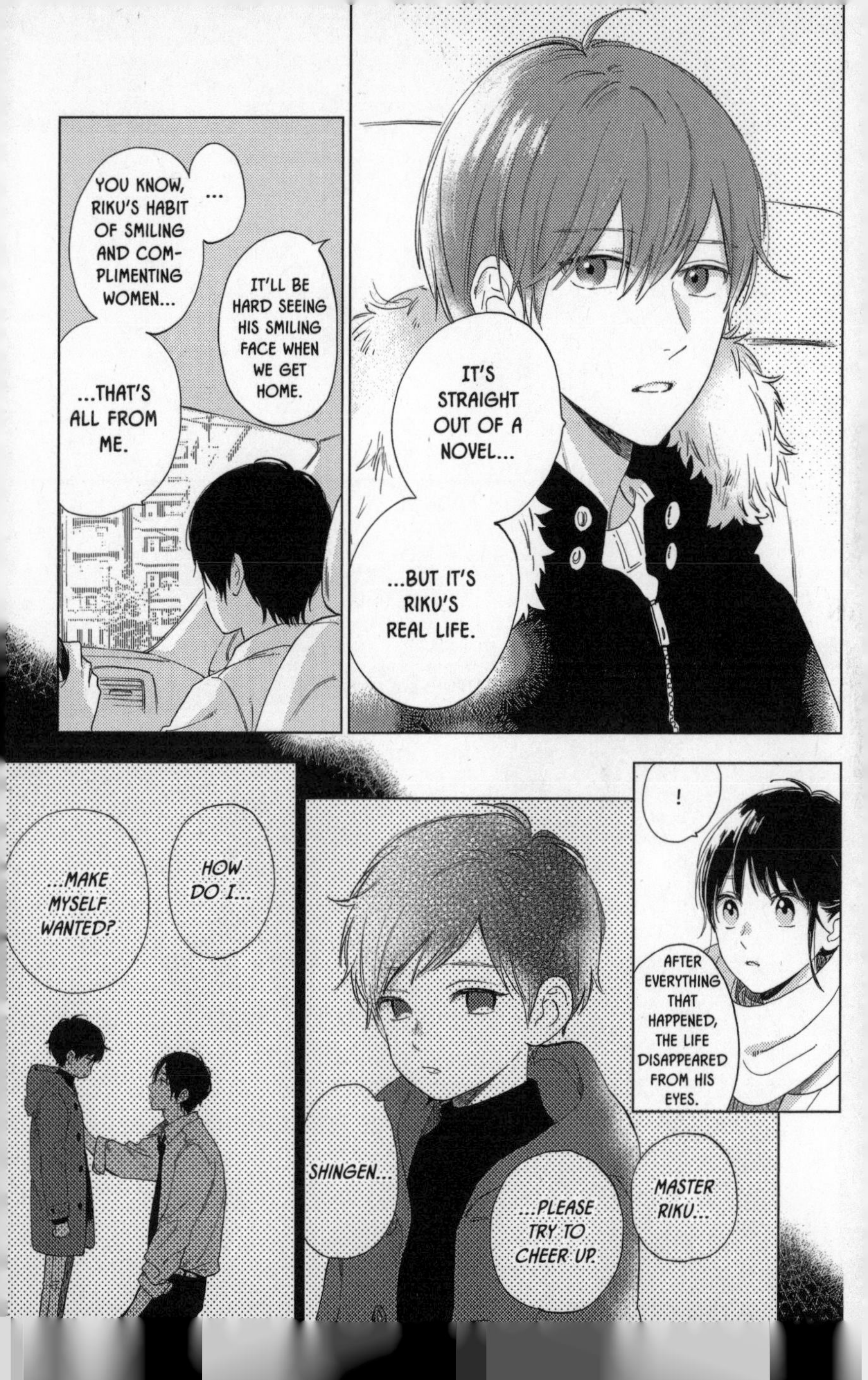
IT'S STRAIGHT OUT OF A NOVEL...
...BUT IT'S RIKU'S REAL LIFE.
...
YOU KNOW, RIKU'S HABIT OF SMILING AND COMPLIMENTING WOMEN...
IT'LL BE HARD SEEING HIS SMILING FACE WHEN WE GET HOME.
...THAT'S ALL FROM ME.
!
AFTER EVERYTHING THAT HAPPENED, THE LIFE DISAPPEARED FROM HIS EYES.
MASTER RIKU...
...PLEASE TRY TO CHEER UP.
SHINGEN...
HOW DO I...
...MAKE MYSELF WANTED?

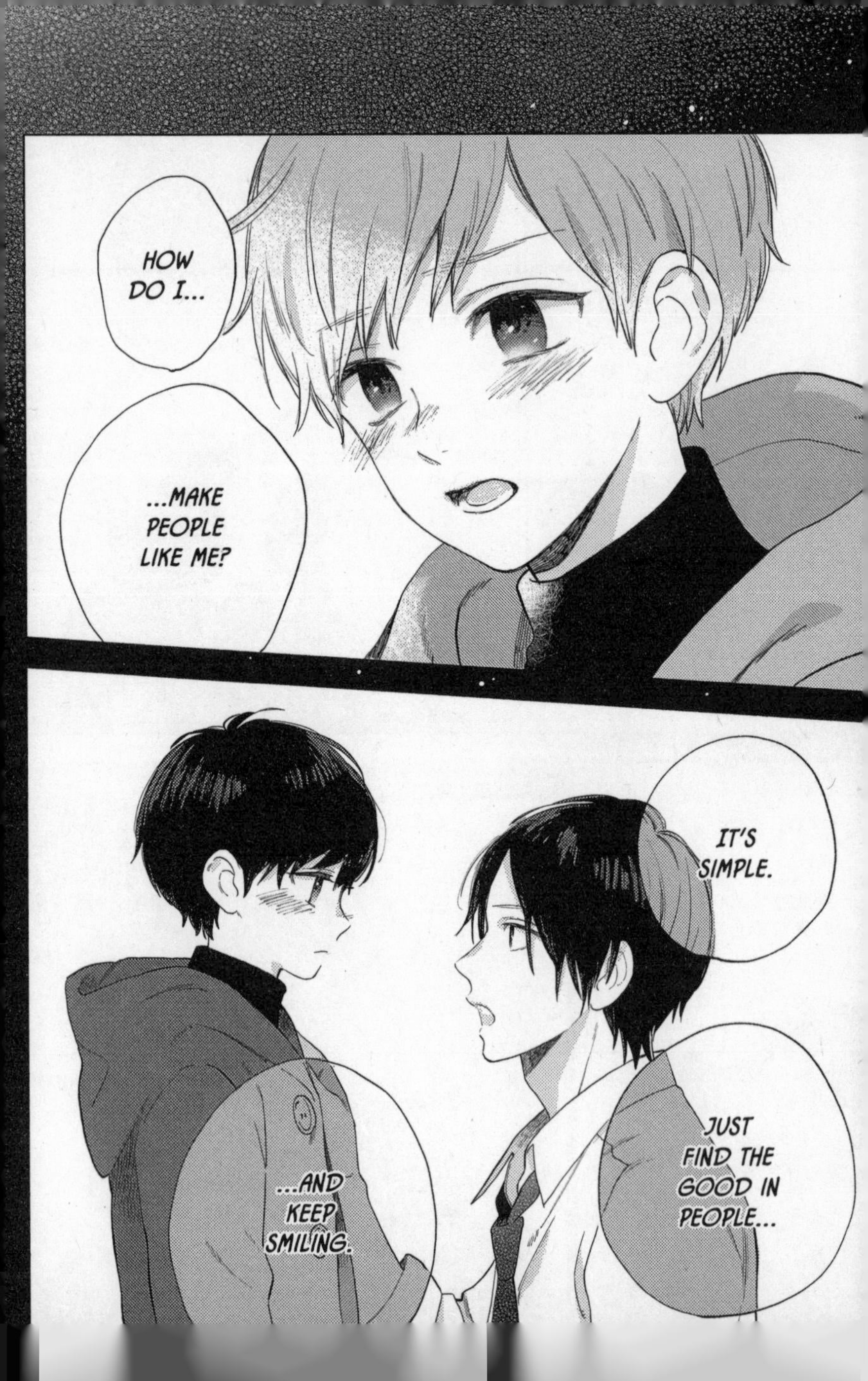
HOW DO I...
...MAKE PEOPLE LIKE ME?
IT'S SIMPLE.
JUST FIND THE GOOD IN PEOPLE...
...AND KEEP SMILING.

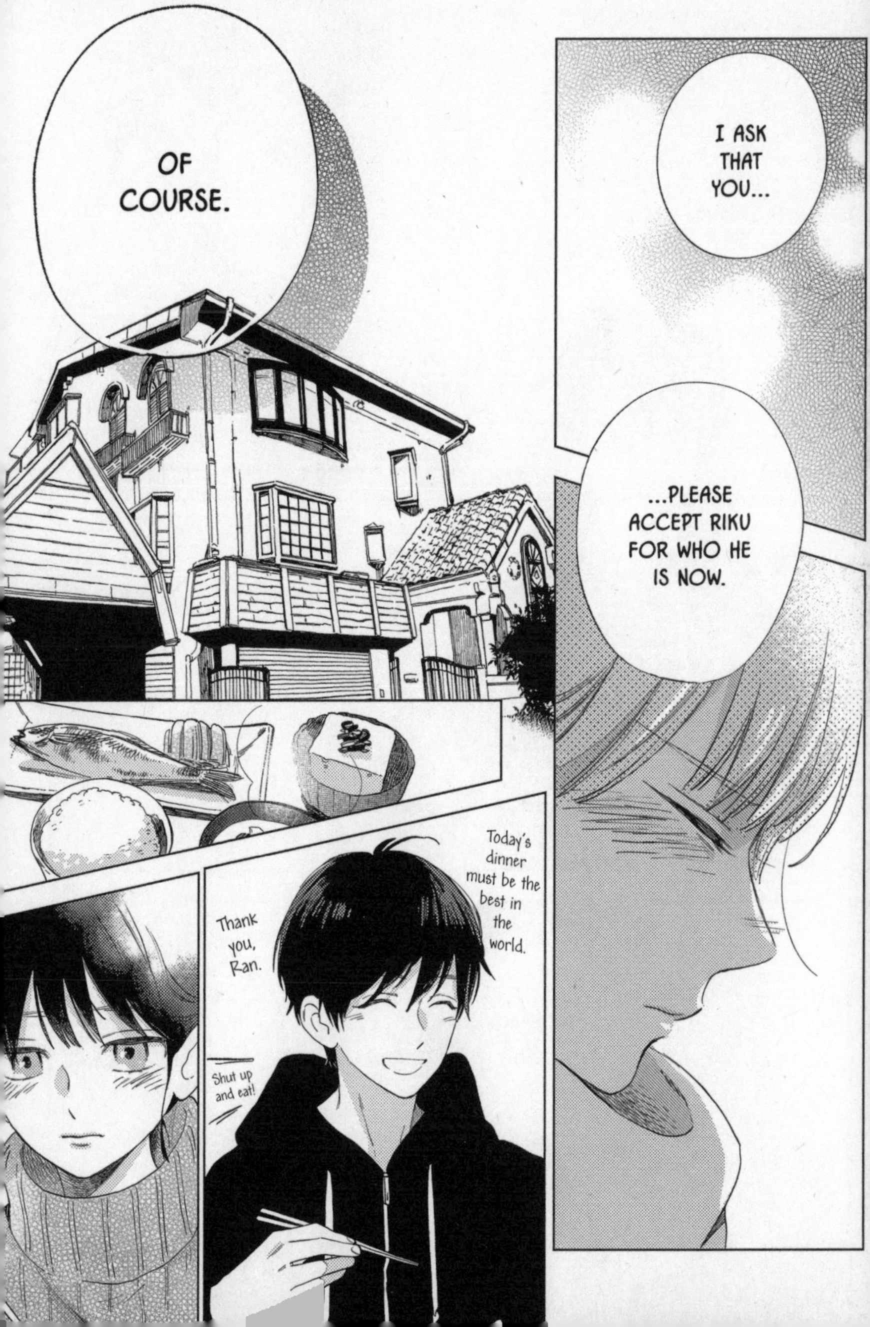
I ASK THAT YOU...
...PLEASE ACCEPT RIKU FOR WHO HE IS NOW.
OF COURSE.
Today's dinner must be the best in the world.
Thank you, Ran.
Shut up and eat!

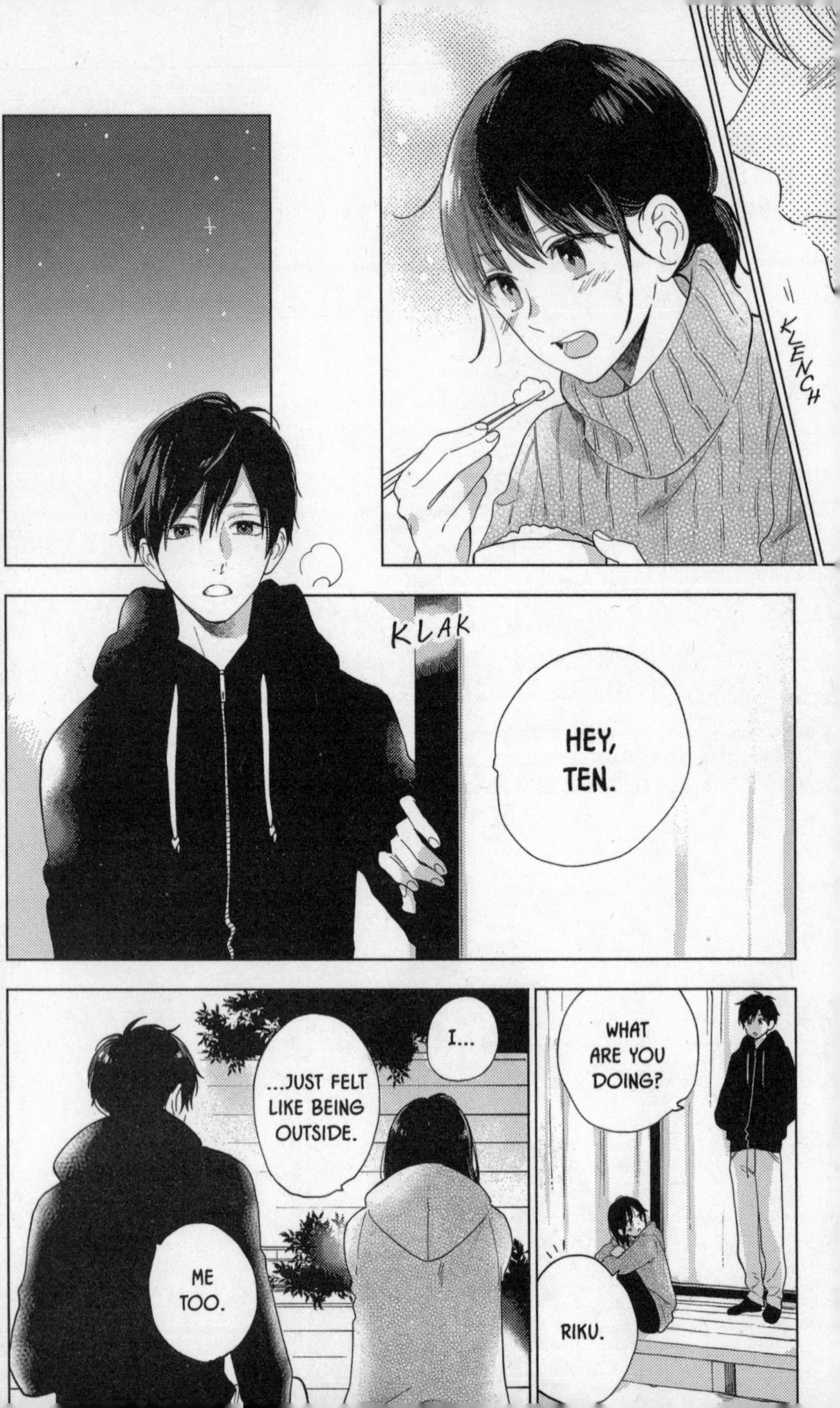
KLENCH
KLAK
HEY, TEN.
WHAT ARE YOU DOING?
RIKU.
I...
...JUST FELT LIKE BEING OUTSIDE.
ME TOO.

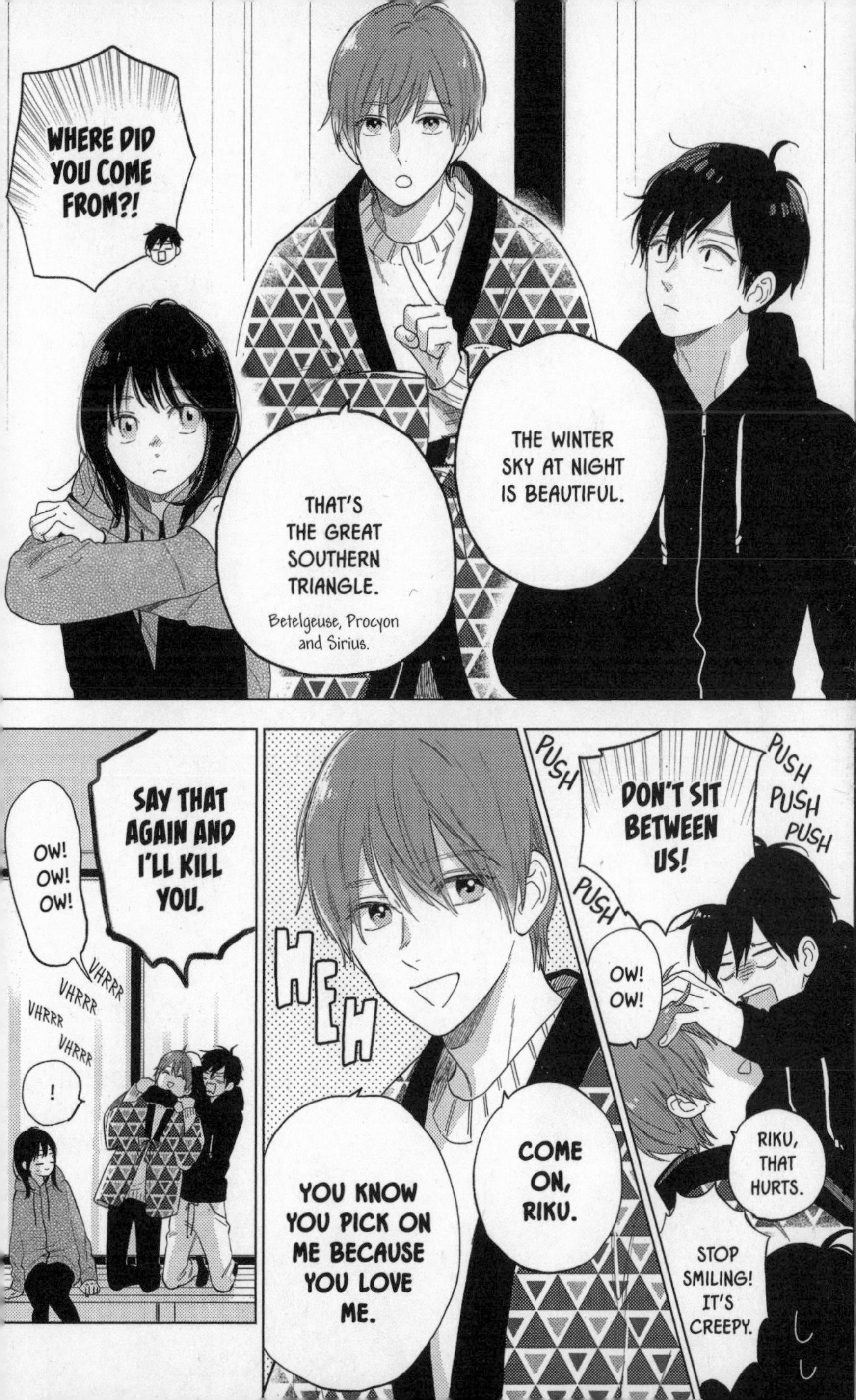
THE WINTER SKY AT NIGHT IS BEAUTIFUL.
THAT'S THE GREAT SOUTHERN TRIANGLE.
Betelgeuse, Procyon and Sirius.
WHERE DID YOU COME FROM?!
PUSH
DON'T SIT BETWEEN US!
PUSH PUSH PUSH
PUSH
OW! OW!
RIKU, THAT HURTS.
STOP SMILING! IT'S CREEPY.
HEH
COME ON, RIKU.
YOU KNOW YOU PICK ON ME BECAUSE YOU LOVE ME.
SAY THAT AGAIN AND I'LL KILL YOU.
OW! OW! OW!
VHRRR
VHRRR
VHRRR
VHRRR
!

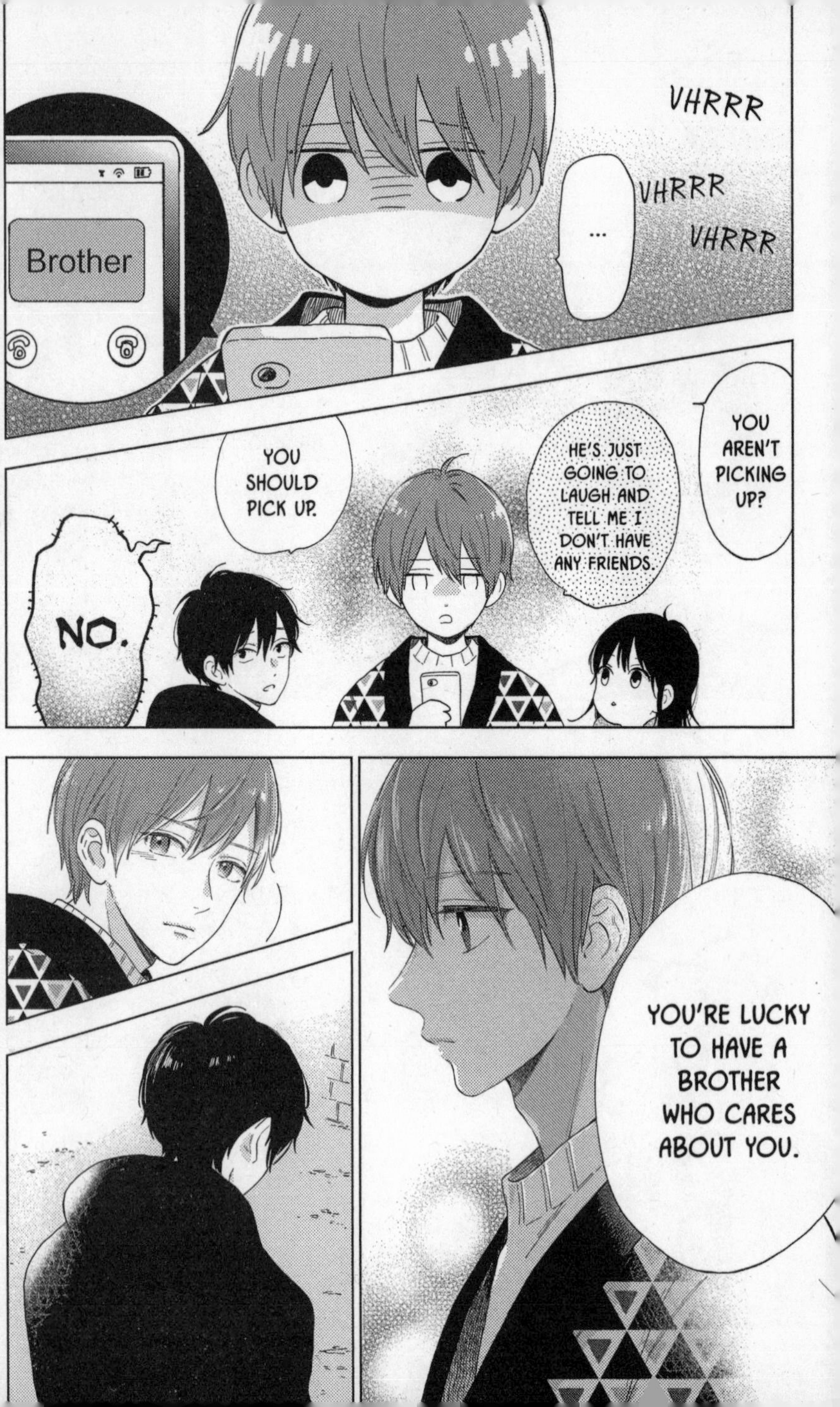
VHRRR
VHRRR
VHRRR
...
Brother
YOU AREN'T PICKING UP?
HE'S JUST GOING TO LAUGH AND TELL ME I DON'T HAVE ANY FRIENDS.
YOU SHOULD PICK UP.
NO.
YOU'RE LUCKY TO HAVE A BROTHER WHO CARES ABOUT YOU.

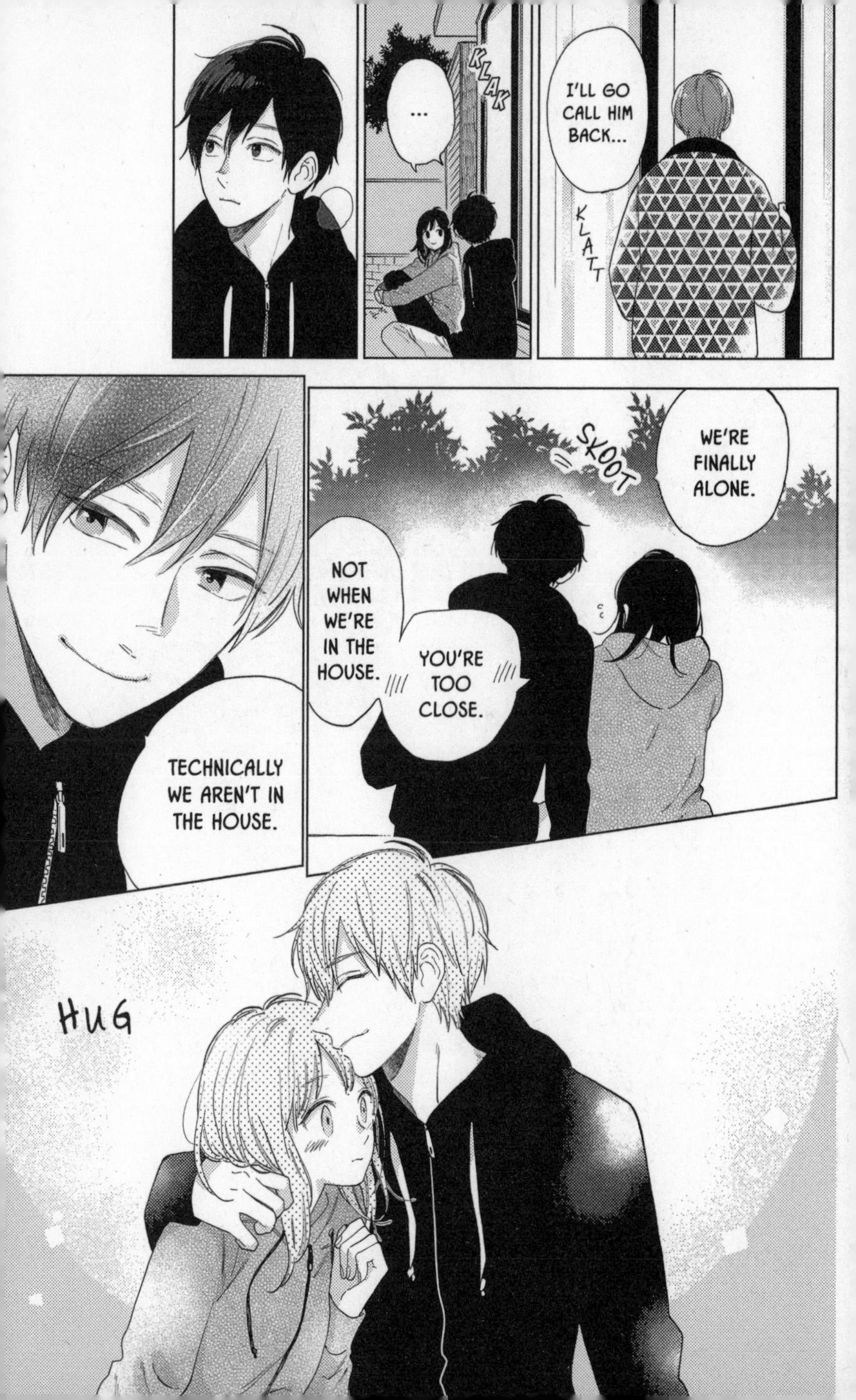
I'LL GO CALL HIM BACK...
KLATT
...
KLAK
WE'RE FINALLY ALONE.
SKOOT
YOU'RE TOO CLOSE.
NOT WHEN WE'RE IN THE HOUSE.
TECHNICALLY WE AREN'T IN THE HOUSE.
HUG

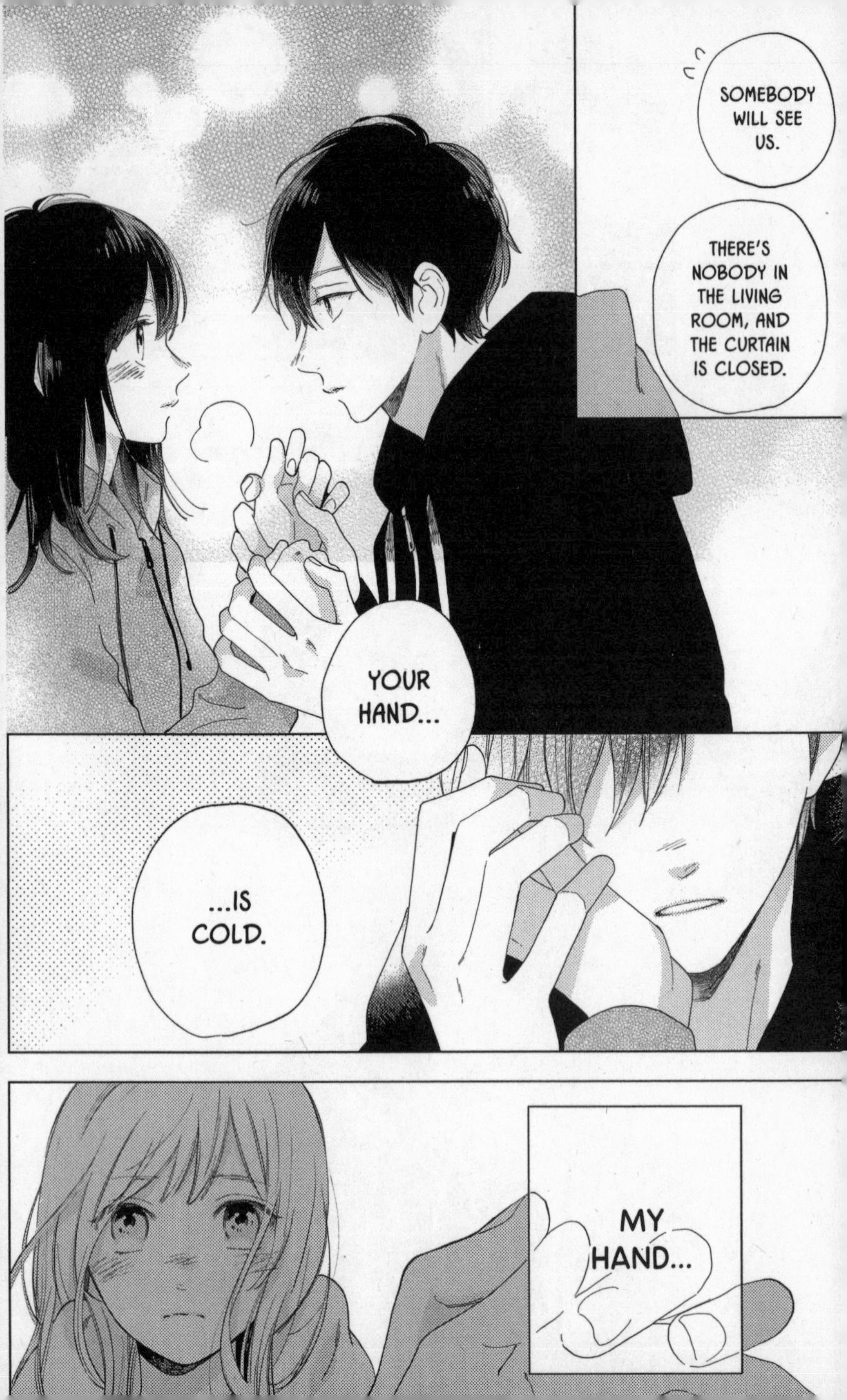
SOMEBODY WILL SEE US.
THERE'S NOBODY IN THE LIVING ROOM, AND THE CURTAIN IS CLOSED.
YOUR HAND...
...IS COLD.
MY HAND...

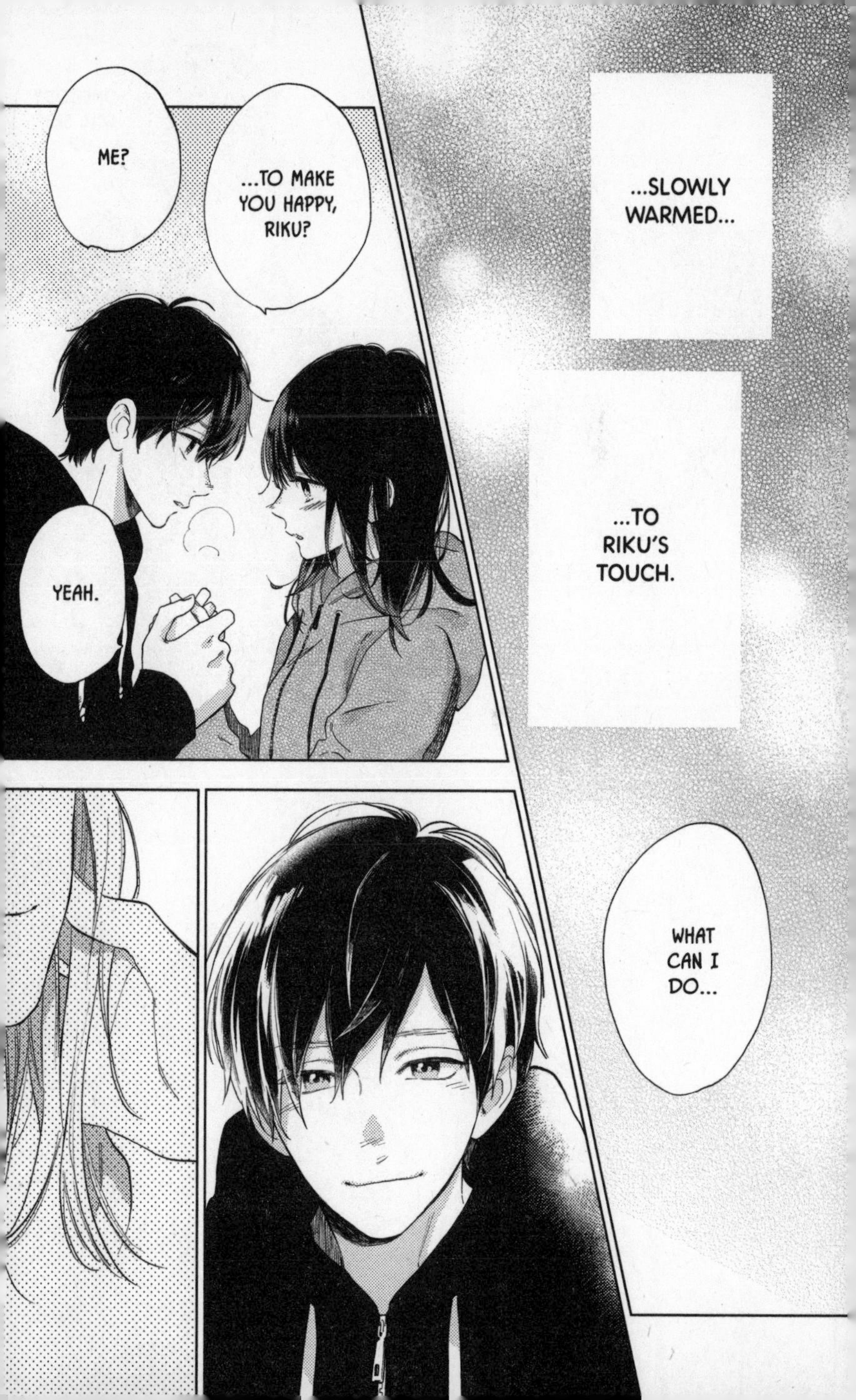
...SLOWLY WARMED...
...TO RIKU'S TOUCH.
WHAT CAN I DO...
...TO MAKE YOU HAPPY, RIKU?
ME?
YEAH.

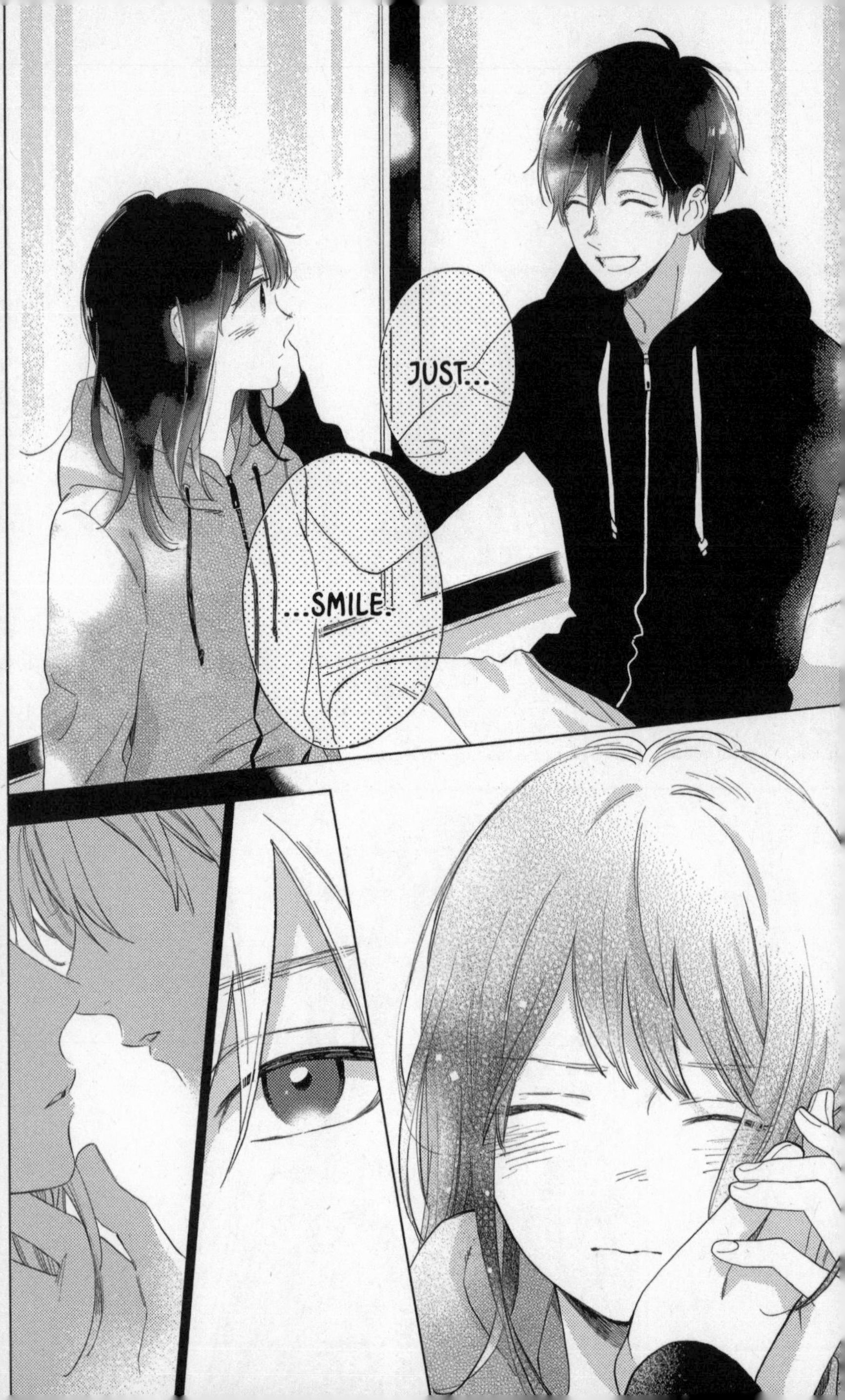
JUST...
...SMILE.

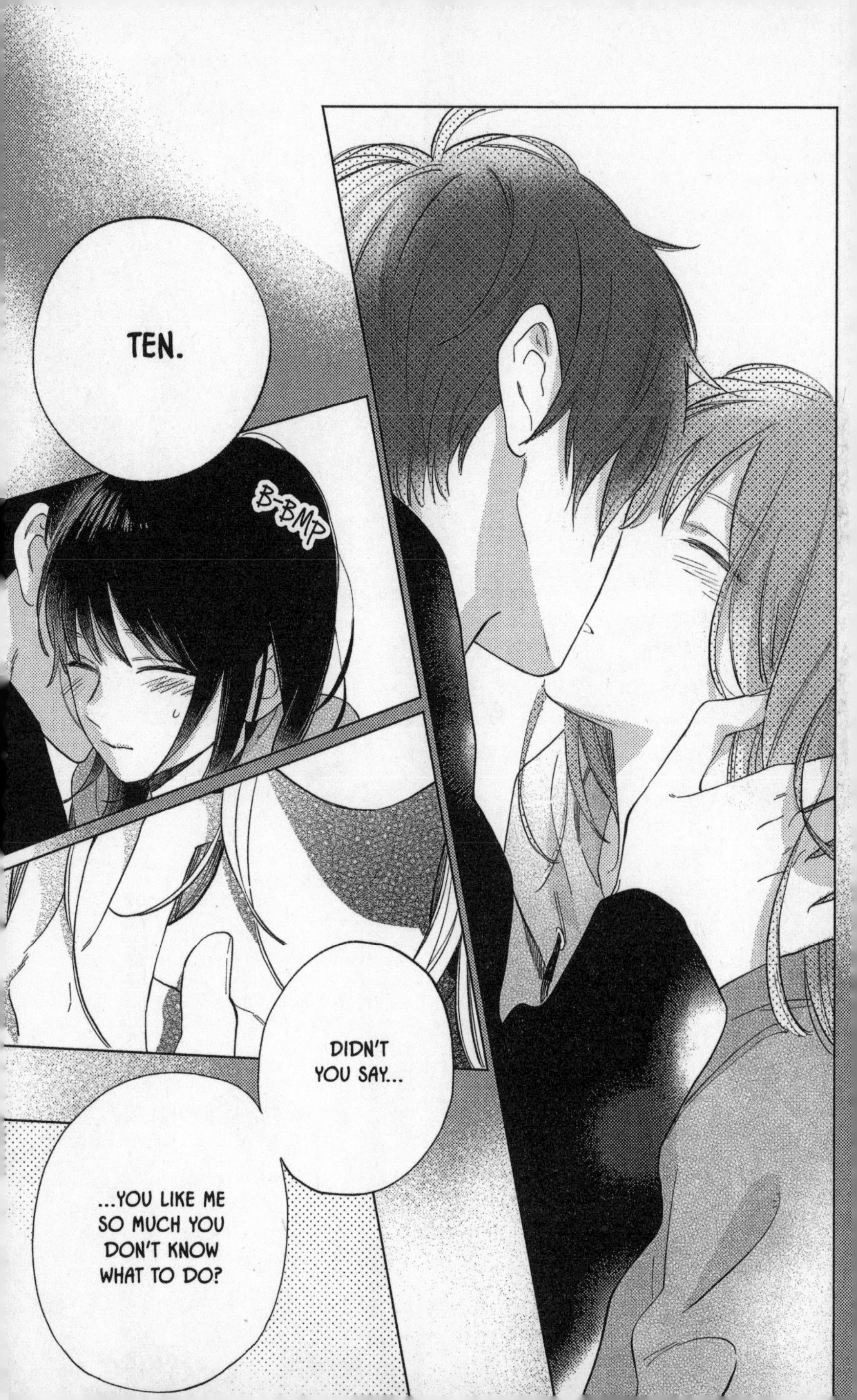
TEN.
B-BMP
DIDN'T YOU SAY...
...YOU LIKE ME SO MUCH YOU DON'T KNOW WHAT TO DO?

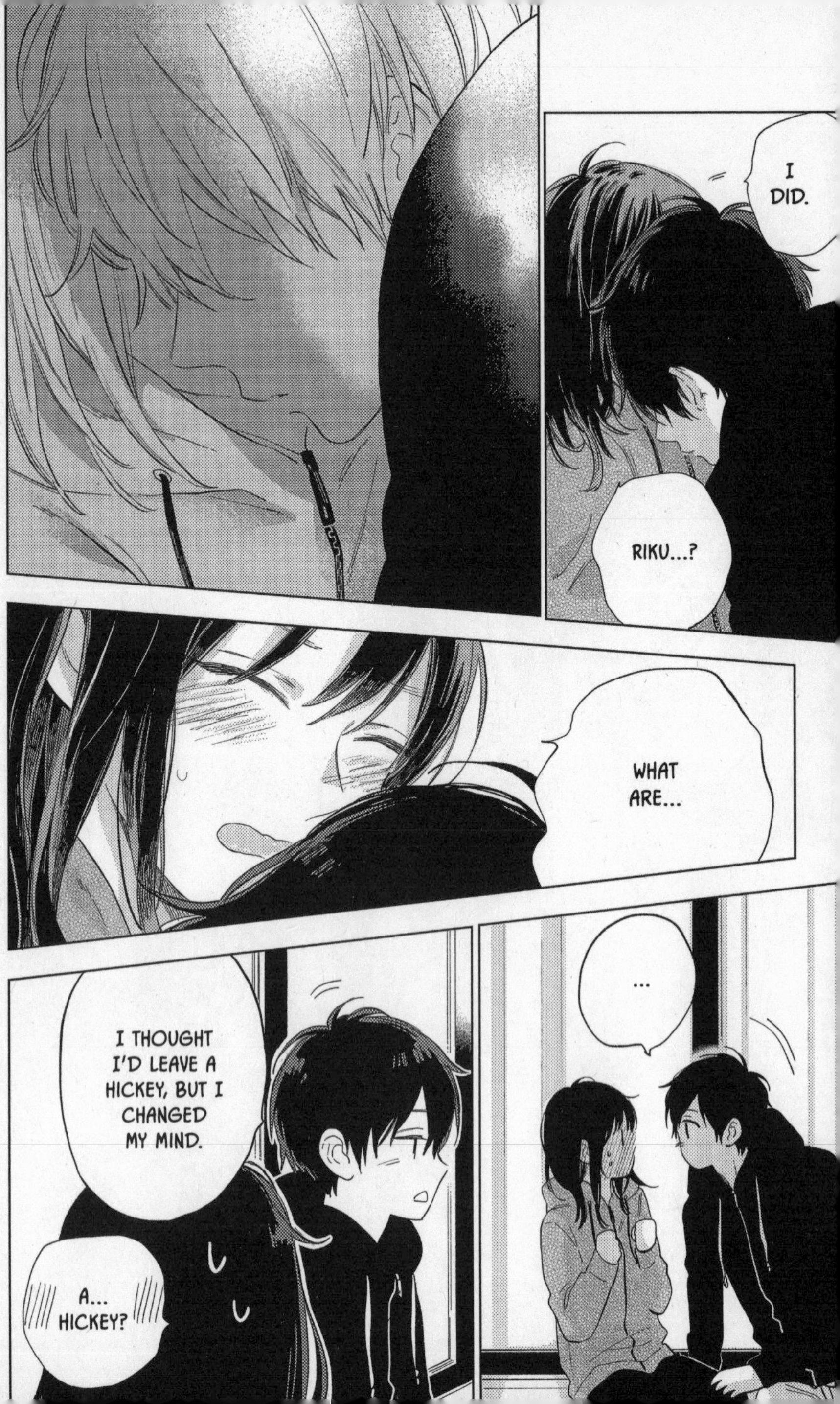
I DID.
RIKU...?
WHAT ARE...
...
I THOUGHT I'D LEAVE A HICKEY, BUT I CHANGED MY MIND.
A... HICKEY?

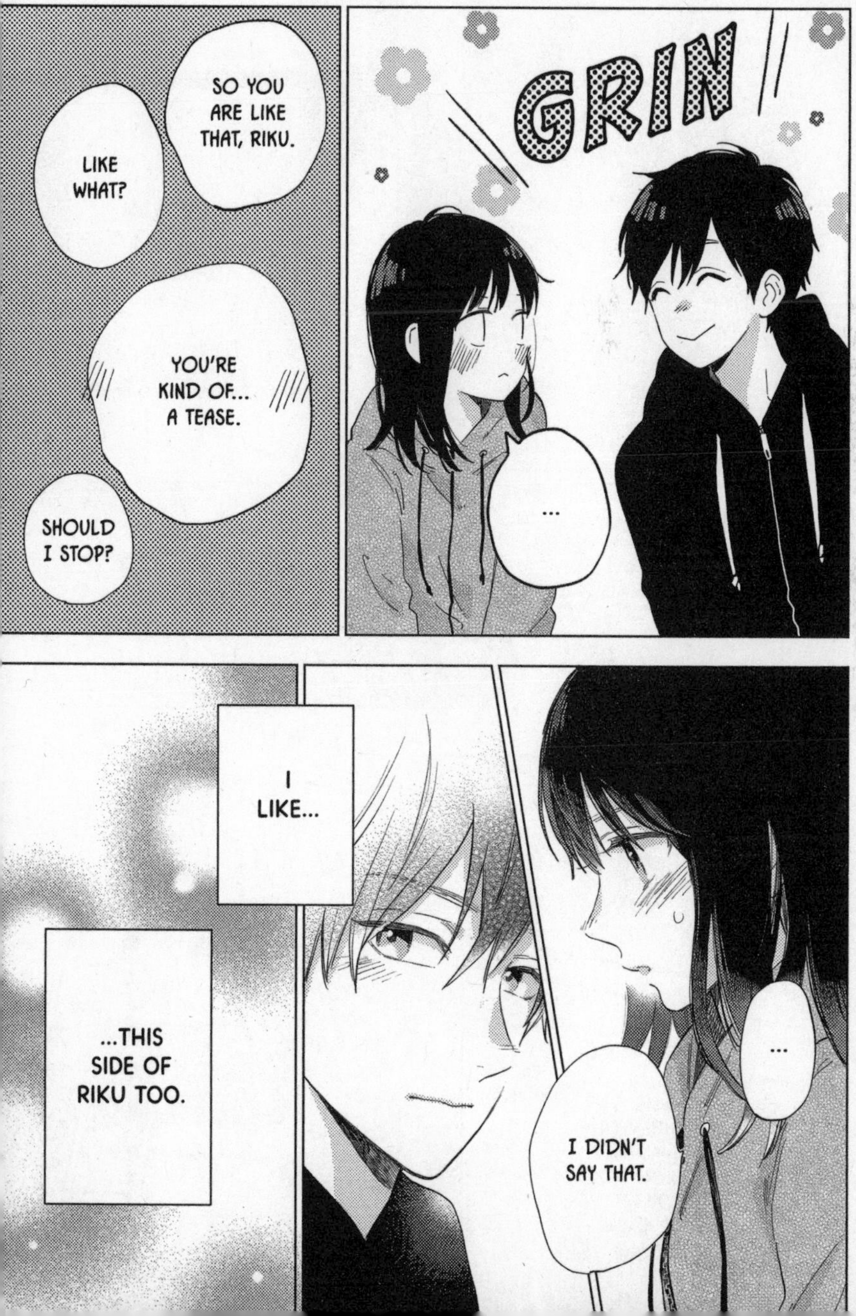
GRIN
...
SO YOU ARE LIKE THAT, RIKU.
LIKE WHAT?
YOU'RE KIND OF... A TEASE.
SHOULD I STOP?
...
I DIDN'T SAY THAT.
I LIKE...
...THIS SIDE OF RIKU TOO.

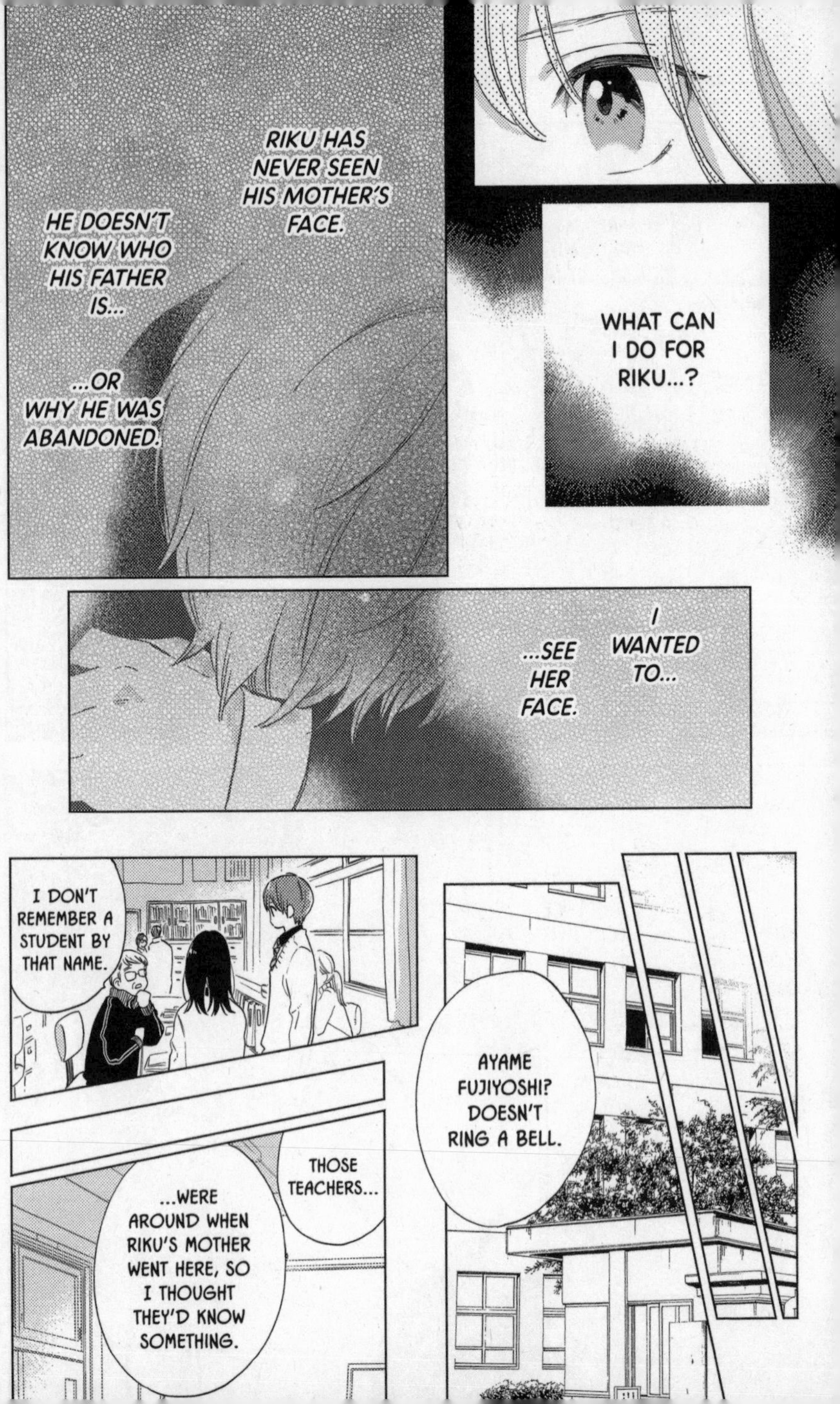
WHAT CAN I DO FOR RIKU...?
RIKU HAS NEVER SEEN HIS MOTHER'S FACE.
HE DOESN'T KNOW WHO HIS FATHER IS...
...OR WHY HE WAS ABANDONED.
I WANTED TO...
...SEE HER FACE.
AYAME FUJIYOSHI? DOESN'T RING A BELL.
I DON'T REMEMBER A STUDENT BY THAT NAME.
THOSE TEACHERS...
...WERE AROUND WHEN RIKU'S MOTHER WENT HERE, SO I THOUGHT THEY'D KNOW SOMETHING.

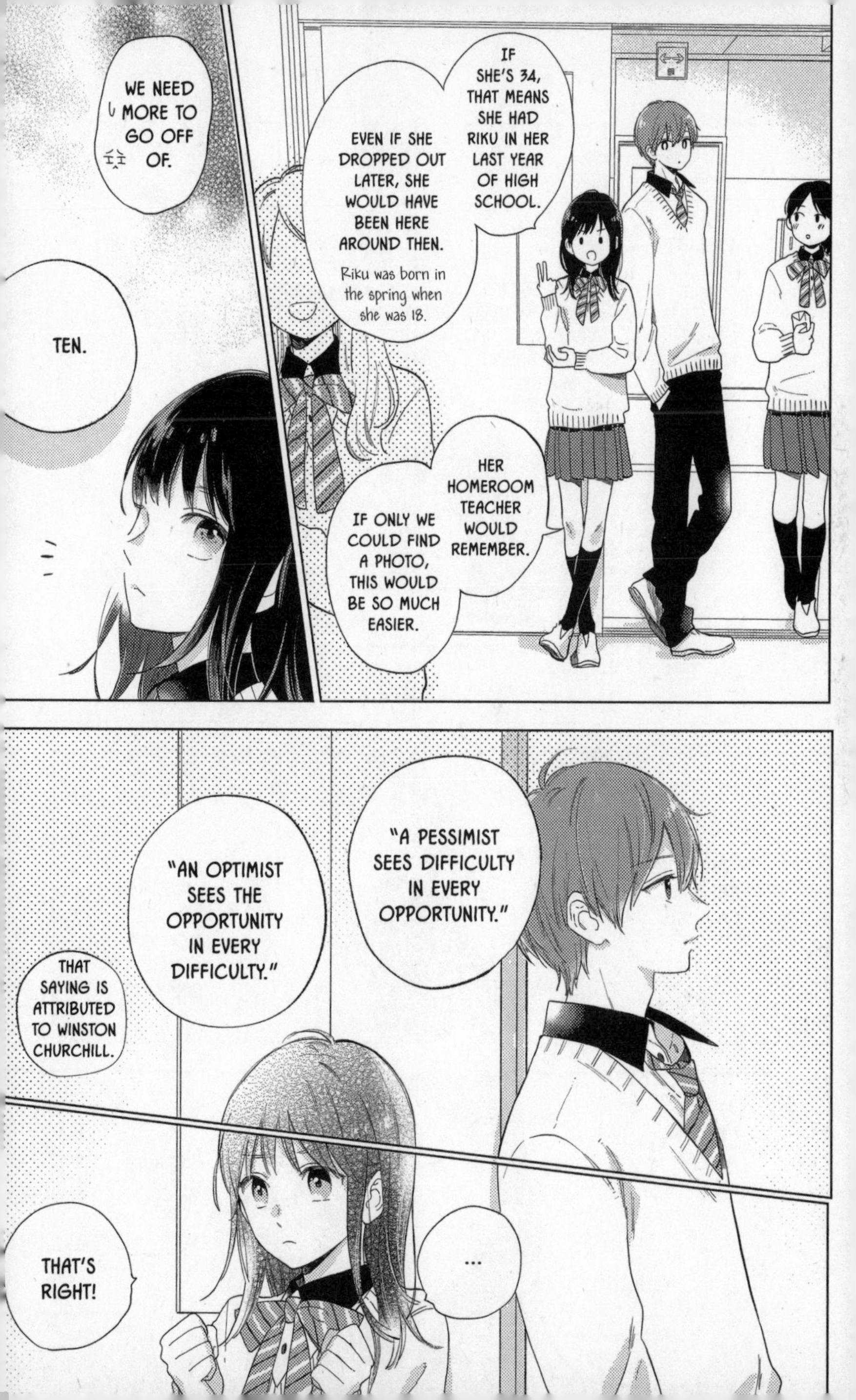
IF SHE'S 34, THAT MEANS SHE HAD RIKU IN HER LAST YEAR OF HIGH SCHOOL.
EVEN IF SHE DROPPED OUT LATER, SHE WOULD HAVE BEEN HERE AROUND THEN.
Riku was born in the spring when she was 18.
HER HOMEROOM TEACHER WOULD REMEMBER.
IF ONLY WE COULD FIND A PHOTO, THIS WOULD BE SO MUCH EASIER.
WE NEED MORE TO GO OFF OF.
TEN.
"A PESSIMIST SEES DIFFICULTY IN EVERY OPPORTUNITY."
"AN OPTIMIST SEES THE OPPORTUNITY IN EVERY DIFFICULTY."
THAT SAYING IS ATTRIBUTED TO WINSTON CHURCHILL.
...
THAT'S RIGHT!

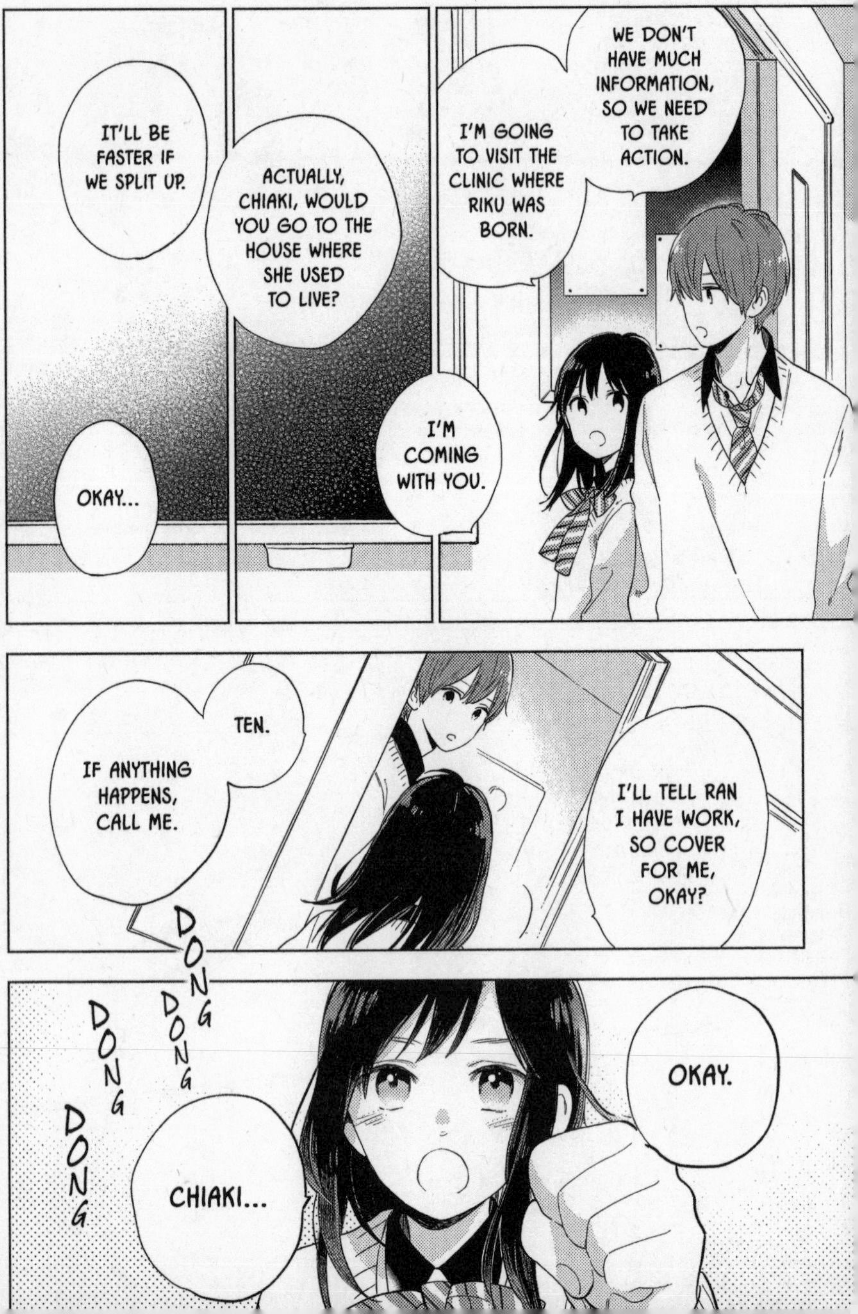
WE DON'T HAVE MUCH INFORMATION, SO WE NEED TO TAKE ACTION.
I'M GOING TO VISIT THE CLINIC WHERE RIKU WAS BORN.
I'M COMING WITH YOU.
ACTUALLY, CHIAKI, WOULD YOU GO TO THE HOUSE WHERE SHE USED TO LIVE?
IT'LL BE FASTER IF WE SPLIT UP.
OKAY...
I'LL TELL RAN I HAVE WORK, SO COVER FOR ME, OKAY?
TEN.
IF ANYTHING HAPPENS, CALL ME.
OKAY.
DONG
DONG
DONG
DONG
CHIAKI...

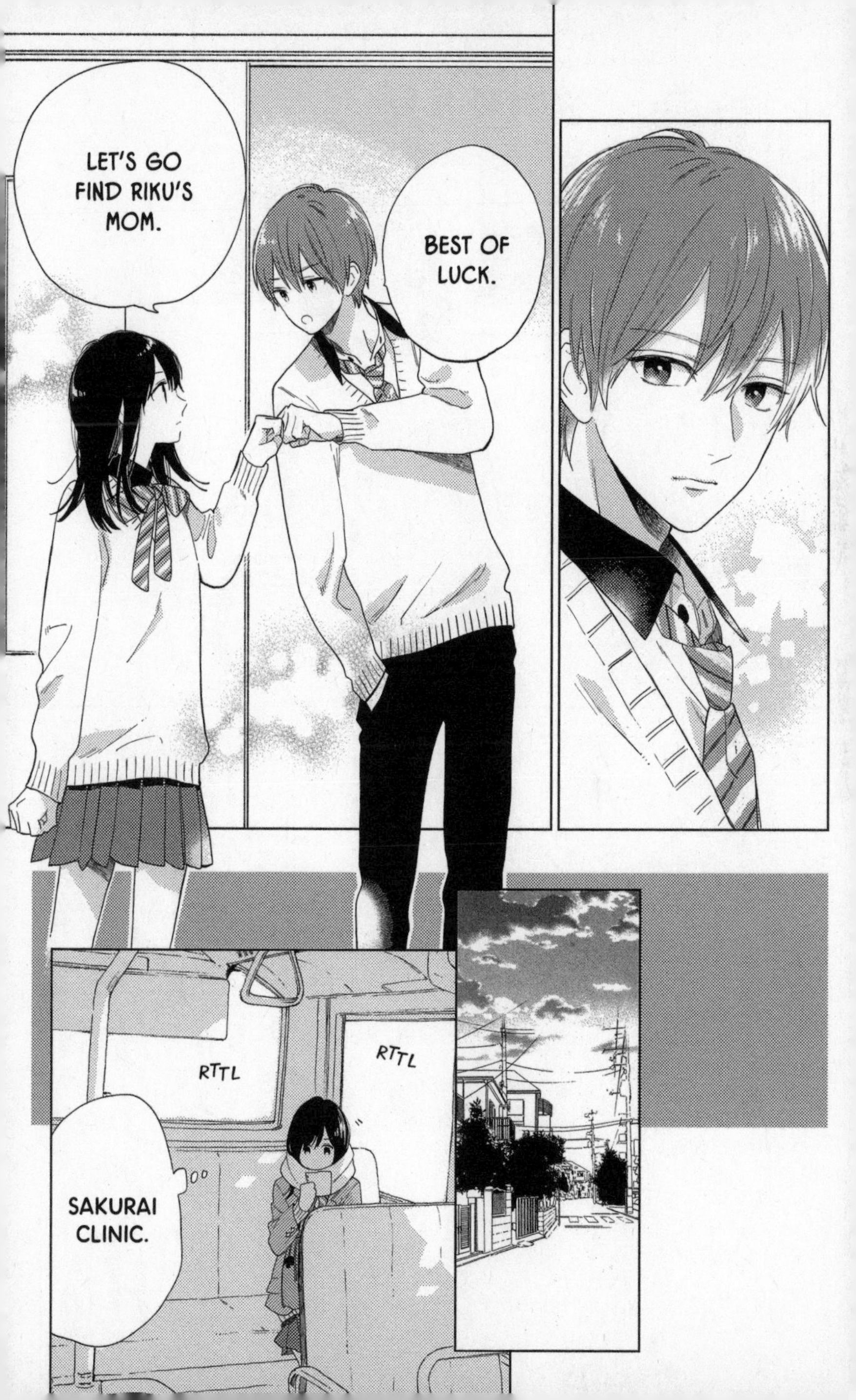
LET'S GO FIND RIKU'S MOM.
BEST OF LUCK.
RTTL
RTTL
SAKURAI CLINIC.

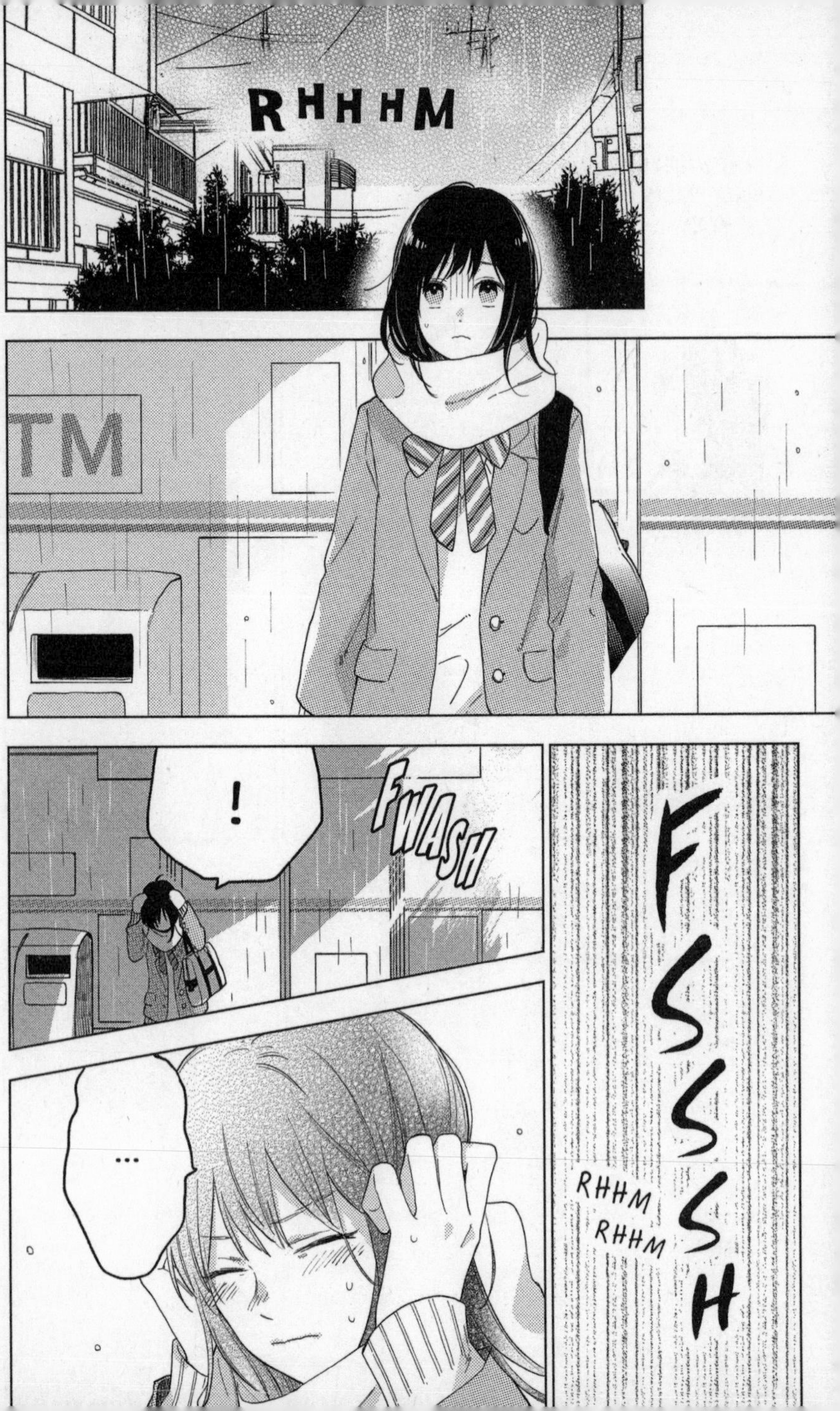
RHHHM
TM
FSSSH
RHHM
RHHM
FWASH
!
...

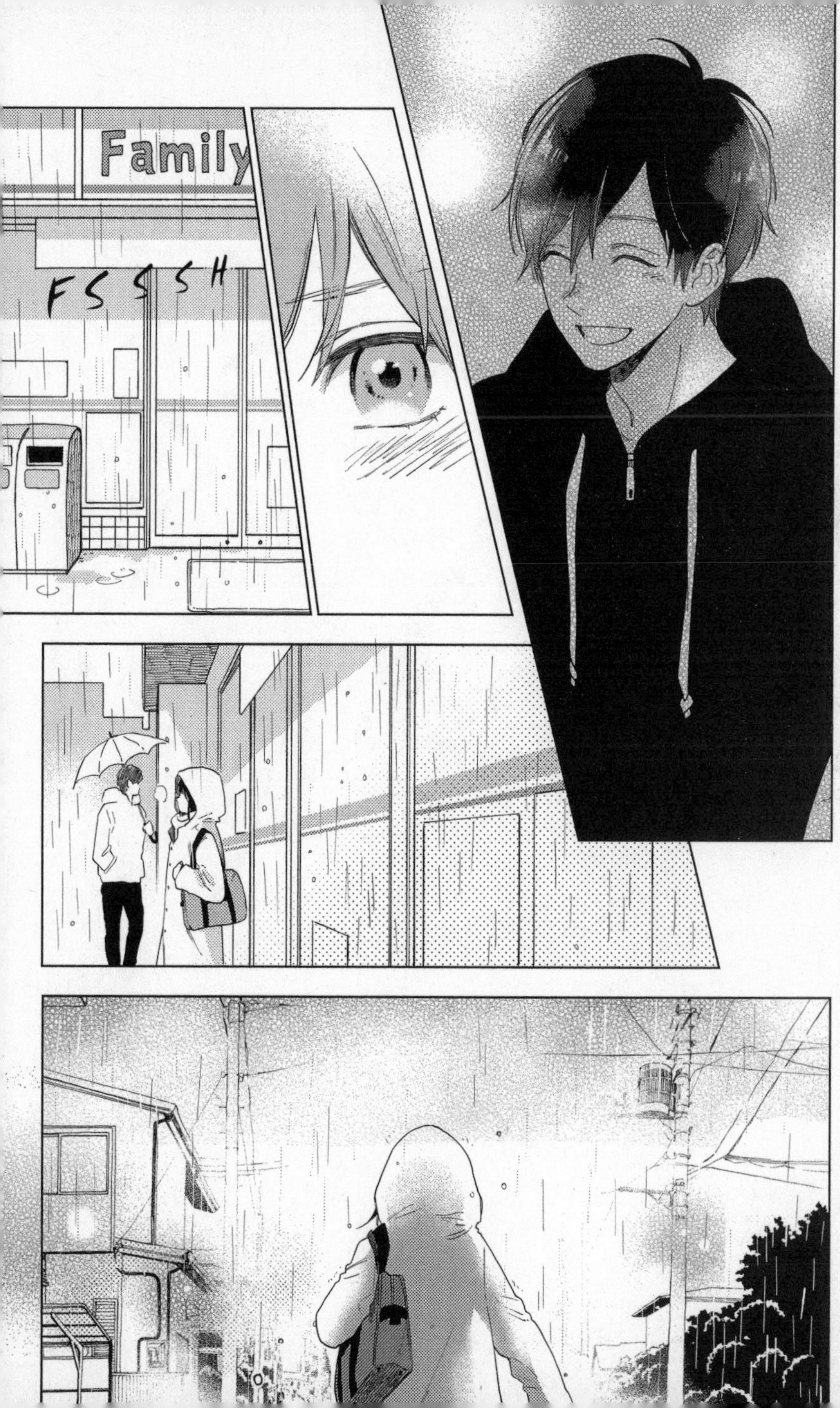
Family
FSSSH

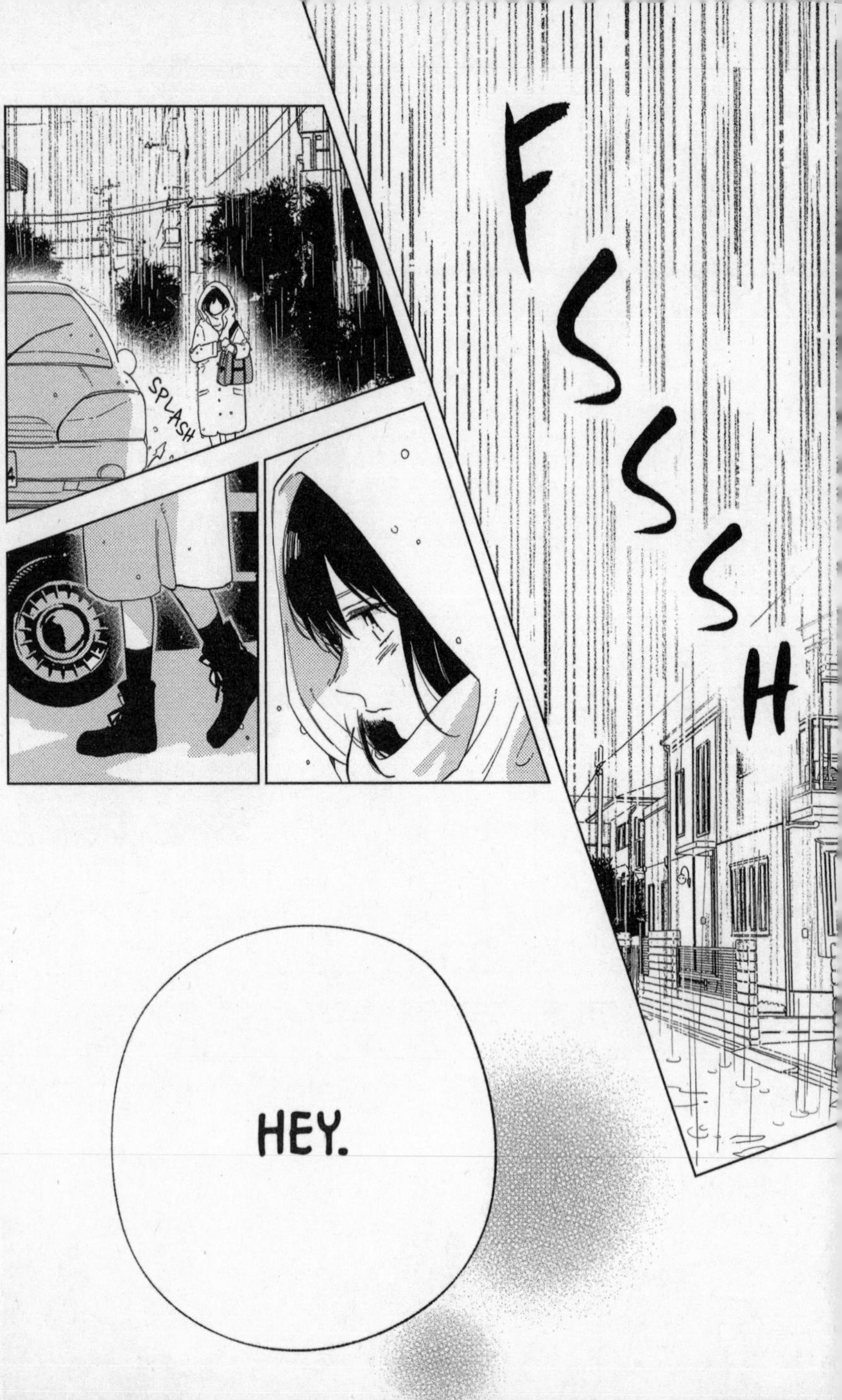
FSSSH
SPLASH
HEY.

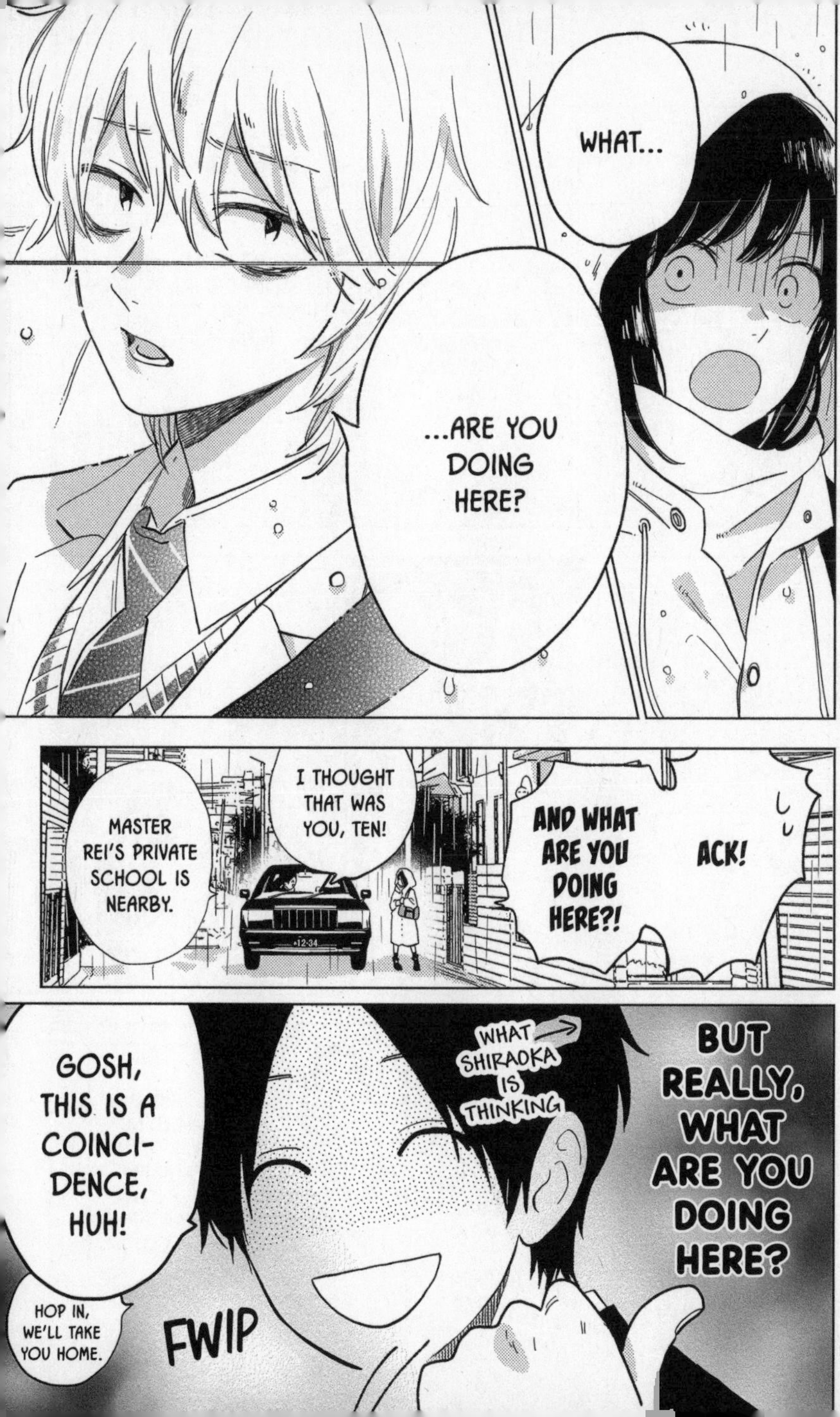
WHAT...
...ARE YOU DOING HERE?
ACK!
AND WHAT ARE YOU DOING HERE?!
I THOUGHT THAT WAS YOU, TEN!
MASTER REI'S PRIVATE SCHOOL IS NEARBY.
BUT REALLY, WHAT ARE YOU DOING HERE?
WHAT SHIRAOKA IS THINKING
GOSH, THIS IS A COINCIDENCE, HUH!
HOP IN, WE'LL TAKE YOU HOME.
FWIP

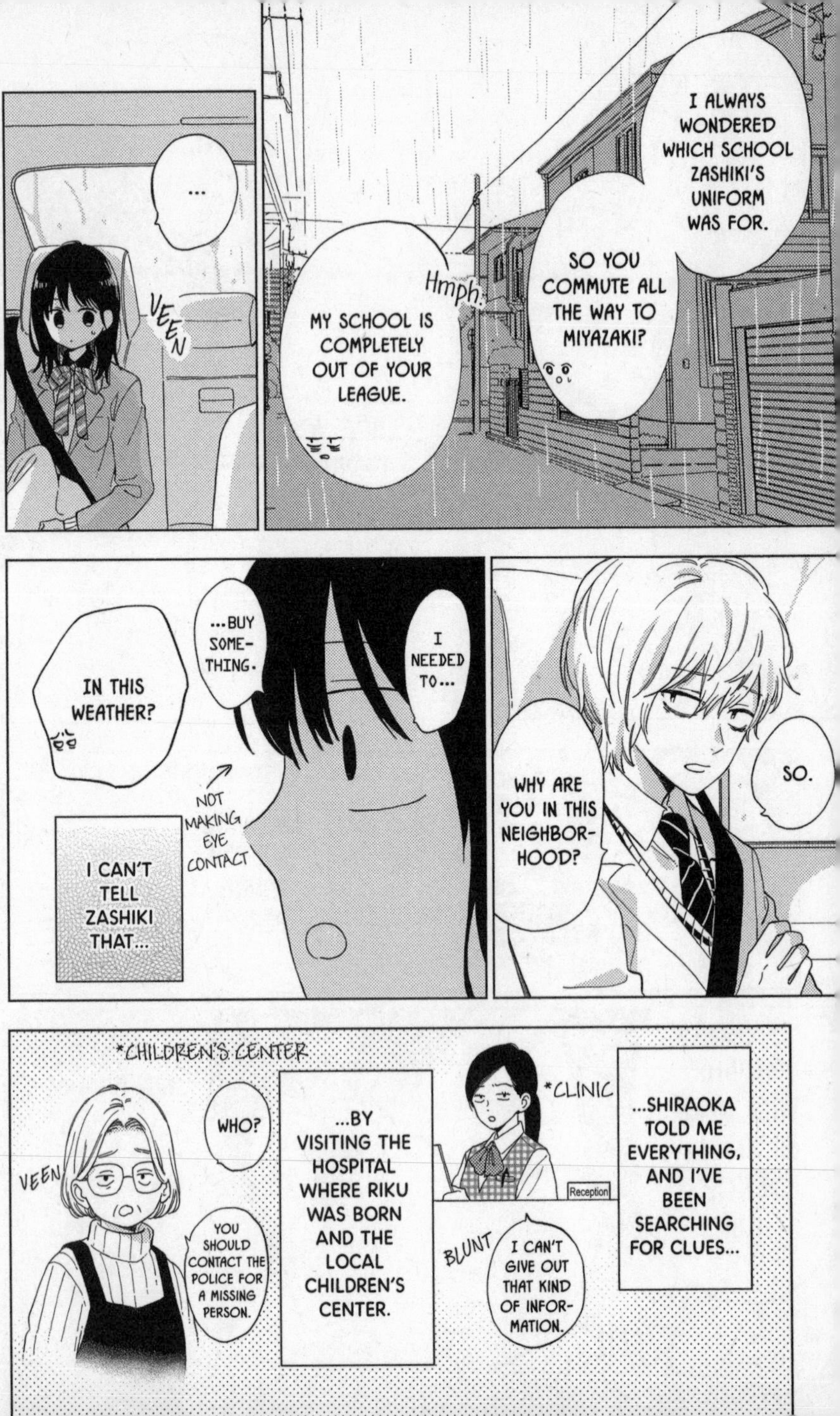
I ALWAYS WONDERED WHICH SCHOOL ZASHIKI'S UNIFORM WAS FOR.
SO YOU COMMUTE ALL THE WAY TO MIYAZAKI?
Hmph.
MY SCHOOL IS COMPLETELY OUT OF YOUR LEAGUE.
...
VEEN
SO.
WHY ARE YOU IN THIS NEIGHBOR-HOOD?
I NEEDED TO...
...BUY SOME-THING.
IN THIS WEATHER?
NOT MAKING EYE CONTACT
I CAN'T TELL ZASHIKI THAT...
...SHIRAOKA TOLD ME EVERYTHING, AND I'VE BEEN SEARCHING FOR CLUES...
*CLINIC
Reception
BLUNT
I CAN'T GIVE OUT THAT KIND OF INFOR-MATION.
...BY VISITING THE HOSPITAL WHERE RIKU WAS BORN AND THE LOCAL CHILDREN'S CENTER.
*CHILDREN'S CENTER
WHO?
VEEN
YOU SHOULD CONTACT THE POLICE FOR A MISSING PERSON.

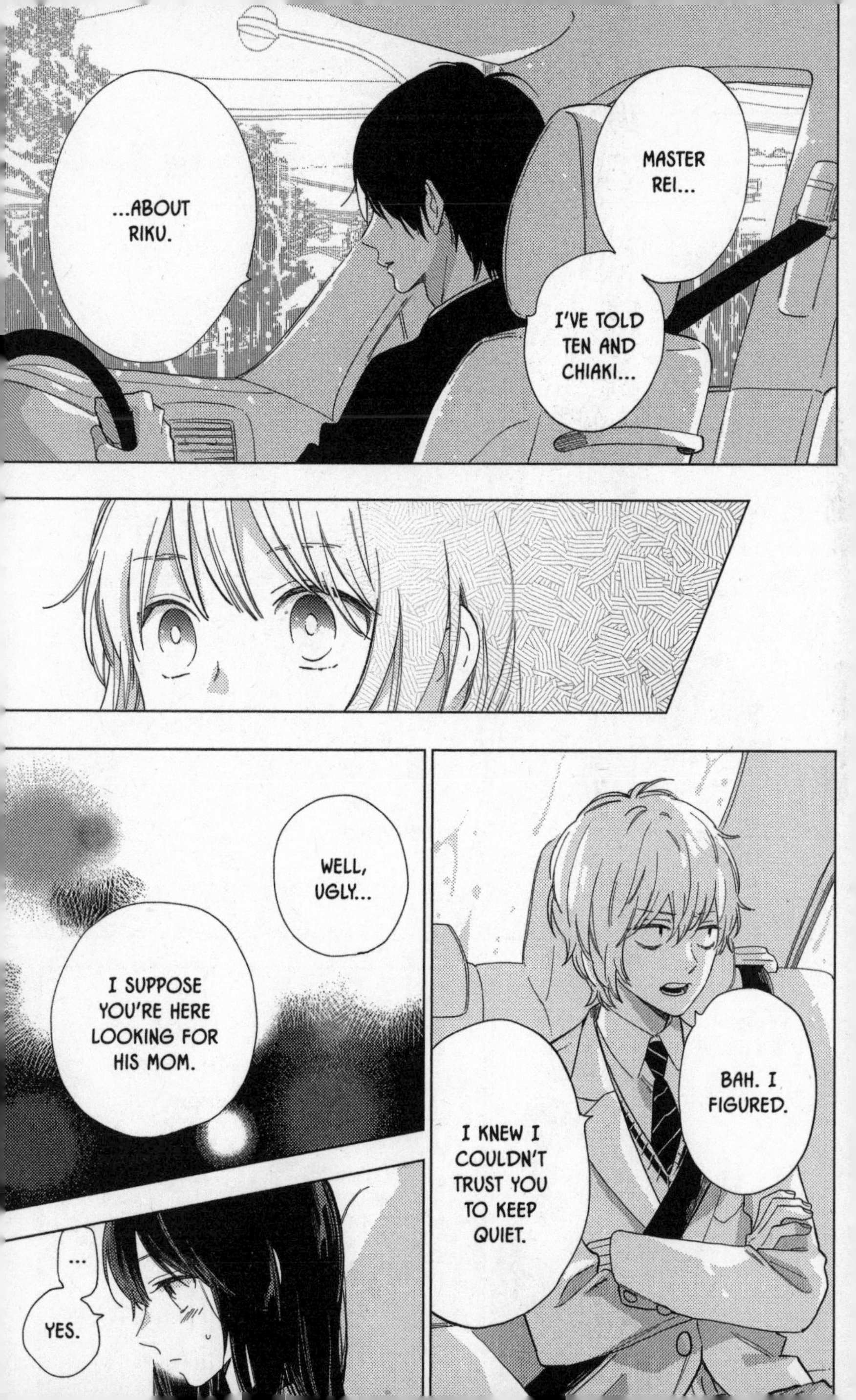
MASTER REI...
I'VE TOLD TEN AND CHIAKI...
...ABOUT RIKU.
BAH. I FIGURED.
I KNEW I COULDN'T TRUST YOU TO KEEP QUIET.
WELL, UGLY...
I SUPPOSE YOU'RE HERE LOOKING FOR HIS MOM.
... YES.

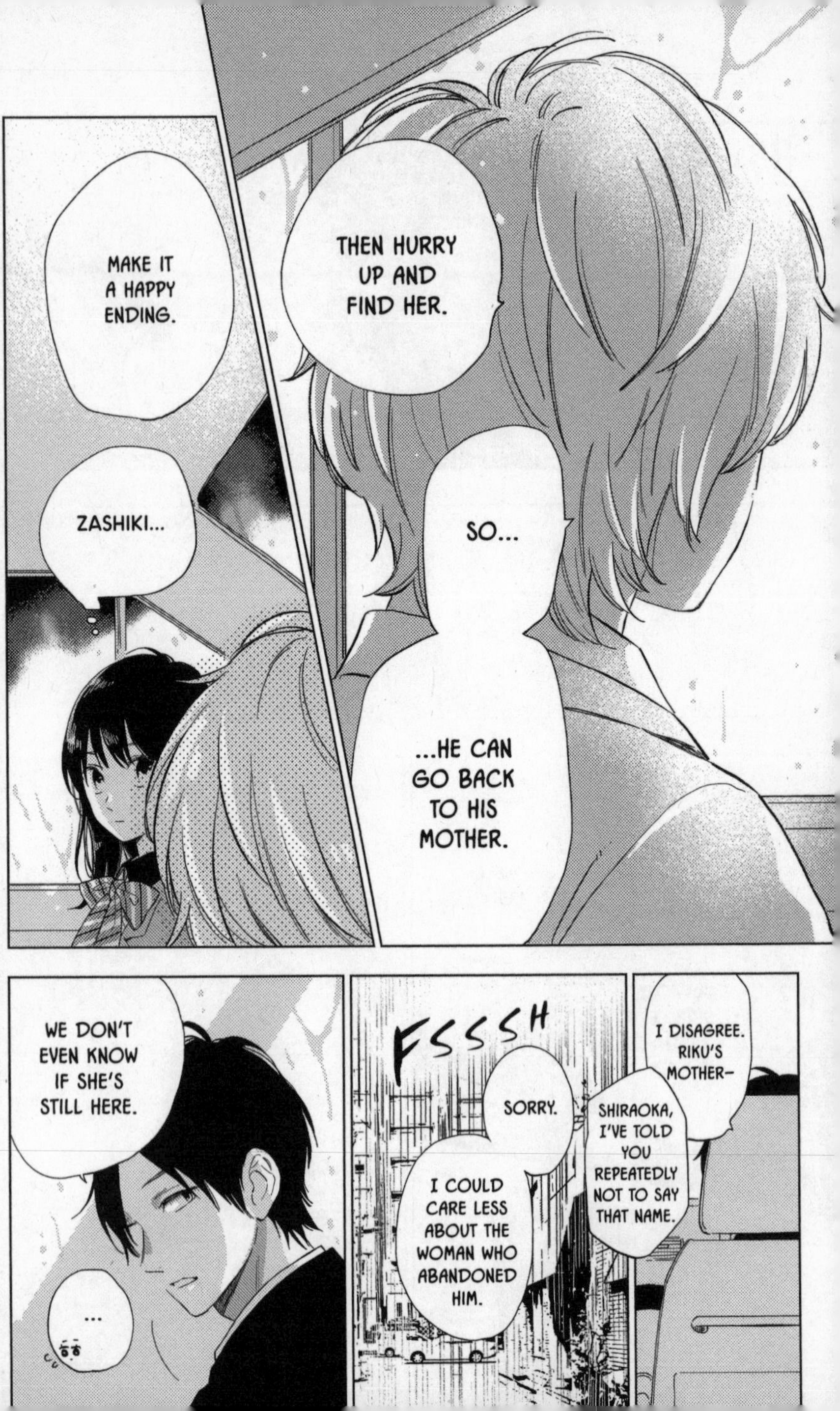
THEN HURRY UP AND FIND HER.
SO...
...HE CAN GO BACK TO HIS MOTHER.
MAKE IT A HAPPY ENDING.
ZASHIKI...
I DISAGREE. RIKU'S MOTHER—
SHIRAOKA, I'VE TOLD YOU REPEATEDLY NOT TO SAY THAT NAME.
FSSSH
SORRY.
I COULD CARE LESS ABOUT THE WOMAN WHO ABANDONED HIM.
WE DON'T EVEN KNOW IF SHE'S STILL HERE.
...

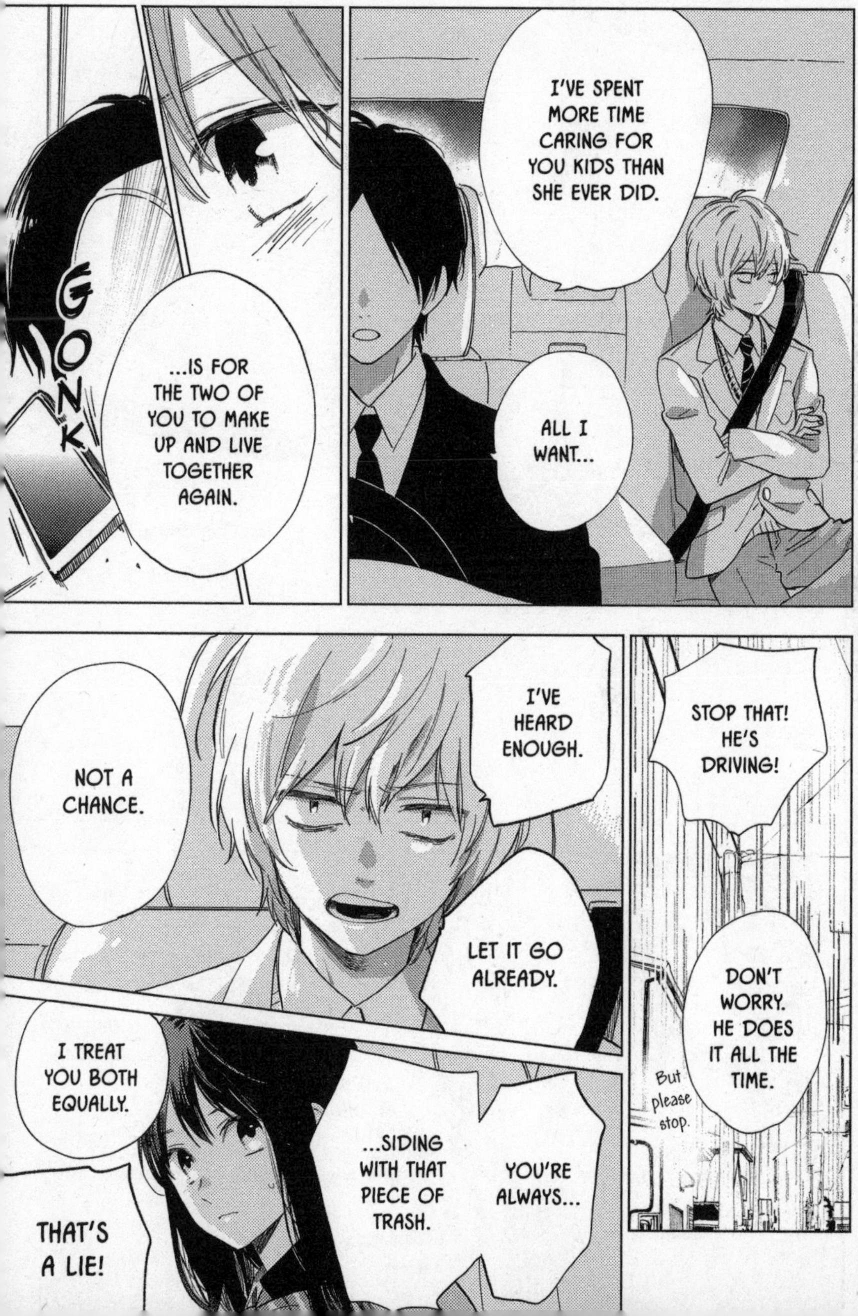
I'VE SPENT MORE TIME CARING FOR YOU KIDS THAN SHE EVER DID.
ALL I WANT...
...IS FOR THE TWO OF YOU TO MAKE UP AND LIVE TOGETHER AGAIN.
GONK
STOP THAT! HE'S DRIVING!
DON'T WORRY. HE DOES IT ALL THE TIME.
But please stop.
I'VE HEARD ENOUGH.
NOT A CHANCE.
LET IT GO ALREADY.
YOU'RE ALWAYS...
...SIDING WITH THAT PIECE OF TRASH.
I TREAT YOU BOTH EQUALLY.
THAT'S A LIE!

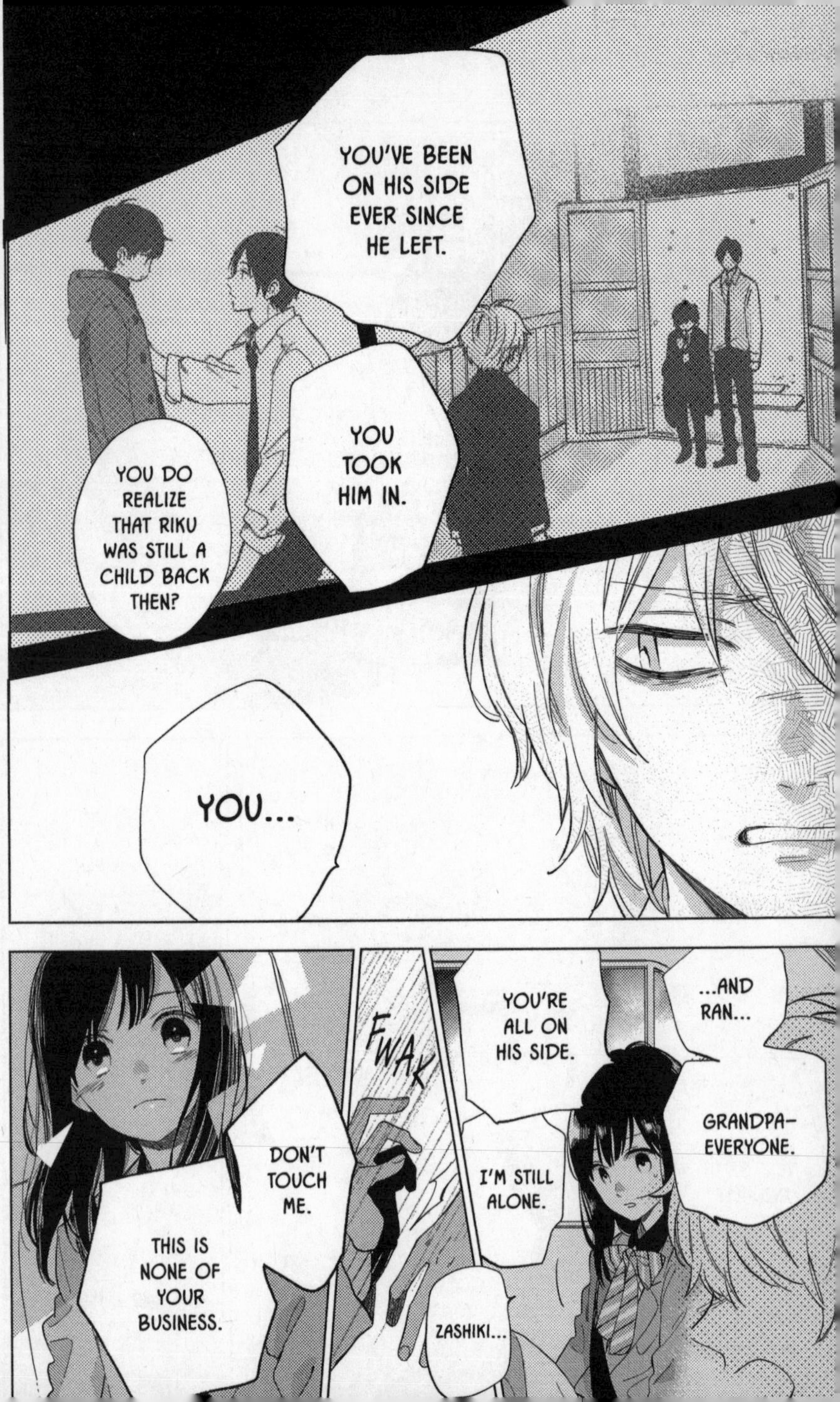
YOU'VE BEEN ON HIS SIDE EVER SINCE HE LEFT.
YOU TOOK HIM IN.
YOU DO REALIZE THAT RIKU WAS STILL A CHILD BACK THEN?
YOU...
...AND RAN...
GRANDPA— EVERYONE.
YOU'RE ALL ON HIS SIDE.
I'M STILL ALONE.
ZASHIKI...
FWAK
DON'T TOUCH ME.
THIS IS NONE OF YOUR BUSINESS.

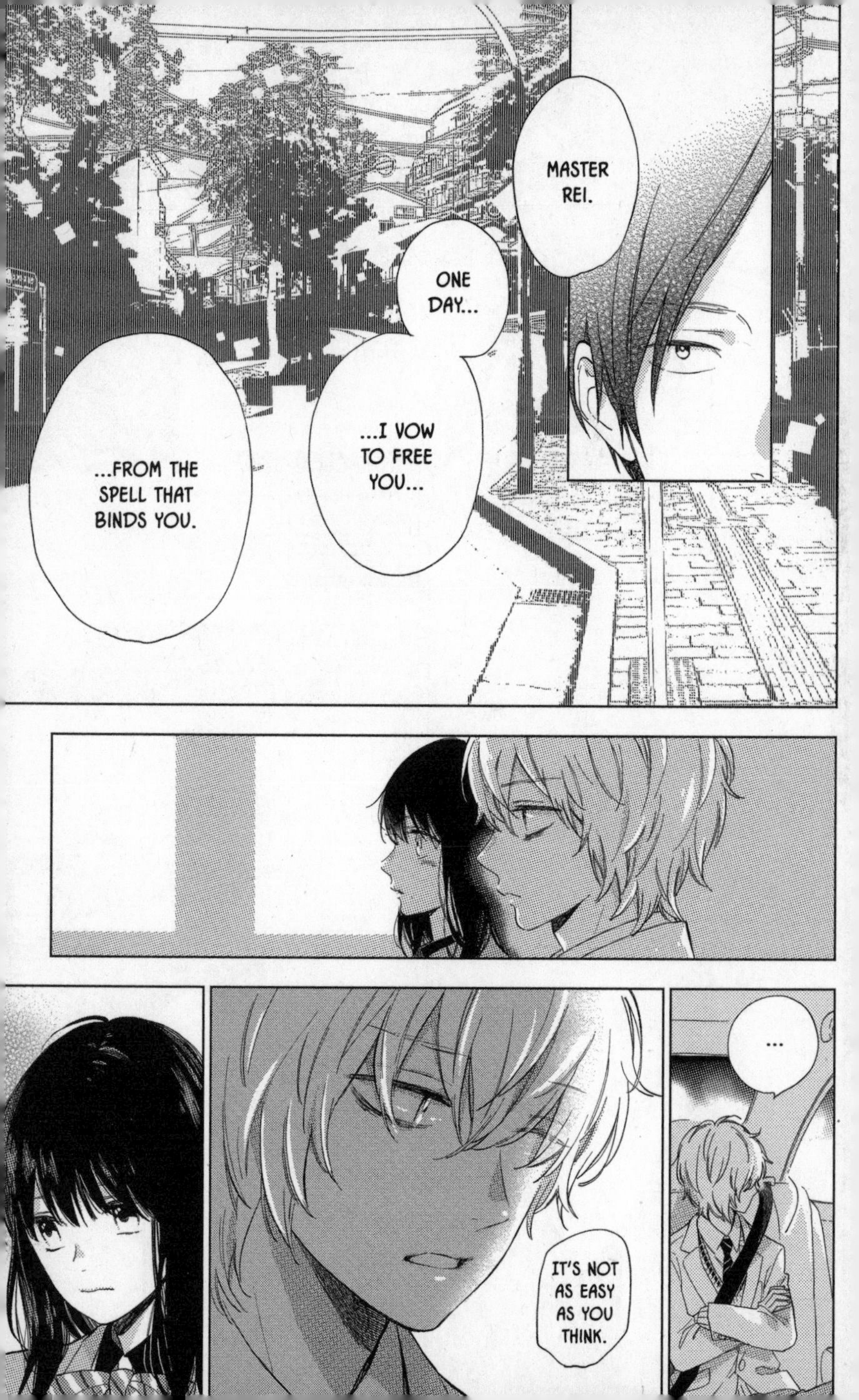
MASTER REI.
ONE DAY...
...I VOW TO FREE YOU...
...FROM THE SPELL THAT BINDS YOU.
...
IT'S NOT AS EASY AS YOU THINK.

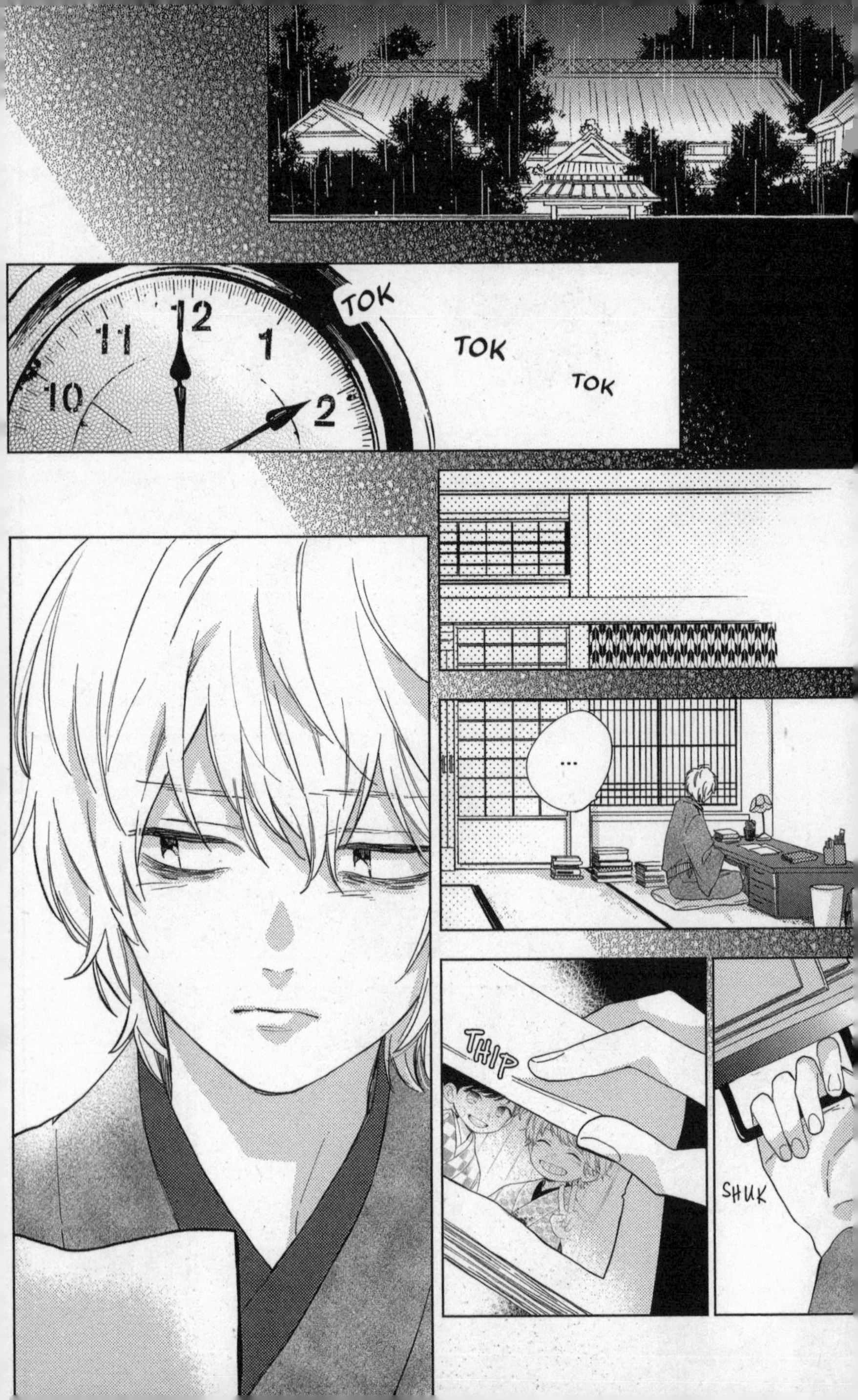
TOK
TOK
TOK
...
THIP
SHUK

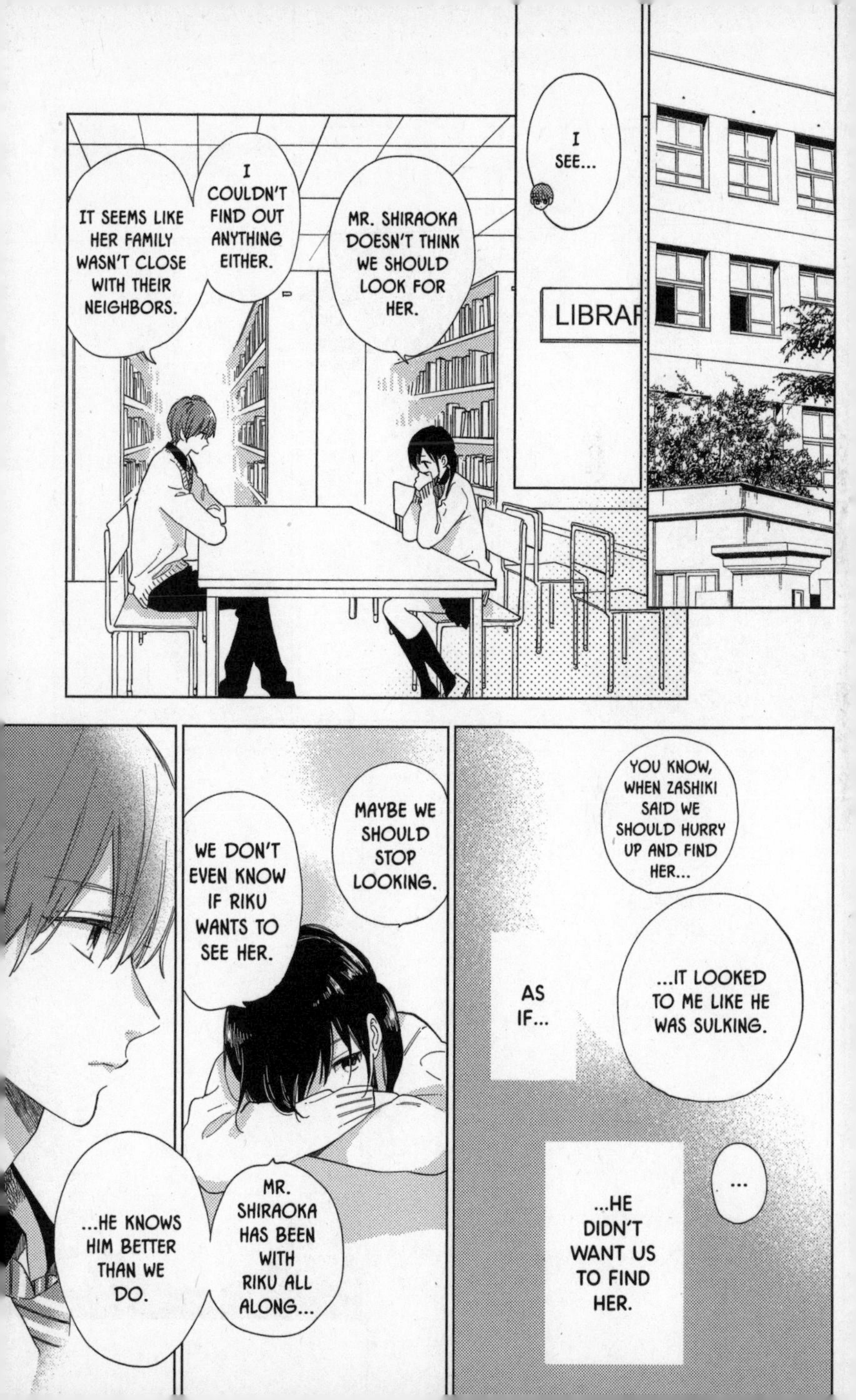
LIBRAR
I SEE...
MR. SHIRAOKA DOESN'T THINK WE SHOULD LOOK FOR HER.
I COULDN'T FIND OUT ANYTHING EITHER.
IT SEEMS LIKE HER FAMILY WASN'T CLOSE WITH THEIR NEIGHBORS.
YOU KNOW, WHEN ZASHIKI SAID WE SHOULD HURRY UP AND FIND HER...
...IT LOOKED TO ME LIKE HE WAS SULKING.
AS IF...
...HE DIDN'T WANT US TO FIND HER.
...
MAYBE WE SHOULD STOP LOOKING.
WE DON'T EVEN KNOW IF RIKU WANTS TO SEE HER.
MR. SHIRAOKA HAS BEEN WITH RIKU ALL ALONG...
...HE KNOWS HIM BETTER THAN WE DO.

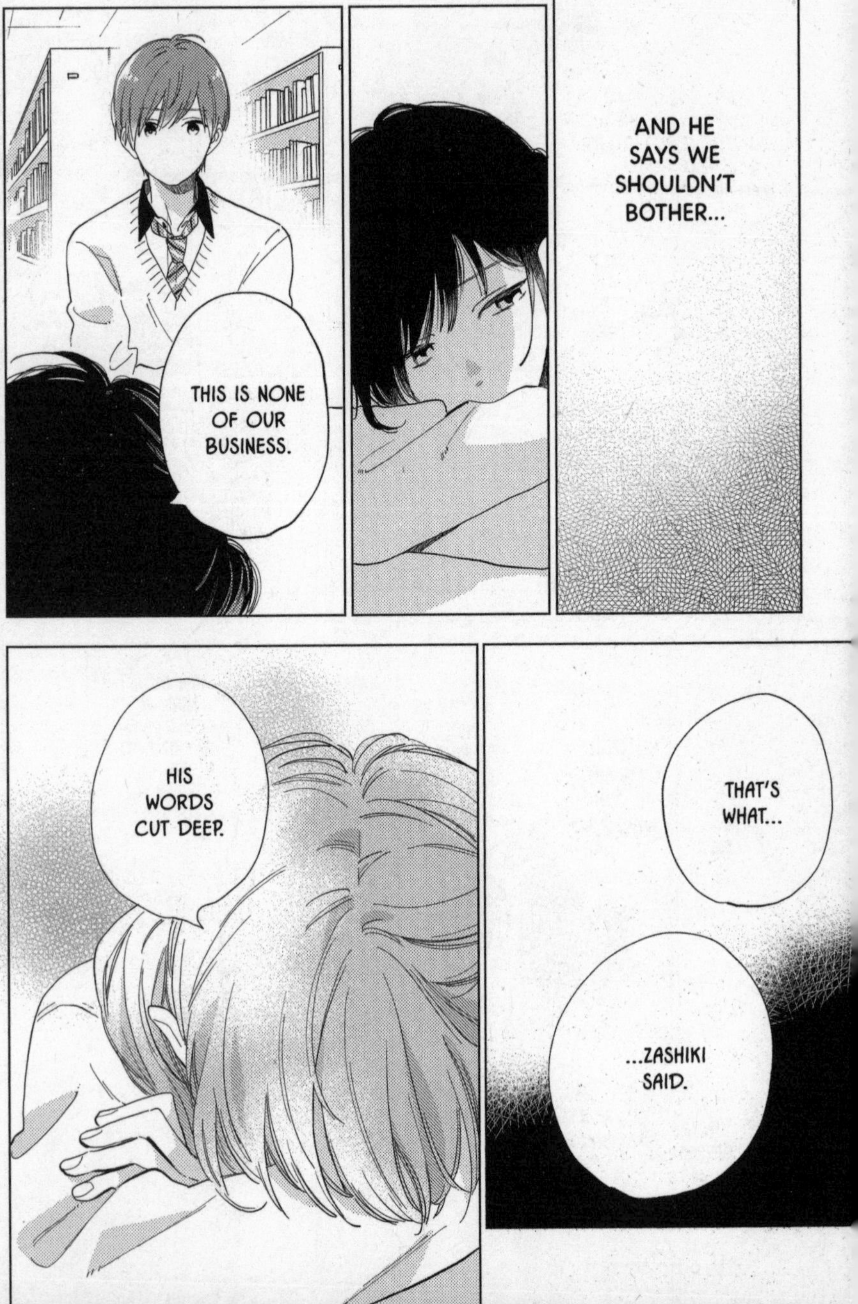
AND HE SAYS WE SHOULDN'T BOTHER...
THIS IS NONE OF OUR BUSINESS.
THAT'S WHAT...
...ZASHIKI SAID.
HIS WORDS CUT DEEP.

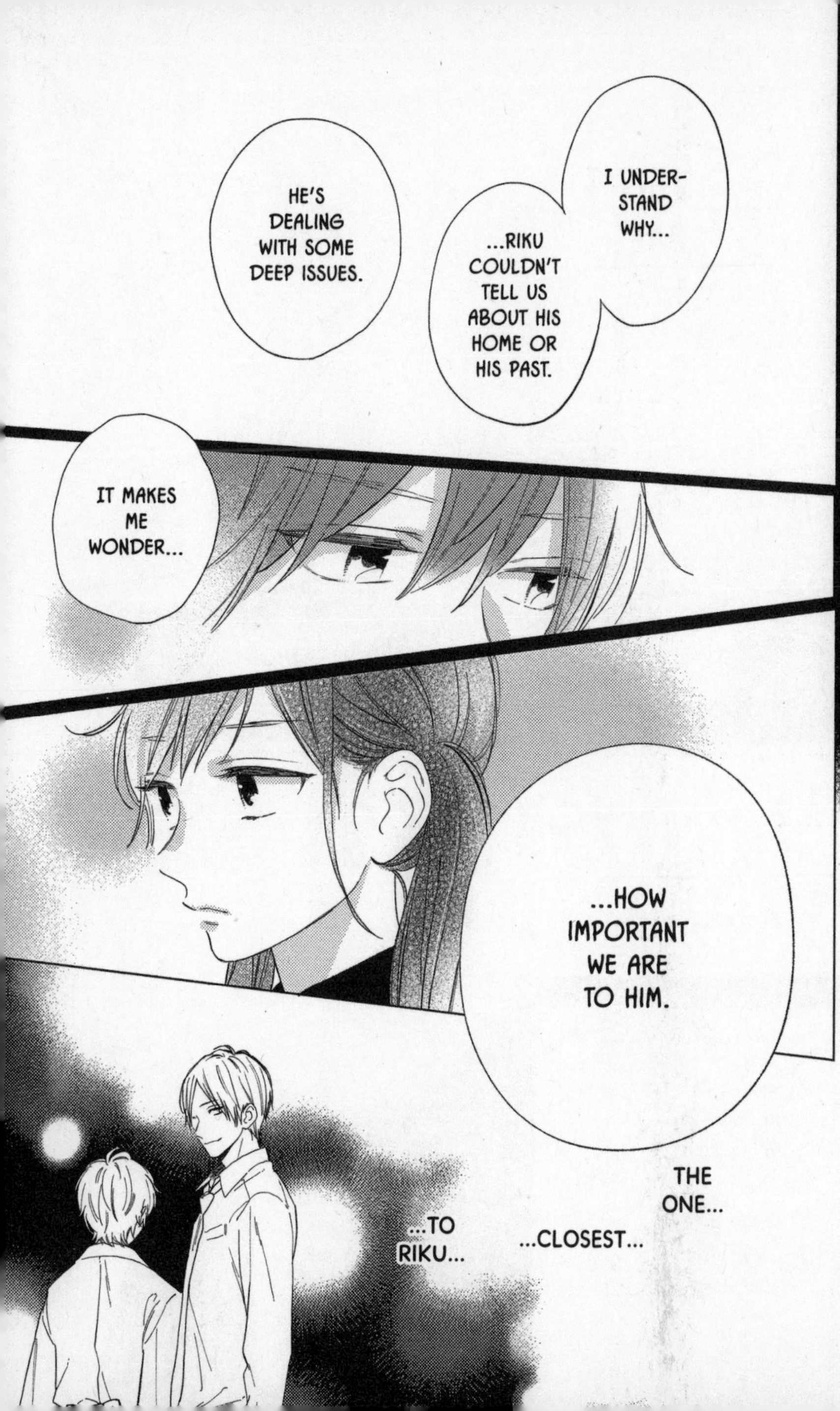
I UNDER-STAND WHY...
...RIKU COULDN'T TELL US ABOUT HIS HOME OR HIS PAST.
HE'S DEALING WITH SOME DEEP ISSUES.
IT MAKES ME WONDER...
...HOW IMPORTANT WE ARE TO HIM.
THE ONE...
...CLOSEST...
...TO RIKU...

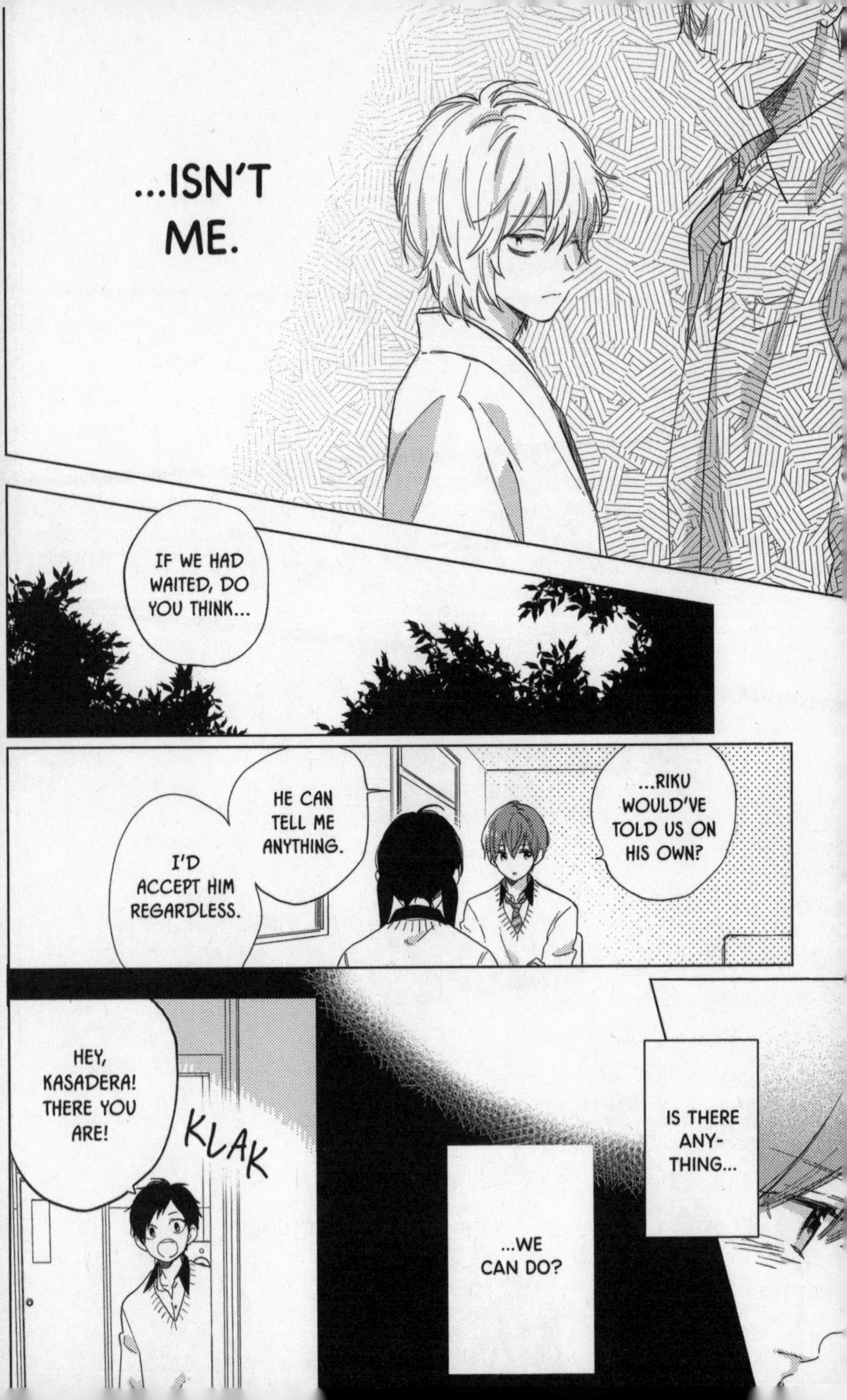
...ISN'T ME.
IF WE HAD WAITED, DO YOU THINK...
...RIKU WOULD'VE TOLD US ON HIS OWN?
HE CAN TELL ME ANYTHING.
I'D ACCEPT HIM REGARDLESS.
IS THERE ANY-THING...
...WE CAN DO?
HEY, KASADERA! THERE YOU ARE!
KLAK

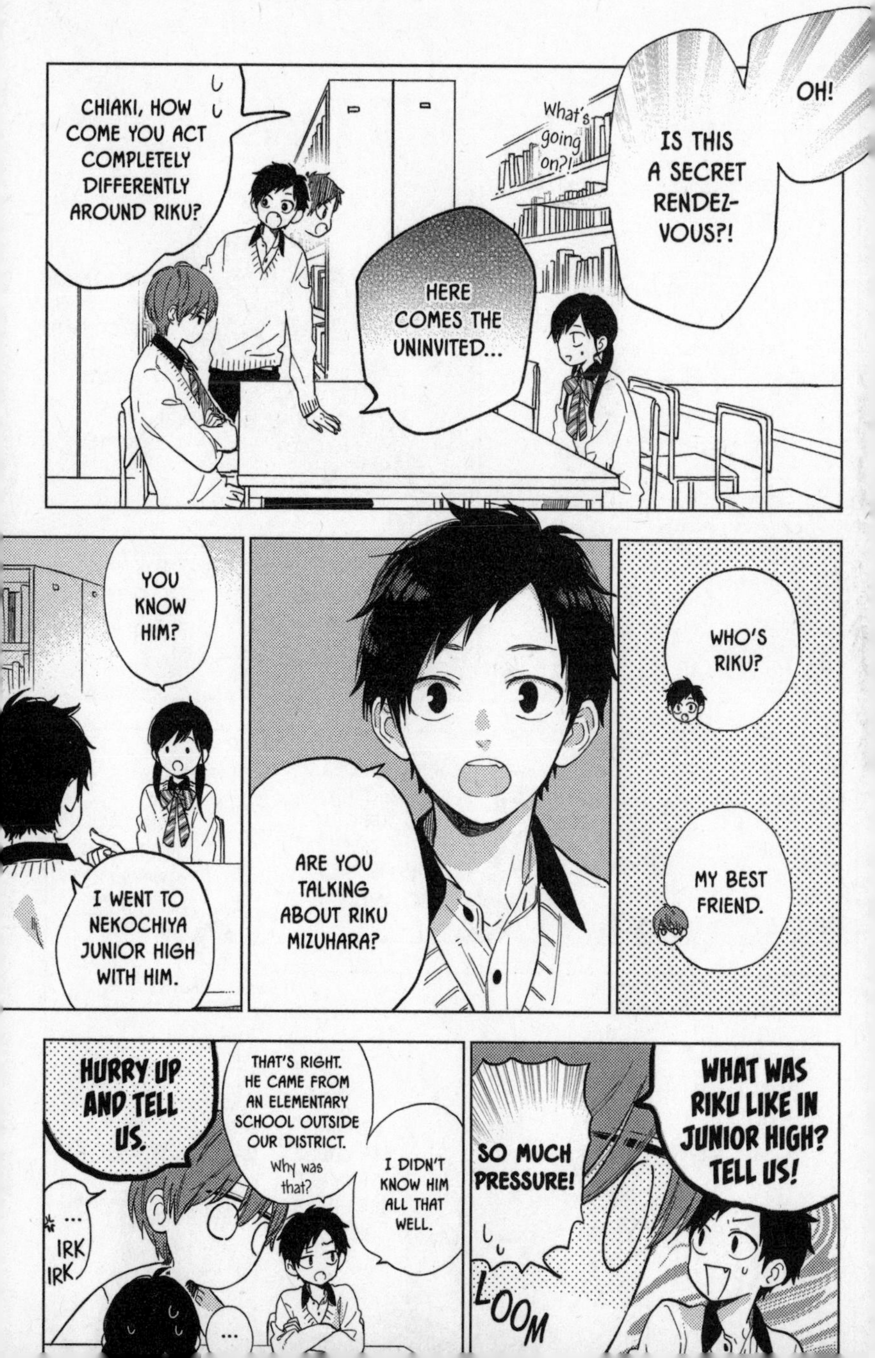
OH!
IS THIS A SECRET RENDEZ-VOUS?!
What's going on?!
HERE COMES THE UNINVITED...
CHIAKI, HOW COME YOU ACT COMPLETELY DIFFERENTLY AROUND RIKU?
WHO'S RIKU?
MY BEST FRIEND.
ARE YOU TALKING ABOUT RIKU MIZUHARA?
YOU KNOW HIM?
I WENT TO NEKOCHIYA JUNIOR HIGH WITH HIM.
WHAT WAS RIKU LIKE IN JUNIOR HIGH? TELL US!
SO MUCH PRESSURE!
LOOM
THAT'S RIGHT. HE CAME FROM AN ELEMENTARY SCHOOL OUTSIDE OUR DISTRICT.
HURRY UP AND TELL US.
I DIDN'T KNOW HIM ALL THAT WELL.
Why was that?
... IRK IRK
...

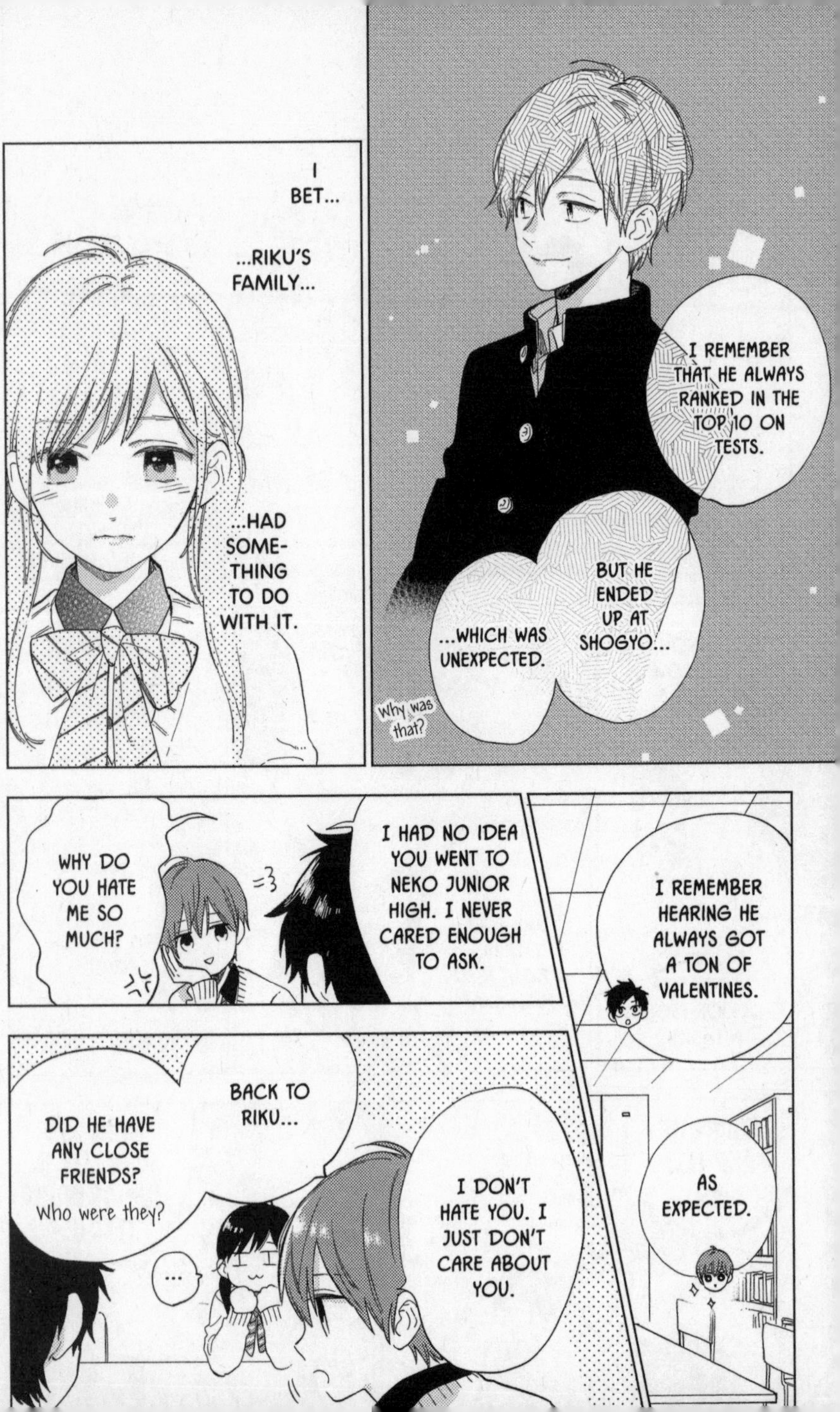
I REMEMBER THAT HE ALWAYS RANKED IN THE TOP 10 ON TESTS.
BUT HE ENDED UP AT SHOGYO...
...WHICH WAS UNEXPECTED.
Why was that?
I BET...
...RIKU'S FAMILY...
...HAD SOME-THING TO DO WITH IT.
I REMEMBER HEARING HE ALWAYS GOT A TON OF VALENTINES.
AS EXPECTED.
I HAD NO IDEA YOU WENT TO NEKO JUNIOR HIGH. I NEVER CARED ENOUGH TO ASK.
WHY DO YOU HATE ME SO MUCH?
I DON'T HATE YOU. I JUST DON'T CARE ABOUT YOU.
...
BACK TO RIKU...
DID HE HAVE ANY CLOSE FRIENDS? Who were they?

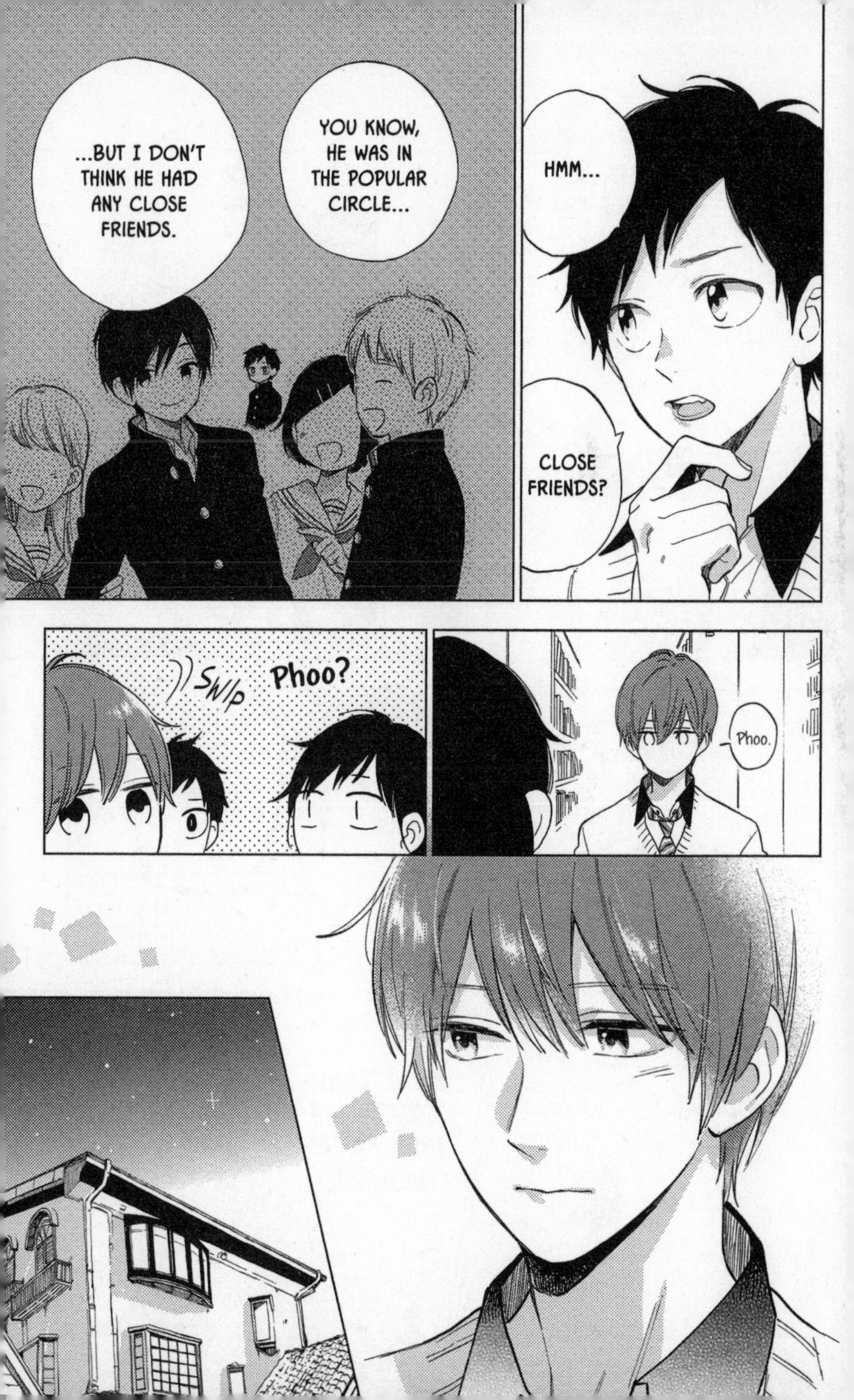
HMM...
CLOSE FRIENDS?
YOU KNOW, HE WAS IN THE POPULAR CIRCLE...
...BUT I DON'T THINK HE HAD ANY CLOSE FRIENDS.
Phoo.
SWIP
Phoo?

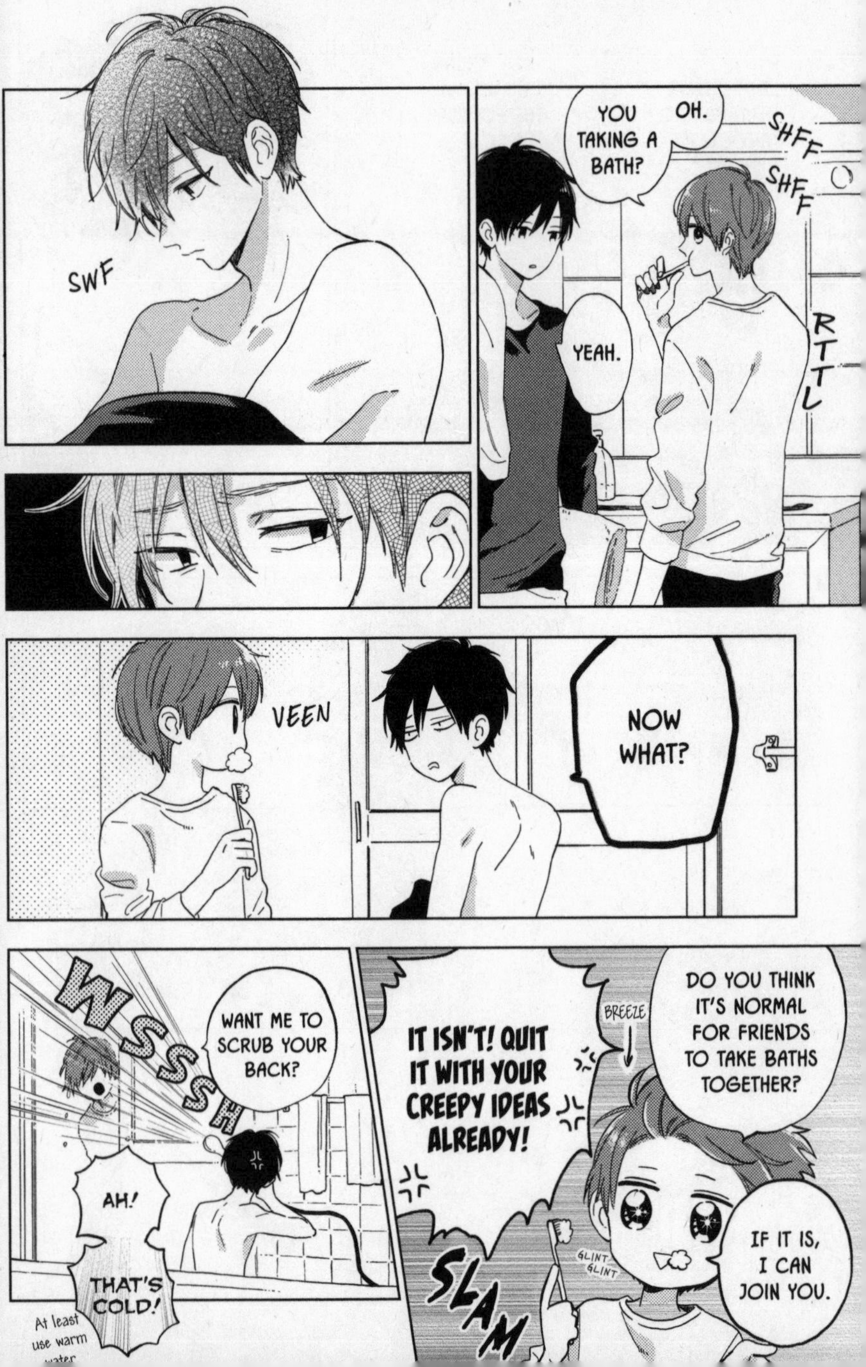
OH.
YOU TAKING A BATH?
SHFF
SHFF
YEAH.
RTTL
SWF
NOW WHAT?
VEEN
DO YOU THINK IT'S NORMAL FOR FRIENDS TO TAKE BATHS TOGETHER?
BREEZE
IF IT IS, I CAN JOIN YOU.
GLINT GLINT
IT ISN'T! QUIT IT WITH YOUR CREEPY IDEAS ALREADY!
SLAM
WANT ME TO SCRUB YOUR BACK?
WSSSH
AH!
THAT'S COLD!
At least use warm

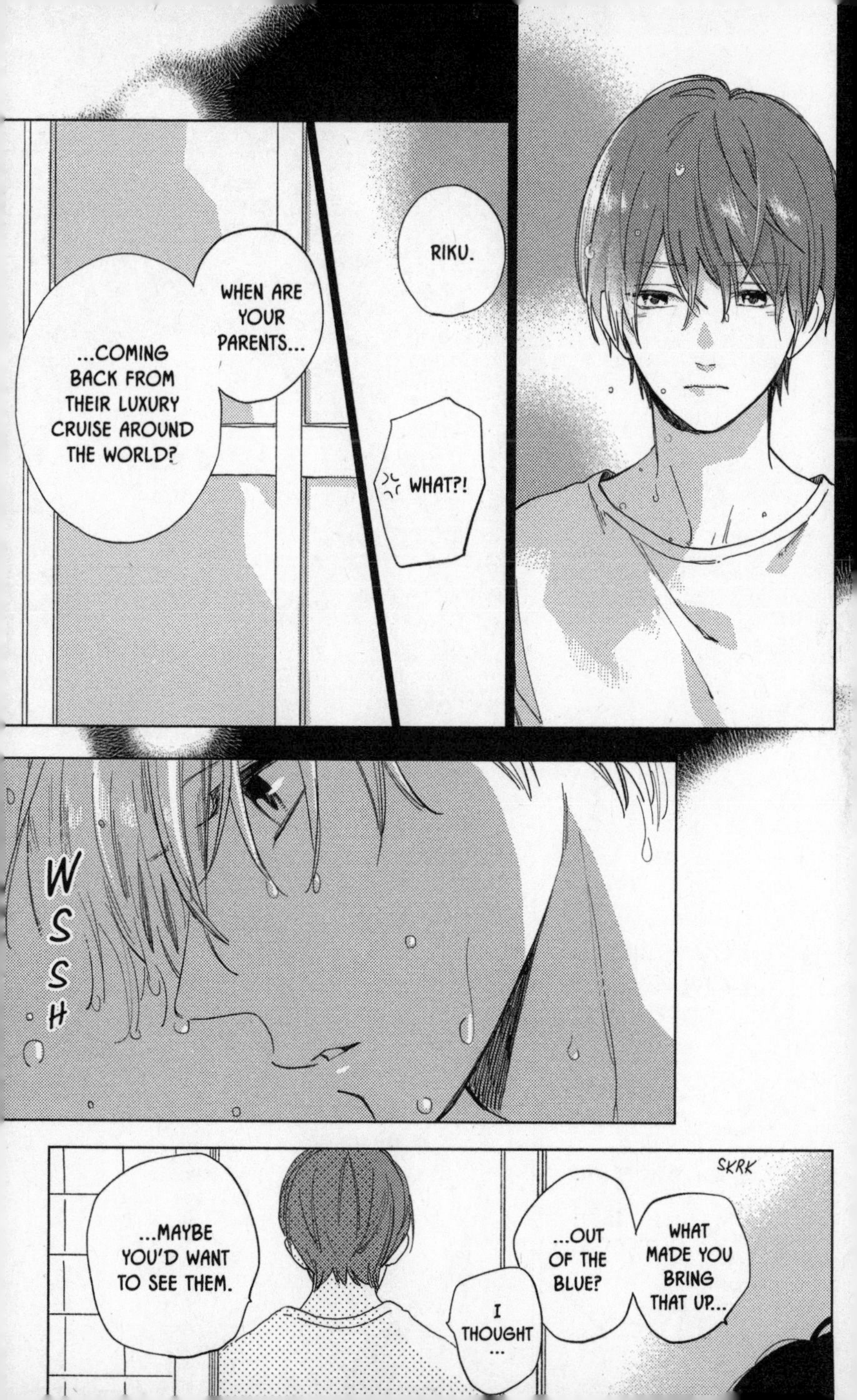
RIKU.
WHAT?!
WHEN ARE YOUR PARENTS...
...COMING BACK FROM THEIR LUXURY CRUISE AROUND THE WORLD?
WSSH
SKRK
WHAT MADE YOU BRING THAT UP...
...OUT OF THE BLUE?
I THOUGHT...
...MAYBE YOU'D WANT TO SEE THEM.

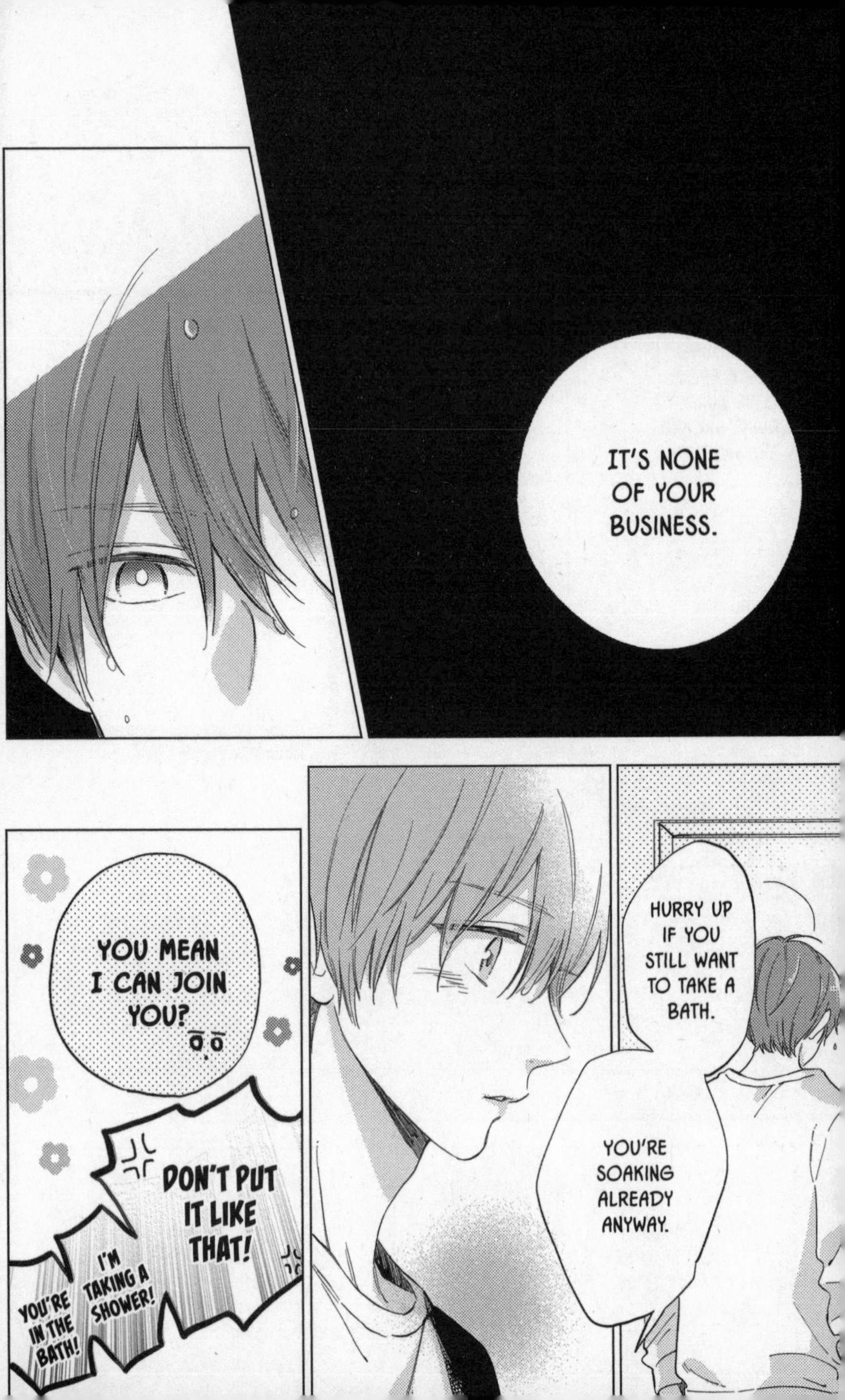
IT'S NONE OF YOUR BUSINESS.
HURRY UP IF YOU STILL WANT TO TAKE A BATH.
YOU'RE SOAKING ALREADY ANYWAY.
YOU MEAN I CAN JOIN YOU?
DON'T PUT IT LIKE THAT!
I'M TAKING A SHOWER!
YOU'RE IN THE BATH!

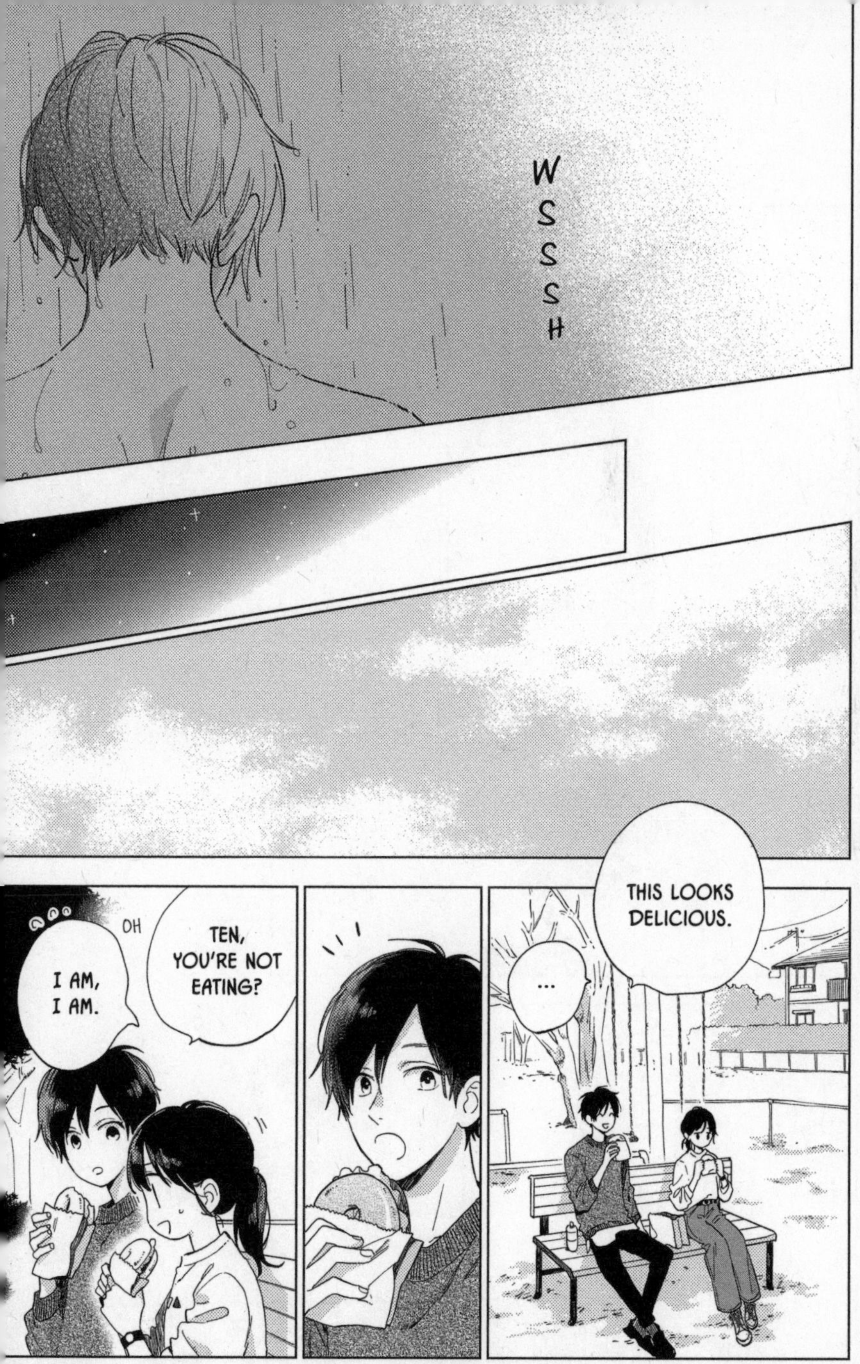
WSSSH
THIS LOOKS DELICIOUS.
...
TEN, YOU'RE NOT EATING?
OH
I AM, I AM.

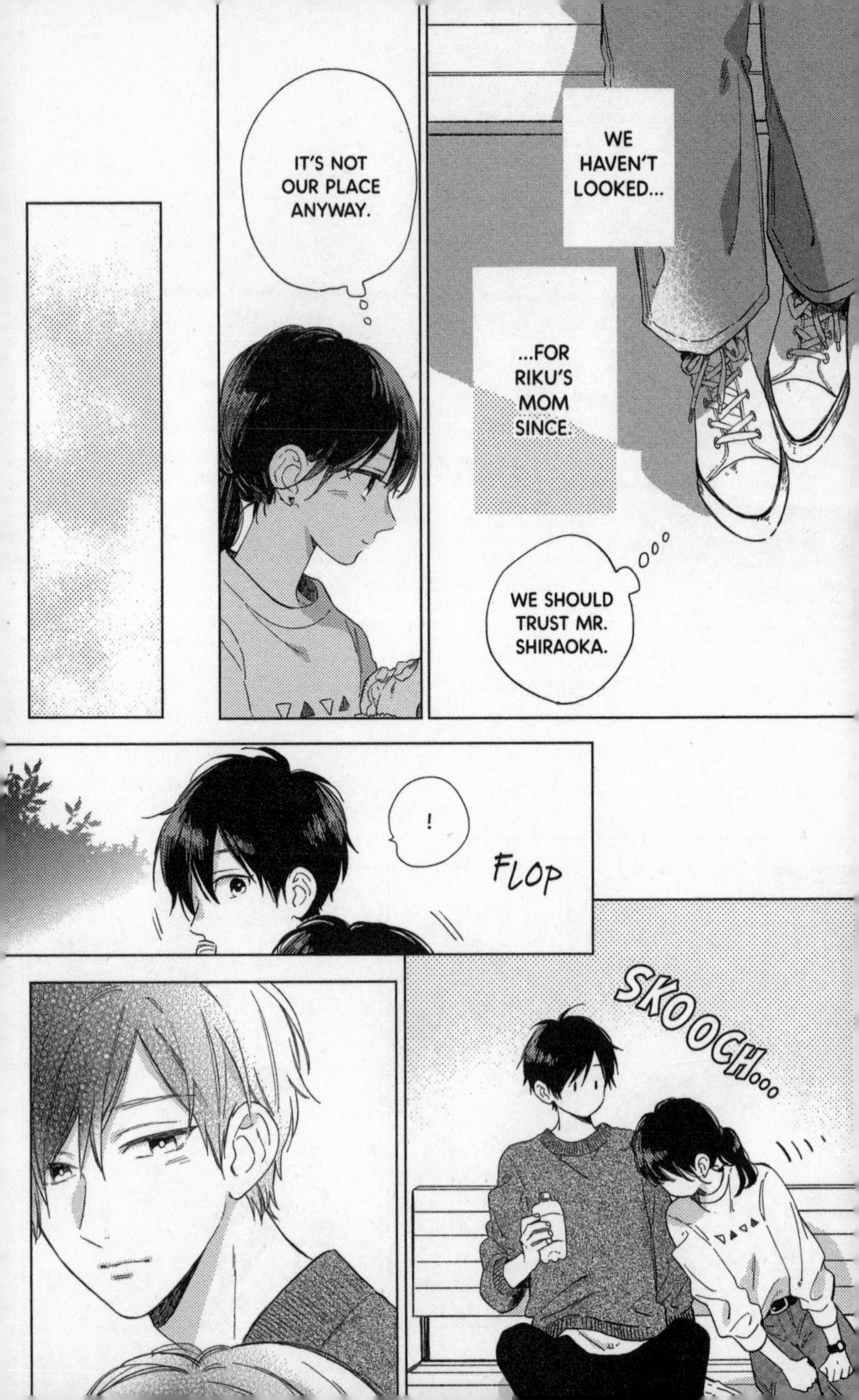
WE HAVEN'T LOOKED...
...FOR RIKU'S MOM SINCE.
WE SHOULD TRUST MR. SHIRAOKA.
IT'S NOT OUR PLACE ANYWAY.
!
FLOP
SKOOCH...

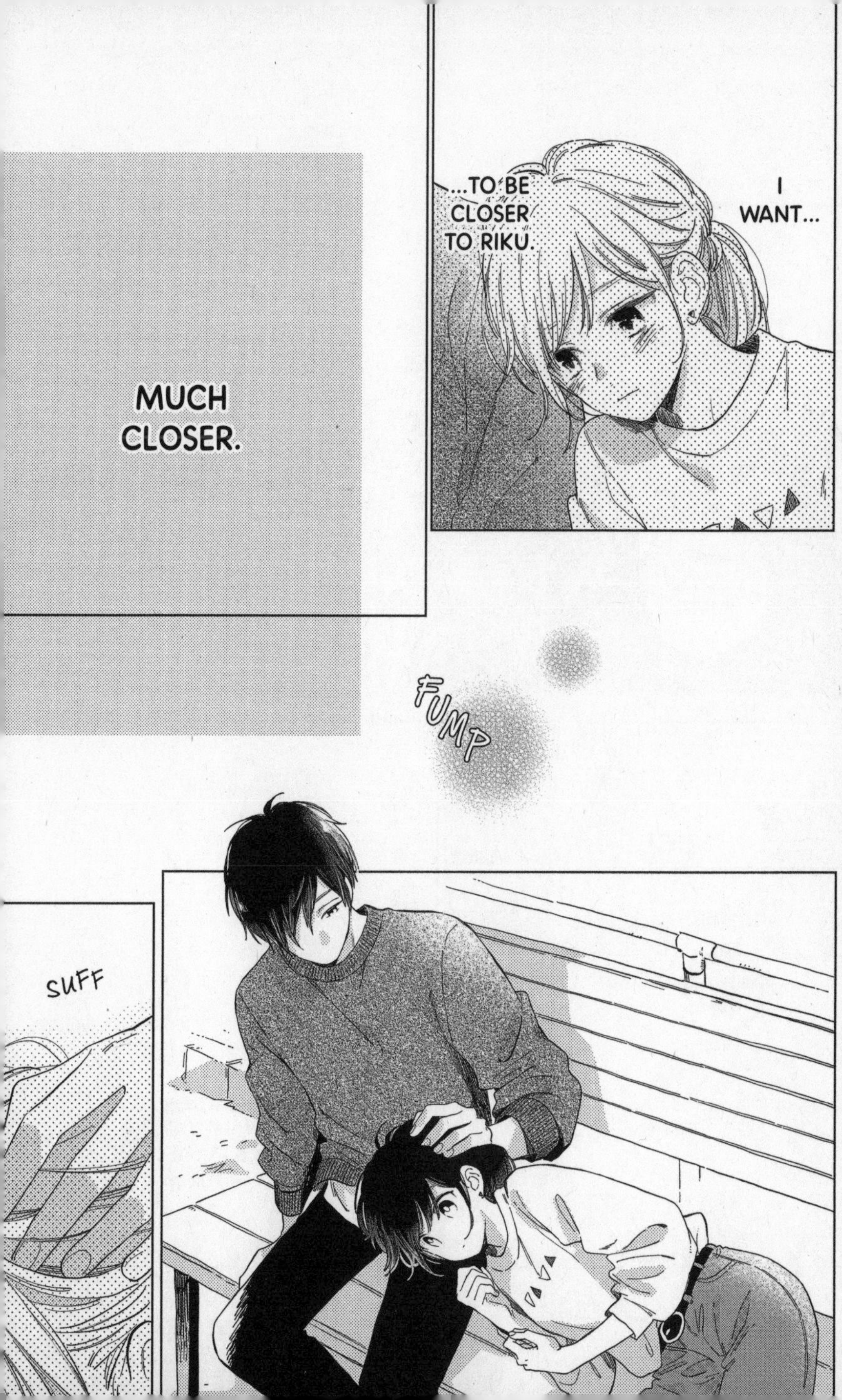
I WANT...
...TO BE CLOSER TO RIKU.
MUCH CLOSER.
FUMP
SUFF

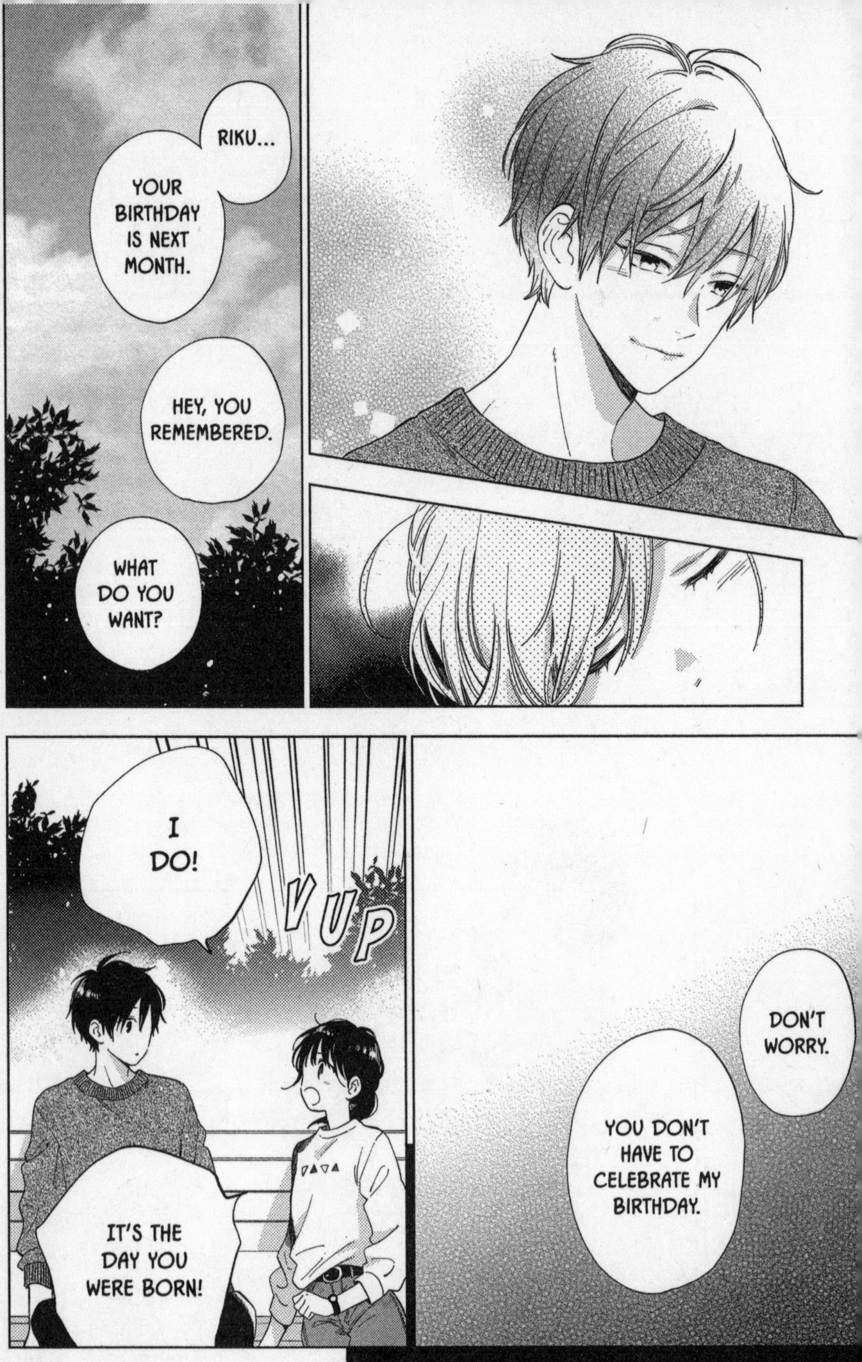
RIKU...
YOUR BIRTHDAY IS NEXT MONTH.
HEY, YOU REMEMBERED.
WHAT DO YOU WANT?
DON'T WORRY.
YOU DON'T HAVE TO CELEBRATE MY BIRTHDAY.
I DO!
VUP
IT'S THE DAY YOU WERE BORN!

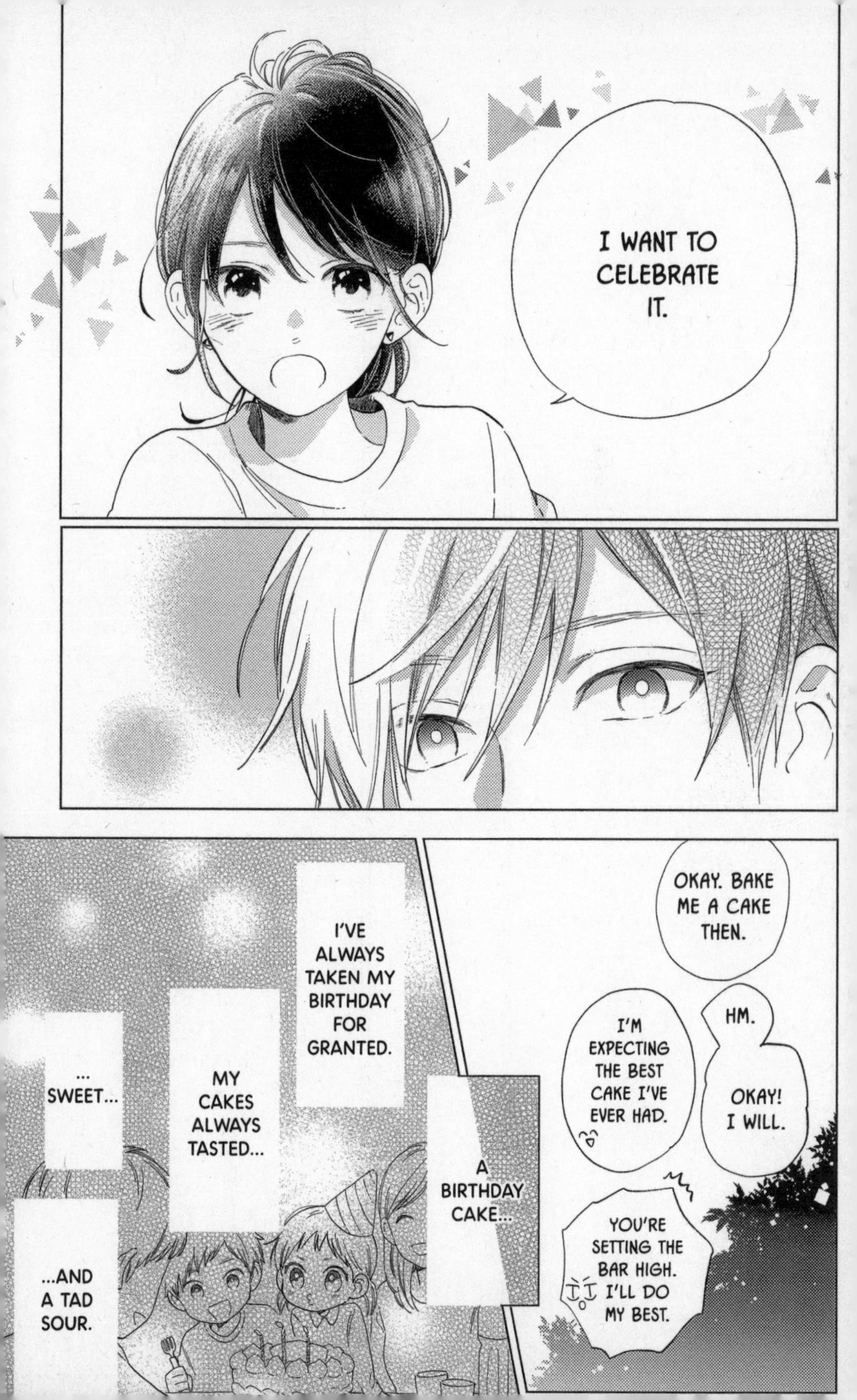
I WANT TO CELEBRATE IT.
OKAY. BAKE ME A CAKE THEN.
HM.
OKAY! I WILL.
I'M EXPECTING THE BEST CAKE I'VE EVER HAD.
YOU'RE SETTING THE BAR HIGH. I'LL DO MY BEST.
A BIRTHDAY CAKE...
I'VE ALWAYS TAKEN MY BIRTHDAY FOR GRANTED.
MY CAKES ALWAYS TASTED...
...SWEET...
...AND A TAD SOUR.

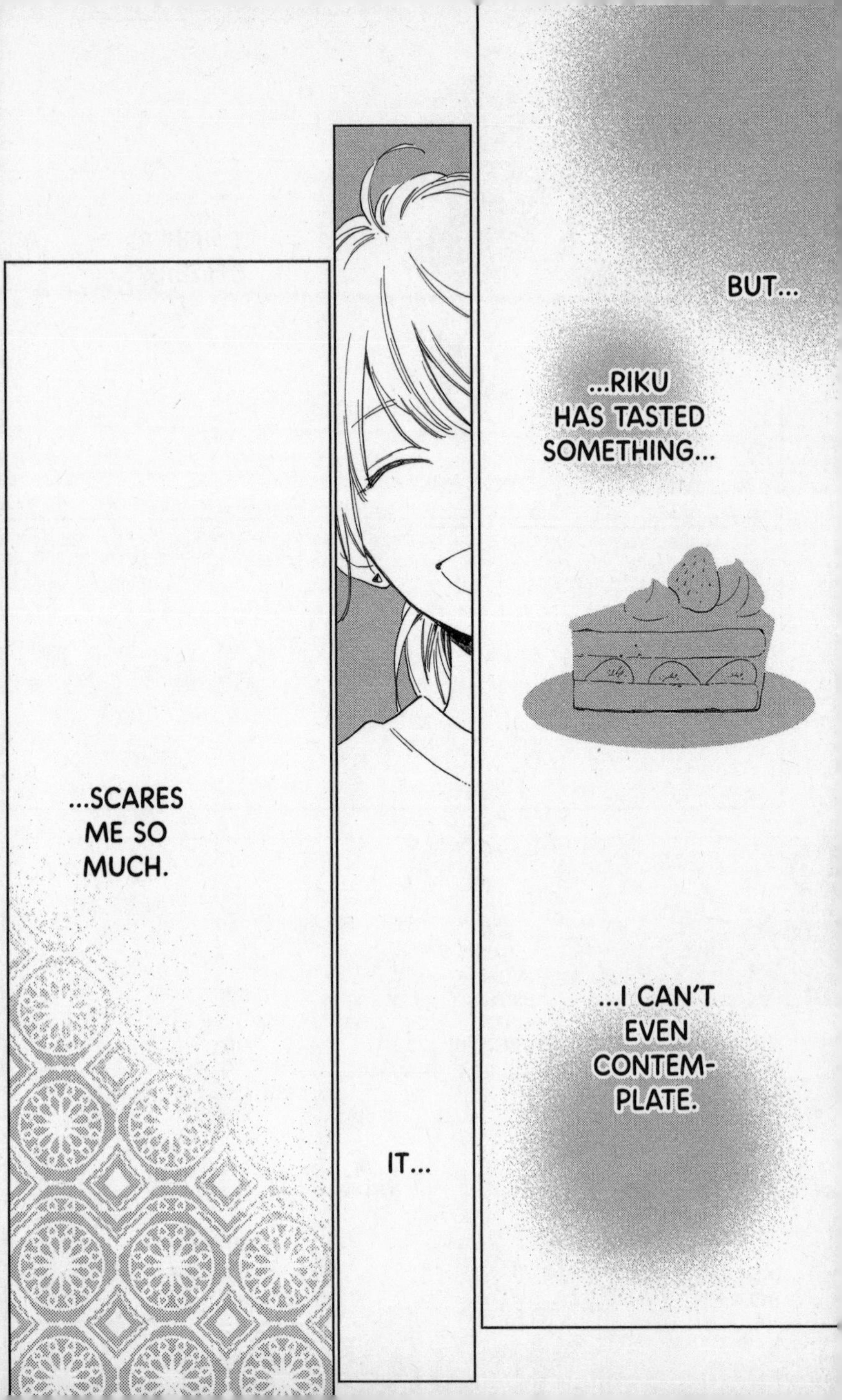
BUT...
...RIKU HAS TASTED SOMETHING...
...I CAN'T EVEN CONTEM-PLATE.
IT...
...SCARES ME SO MUCH.

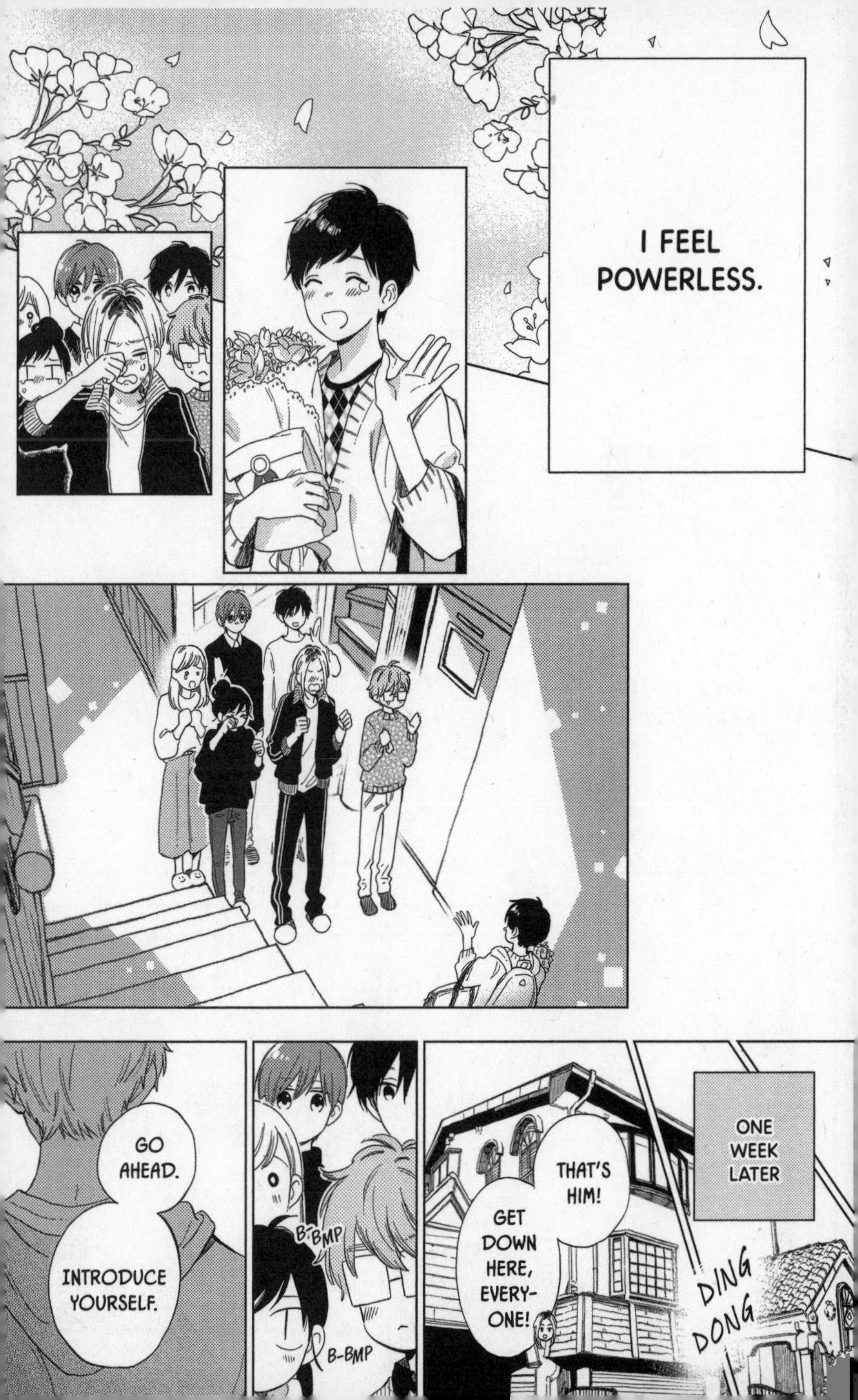
I FEEL POWERLESS.
ONE WEEK LATER
DING DONG
THAT'S HIM!
GET DOWN HERE, EVERY-ONE!
B-BMP
B-BMP
GO AHEAD.
INTRODUCE YOURSELF.

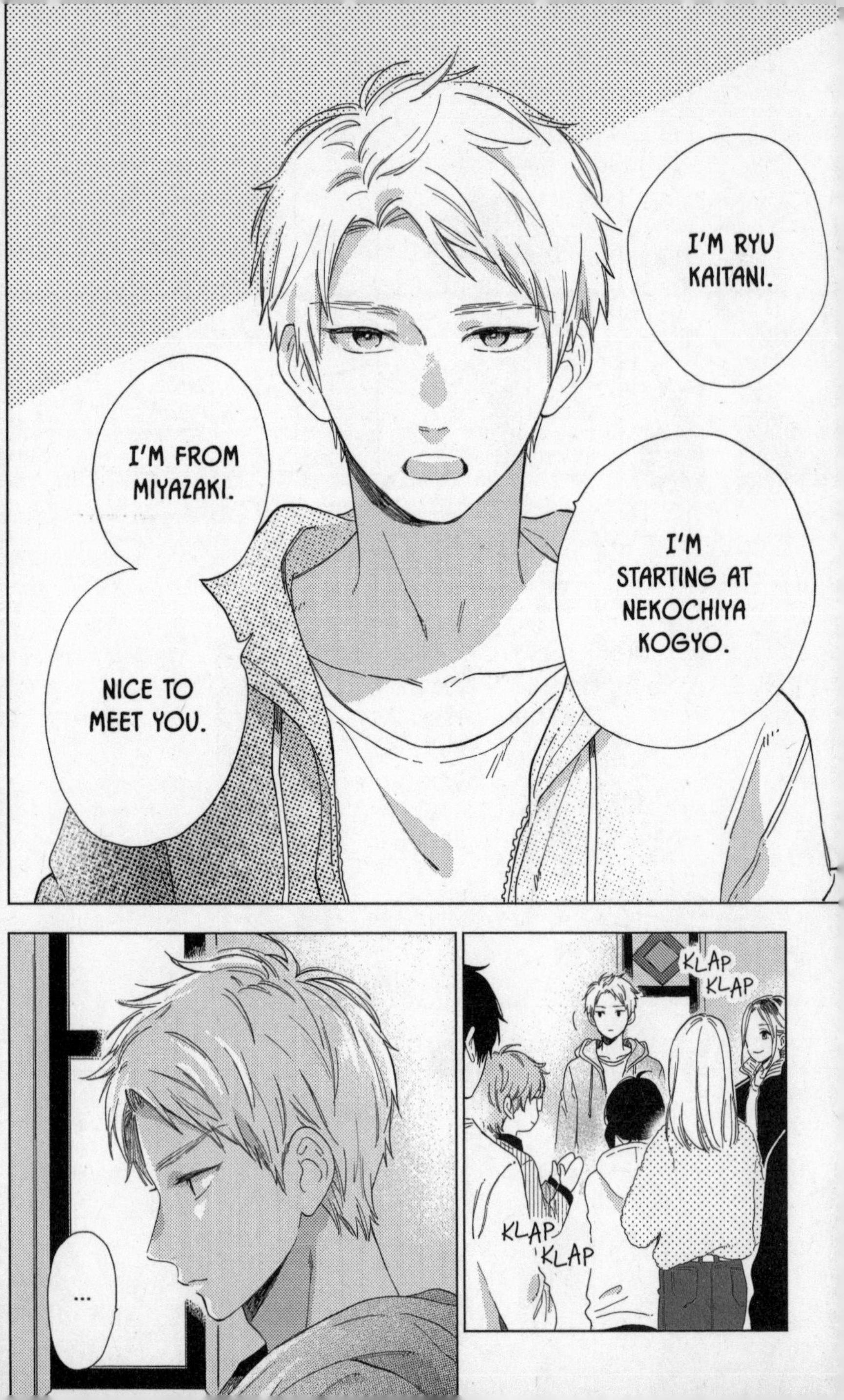
I'M RYU KAITANI.
I'M FROM MIYAZAKI.
I'M STARTING AT NEKOCHIYA KOGYO.
NICE TO MEET YOU.
KLAP KLAP
KLAP KLAP
...

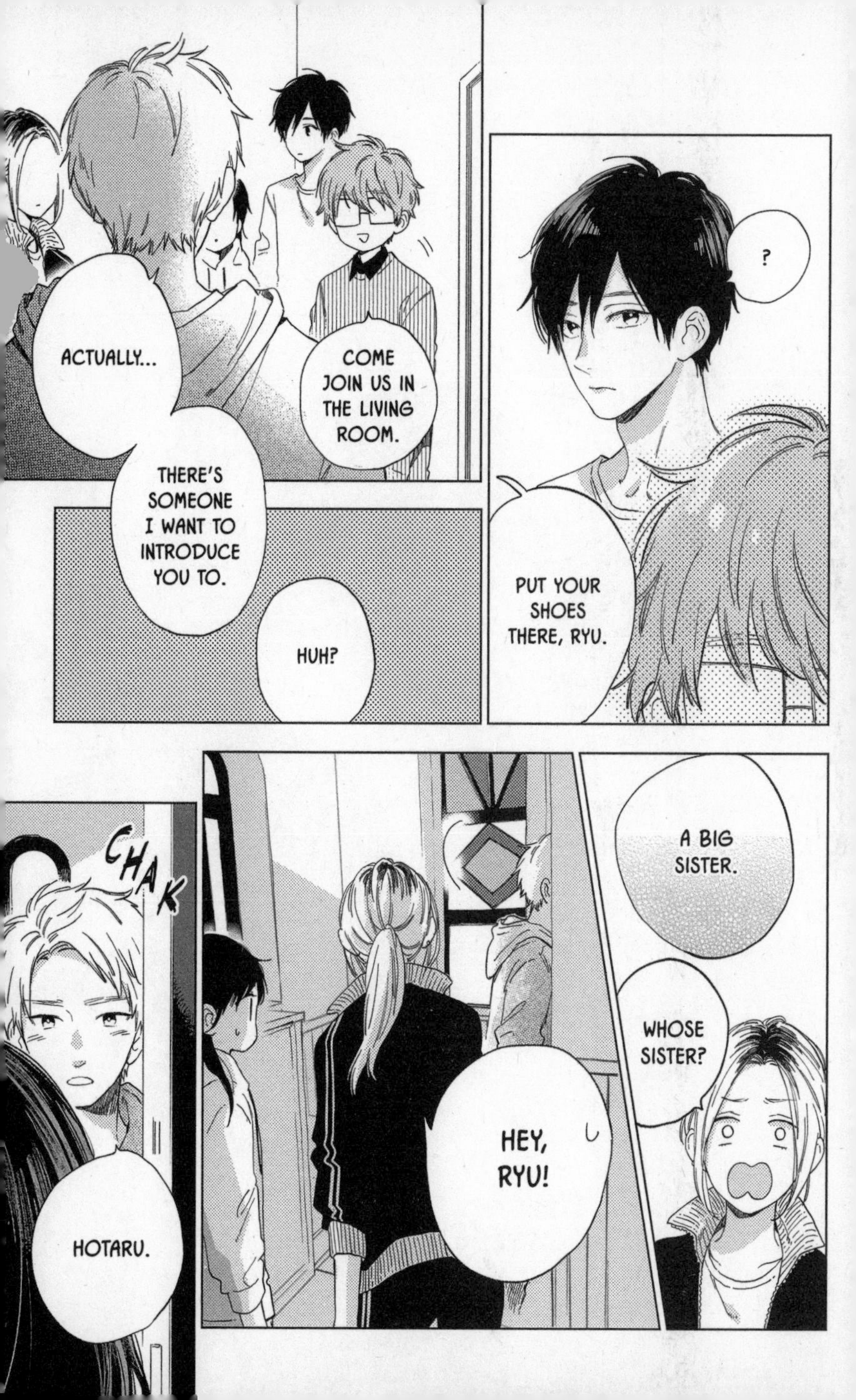
?
PUT YOUR SHOES THERE, RYU.
COME JOIN US IN THE LIVING ROOM.
ACTUALLY...
THERE'S SOMEONE I WANT TO INTRODUCE YOU TO.
HUH?
A BIG SISTER.
WHOSE SISTER?
HEY, RYU!
CHAK
HOTARU.

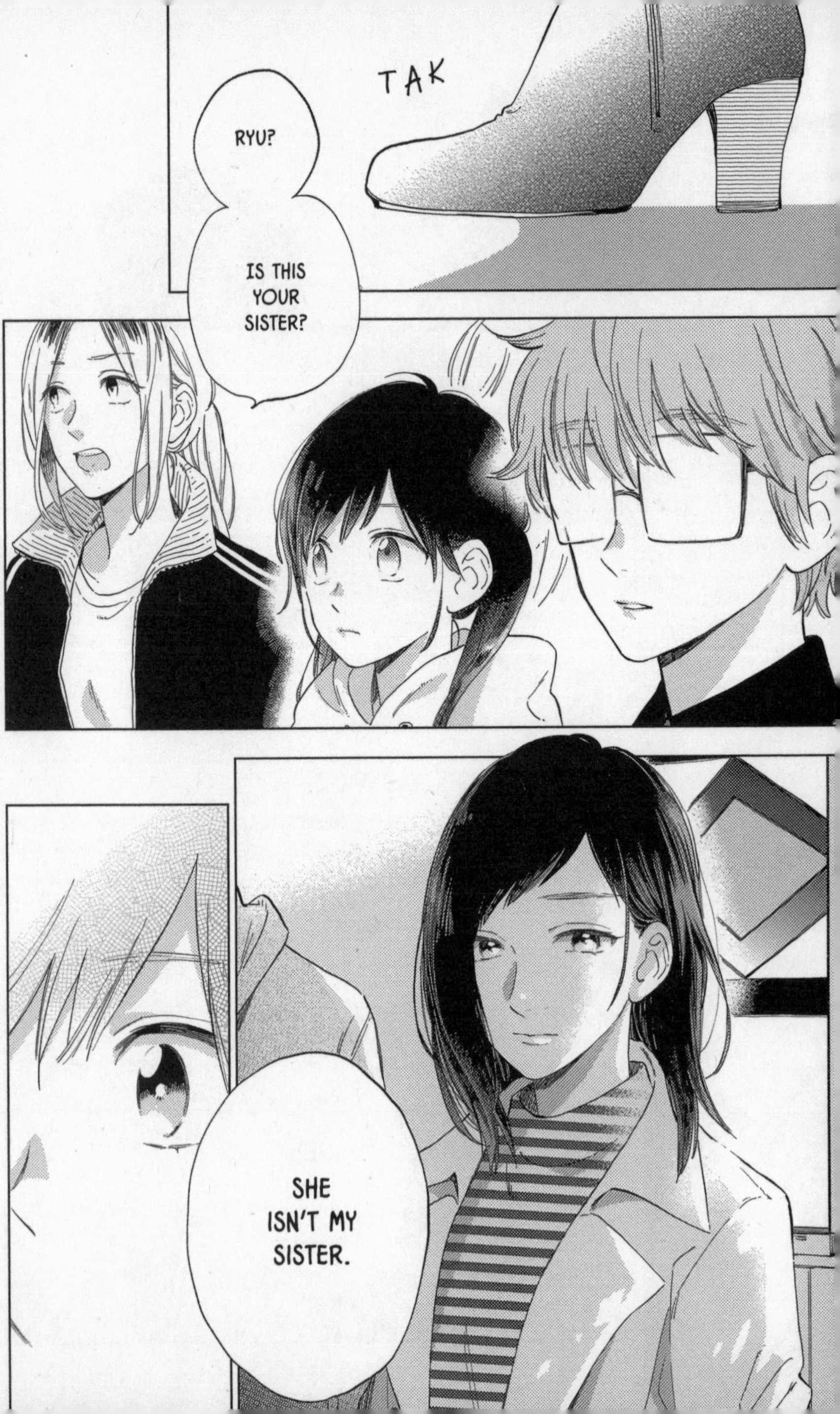
TAK
RYU?
IS THIS YOUR SISTER?
SHE ISN'T MY SISTER.

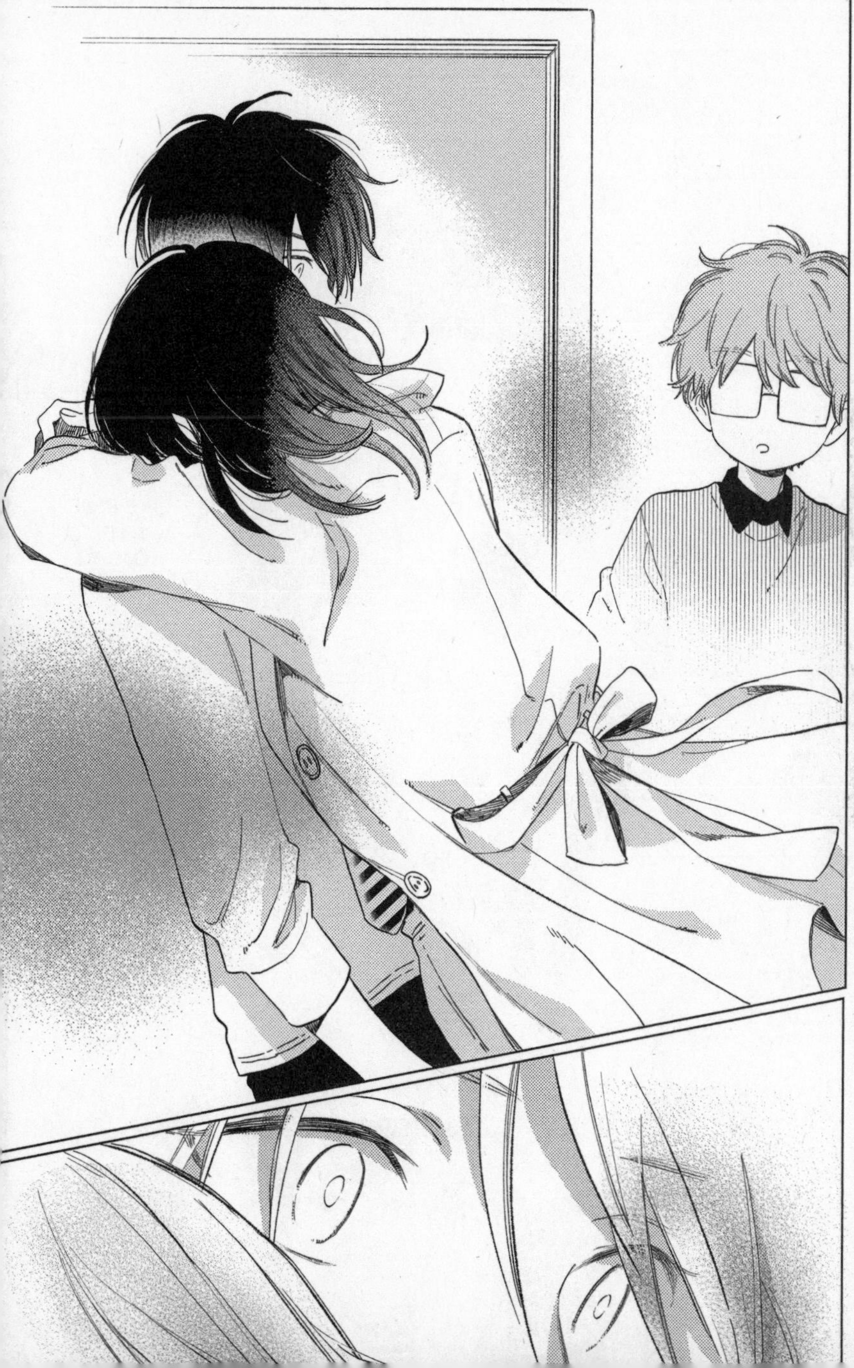

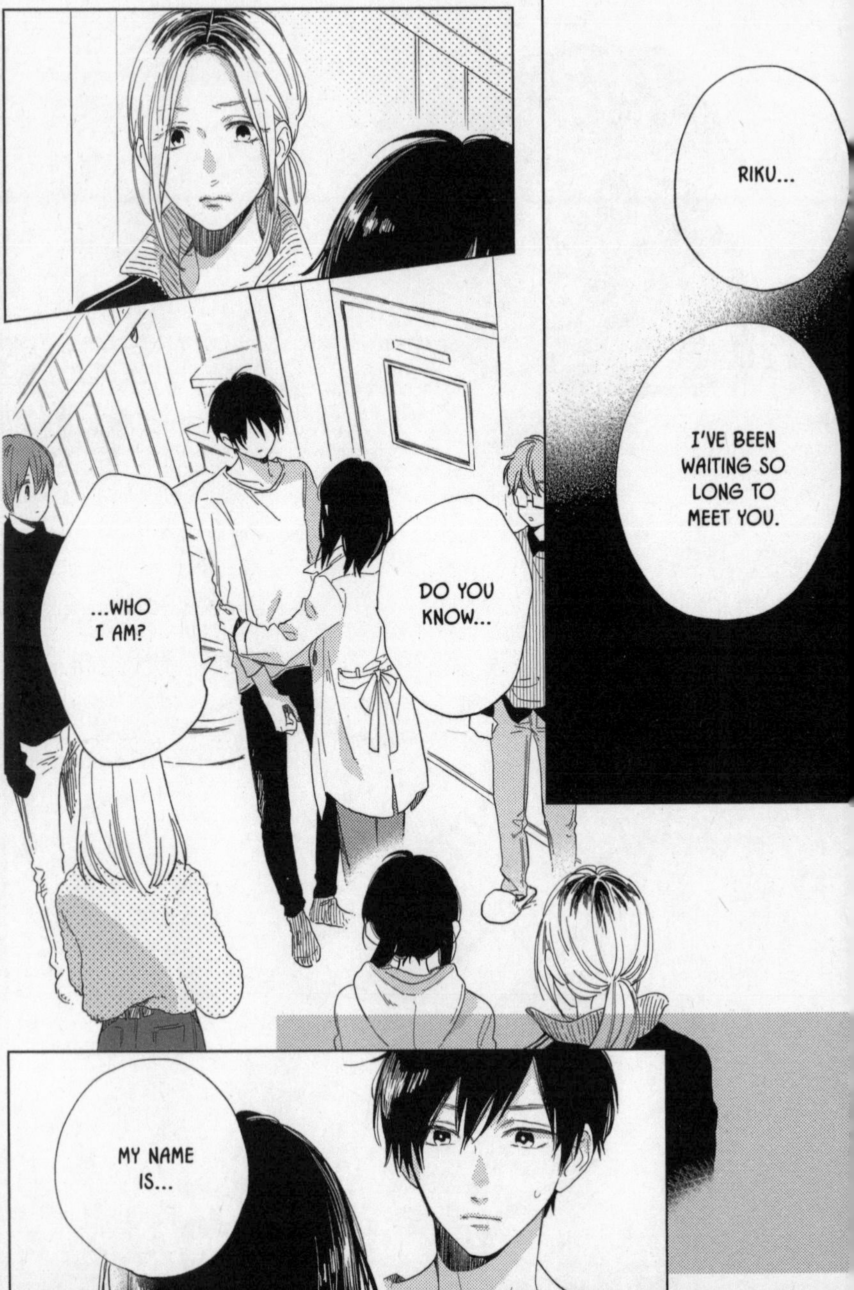
RIKU...
I'VE BEEN WAITING SO LONG TO MEET YOU.
DO YOU KNOW...
...WHO I AM?
MY NAME IS...

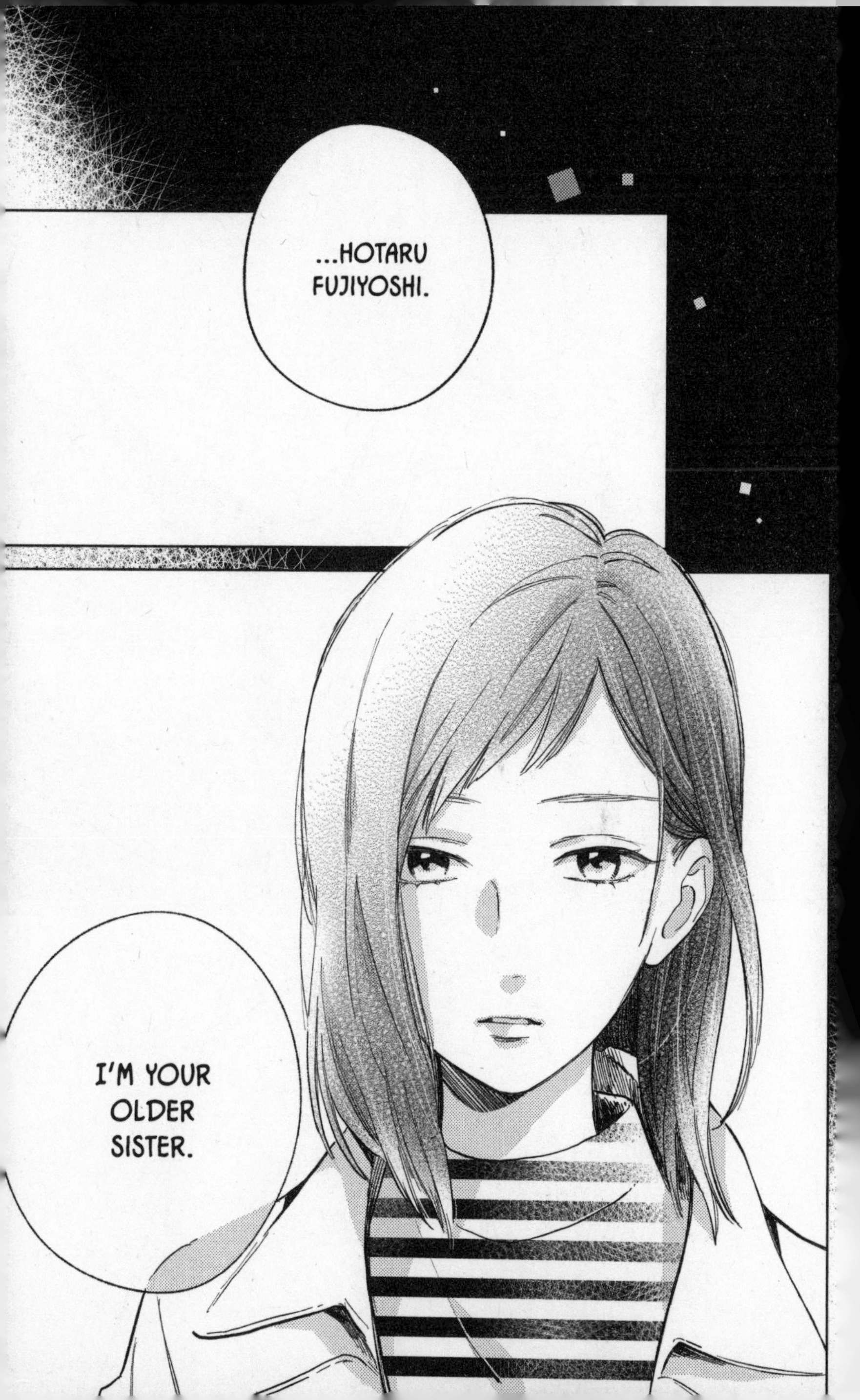
...HOTARU FUJIYOSHI.
I'M YOUR OLDER SISTER.

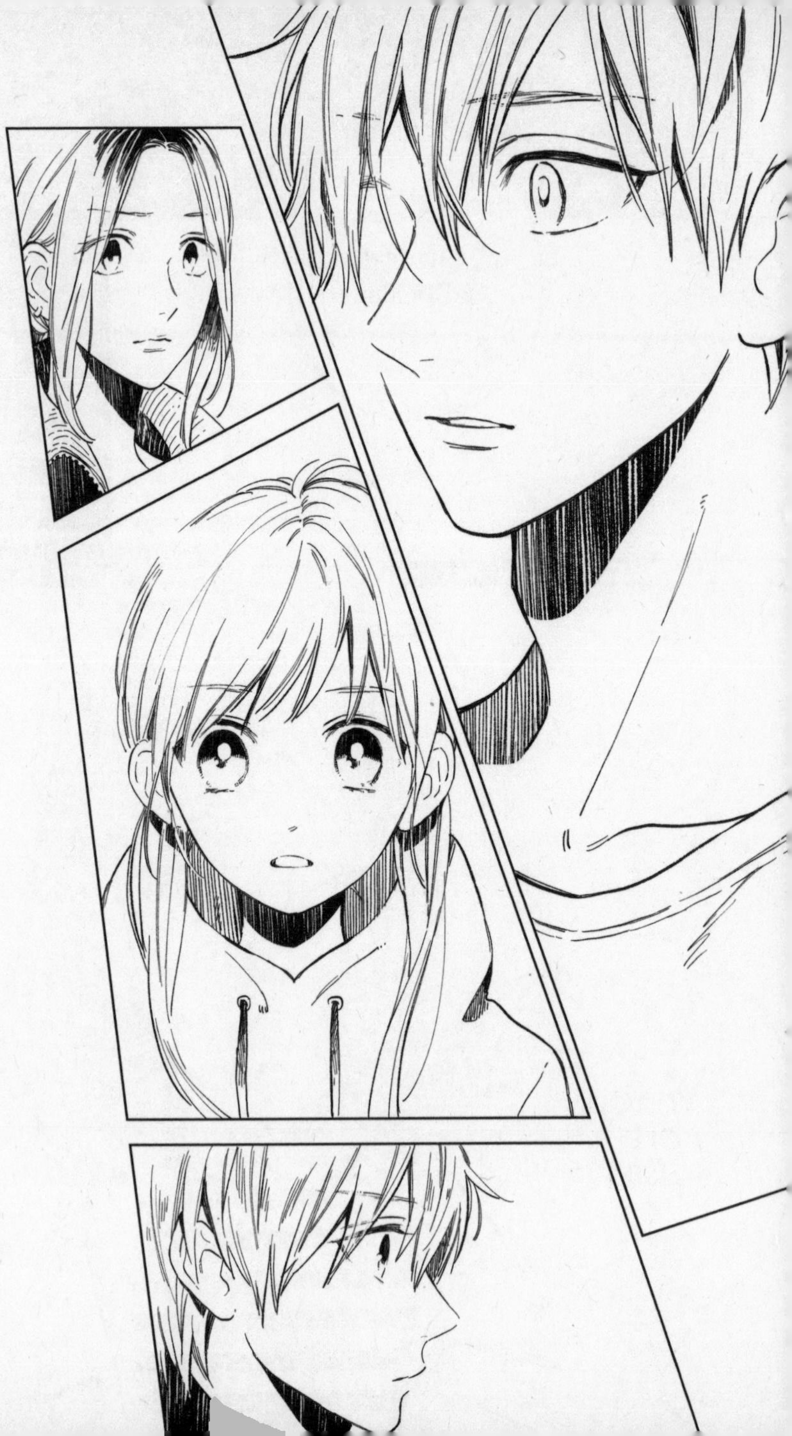

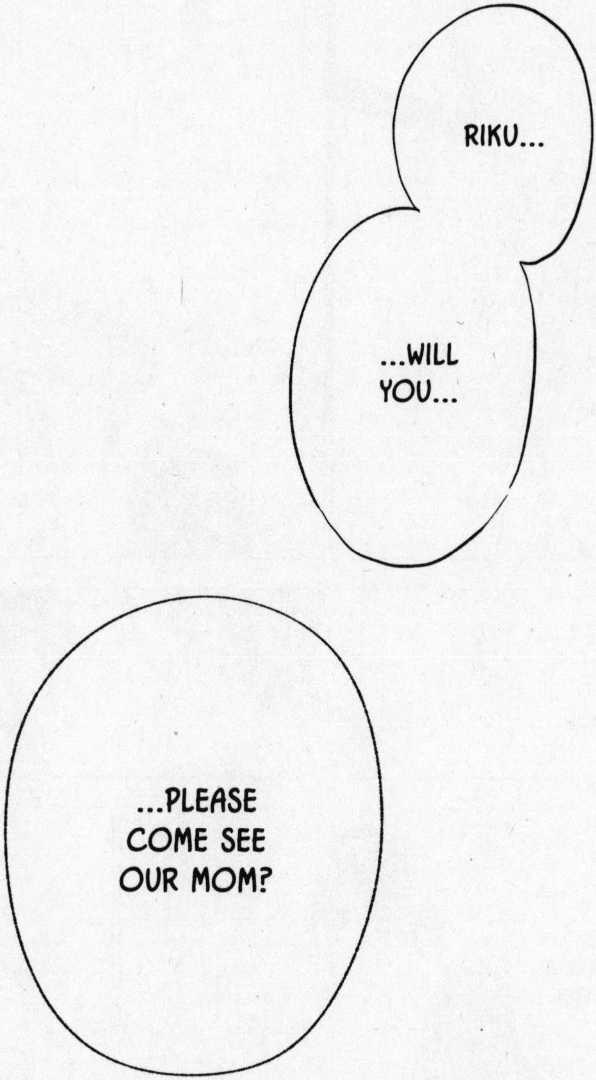
RIKU...
...WILL YOU...
...PLEASE COME SEE OUR MOM?

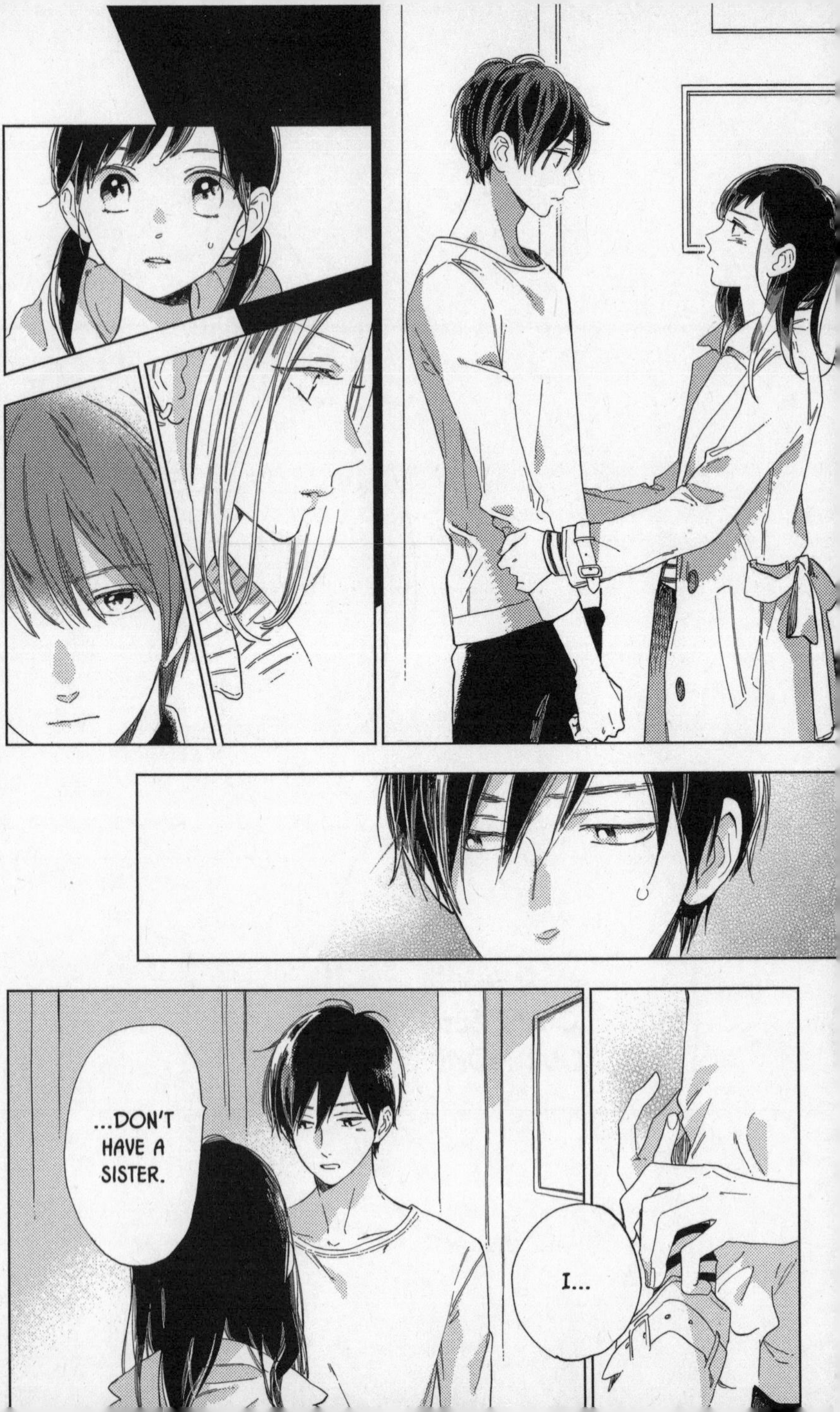
I...
...DON'T HAVE A SISTER.

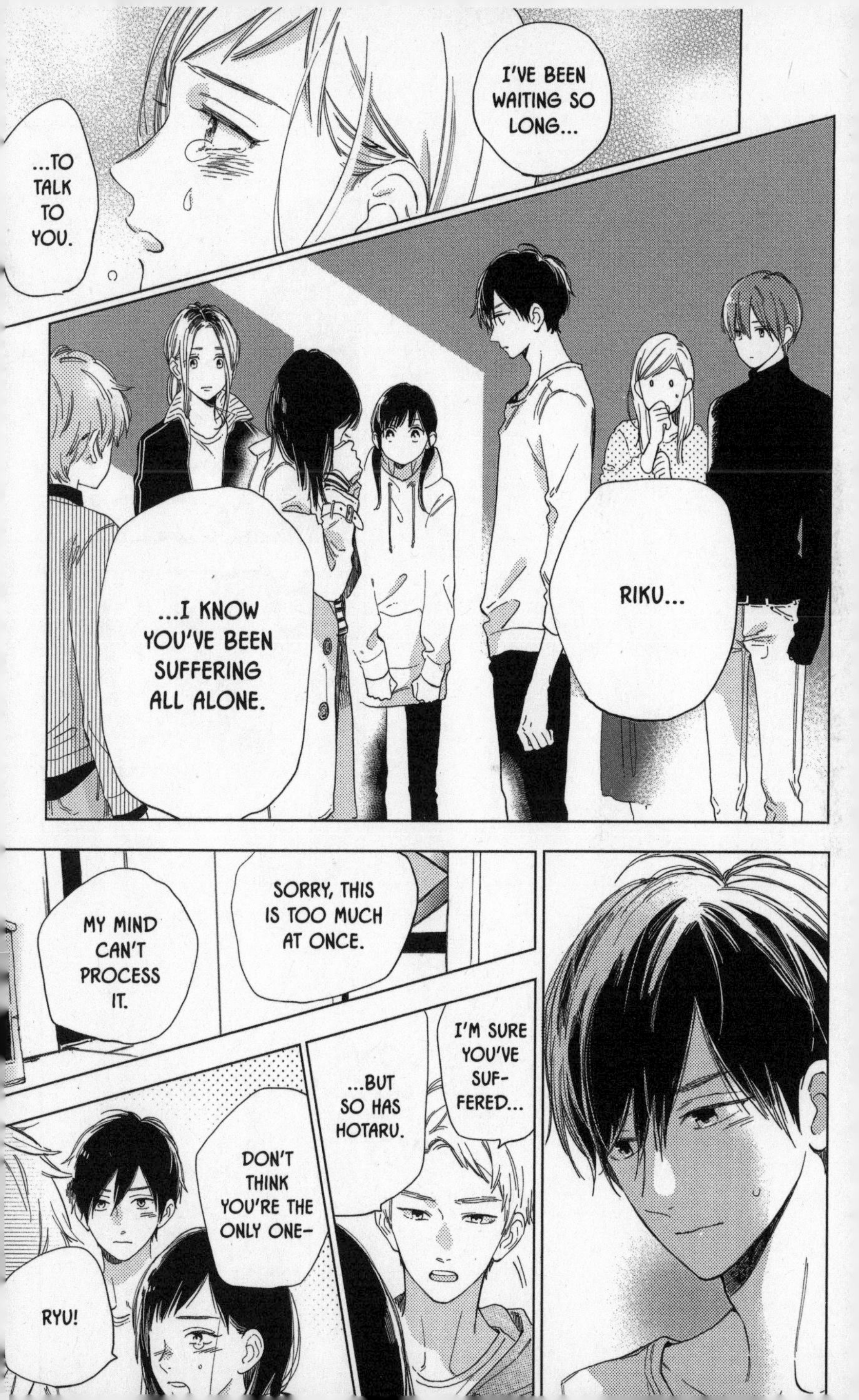
I'VE BEEN WAITING SO LONG...
...TO TALK TO YOU.
RIKU...
...I KNOW YOU'VE BEEN SUFFERING ALL ALONE.
SORRY, THIS IS TOO MUCH AT ONCE.
MY MIND CAN'T PROCESS IT.
I'M SURE YOU'VE SUF-FERED...
...BUT SO HAS HOTARU.
DON'T THINK YOU'RE THE ONLY ONE–
RYU!

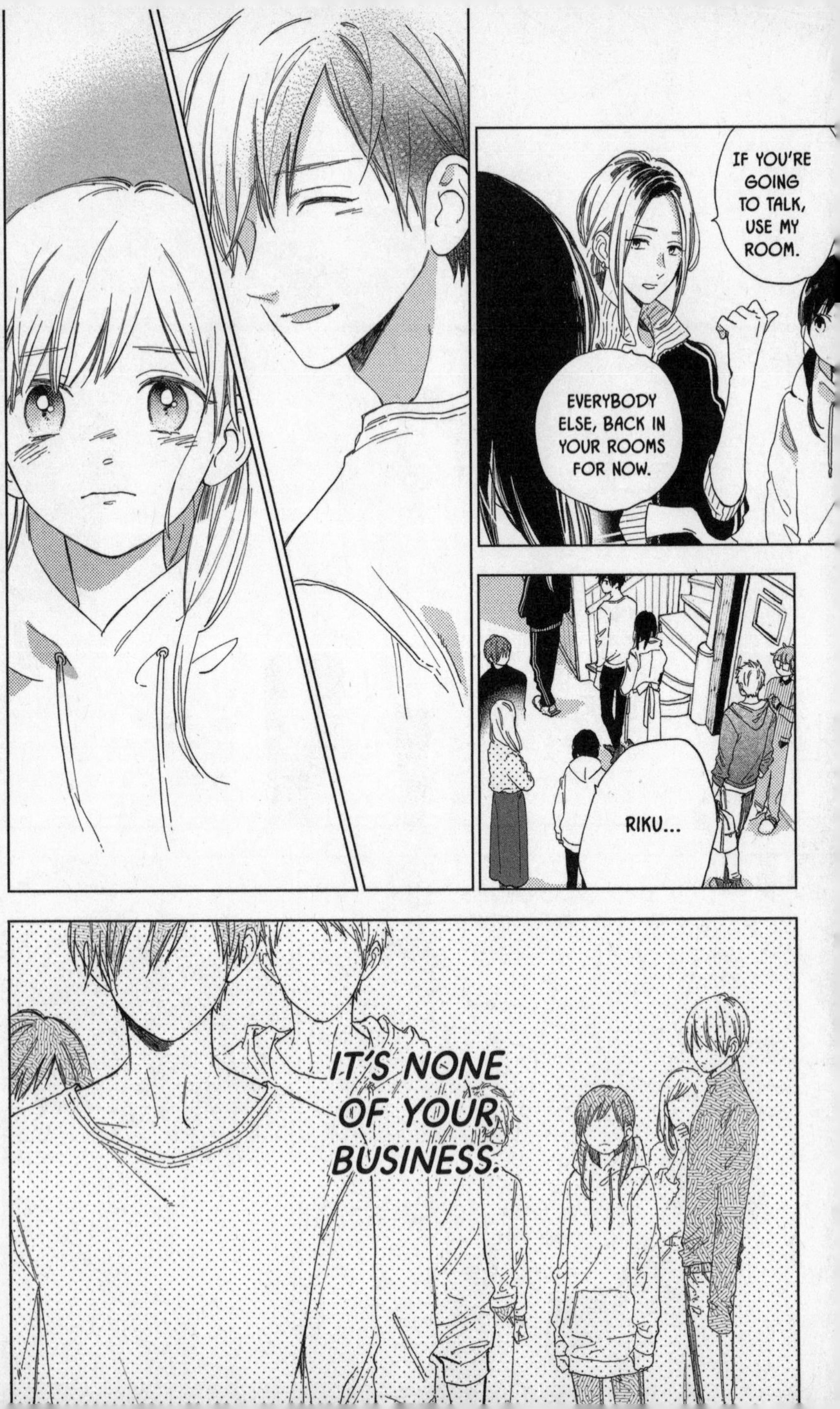
IF YOU'RE GOING TO TALK, USE MY ROOM.
EVERYBODY ELSE, BACK IN YOUR ROOMS FOR NOW.
RIKU...
IT'S NONE OF YOUR BUSINESS.

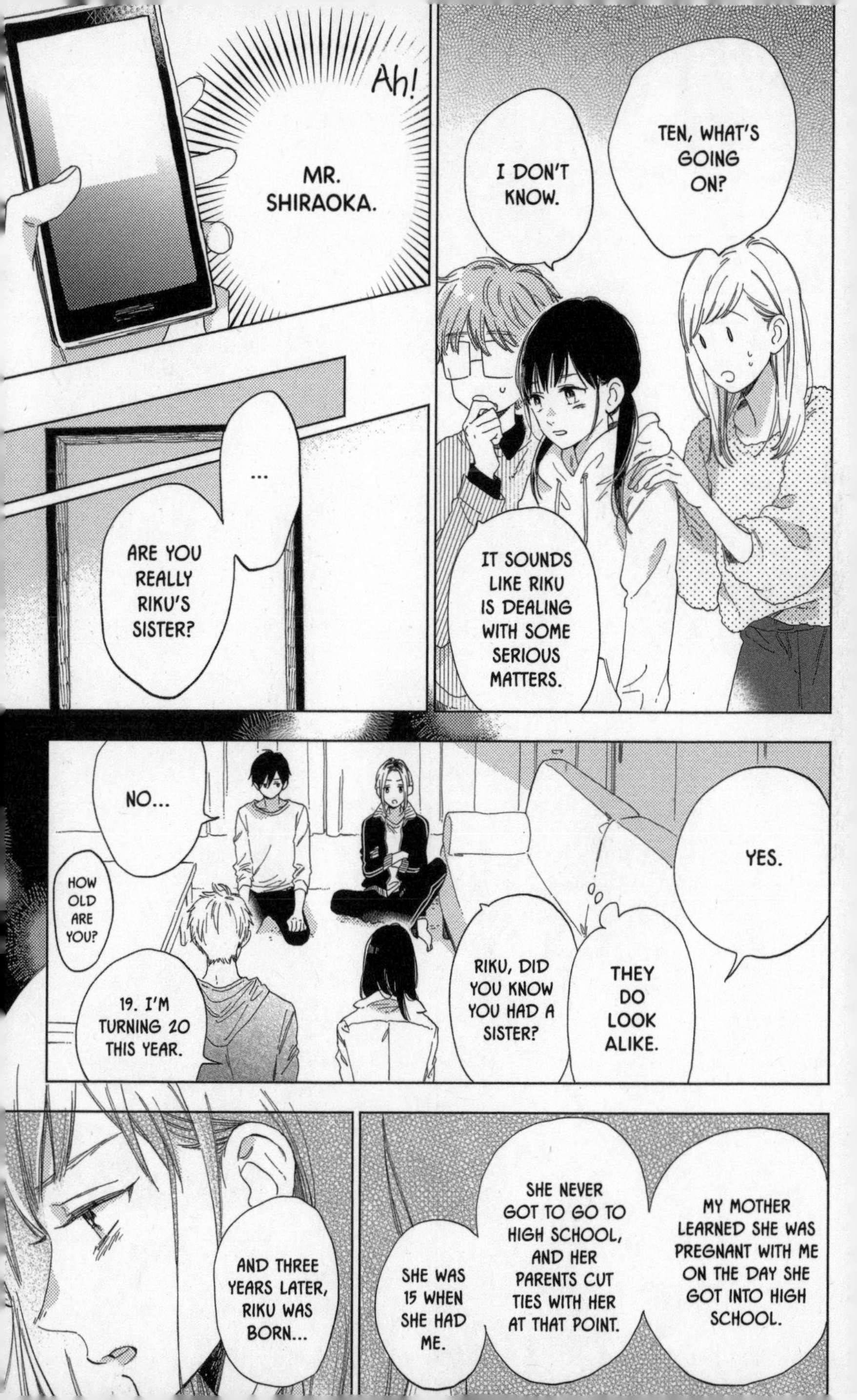
TEN, WHAT'S GOING ON?
I DON'T KNOW.
IT SOUNDS LIKE RIKU IS DEALING WITH SOME SERIOUS MATTERS.
Ah!
MR. SHIRAOKA.
...
ARE YOU REALLY RIKU'S SISTER?
YES.
THEY DO LOOK ALIKE.
RIKU, DID YOU KNOW YOU HAD A SISTER?
NO...
HOW OLD ARE YOU?
19. I'M TURNING 20 THIS YEAR.
MY MOTHER LEARNED SHE WAS PREGNANT WITH ME ON THE DAY SHE GOT INTO HIGH SCHOOL.
SHE NEVER GOT TO GO TO HIGH SCHOOL, AND HER PARENTS CUT TIES WITH HER AT THAT POINT.
SHE WAS 15 WHEN SHE HAD ME.
AND THREE YEARS LATER, RIKU WAS BORN...

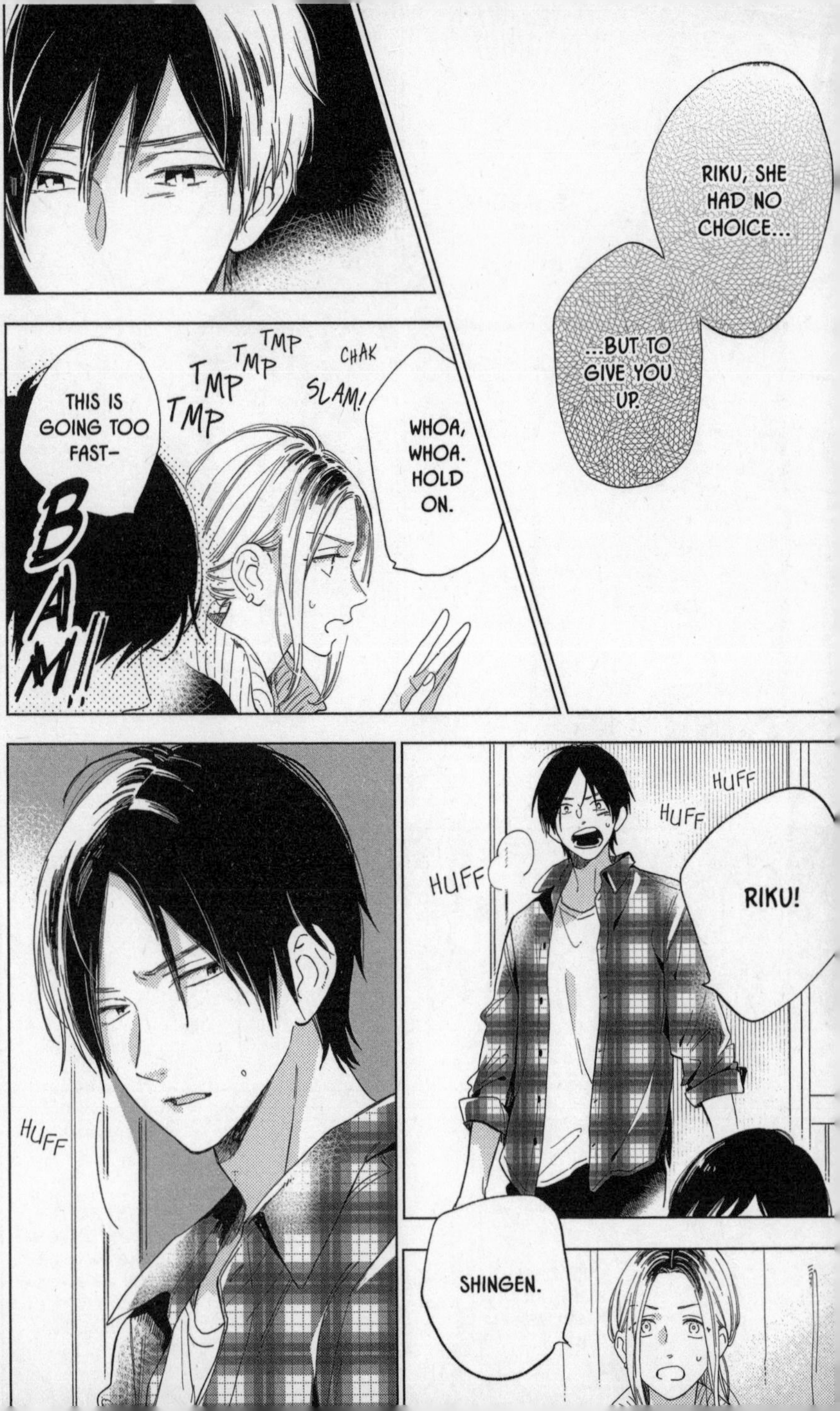
RIKU, SHE HAD NO CHOICE...
...BUT TO GIVE YOU UP.
WHOA, WHOA. HOLD ON.
CHAK
SLAM!
TMP
TMP
TMP
TMP
THIS IS GOING TOO FAST-
BAM!!
RIKU!
HUFF
HUFF
HUFF
SHINGEN.
HUFF

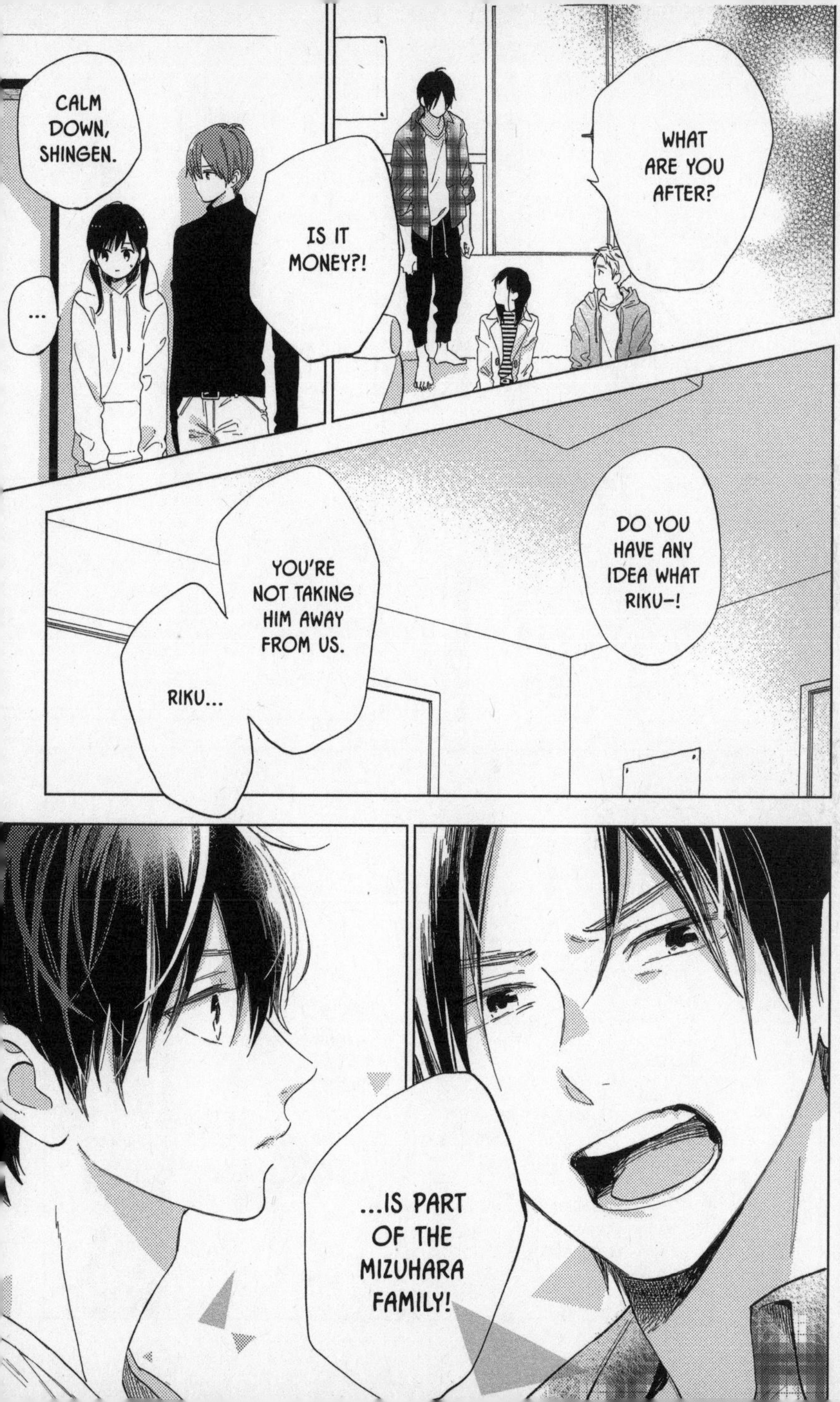
WHAT ARE YOU AFTER?
IS IT MONEY?!
CALM DOWN, SHINGEN.
...
DO YOU HAVE ANY IDEA WHAT RIKU—!
YOU'RE NOT TAKING HIM AWAY FROM US.
RIKU...
...IS PART OF THE MIZUHARA FAMILY!

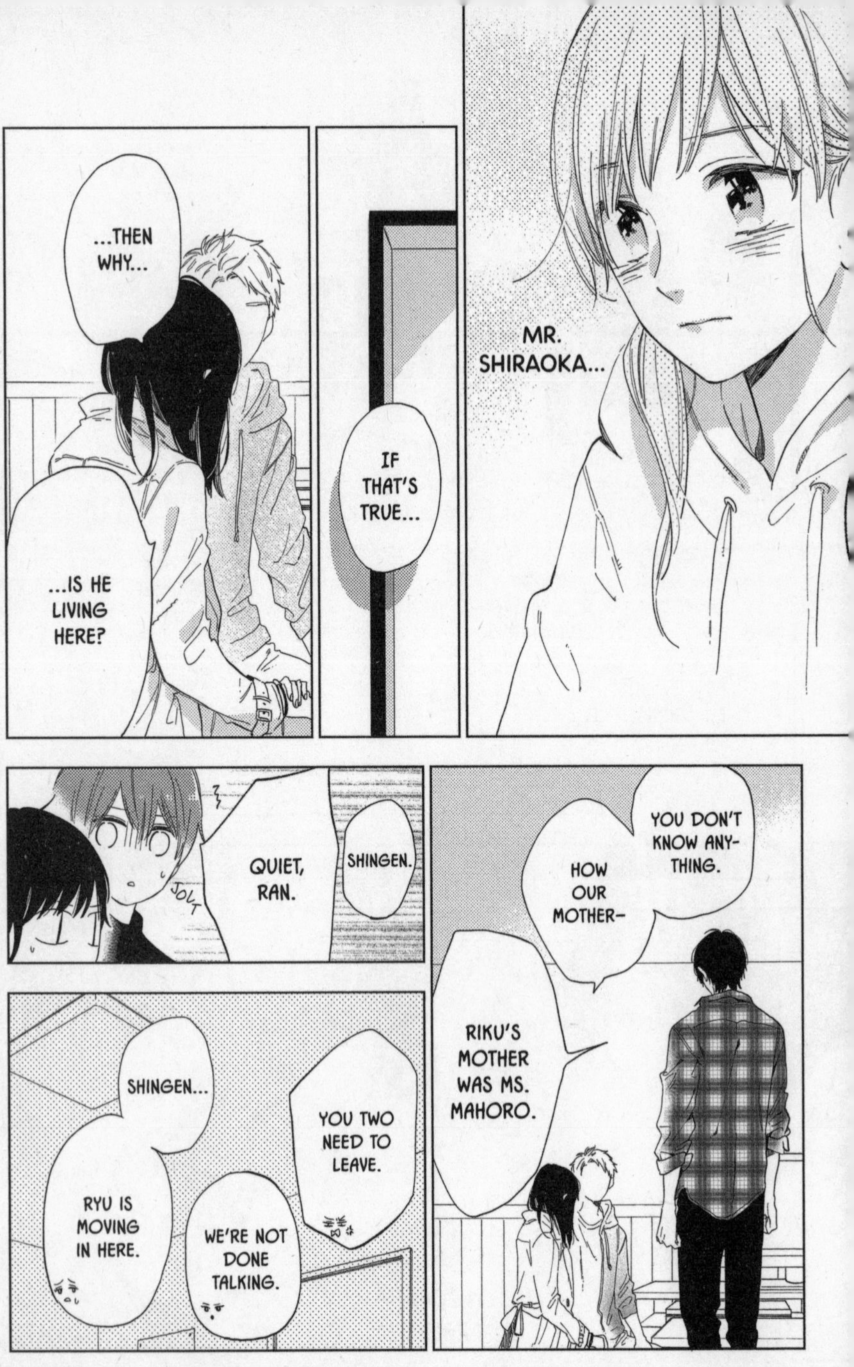
MR. SHIRAOKA...
IF THAT'S TRUE...
...THEN WHY...
...IS HE LIVING HERE?
YOU DON'T KNOW ANY-THING.
HOW OUR MOTHER—
RIKU'S MOTHER WAS MS. MAHORO.
SHINGEN.
QUIET, RAN.
JOLT
YOU TWO NEED TO LEAVE.
SHINGEN...
WE'RE NOT DONE TALKING.
RYU IS MOVING IN HERE.

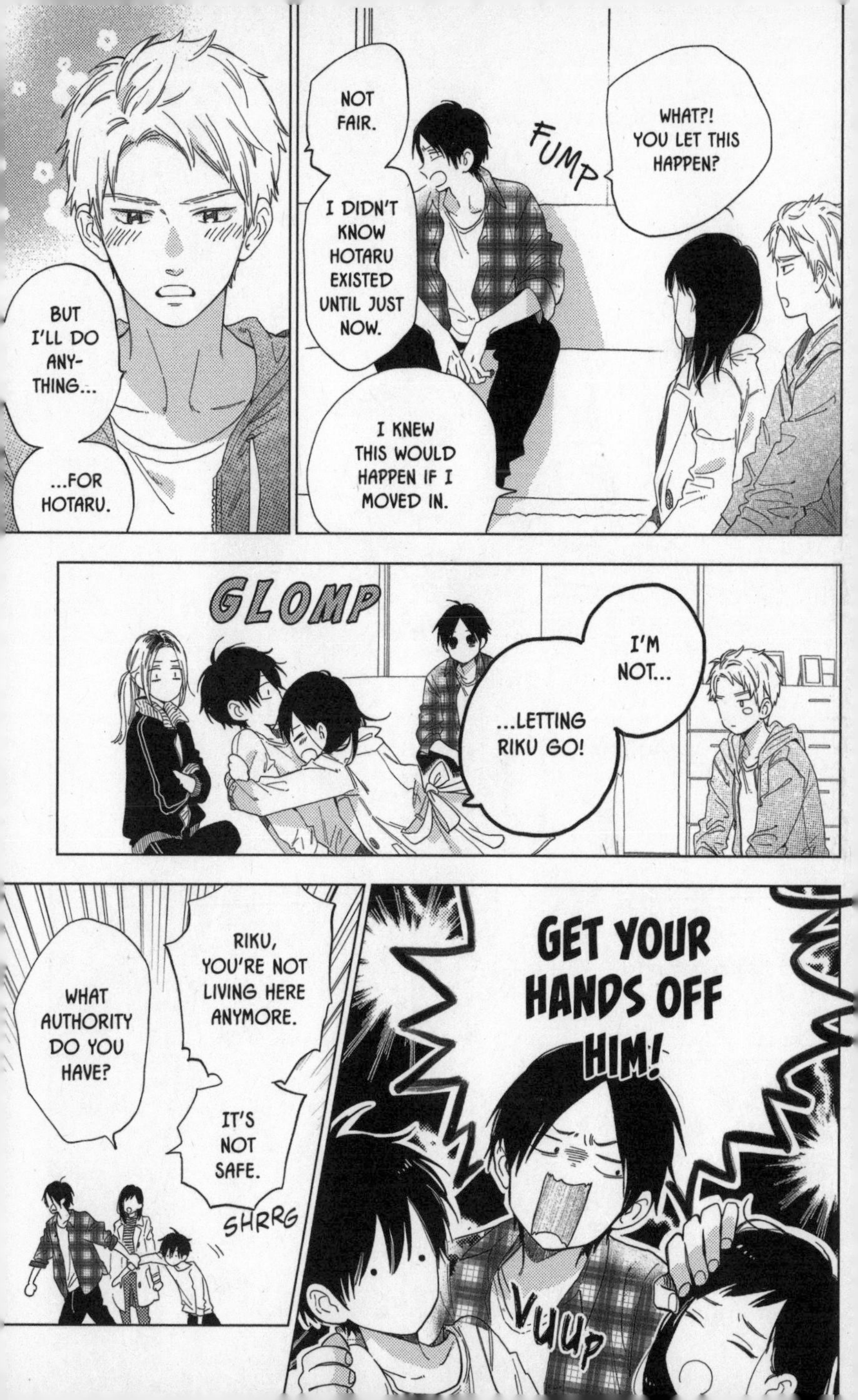
WHAT?! YOU LET THIS HAPPEN?
FUMP
NOT FAIR.
I DIDN'T KNOW HOTARU EXISTED UNTIL JUST NOW.
I KNEW THIS WOULD HAPPEN IF I MOVED IN.
BUT I'LL DO ANY-THING...
...FOR HOTARU.
I'M NOT...
...LETTING RIKU GO!
GLOMP
GET YOUR HANDS OFF HIM!
VUUP
RIKU, YOU'RE NOT LIVING HERE ANYMORE.
WHAT AUTHORITY DO YOU HAVE?
IT'S NOT SAFE.
SHRRG

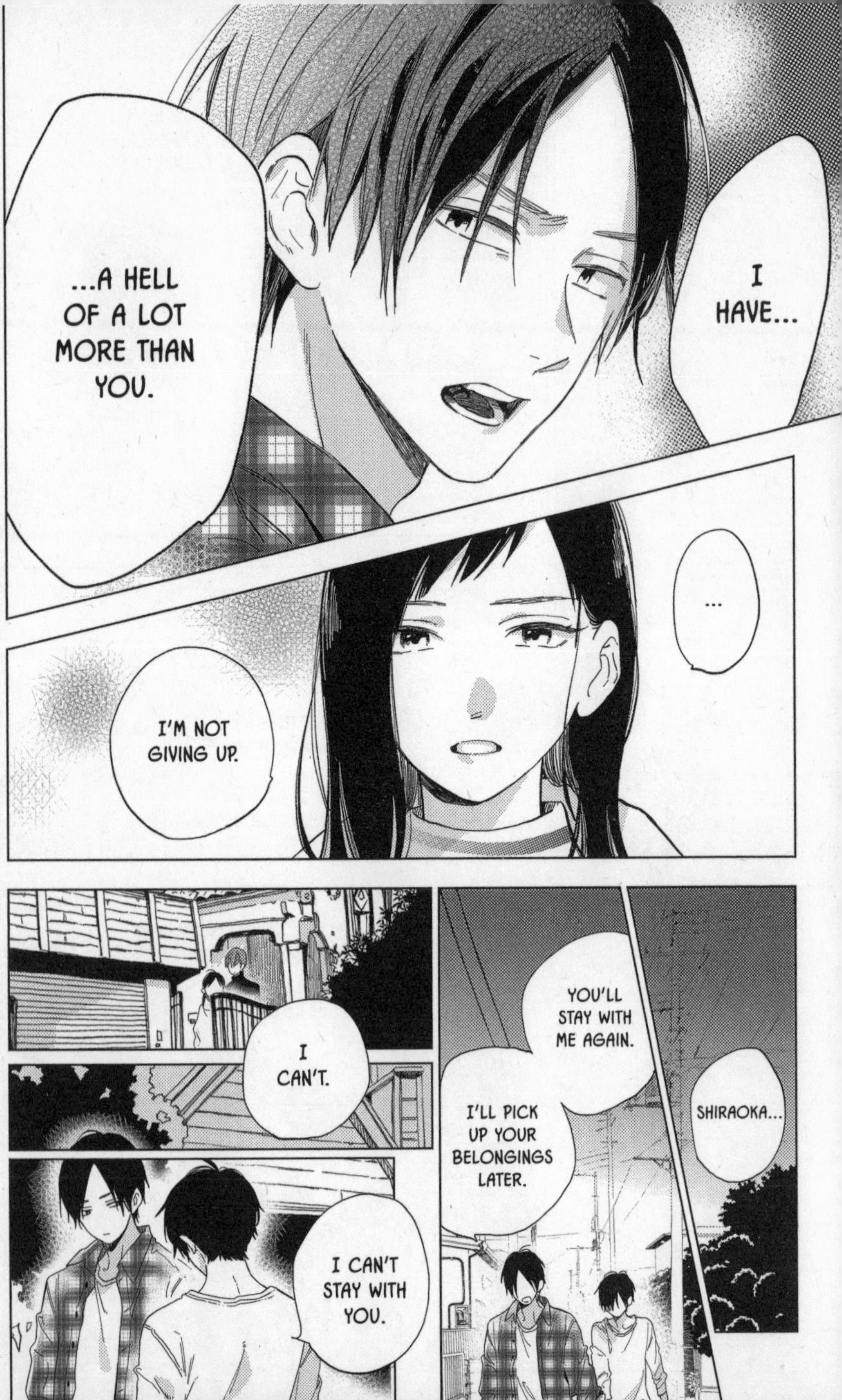
I HAVE...
...A HELL OF A LOT MORE THAN YOU.
...
I'M NOT GIVING UP.
YOU'LL STAY WITH ME AGAIN.
I'LL PICK UP YOUR BELONGINGS LATER.
SHIRAOKA...
I CAN'T.
I CAN'T STAY WITH YOU.

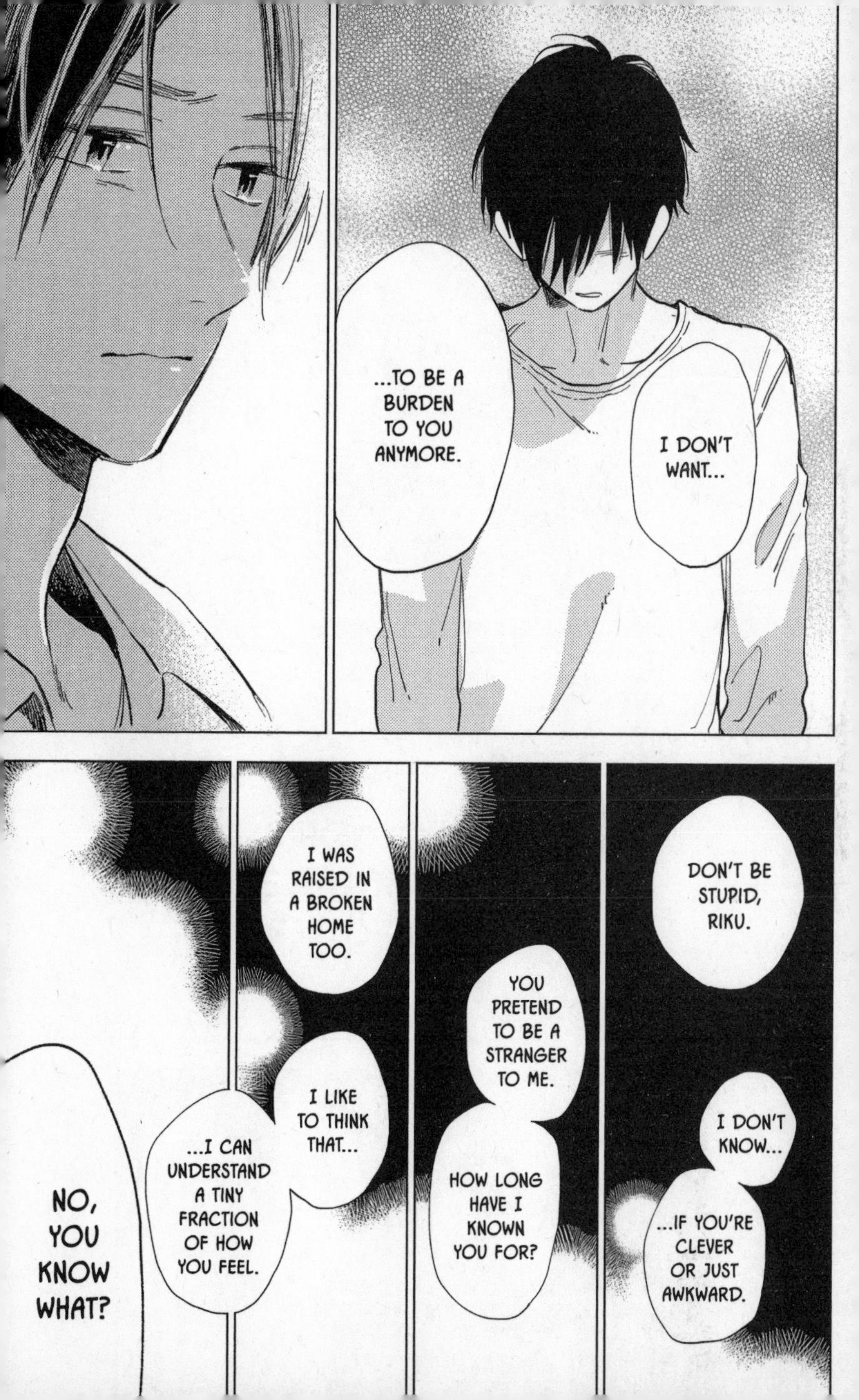
I DON'T WANT...
...TO BE A BURDEN TO YOU ANYMORE.
DON'T BE STUPID, RIKU.
I DON'T KNOW...
...IF YOU'RE CLEVER OR JUST AWKWARD.
YOU PRETEND TO BE A STRANGER TO ME.
HOW LONG HAVE I KNOWN YOU FOR?
I WAS RAISED IN A BROKEN HOME TOO.
I LIKE TO THINK THAT...
...I CAN UNDERSTAND A TINY FRACTION OF HOW YOU FEEL.
NO, YOU KNOW WHAT?

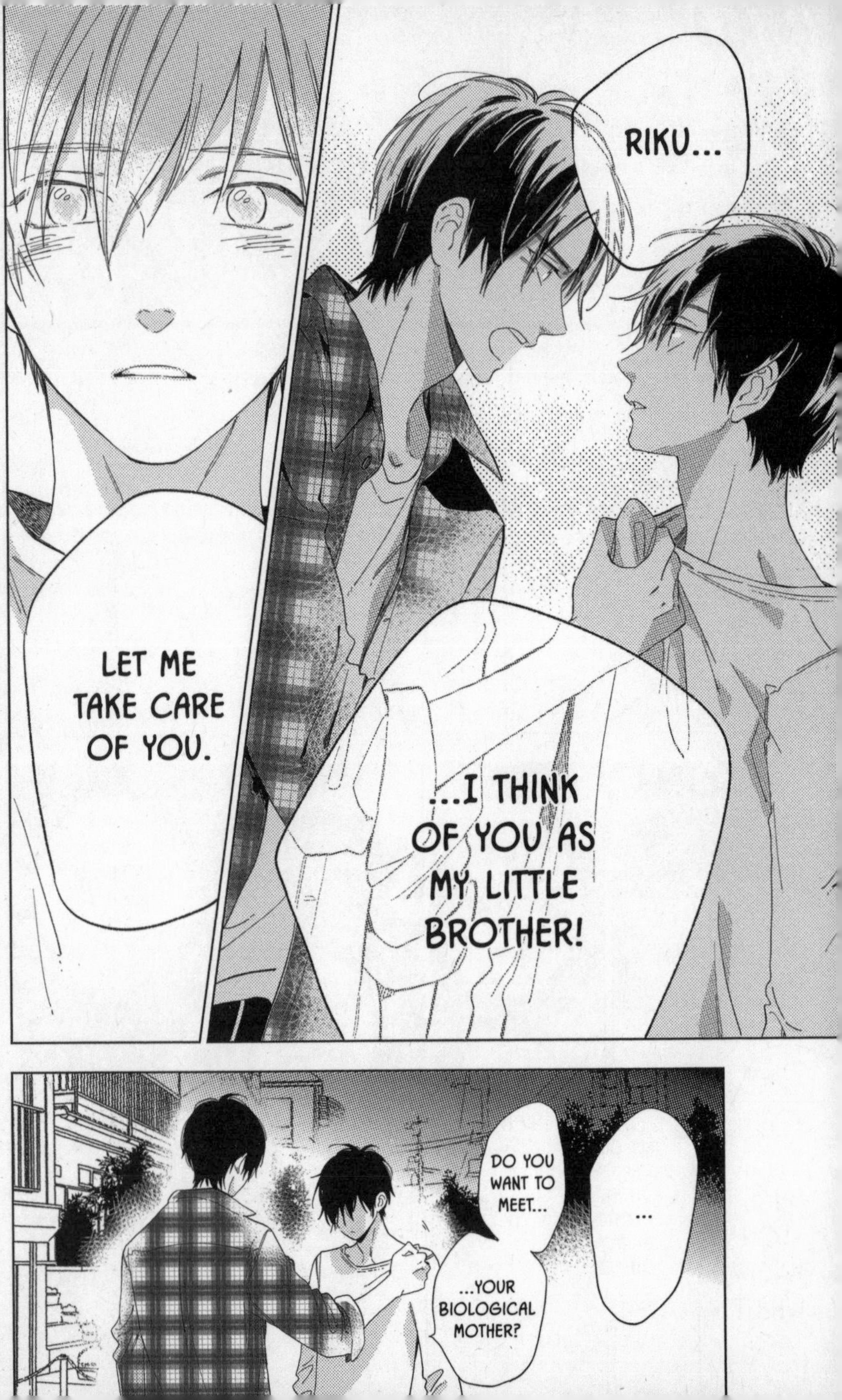
RIKU...
...I THINK OF YOU AS MY LITTLE BROTHER!
LET ME TAKE CARE OF YOU.
...
DO YOU WANT TO MEET...
...YOUR BIOLOGICAL MOTHER?

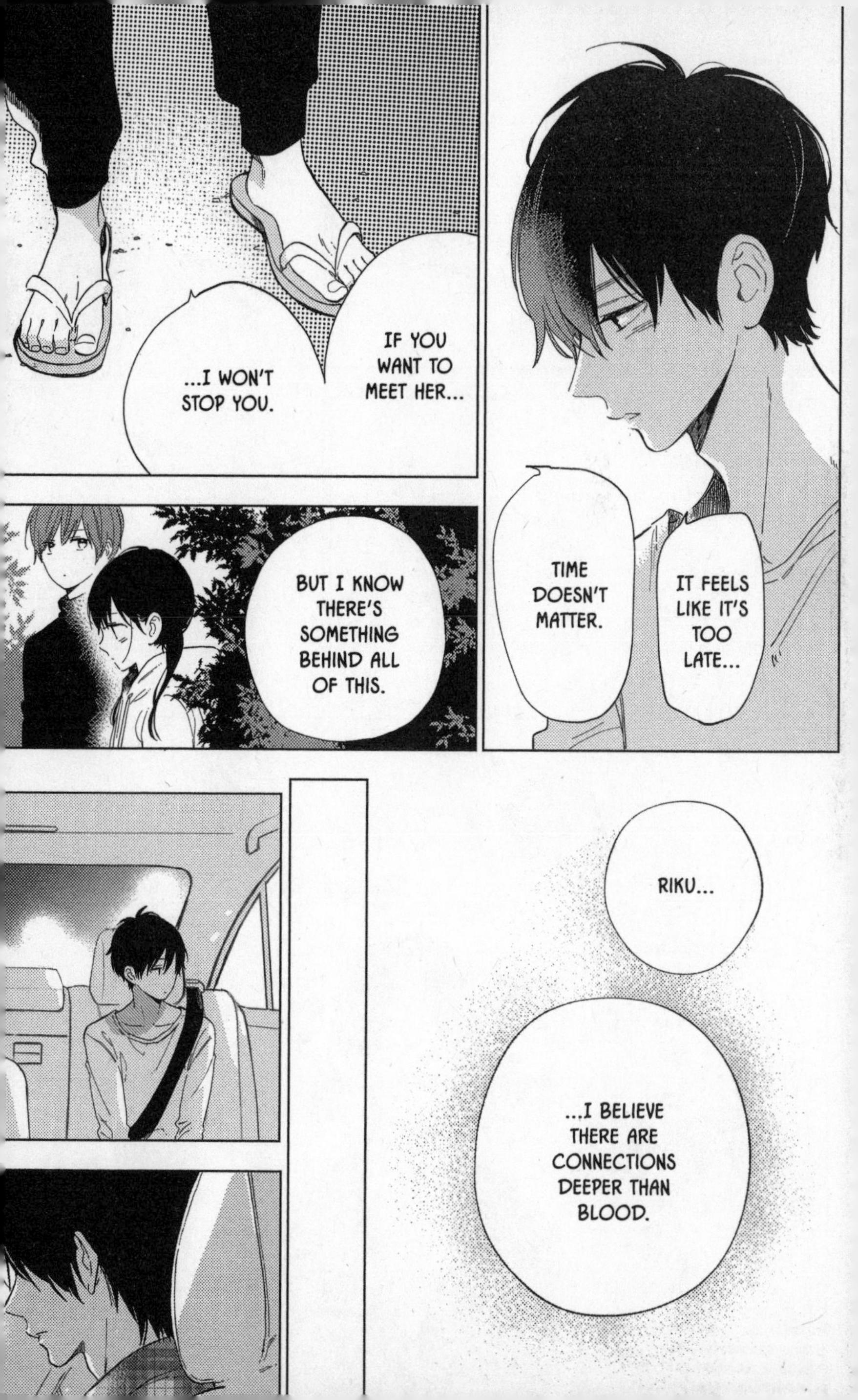
IT FEELS LIKE IT'S TOO LATE...
TIME DOESN'T MATTER.
IF YOU WANT TO MEET HER...
...I WON'T STOP YOU.
BUT I KNOW THERE'S SOMETHING BEHIND ALL OF THIS.
RIKU...
...I BELIEVE THERE ARE CONNECTIONS DEEPER THAN BLOOD.

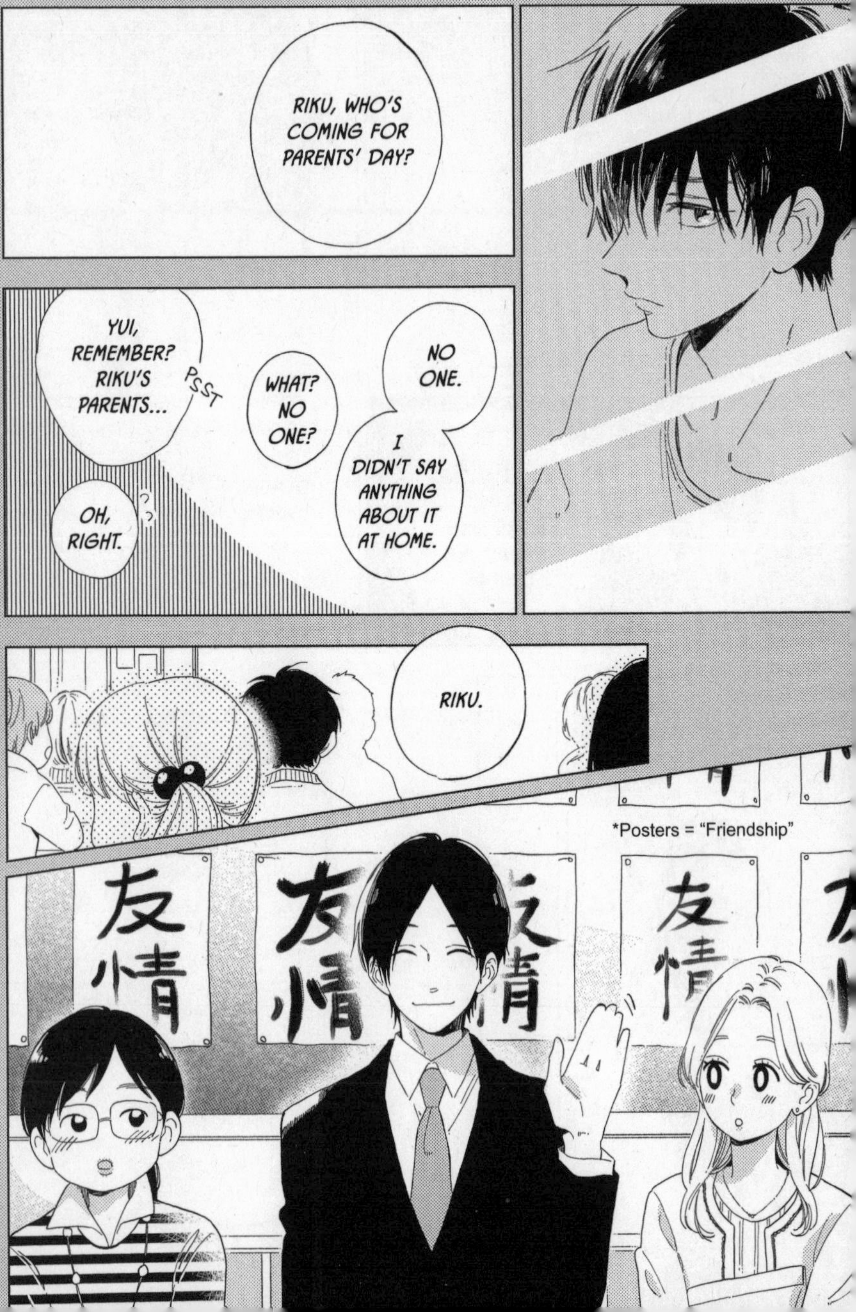
RIKU, WHO'S COMING FOR PARENTS' DAY?
NO ONE.
I DIDN'T SAY ANYTHING ABOUT IT AT HOME.
WHAT? NO ONE?
YUI, REMEMBER? RIKU'S PARENTS...
PSST
OH, RIGHT.
RIKU.
*Posters = "Friendship"
友情

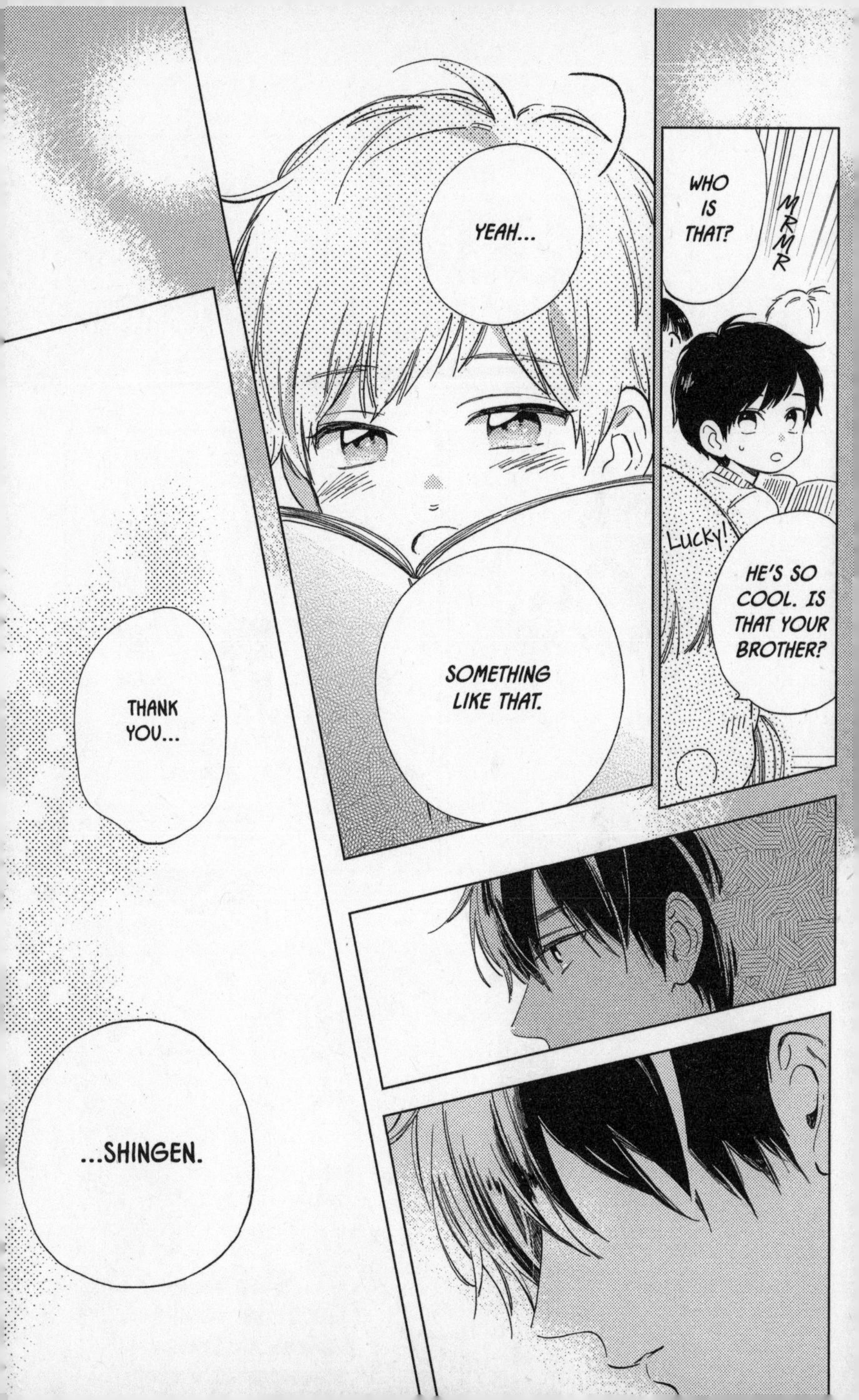
WHO IS THAT?
MRMR
Lucky!
HE'S SO COOL. IS THAT YOUR BROTHER?
YEAH...
SOMETHING LIKE THAT.
THANK YOU...
...SHINGEN.

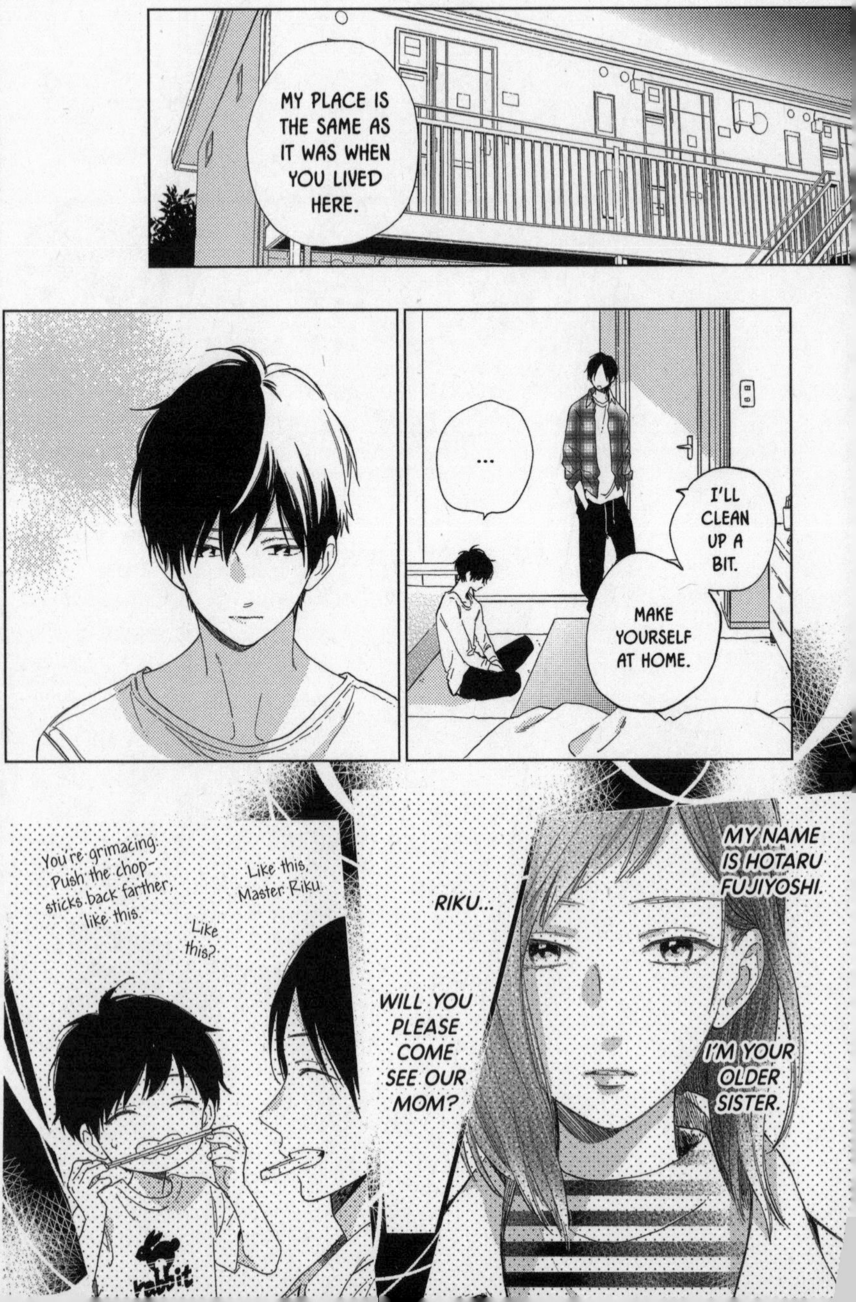
MY PLACE IS THE SAME AS IT WAS WHEN YOU LIVED HERE.
I'LL CLEAN UP A BIT.
MAKE YOURSELF AT HOME.
...
MY NAME IS HOTARU FUJIYOSHI.
I'M YOUR OLDER SISTER.
RIKU...
WILL YOU PLEASE COME SEE OUR MOM?
Like this, Master Riku.
You're grimacing. Push the chopsticks back farther, like this.
Like this?

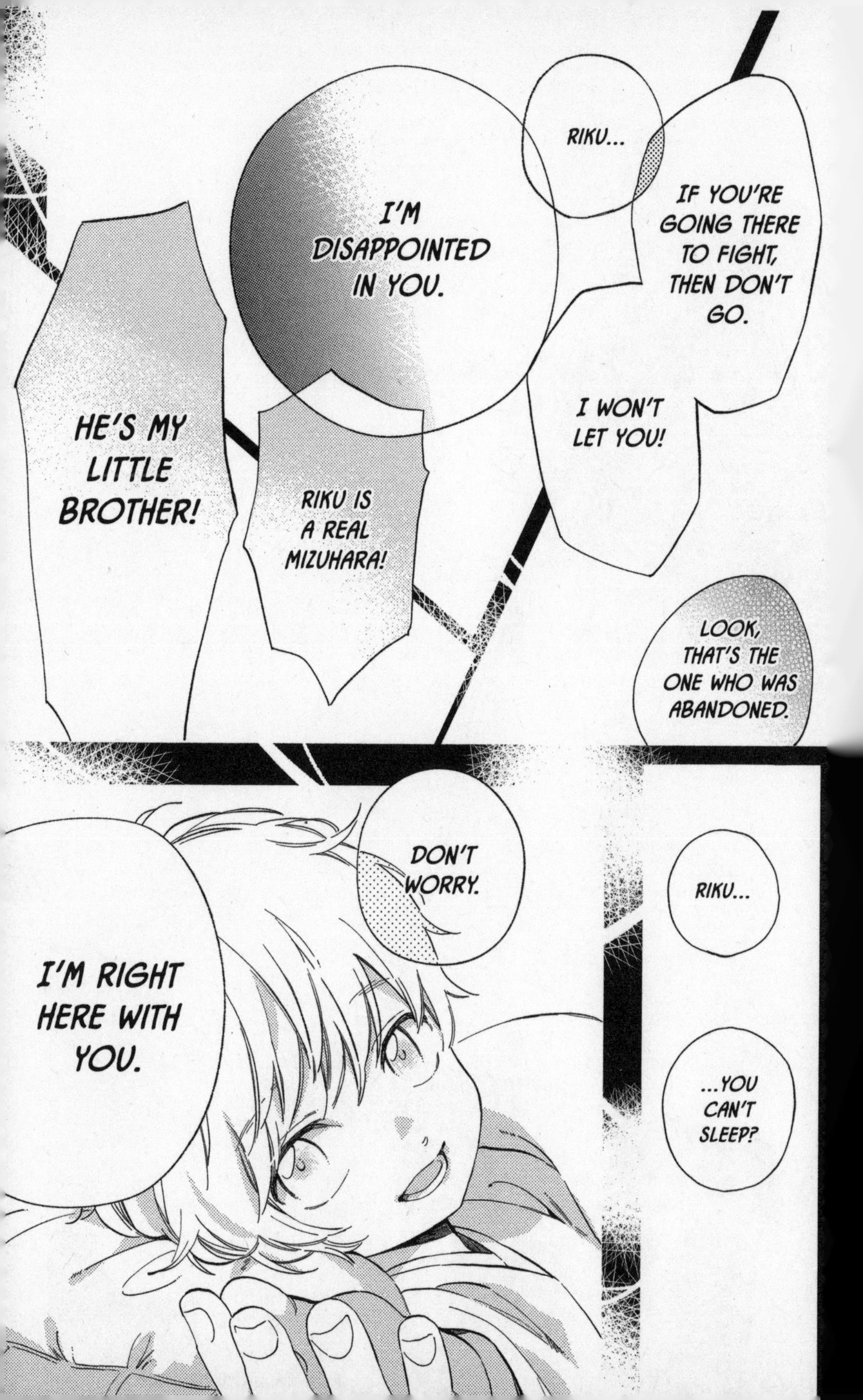
IF YOU'RE GOING THERE TO FIGHT, THEN DON'T GO.
RIKU...
I WON'T LET YOU!
I'M DISAPPOINTED IN YOU.
LOOK, THAT'S THE ONE WHO WAS ABANDONED.
RIKU IS A REAL MIZUHARA!
HE'S MY LITTLE BROTHER!
RIKU...
...YOU CAN'T SLEEP?
DON'T WORRY.
I'M RIGHT HERE WITH YOU.

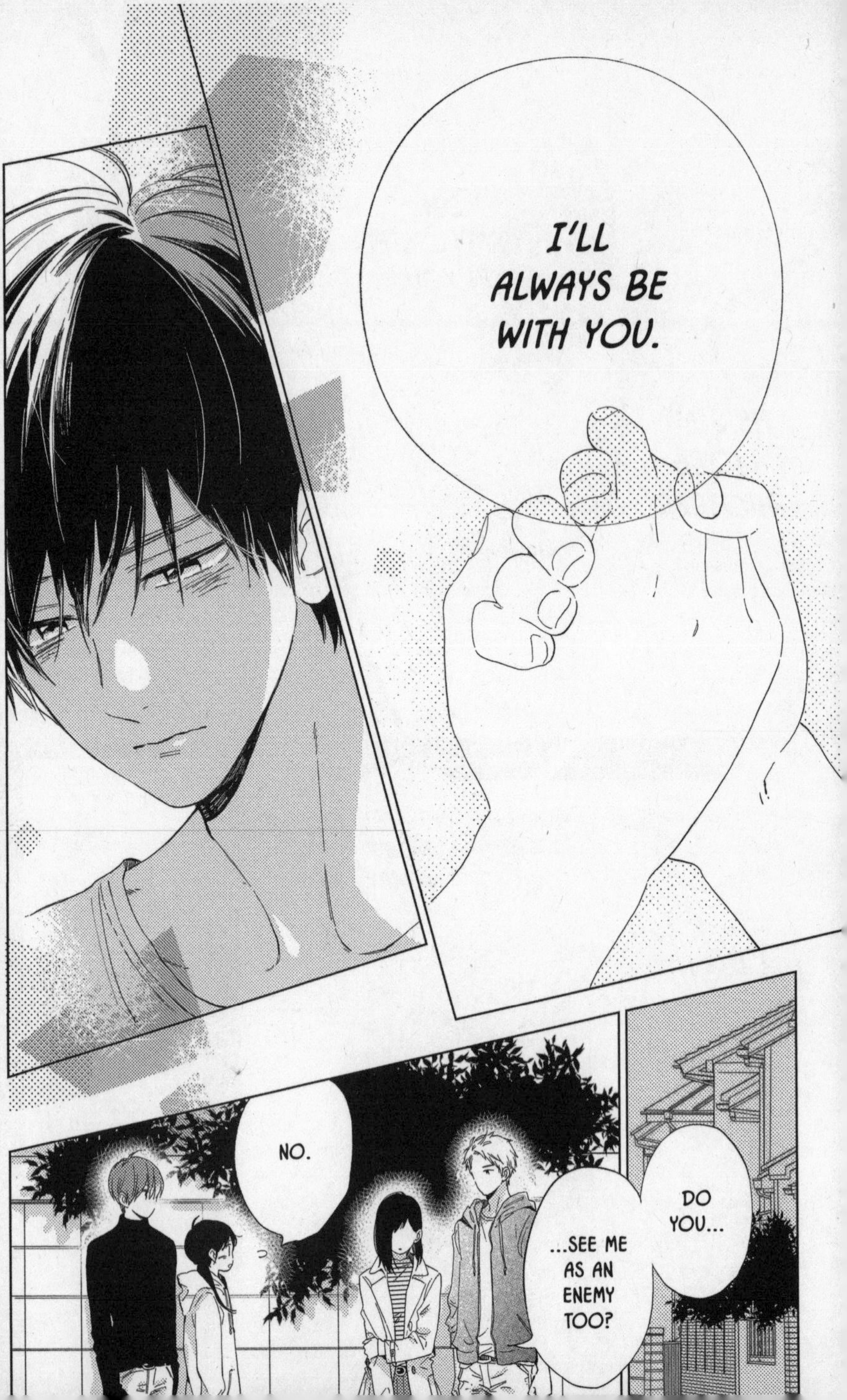
I'LL ALWAYS BE WITH YOU.
DO YOU...
...SEE ME AS AN ENEMY TOO?
NO.

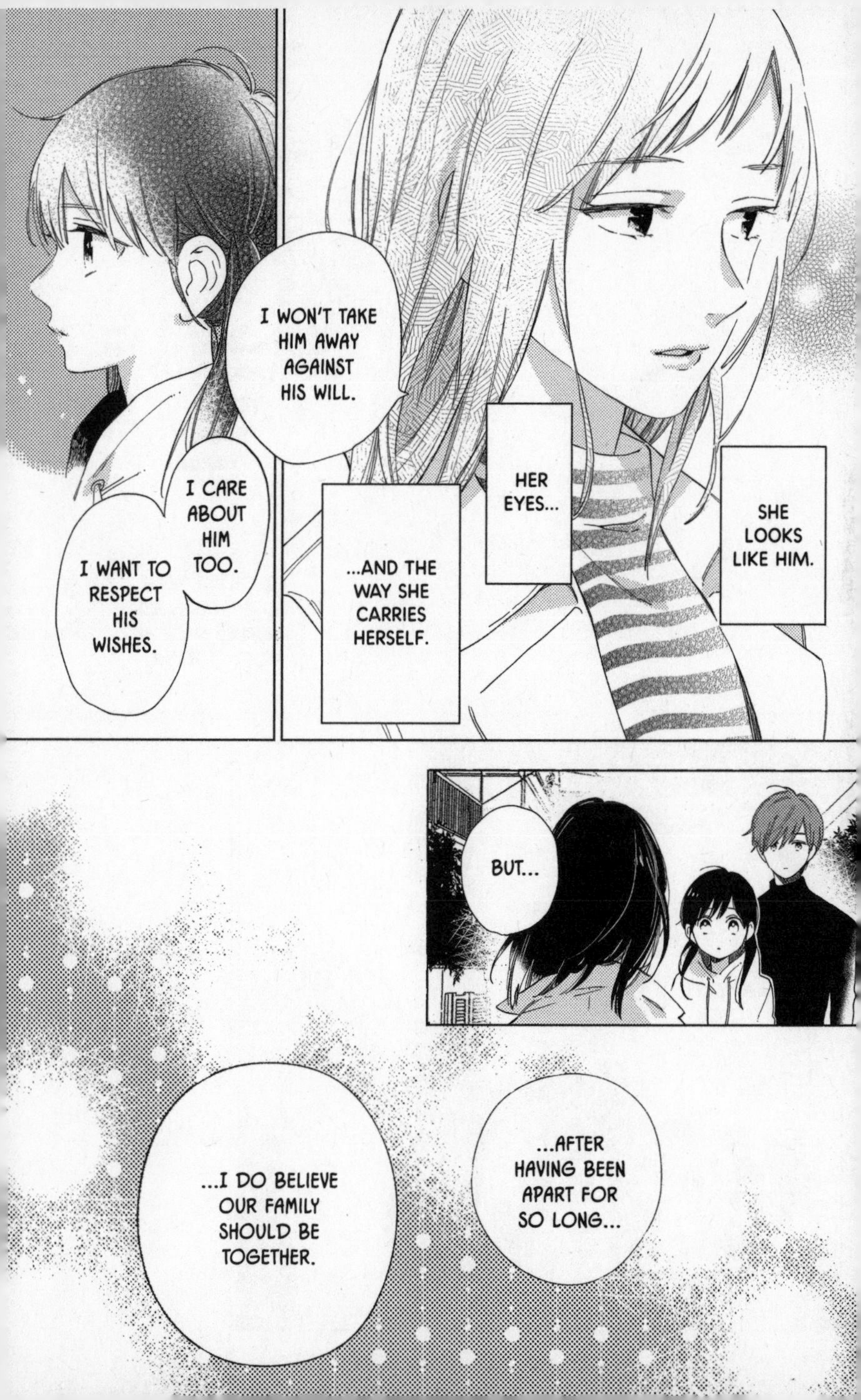
SHE LOOKS LIKE HIM.
HER EYES...
...AND THE WAY SHE CARRIES HERSELF.
I WON'T TAKE HIM AWAY AGAINST HIS WILL.
I CARE ABOUT HIM TOO.
I WANT TO RESPECT HIS WISHES.
BUT...
...AFTER HAVING BEEN APART FOR SO LONG...
...I DO BELIEVE OUR FAMILY SHOULD BE TOGETHER.

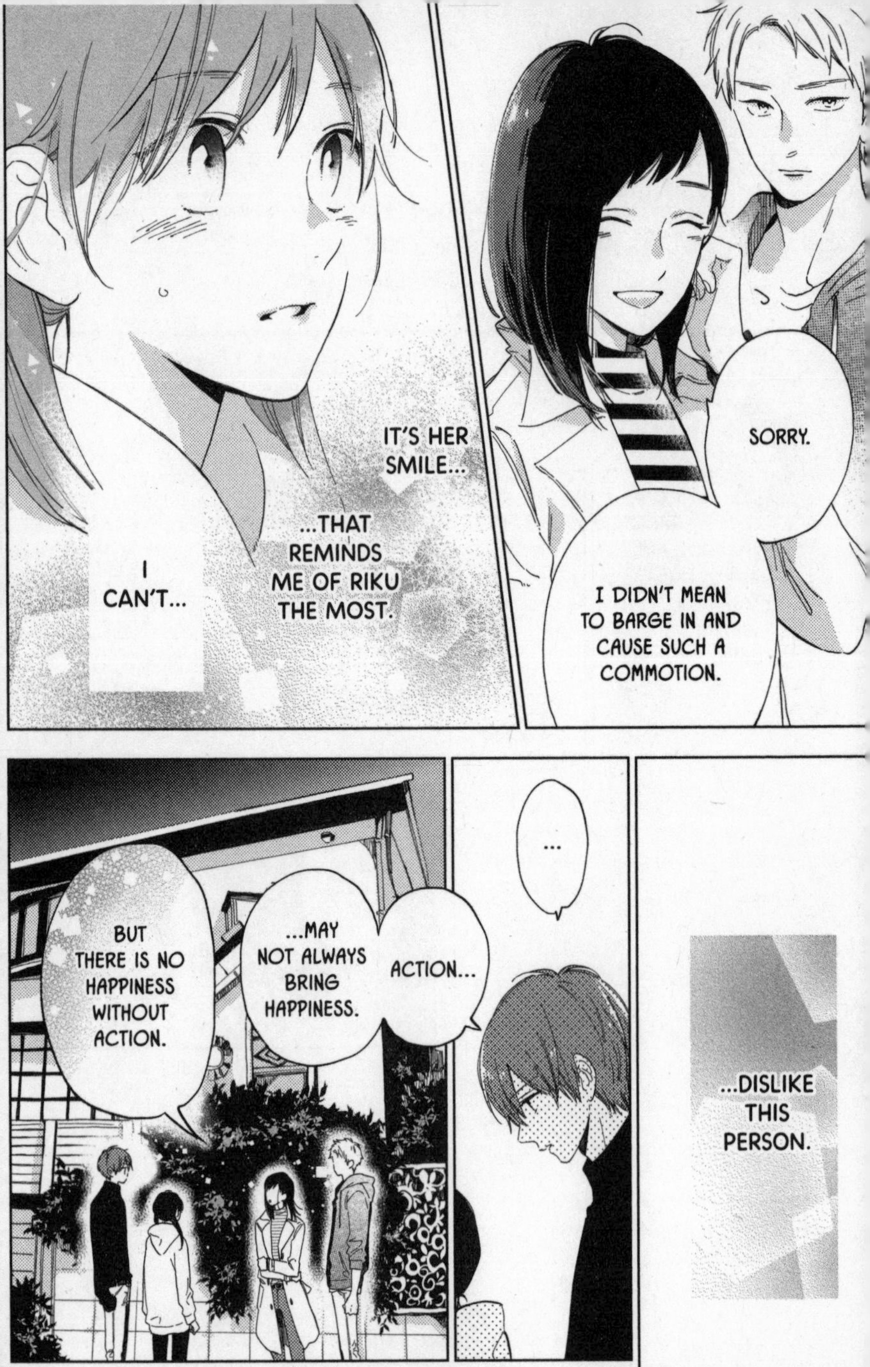
SORRY.
I DIDN'T MEAN TO BARGE IN AND CAUSE SUCH A COMMOTION.
IT'S HER SMILE...
...THAT REMINDS ME OF RIKU THE MOST.
I CAN'T...
...DISLIKE THIS PERSON.
...
ACTION...
...MAY NOT ALWAYS BRING HAPPINESS.
BUT THERE IS NO HAPPINESS WITHOUT ACTION.

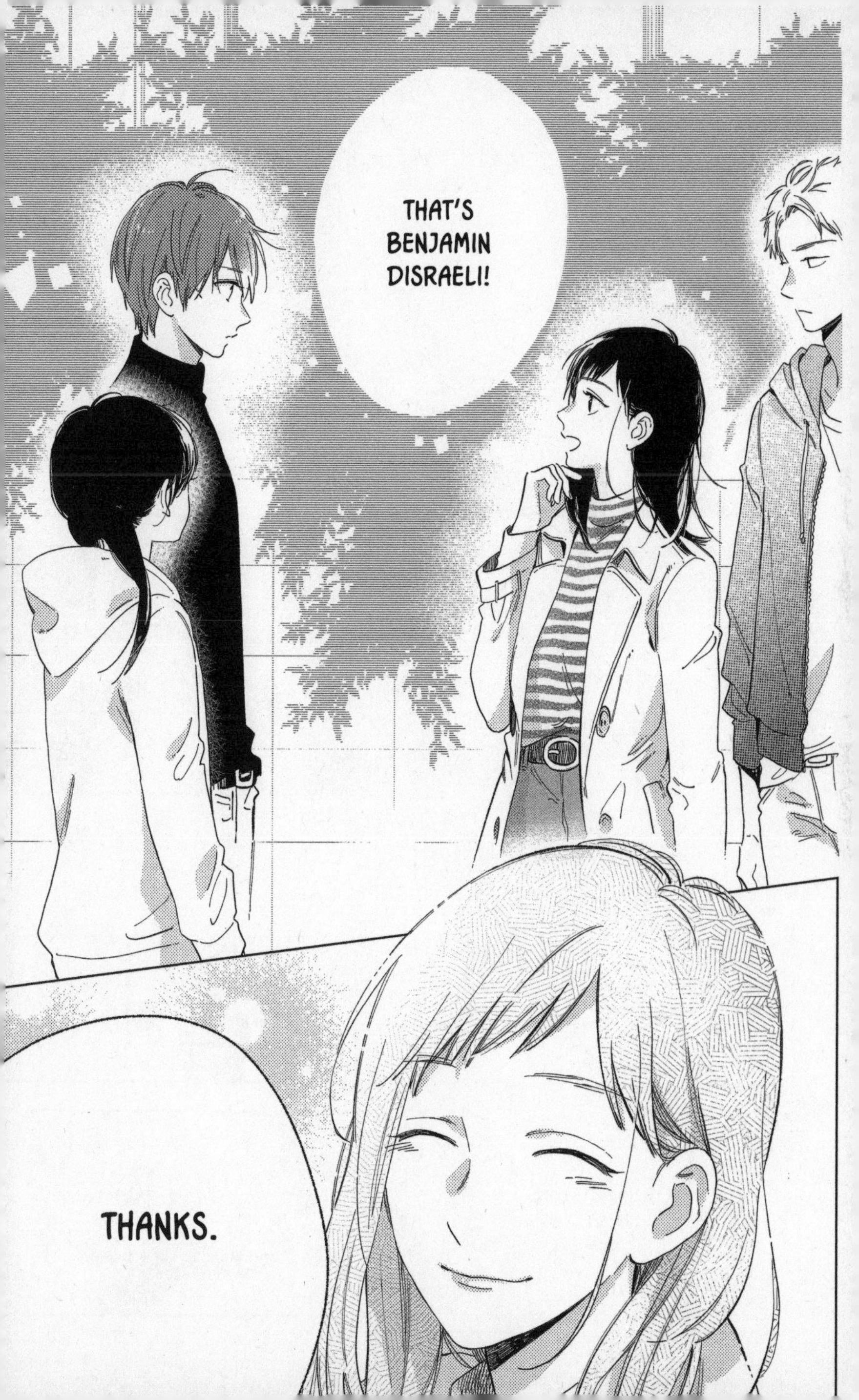
THAT'S BENJAMIN DISRAELI!
THANKS.

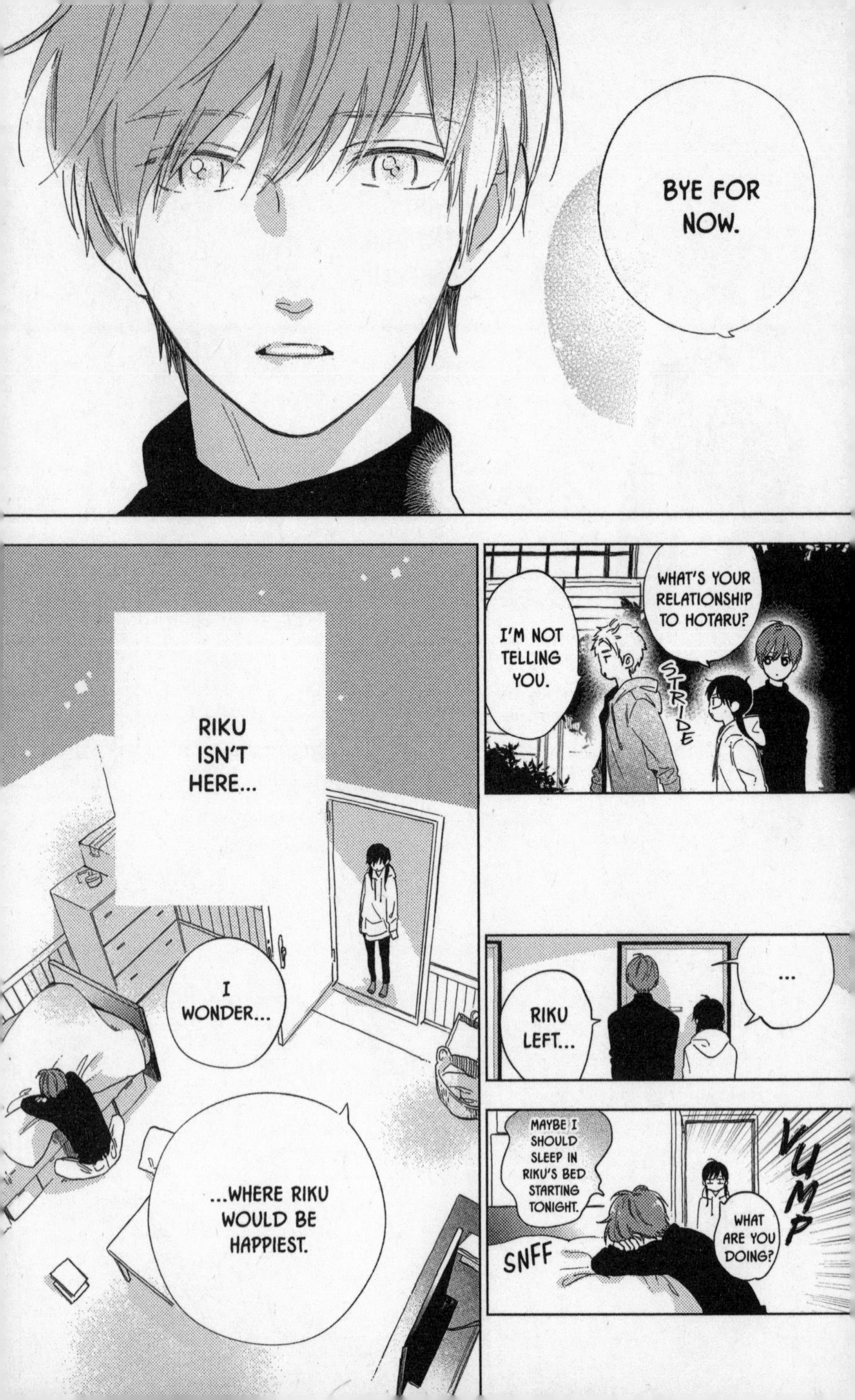
BYE FOR NOW.
WHAT'S YOUR RELATIONSHIP TO HOTARU?
STRIDE
I'M NOT TELLING YOU.
...
RIKU LEFT...
VUMP
WHAT ARE YOU DOING?
MAYBE I SHOULD SLEEP IN RIKU'S BED STARTING TONIGHT.
SNFF
RIKU ISN'T HERE...
I WONDER...
...WHERE RIKU WOULD BE HAPPIEST.

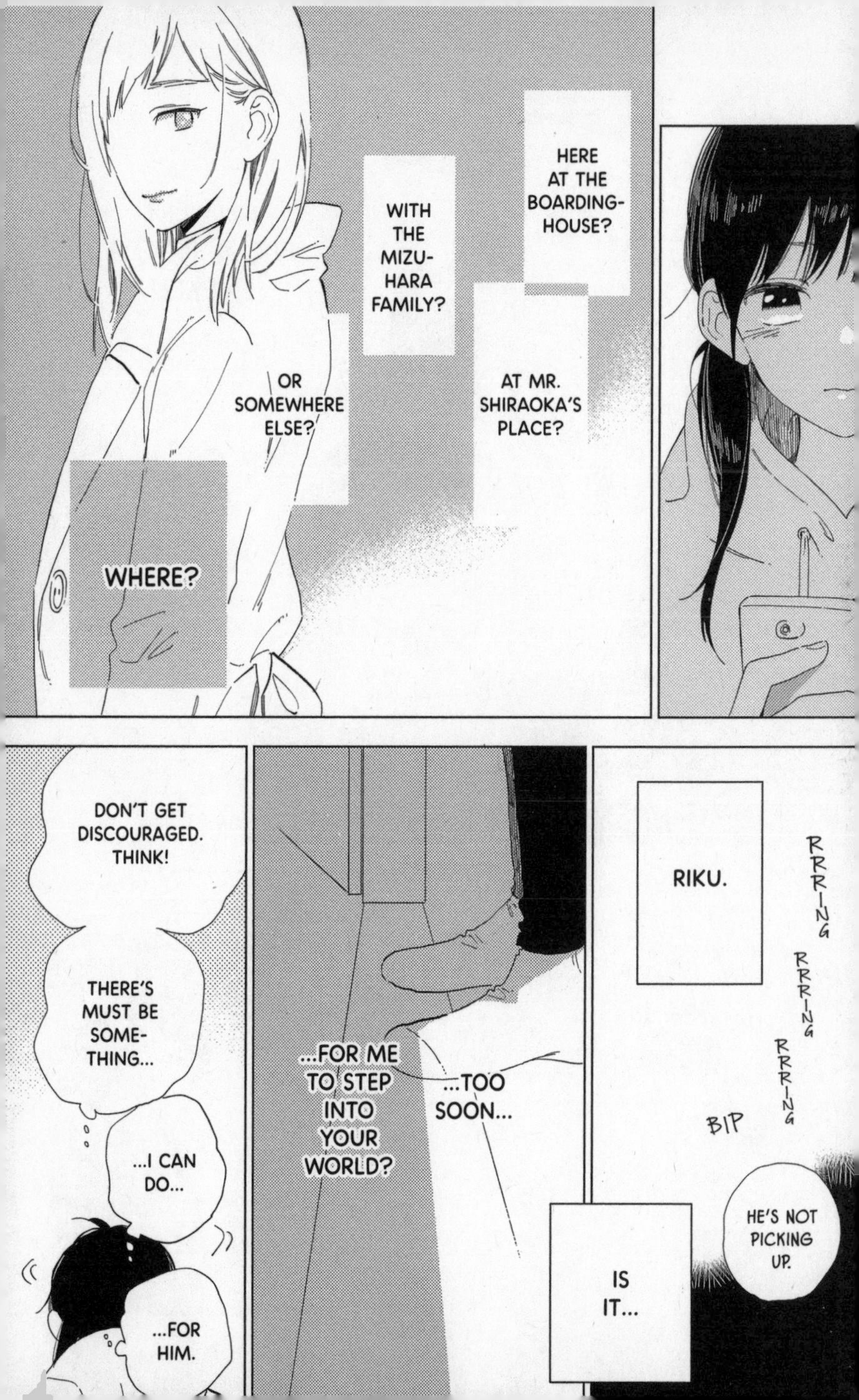
HERE AT THE BOARDING-HOUSE?
WITH THE MIZU-HARA FAMILY?
AT MR. SHIRAOKA'S PLACE?
OR SOMEWHERE ELSE?
WHERE?
RIKU.
RRRING
RRRING
RRRING
BIP
HE'S NOT PICKING UP.
IS IT...
...TOO SOON...
...FOR ME TO STEP INTO YOUR WORLD?
DON'T GET DISCOURAGED. THINK!
THERE'S MUST BE SOME-THING...
...I CAN DO...
...FOR HIM.

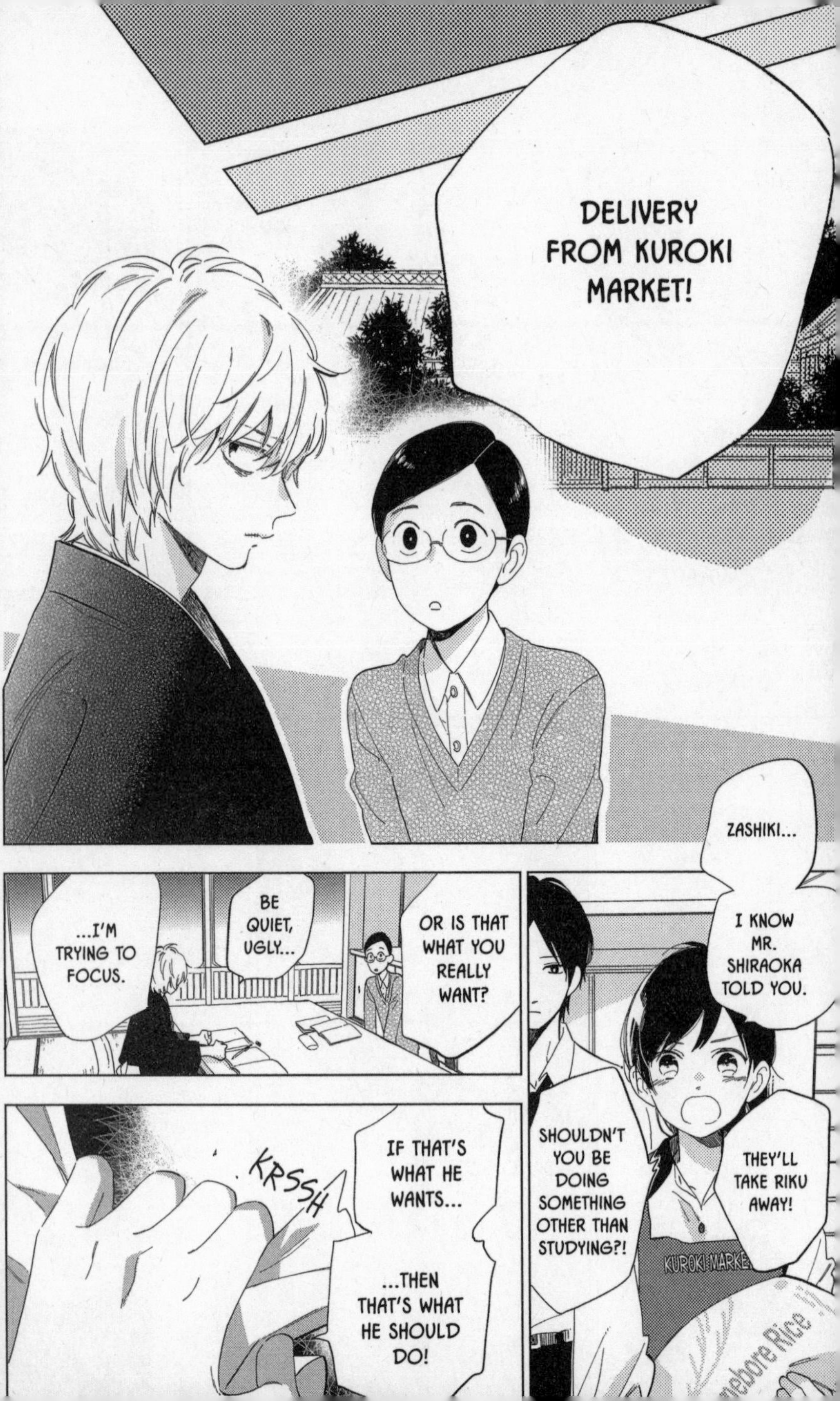
DELIVERY FROM KUROKI MARKET!
ZASHIKI...
I KNOW MR. SHIRAOKA TOLD YOU.
THEY'LL TAKE RIKU AWAY!
SHOULDN'T YOU BE DOING SOMETHING OTHER THAN STUDYING?!
KUROKI MARKET
OR IS THAT WHAT YOU REALLY WANT?
BE QUIET, UGLY...
...I'M TRYING TO FOCUS.
KRSSH
IF THAT'S WHAT HE WANTS...
...THEN THAT'S WHAT HE SHOULD DO!

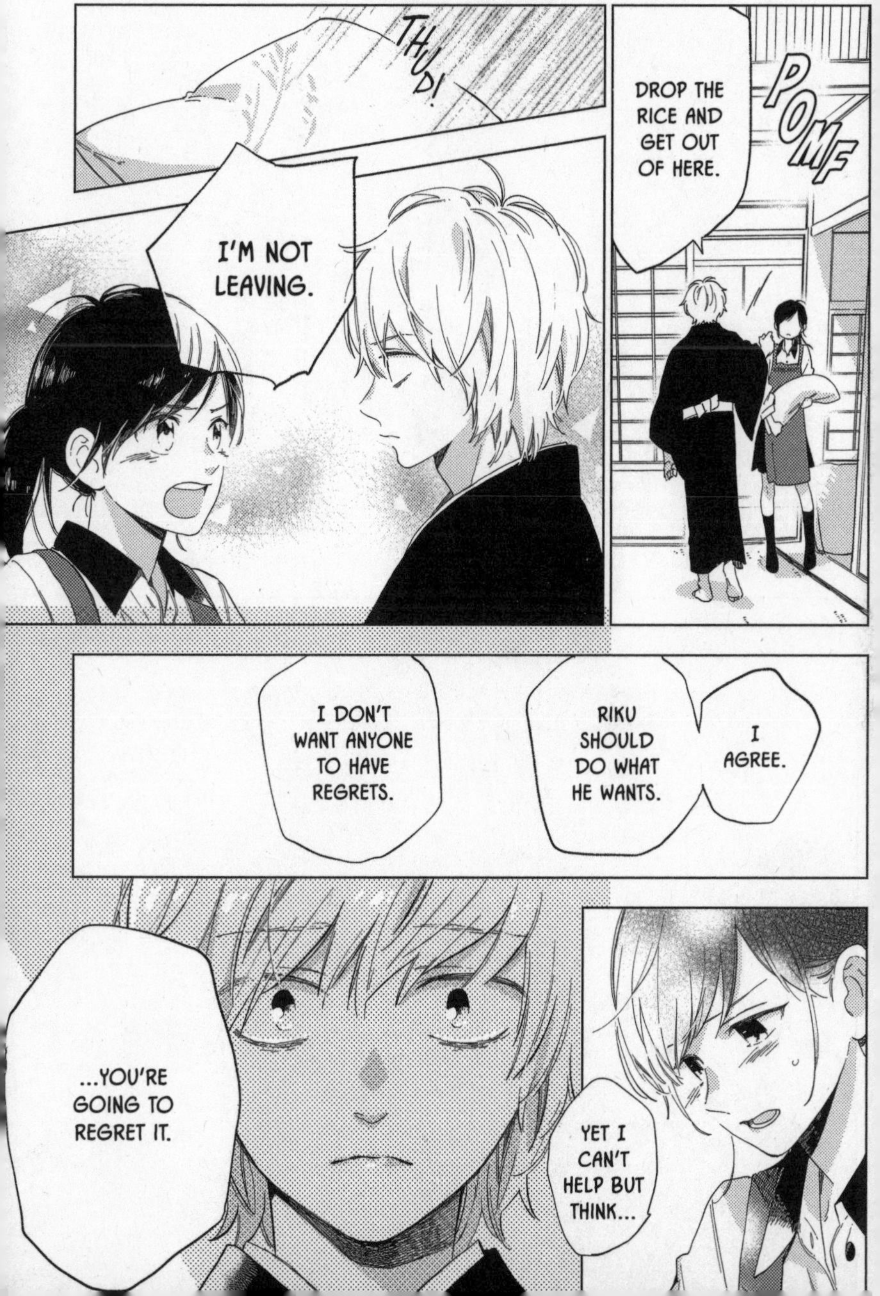
POMF
DROP THE RICE AND GET OUT OF HERE.
THUD!
I'M NOT LEAVING.
I AGREE.
RIKU SHOULD DO WHAT HE WANTS.
I DON'T WANT ANYONE TO HAVE REGRETS.
YET I CAN'T HELP BUT THINK...
...YOU'RE GOING TO REGRET IT.

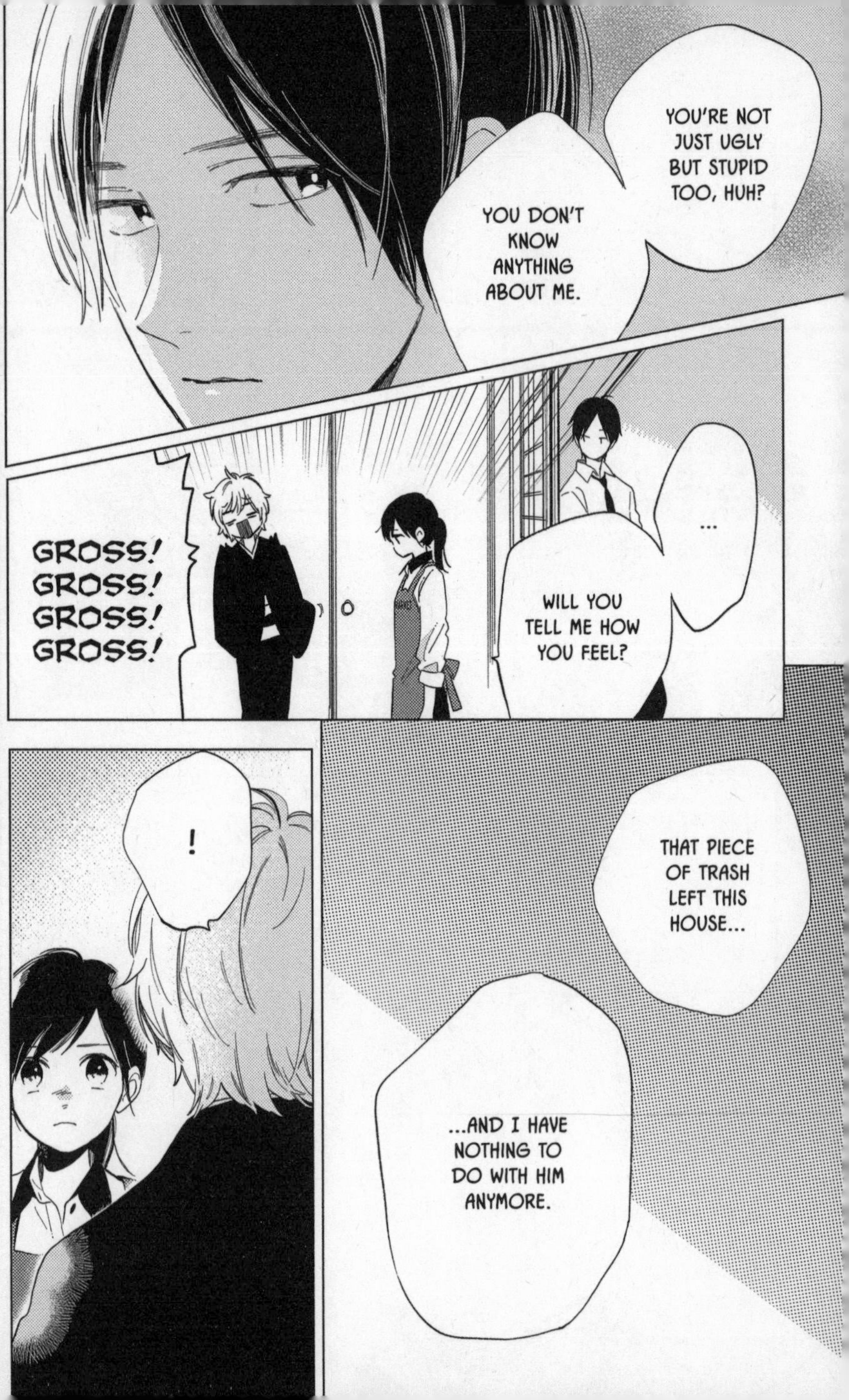
YOU'RE NOT JUST UGLY BUT STUPID TOO, HUH?
YOU DON'T KNOW ANYTHING ABOUT ME.
...
WILL YOU TELL ME HOW YOU FEEL?
GROSS! GROSS! GROSS! GROSS!
THAT PIECE OF TRASH LEFT THIS HOUSE...
...AND I HAVE NOTHING TO DO WITH HIM ANYMORE.
!

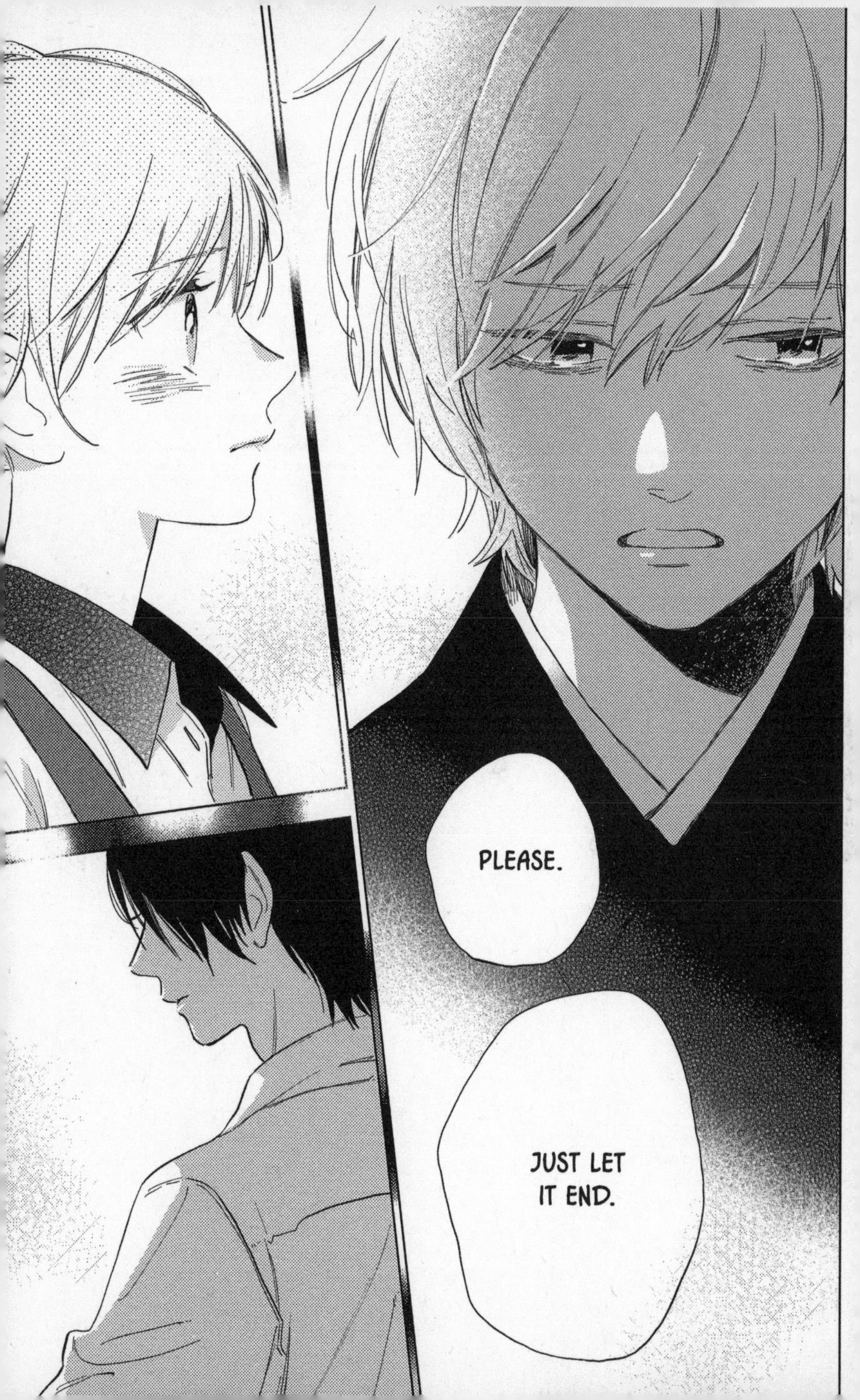
PLEASE.
JUST LET IT END.

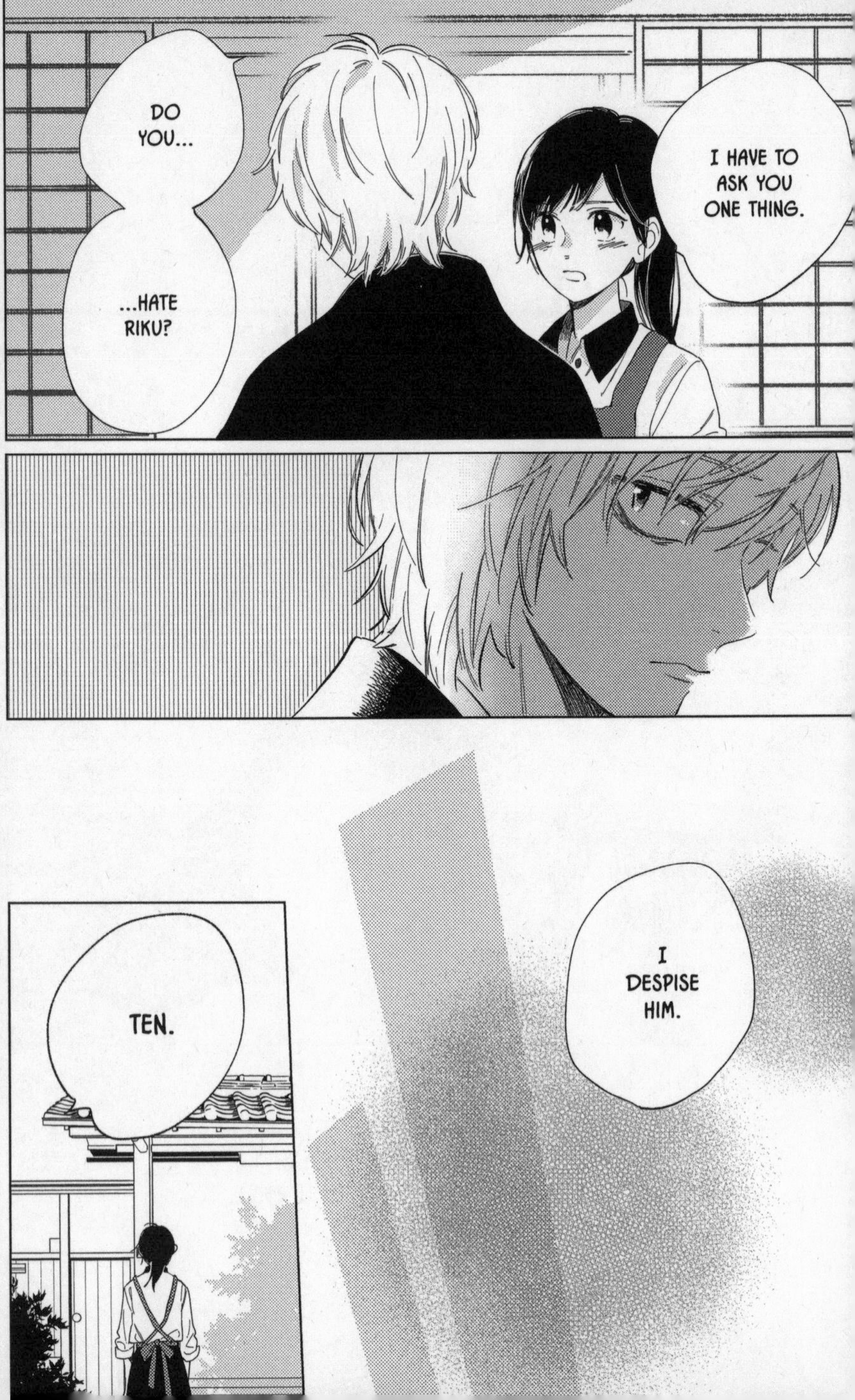
I HAVE TO ASK YOU ONE THING.
DO YOU...
...HATE RIKU?
I DESPISE HIM.
TEN.

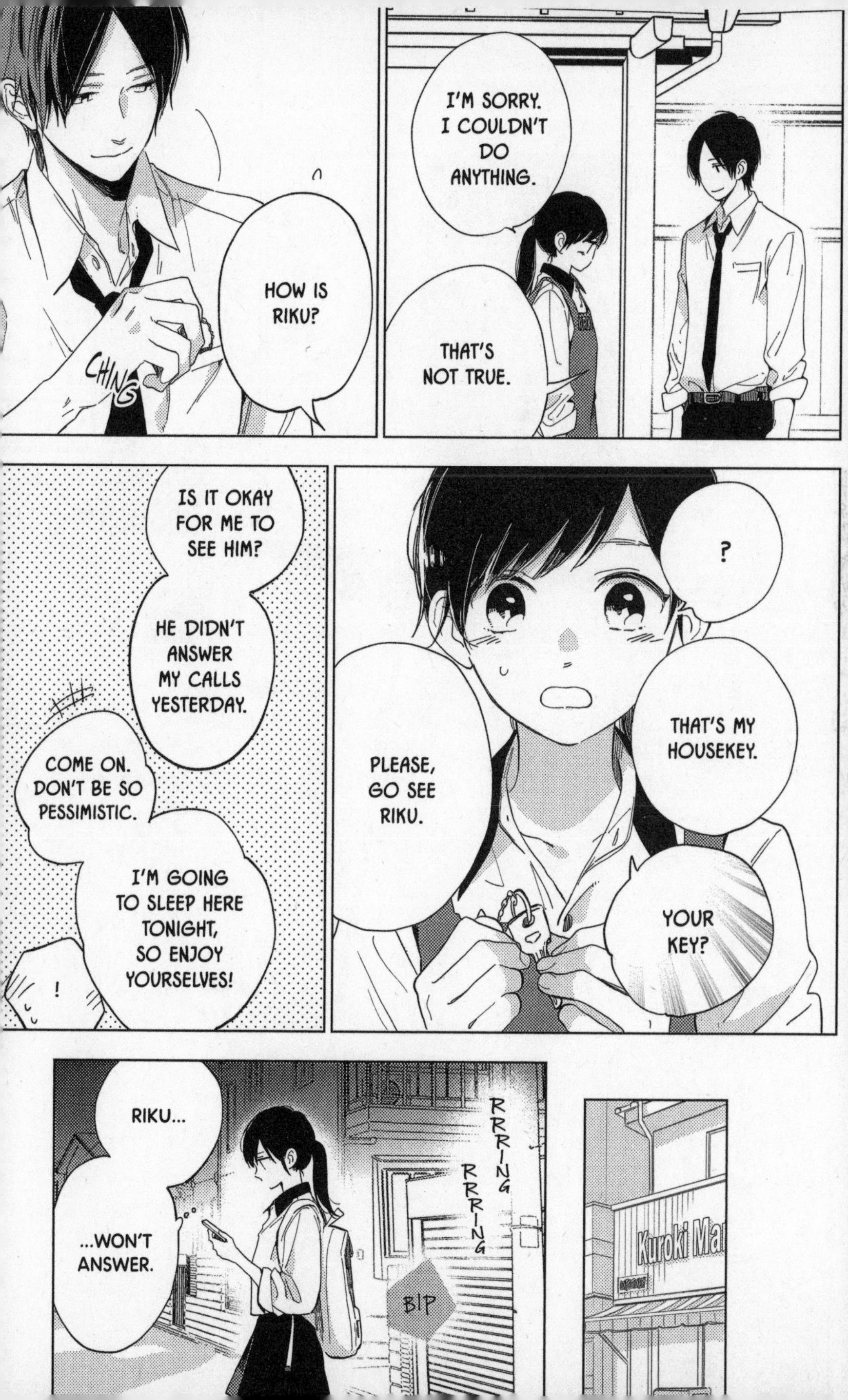
I'M SORRY. I COULDN'T DO ANYTHING.
THAT'S NOT TRUE.
HOW IS RIKU?
CHING
?
YOUR KEY?
THAT'S MY HOUSEKEY.
PLEASE, GO SEE RIKU.
IS IT OKAY FOR ME TO SEE HIM?
HE DIDN'T ANSWER MY CALLS YESTERDAY.
COME ON. DON'T BE SO PESSIMISTIC.
I'M GOING TO SLEEP HERE TONIGHT, SO ENJOY YOURSELVES!
!
Kuroki Mar
RRRING
RRRING
BIP
RIKU...
...WON'T ANSWER.

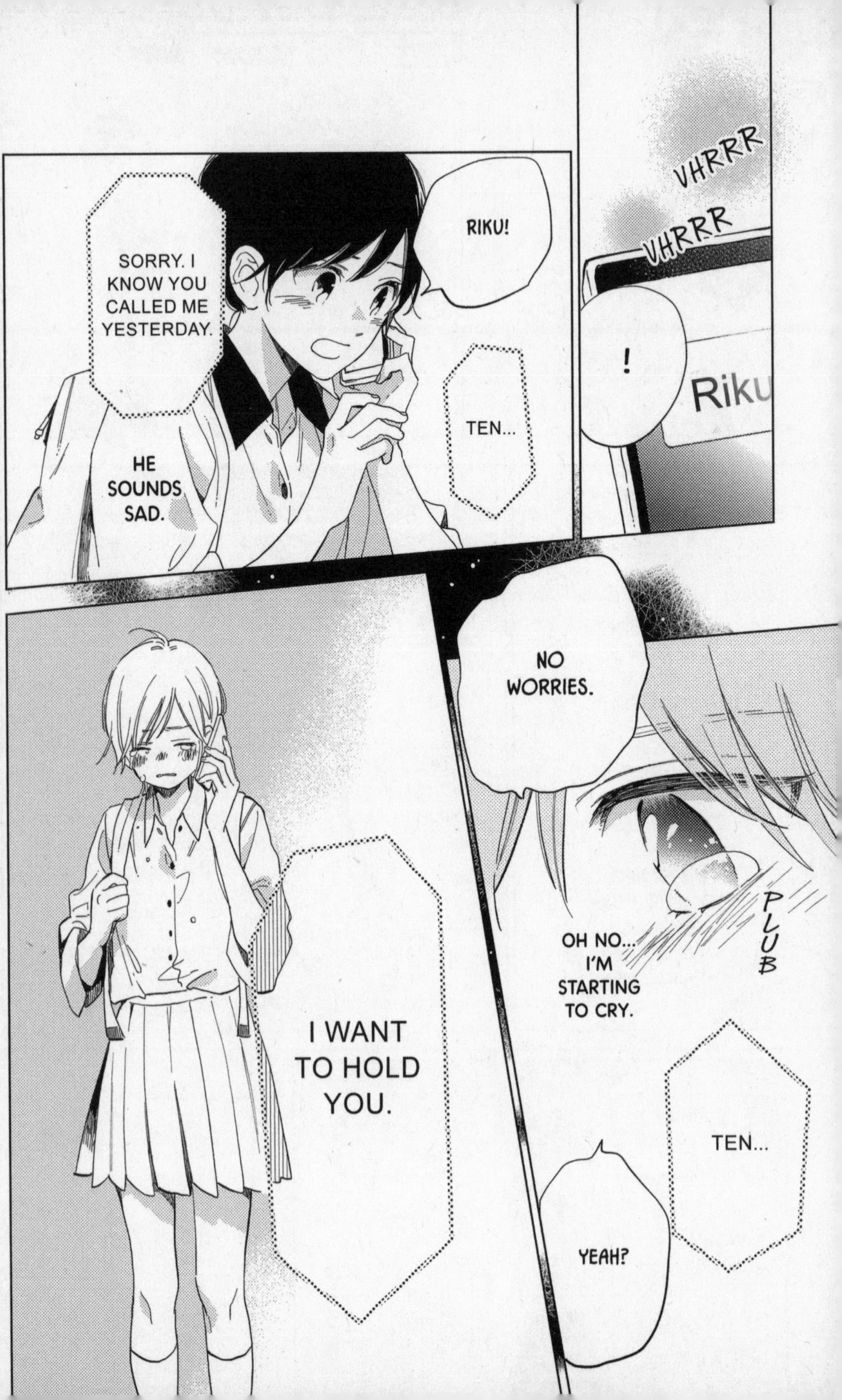
VHRRR
VHRRR
!
Riku
RIKU!
TEN...
SORRY. I KNOW YOU CALLED ME YESTERDAY.
HE SOUNDS SAD.
NO WORRIES.
PLUB
OH NO... I'M STARTING TO CRY.
TEN...
YEAH?
I WANT TO HOLD YOU.

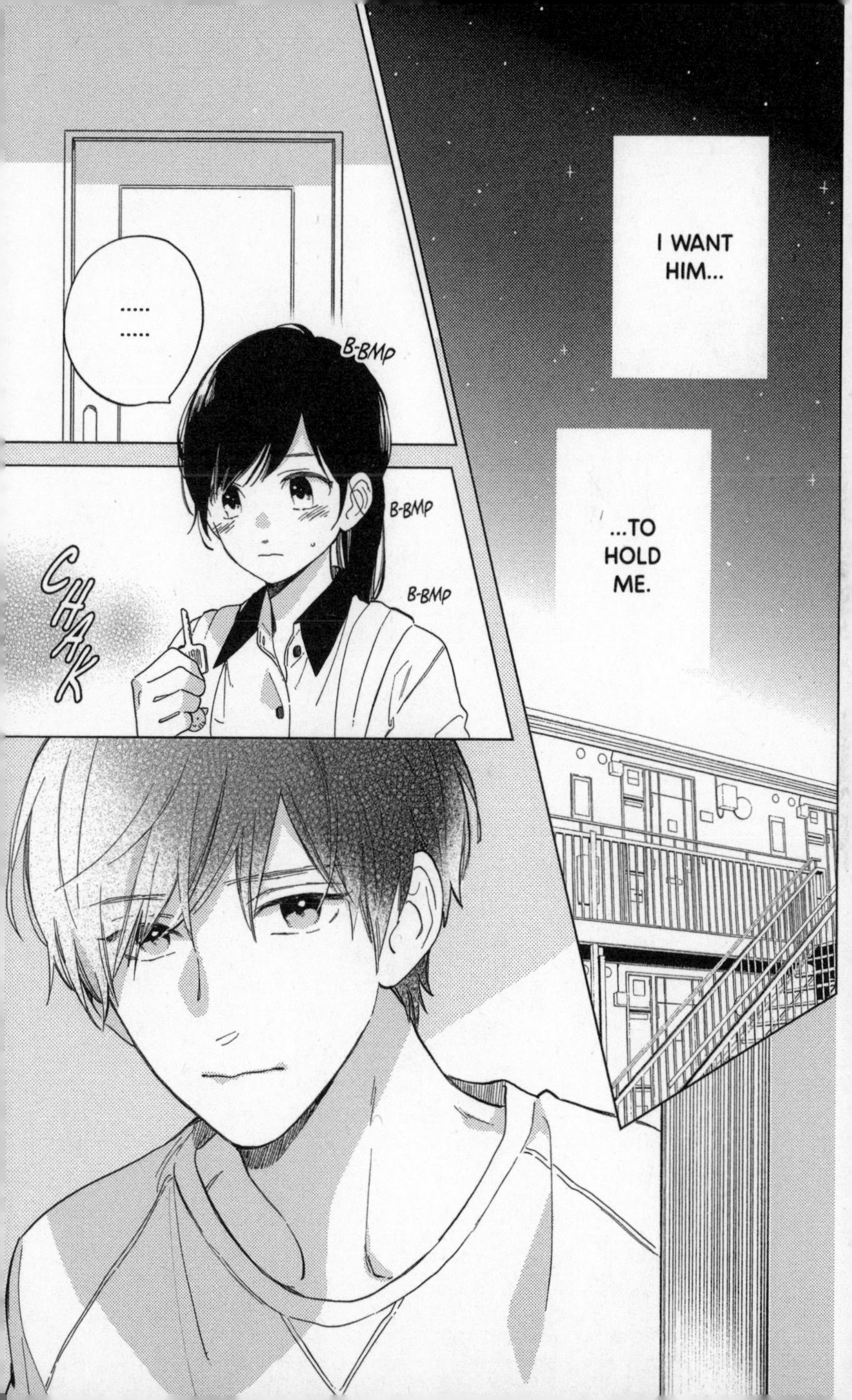
I WANT HIM...
...TO HOLD ME.
......
......
B-BMP
B-BMP
B-BMP
CHAK

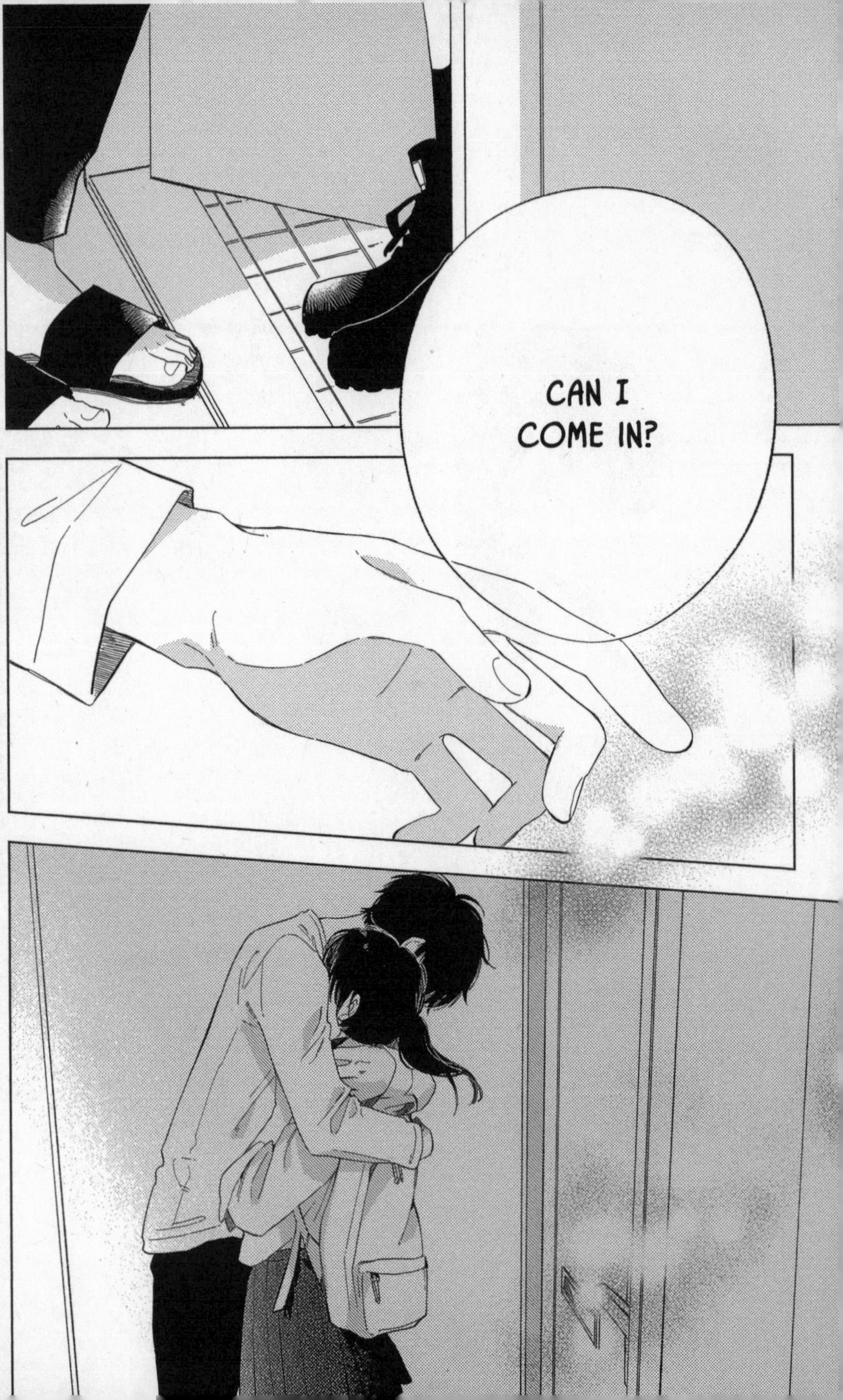
CAN I COME IN?

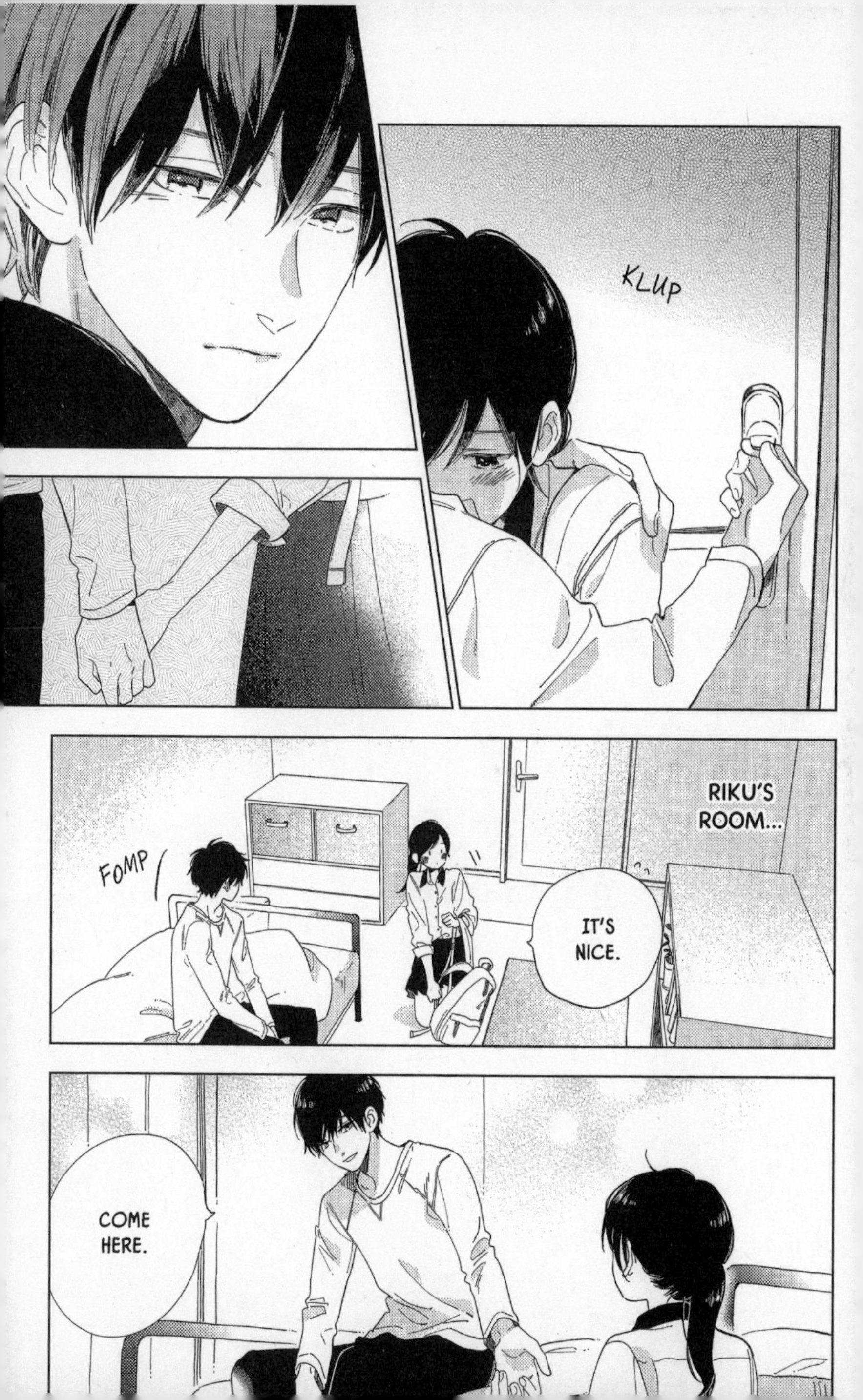
KLUP
RIKU'S ROOM...
IT'S NICE.
FOMP
COME HERE.

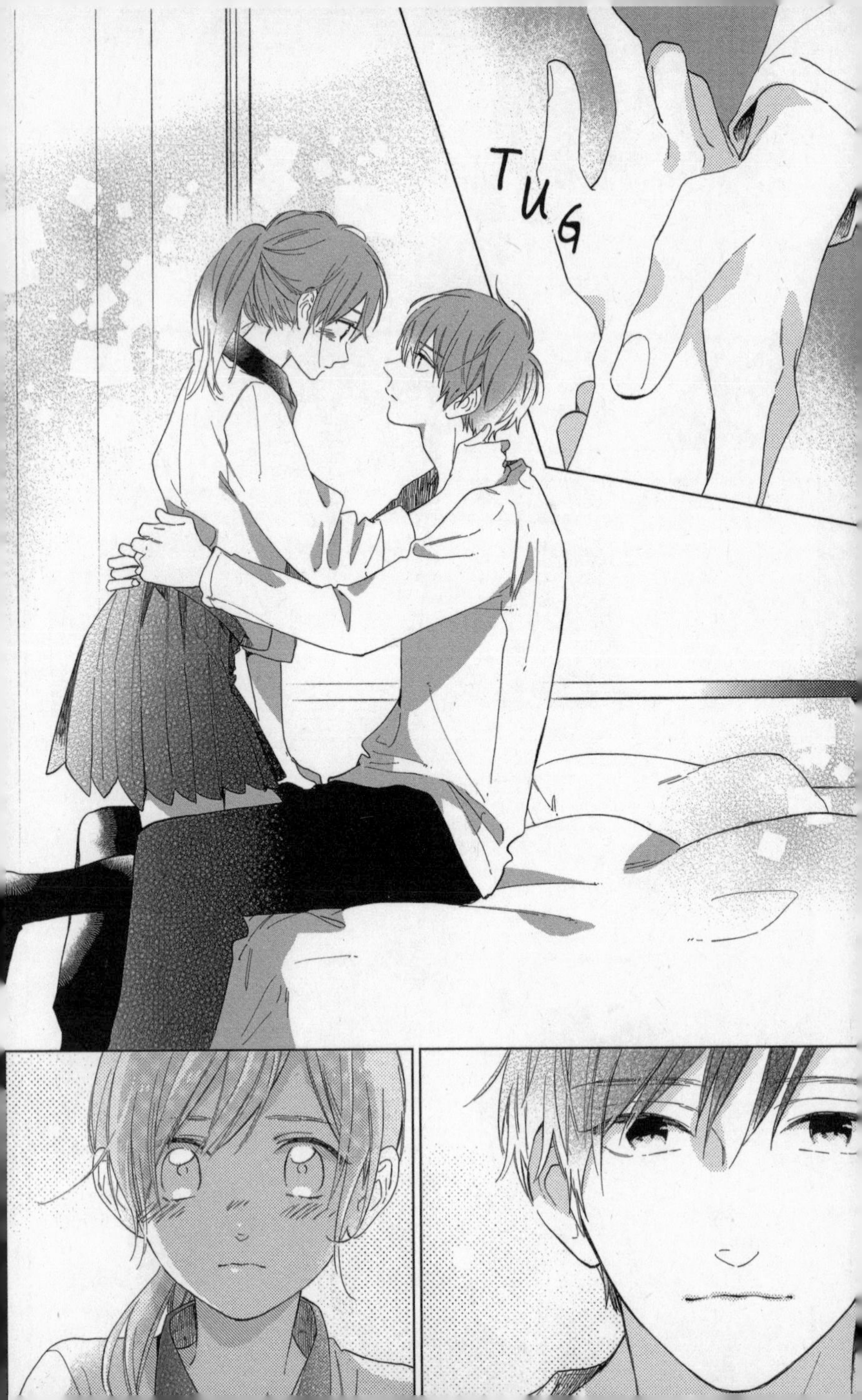
TUG

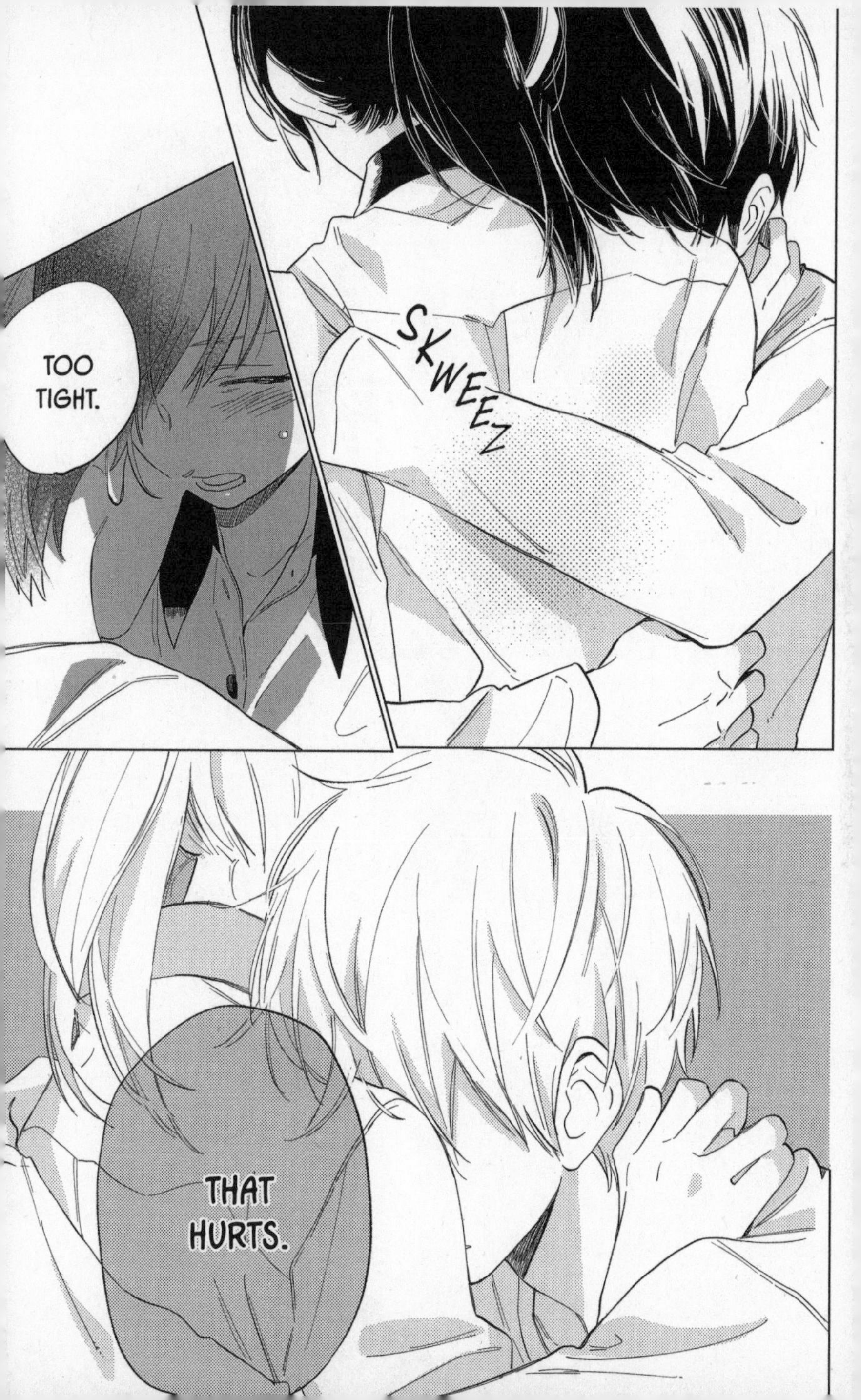
SKWEEZ
TOO TIGHT.
THAT HURTS.

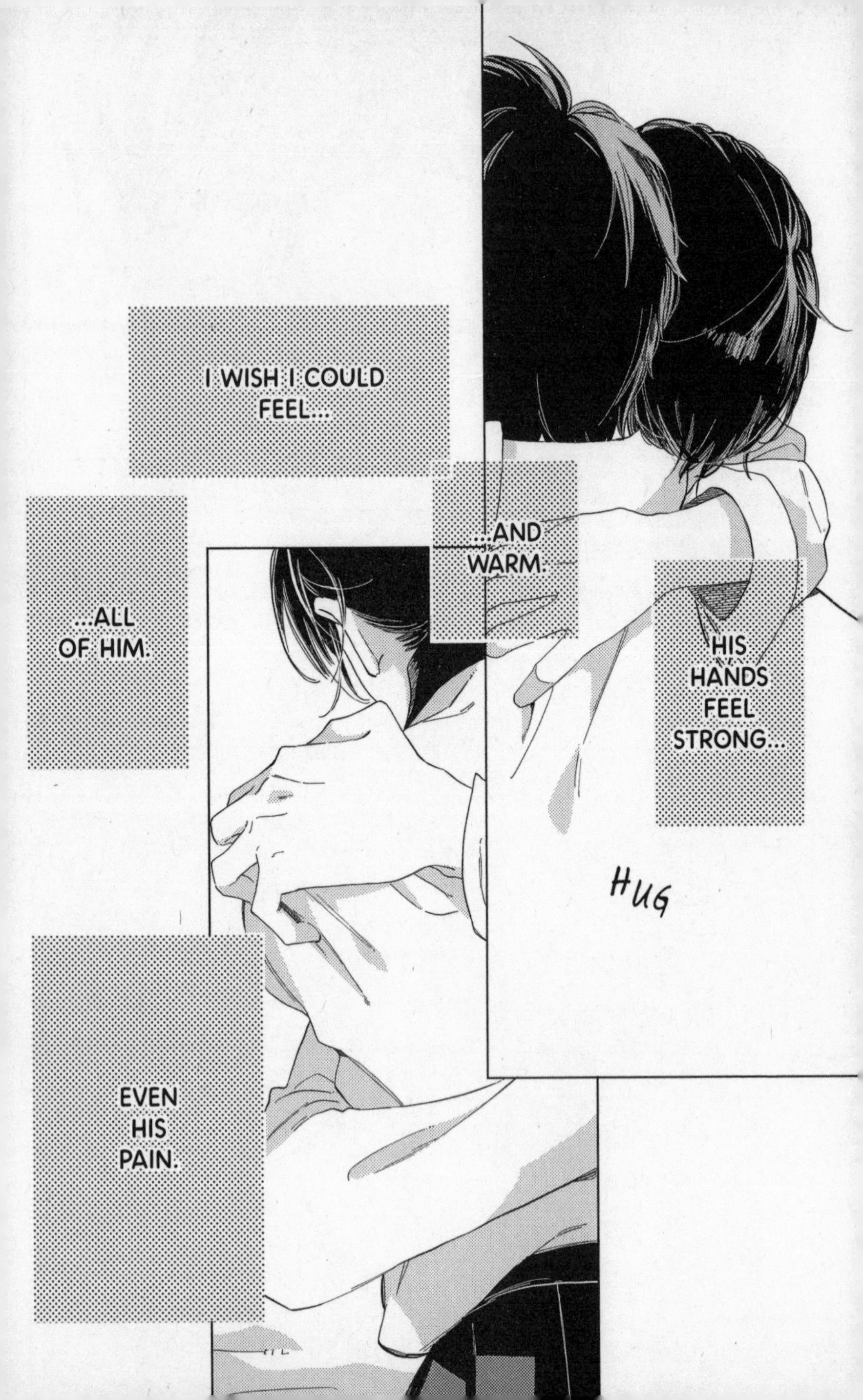

HIS HANDS FEEL STRONG...
...AND WARM.
HUG
I WISH I COULD FEEL...
...ALL OF HIM.
EVEN HIS PAIN.

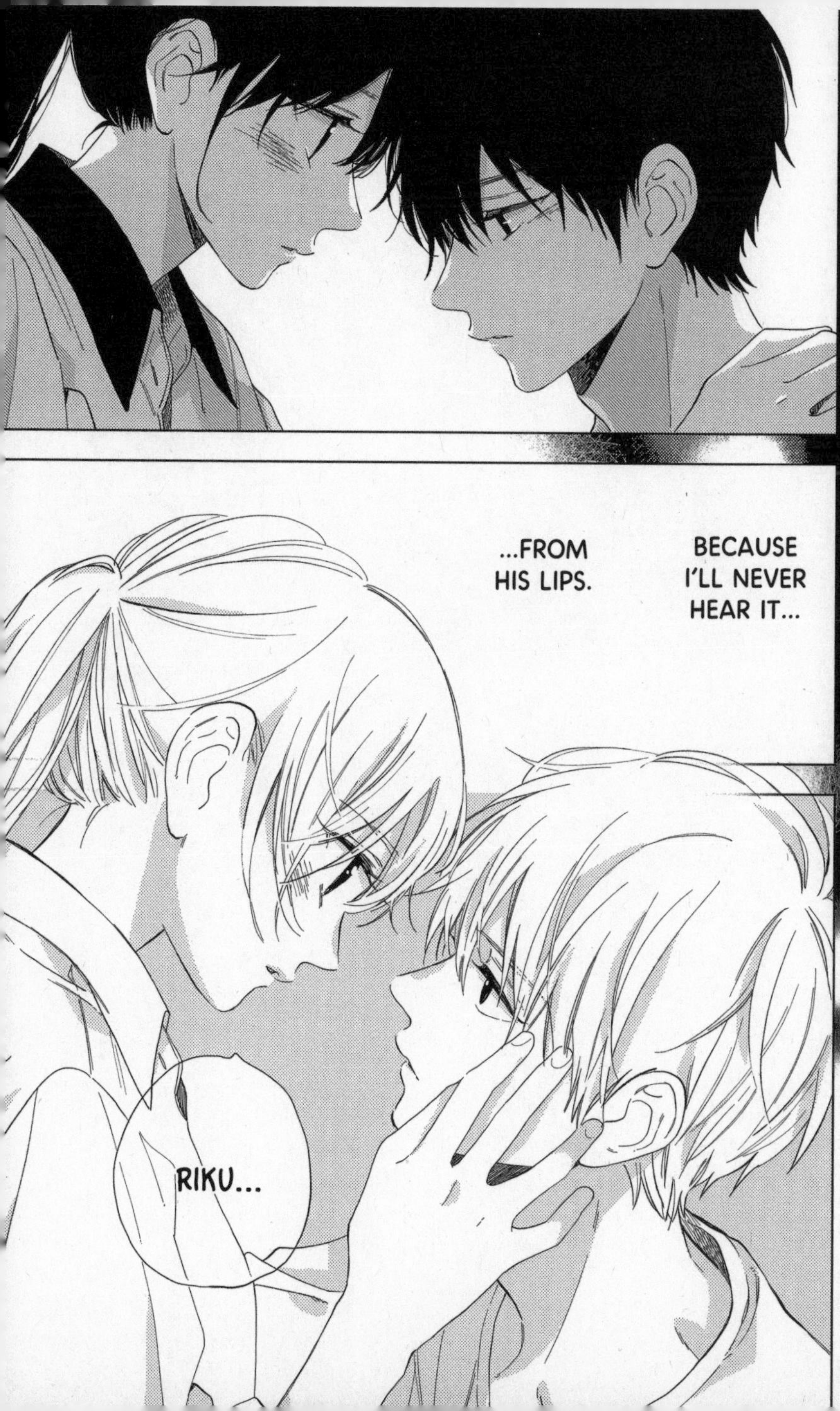
BECAUSE I'LL NEVER HEAR IT...
...FROM HIS LIPS.
RIKU...

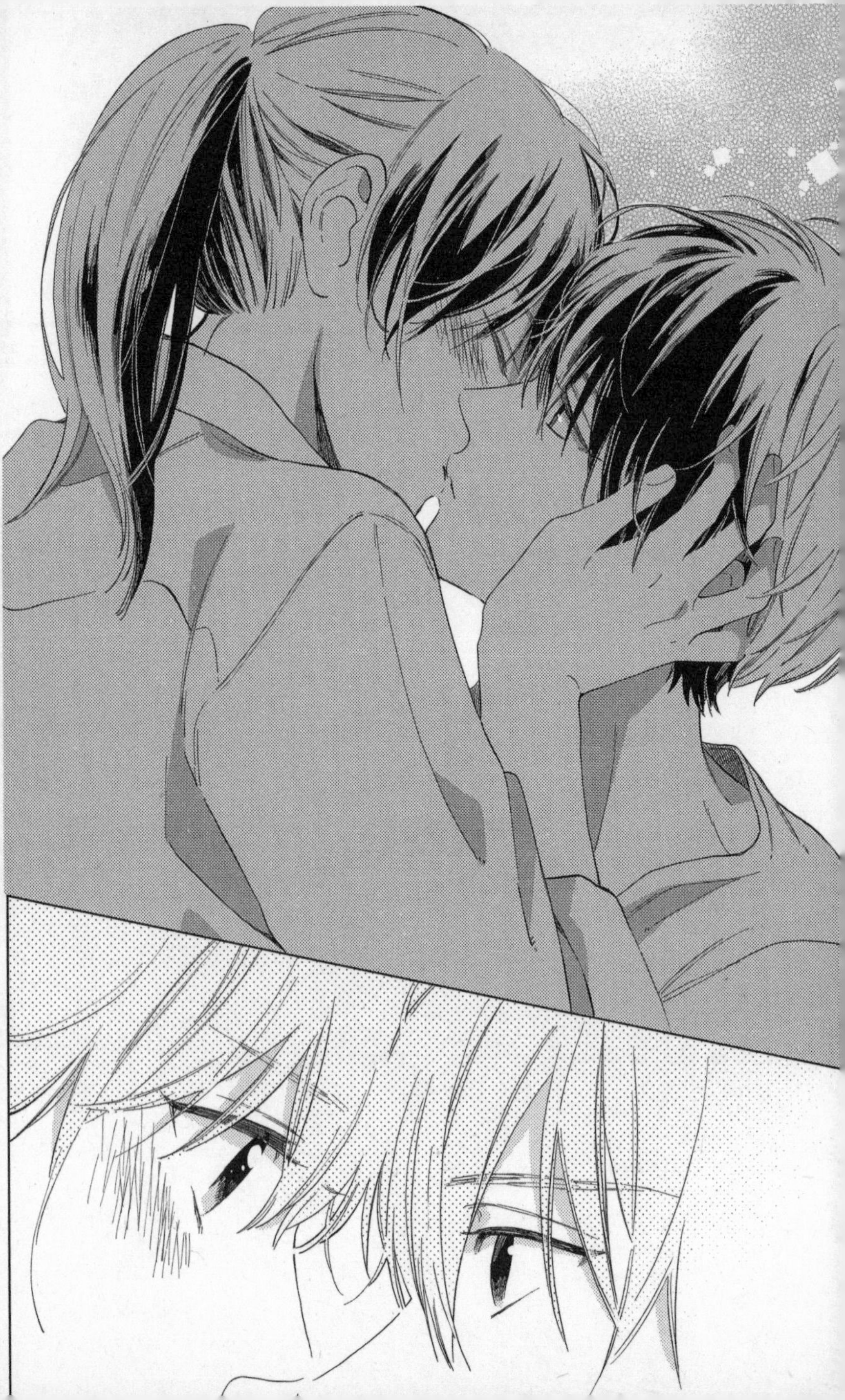

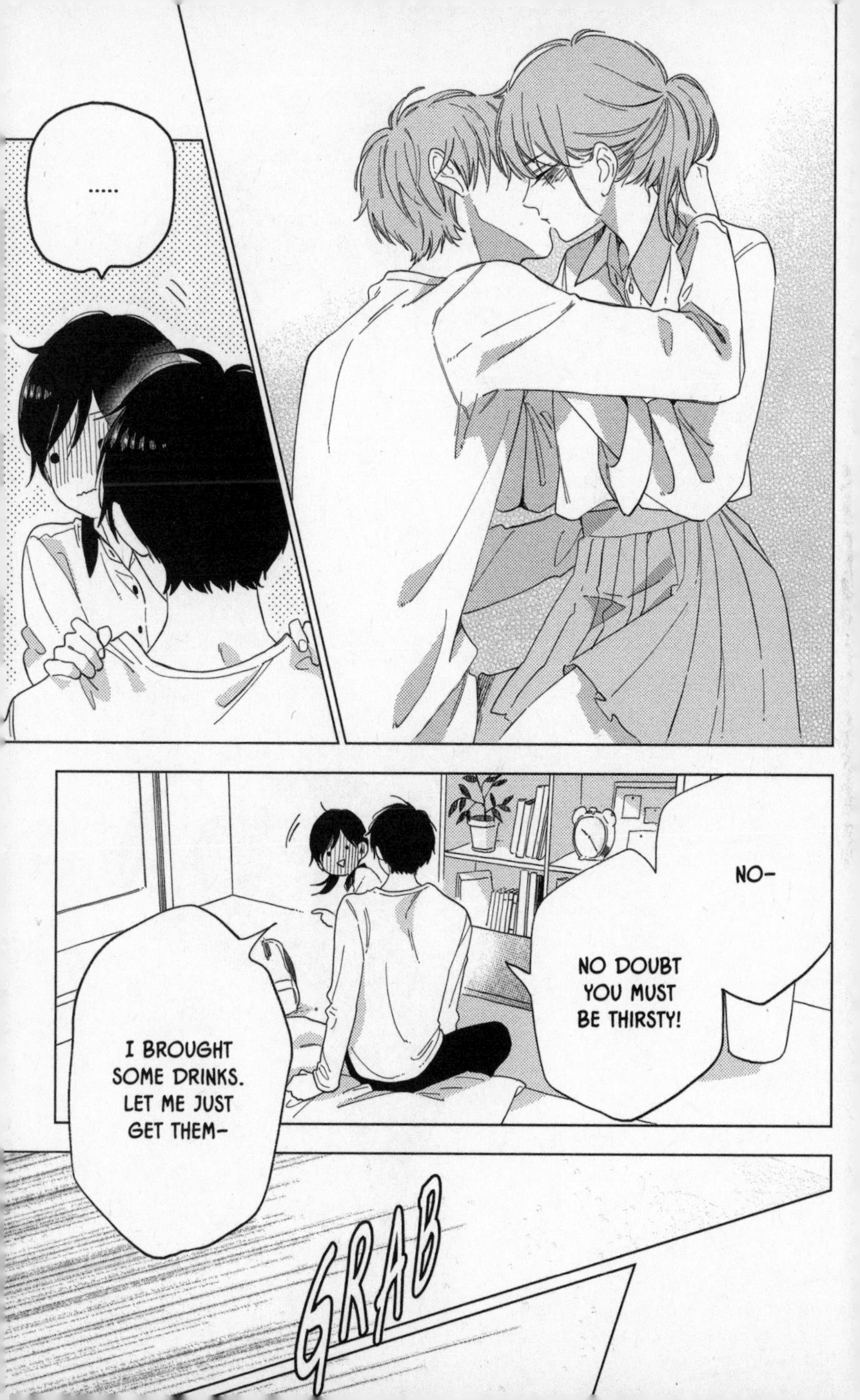
......
NO-
NO DOUBT YOU MUST BE THIRSTY!
I BROUGHT SOME DRINKS. LET ME JUST GET THEM-
GRAB

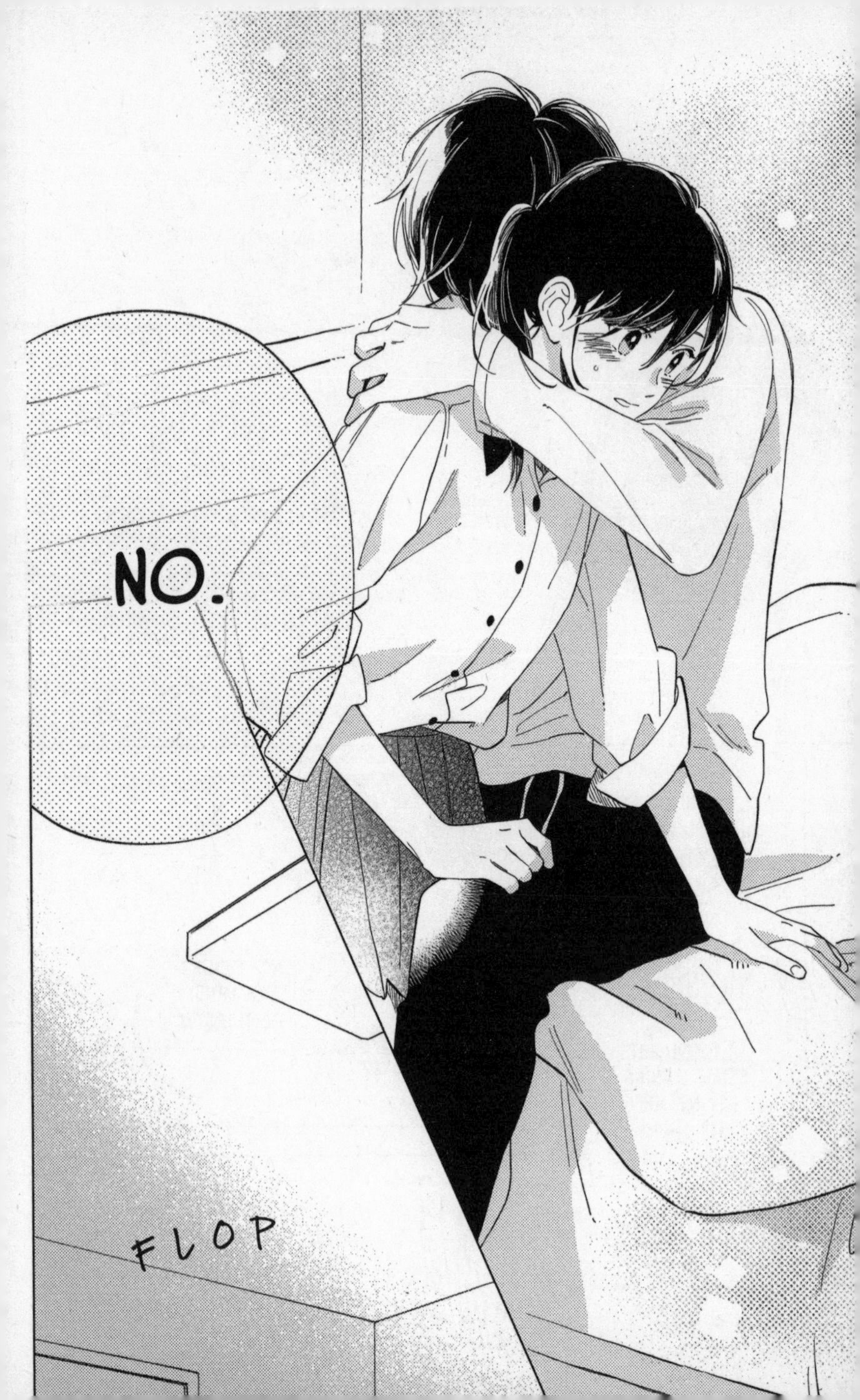
NO.
FLOP

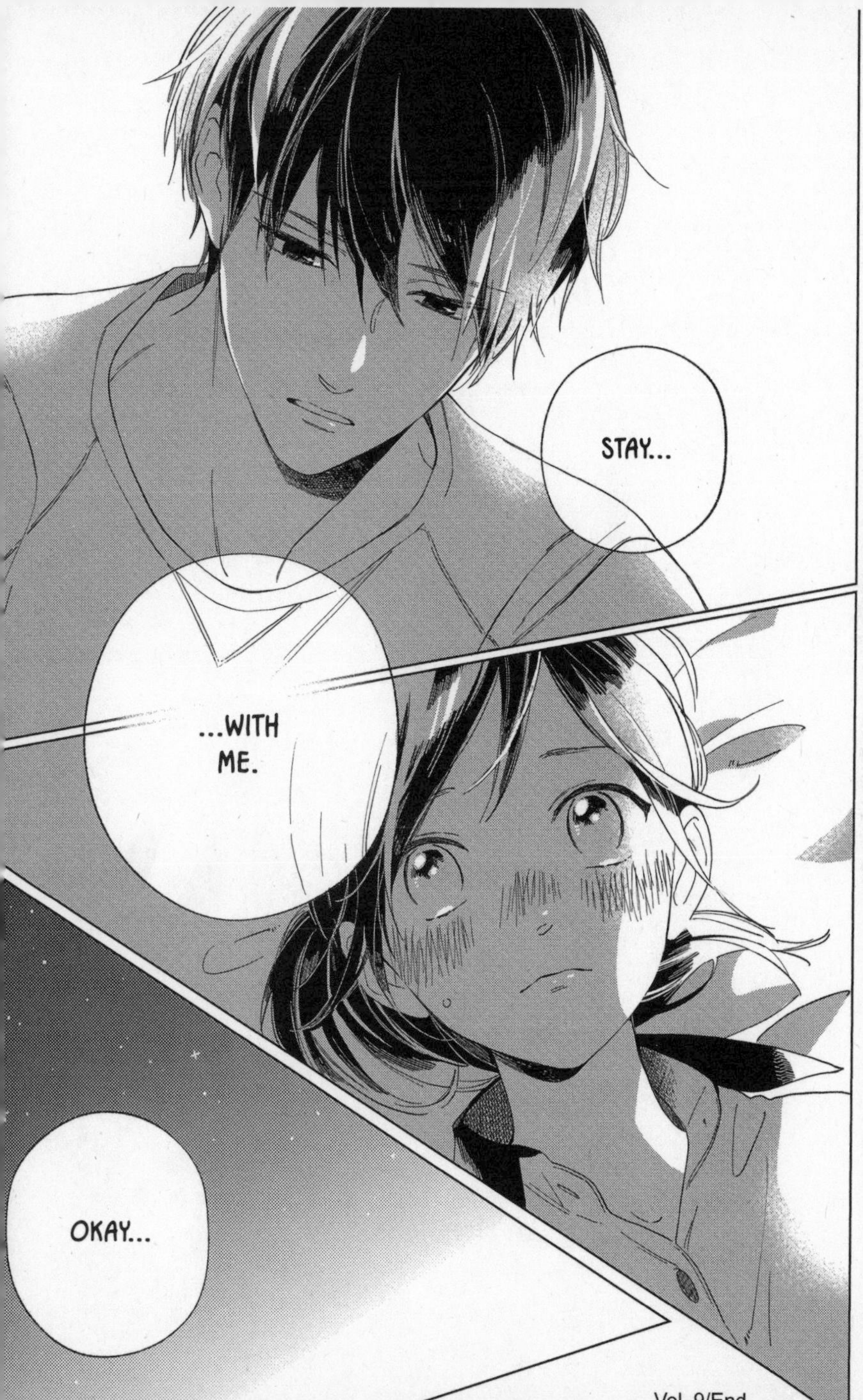
STAY...
...WITH ME.
OKAY...

Vol. 9/End

SHORTCAKE CAKE

Thank you for purchasing volume 9!

As a team, we divvy up the work between writing and illustrating. We'll tell you a little bit about how we do it. (˘˘)୨

Makiro
STORY

Nachiyan
ART

① Storyboard

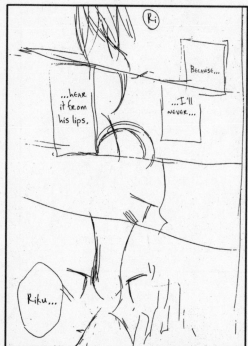

Ri

Because...

...HEAR it from his lips.

...I'll NEVER...

Riku...

Makiro meets with our editor.
(Nachiyan gets looped in first if there's a big plot twist.)

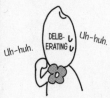

DELIB-ERATING

Uh-huh.

Uh-huh.

Once the story is settled, we fax each other because one of us lives in Fukuoka, and the other lives in Nagoya. They're pretty far apart.

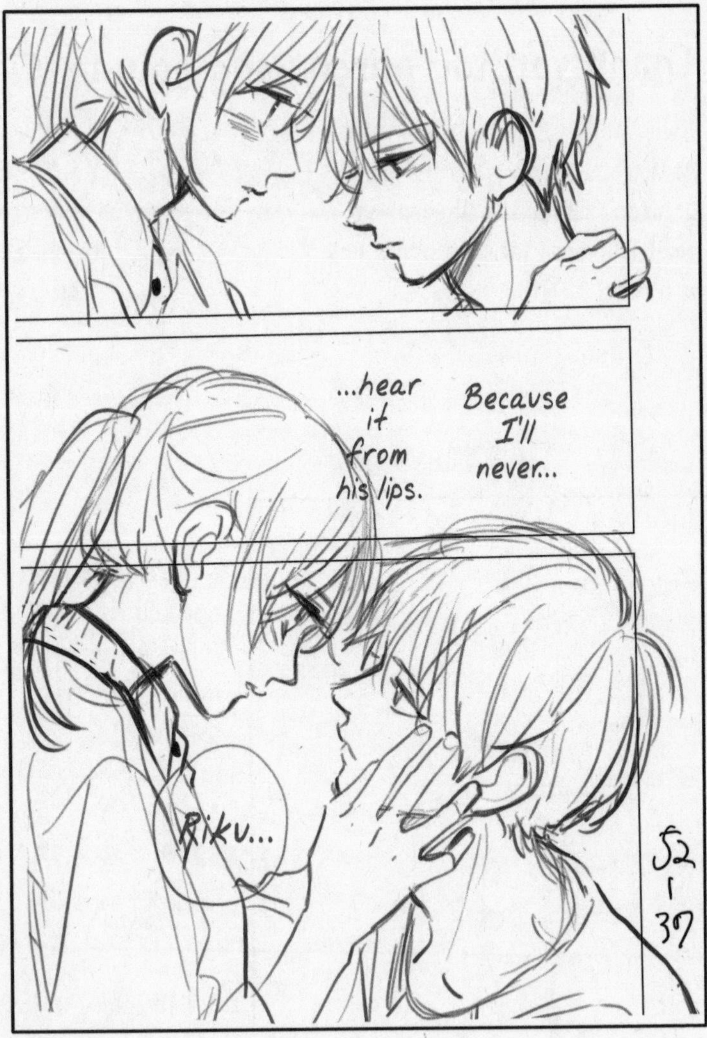
Because I'll never...
...hear it from his lips.
Riku...

② Draft

We're pretty thorough at this stage, because we don't want to be guessing when we start inking.

(We use MediBang Paint Pro software for the iPad Pro.)

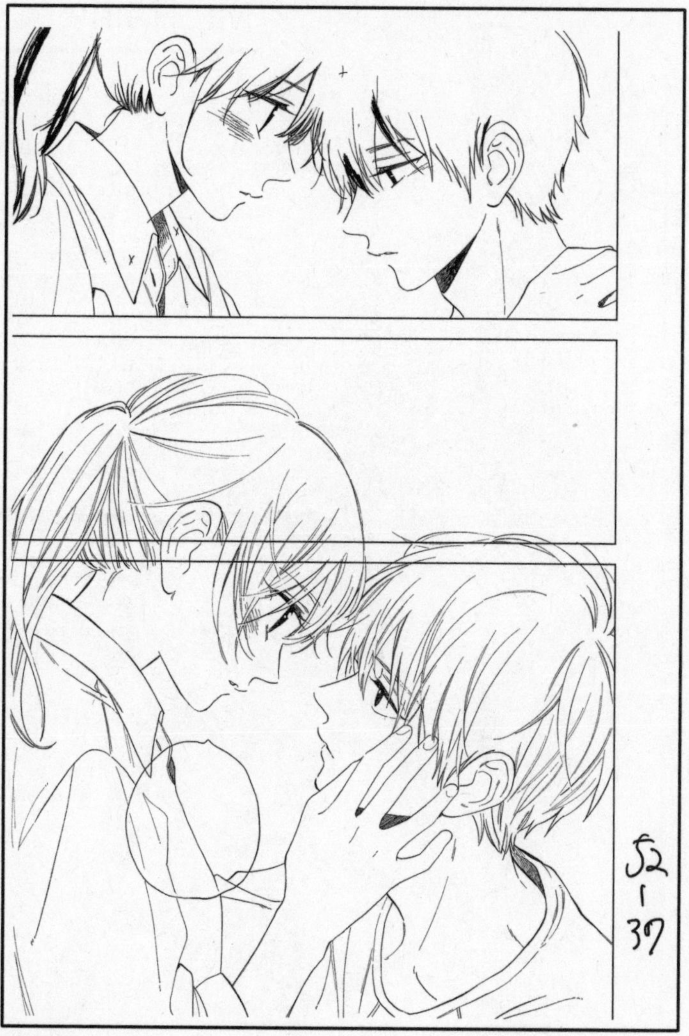
52
1
37

③ Inking

Up until this stage we work on the iPad Pro.
Nachiyan uses a G Pen. Right now, inking is her favorite part.
She draws 90% of the panels—even the background. After our assistants cover everything with tone, she uses a Wacom tablet for the final touches!
Please check out the finished illustrations in the pages of this book! (^3^) ~♫

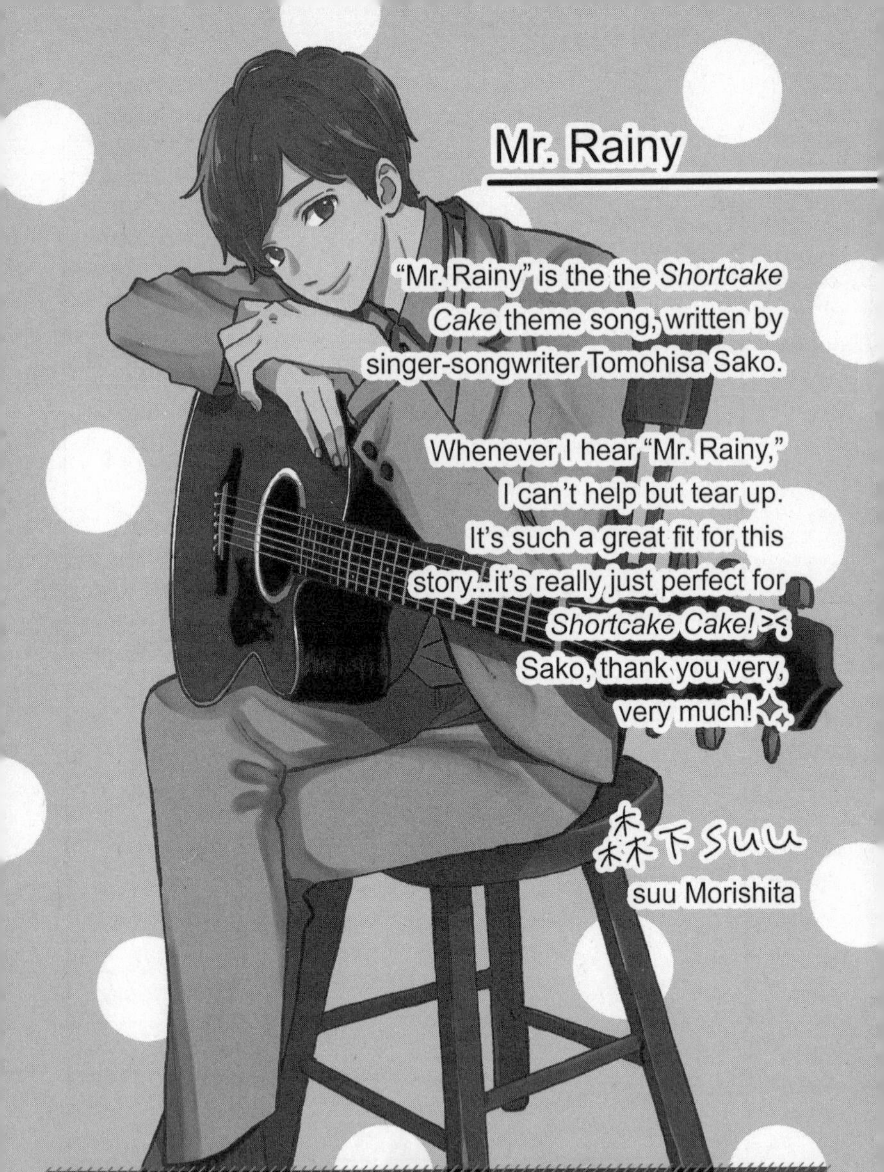

Mr. Rainy

"Mr. Rainy" is the the *Shortcake Cake* theme song, written by singer-songwriter Tomohisa Sako.

Whenever I hear "Mr. Rainy," I can't help but tear up. It's such a great fit for this story...it's really just perfect for *Shortcake Cake!* >< Sako, thank you very, very much! ✧

森下suu
suu Morishita

Watch a music video featuring *Shortcake Cake* and "Mr. Rainy" on the official *Margaret* YouTube channel!

"Mr. Rainy" is available on Tomohisa Sako's mini-album, *Kimi no Mimi ni Rabu Songu wo*. The cover illustration is a suu Morishita original!

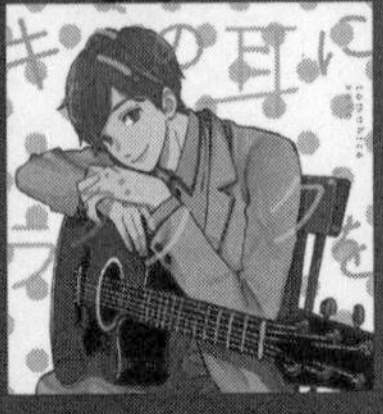

Special Thanks

- Editor J
- Yasuhisa Kawatani (Kawatani Design)
- Nao Hamaguchi (assistant)
- Everyone who helped make this book possible

- All our readers!! ◇ ◇

← **The following two pages were created in commemoration of reaching 50 chapters. It's an illustrated recap of the boys in *Shortcake Cake!* Please enjoy!**

Connected

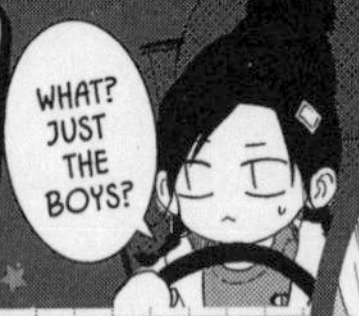
WHAT? JUST THE BOYS?

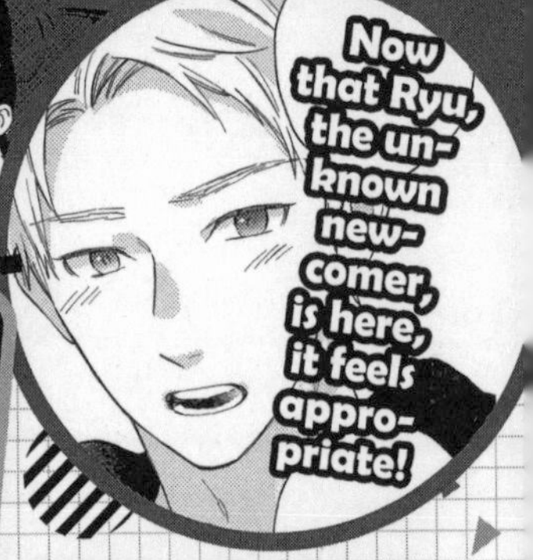
Now that Ryu, the unknown newcomer, is here, it feels appropriate!

We'll recap the story by diagraming the boys in this story. Which relationship is the most interesting to you?

Yuto

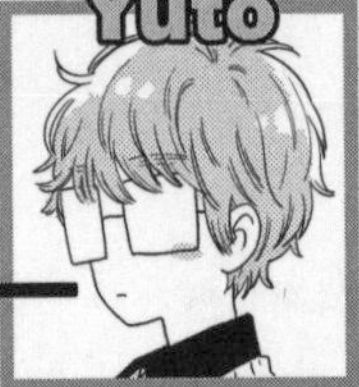

Second-year. Tutors Riku and the other first-years. A bespectacled boy with a kind heart. He doesn't know that Ten is hiding her relationship with Riku. He worries about her change in behavior.

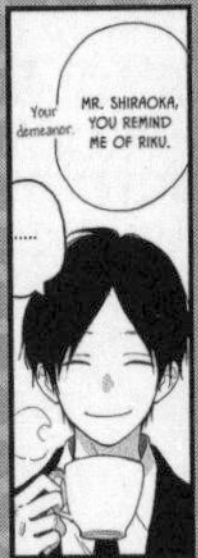
MR. SHIRAOKA, YOU REMIND ME OF RIKU.
Your demeanor.

As Chiaki noted, Shiraoka and Riku share a smile and kind demeanor. The reason for their similarity is in this volume!

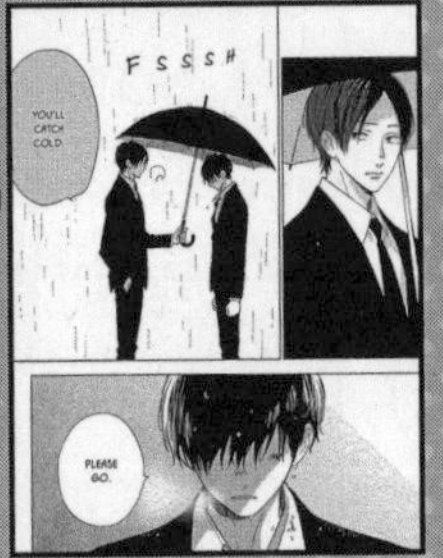
FSSSH
YOU'LL CATCH COLD.
PLEASE GO.

Riku and Shiraoka are...

Teacher & Disciple?!

Ever since Shiraoka was hired he's been watching over Riku. He waited a long time to find someone who could save Riku. Putting his trust in Ten and Chiaki, he tells them to stop Riku and Rei's sibling feud.

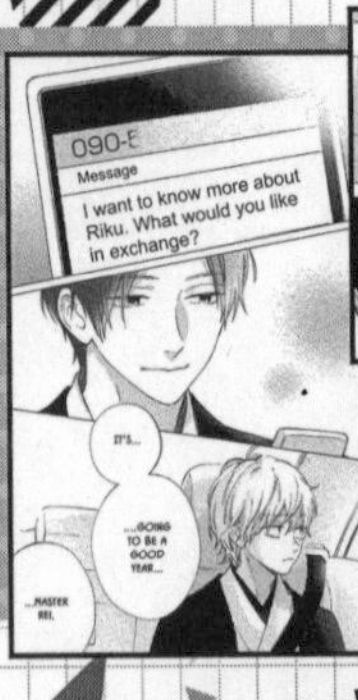
090-8
Message
I want to know more about Riku. What would you like in exchange?
IT'S...
...GOING TO BE A GOOD YEAR...
...MASTER REI.

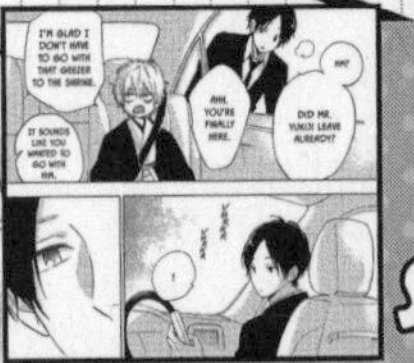
I'M GLAD I DON'T HAVE TO GO WITH THAT GEEZER TO THE SHRINE.
IT SOUNDS LIKE YOU WANTED TO GO WITH HIM.
AHH, YOU'RE FINALLY HERE.
DID MR. YUKIO LEAVE ALREADY?

Rei and Shiraoka are...

Master & Servant

Shiraoka is Rei's driver. He does anything Rei commands, and no matter how insolent Rei is, he responds to every request without complaint. Surely it's because he knows Rei has his own share of sadness. He hopes Ten can help change Riku, but he may be hoping for the same for Rei.

Shiraoka

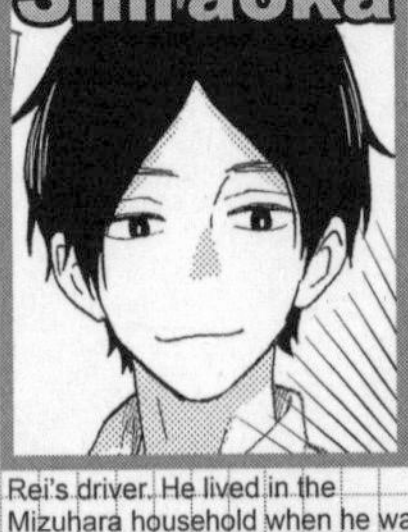

Rei's driver. He lived in the Mizuhara household when he was young, and he knows all about the history between Riku and Rei.

Just do what I say!

Yes, Sir.

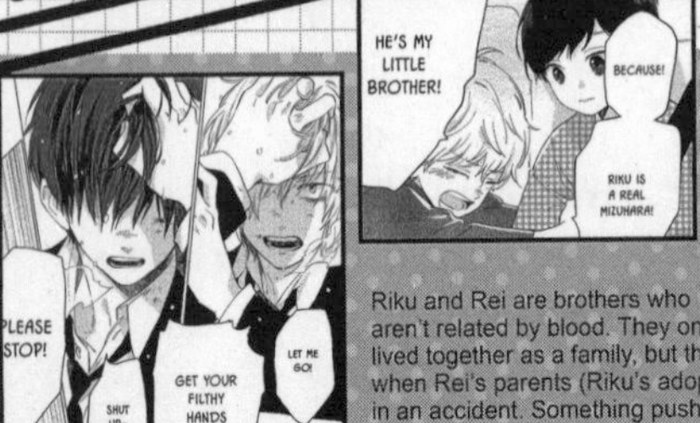
HE'S MY LITTLE BROTHER!
BECAUSE!
RIKU IS A REAL MIZUHARA!
PLEASE STOP!
SHUT UP-
GET YOUR FILTHY HANDS OFF ME!
LET ME GO!

Riku and Rei's relationship is...

Hate-Filled

Riku and Rei are brothers who aren't related by blood. They once lived together as a family, but the situation changed when Rei's parents (Riku's adoptive parents) were killed in an accident. Something pushed Rei to despise Riku and eventually throw him out of the house.

Which relationship do you want to understand first?

Shortcake Cake How All the Boys Are

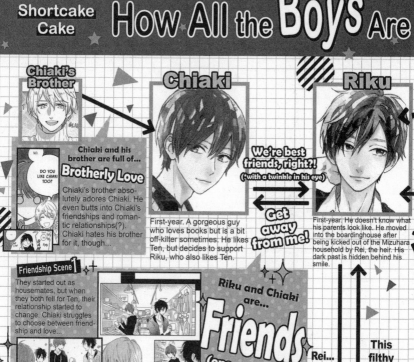

Chiaki's Brother

GLIN

Chiaki

Riku

We're best friends, right?!
(*with a twinkle in his eye)

Get away from me!

First-year. A gorgeous guy who loves books but is a bit off-kilter sometimes. He likes Ten, but decides to support Riku, who also likes Ten.

First-year. He doesn't know what his parents look like. He moved into the boardinghouse after being kicked out of the Mizuhara household by Rei, the heir. His dark past is hidden behind his smile.

SO.
DO YOU LIKE CHIAKI TOO?
BAM
POW

Chiaki and his brother are full of...
Brotherly Love

Chiaki's brother absolutely adores Chiaki. He even butts into Chiaki's friendships and romantic relationships(?). Chiaki hates his brother for it, though...

Friendship Scene 1

They started out as housemates, but when they both fell for Ten, their relationship started to change. Chiaki struggles to choose between friendship and love...

WHY DID RIKU AND I...
HEY.
HEY.
...FOR THE SAME GIRL?
...HAVE TO FALL...

Riku and Chiaki are...
Friends
(one-way only)
!?

Rei... Do you really mean it?

This filthy piece of trash isn't my brother.

Friendship Scene 2

Chiaki kisses Ten after she starts liking Riku. When he confesses what happened, Riku is nice (sort of?)...

YANK
HIT ME!
SAY WHATEVER YOU WANT!
FWAK
DON'T TOUCH ME!
DON'T WORRY.
I'VE NEVER THOUGHT OF US AS FRIENDS ANYWAY.
...I HAVE NO RIGHT TO BE YOUR FRIEND ANYMORE.
IF YOU DON'T...
SHOCK

Friendship Scene 3

KRIK

When Ten tells Riku her feelings, Chiaki urges her along. (For some reason he was there to see it go down!) He becomes a supporter of their relationship.

Chiaki has one other "friend"...

Rei

Friendship Scene 4

Together with Ten, Chiaki learns about Riku's past. Knowing that Riku won't be pleased, he and Ten decide to take action.

I'M PRETTY GOOD AT MAKING HIM MAD AT ME, YOU KNOW.

WHAT? FOR ME?
WHO'S THAT FOR?
AHA! FOUND YOU!
SINCE WHEN HAVE WE BEEN FRIENDS?
MY BEST FRIEND.

Eita

Chiaki acts extremely cold towards just about everybody besides Riku. Is this because of his "love" for Riku?

Second-year. Heir to the Mizuhara family. Selfish and insensitive, he's constantly

SHORTCAKE CAKE

SHORTCAKE CAKE
Title Page Collection
Chapter 48

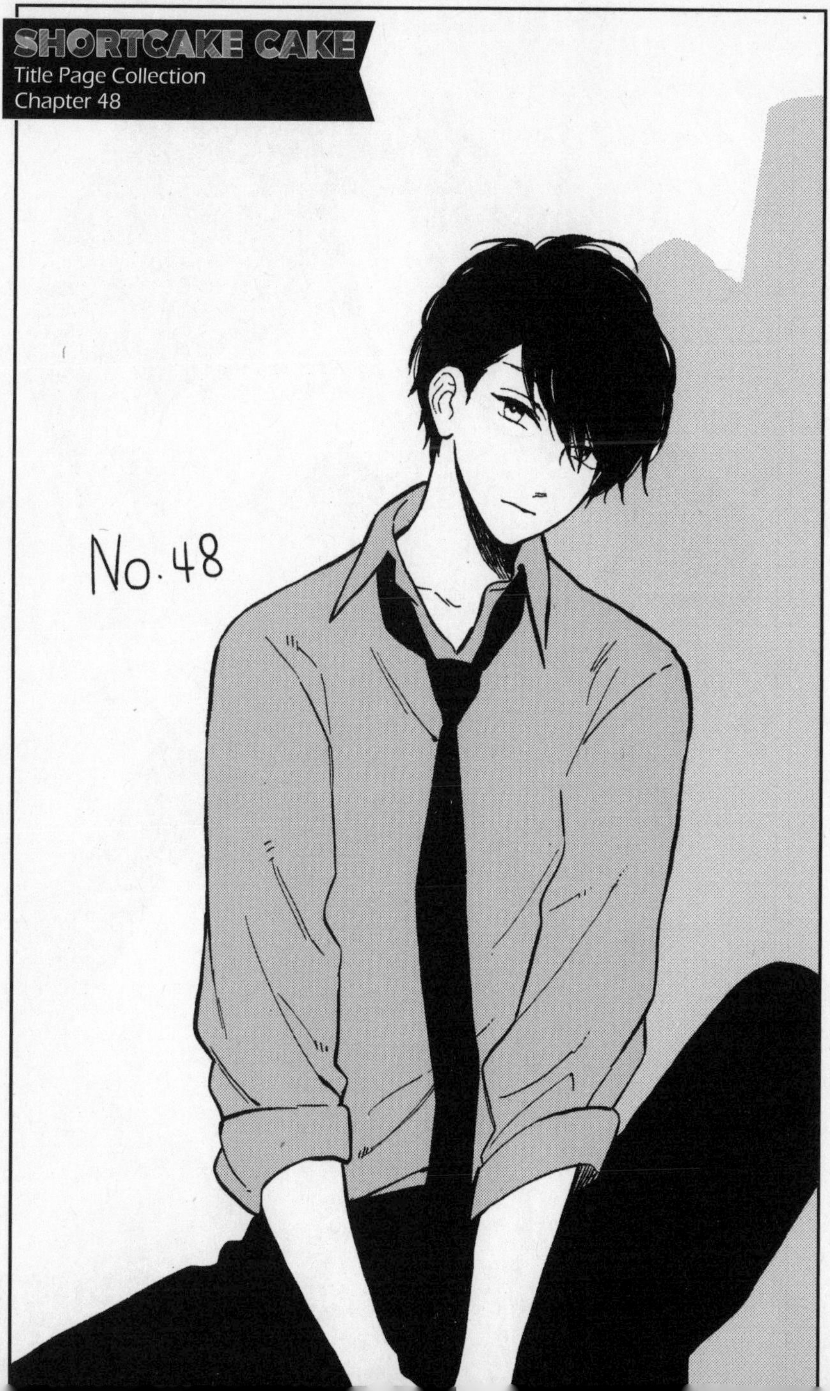
No.48

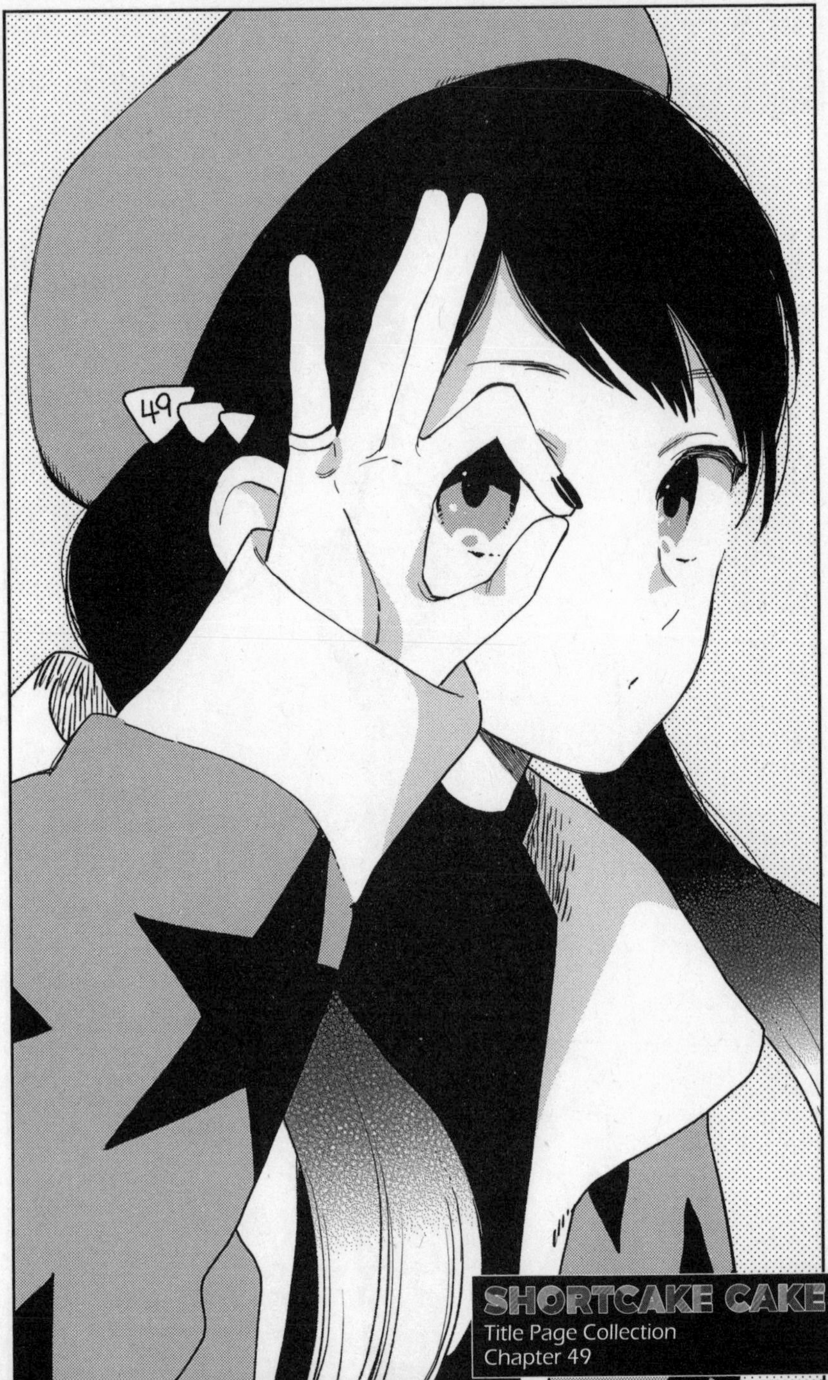
49

SHORTCAKE CAKE
Title Page Collection
Chapter 49

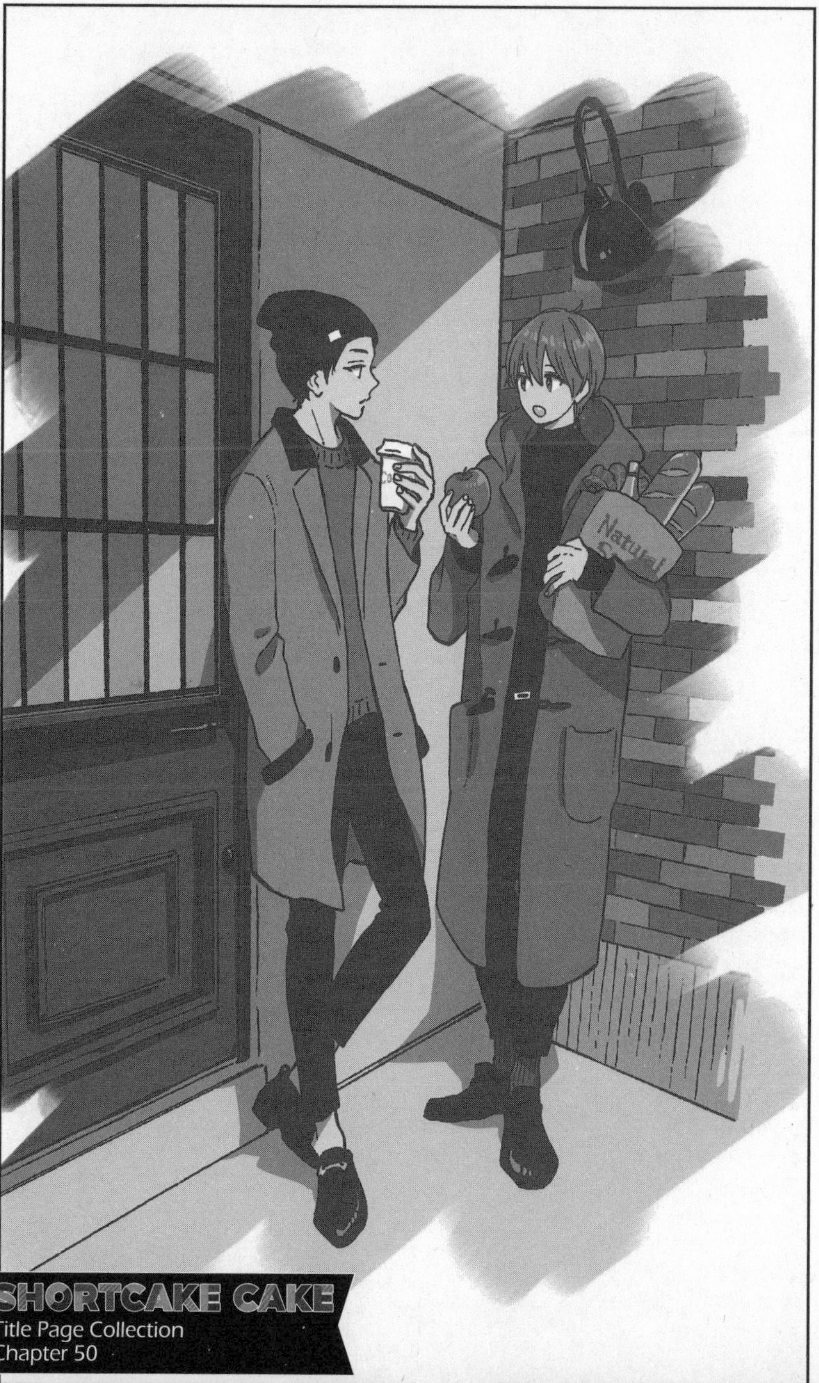
Natural

SHORTCAKE CAKE
Title Page Collection
Chapter 50

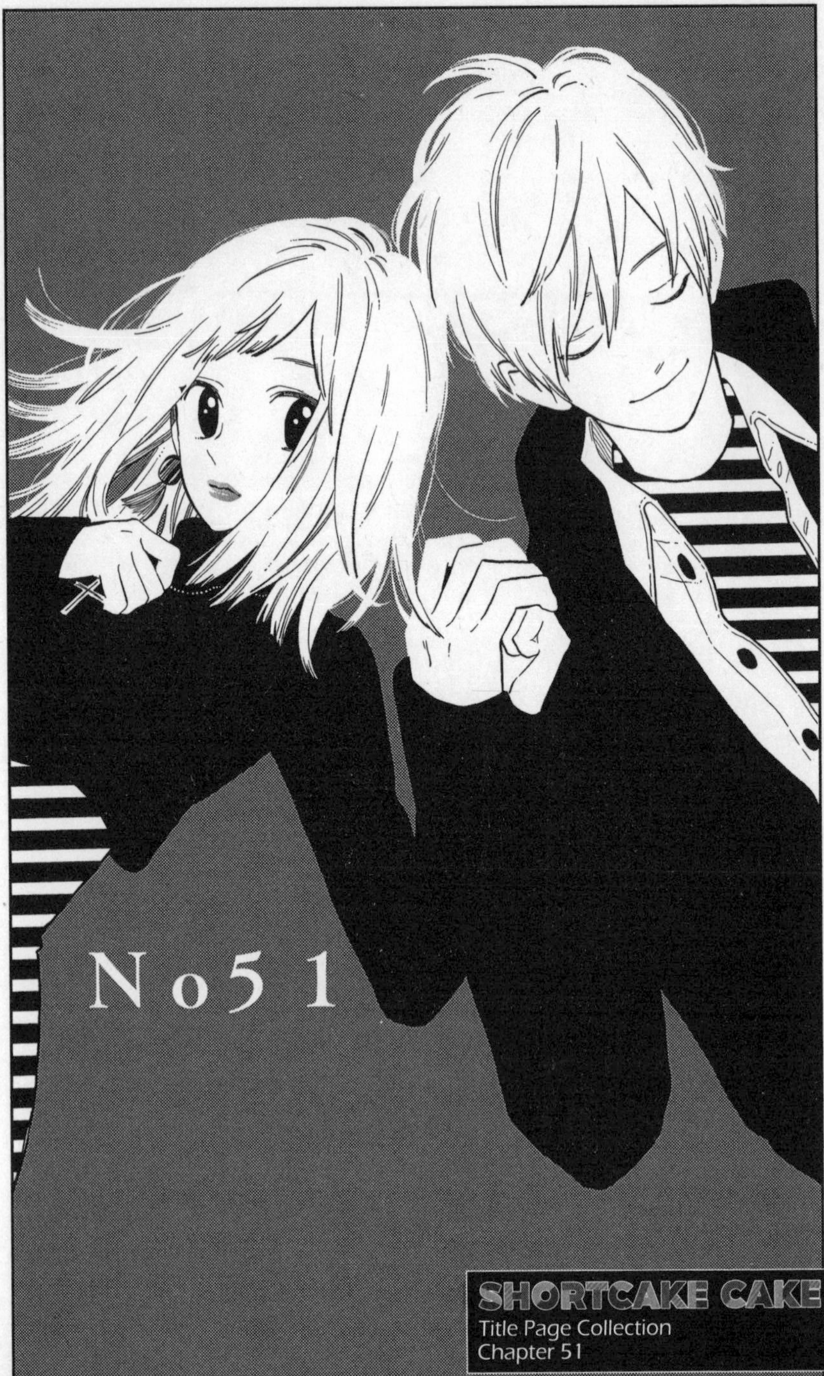
No51
SHORTCAKE CAKE
Title Page Collection
Chapter 51

SHORTCAKE CAKE
Title Page Collection
Chapter 52

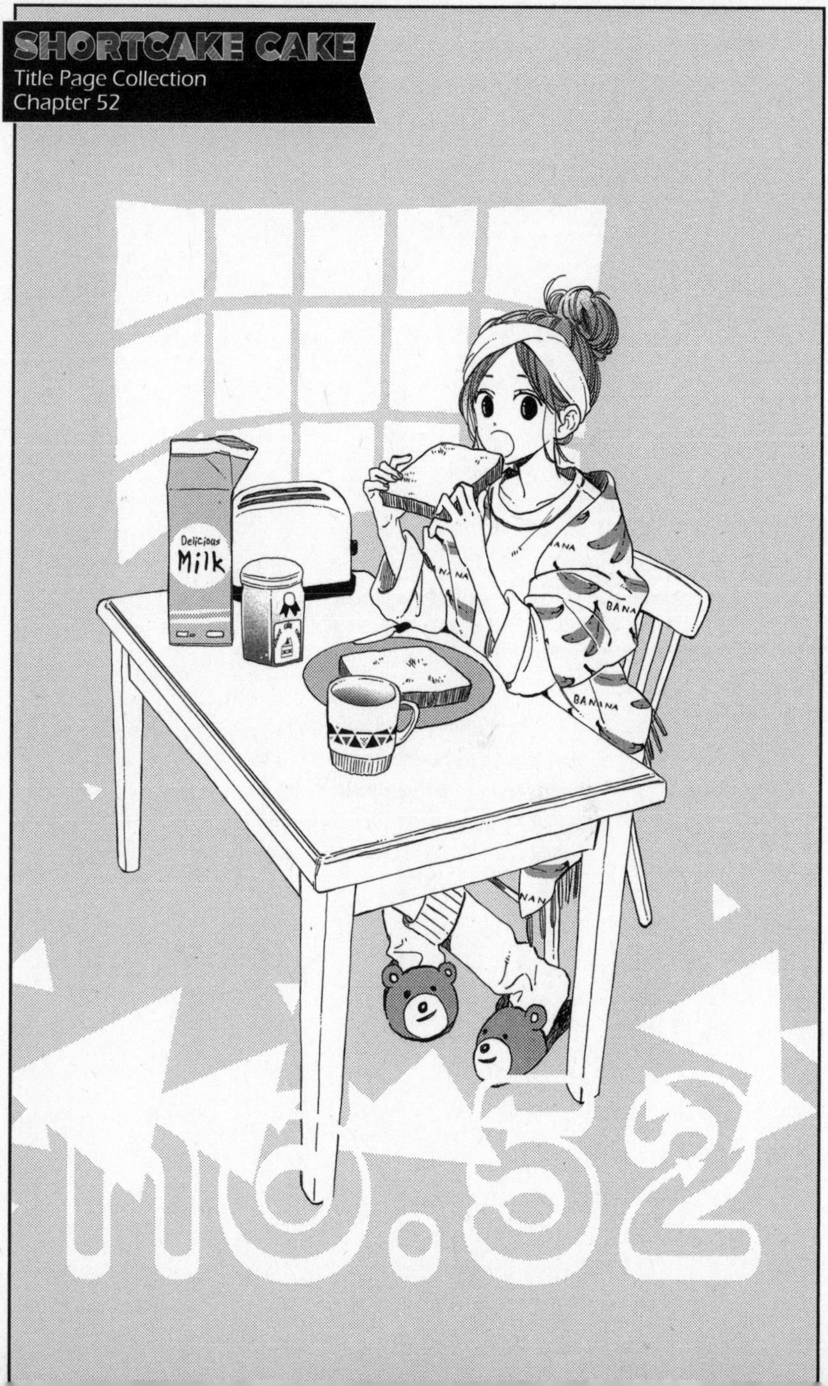
Delicious
Milk
no.52

We started using Twitter.

—suu Morishita

suu Morishita is a creator duo.
The story is by Makiro, and the art is by
Nachiyan. In 2010 they debuted with the
one-shot "Anote Konote." Their works include
Hibi Chouchou and *Shortcake Cake*.

VOLUME 9
SHOJO BEAT EDITION

STORY + ART BY **suu Morishita**

TRANSLATION **Emi Louie-Nishikawa**
TOUCH-UP ART + LETTERING **Inori Fukuda Trant**
DESIGN **Joy Zhang**
EDITOR **Nancy Thistlethwaite**

SHORTCAKE CAKE © 2015 by Suu Morishita
All rights reserved.
First published in Japan in 2015 by SHUEISHA Inc., Tokyo.
English translation rights arranged by SHUEISHA Inc.

The stories, characters and incidents mentioned
in this publication are entirely fictional.

Printed in the U.S.A.

Published by VIZ Media, LLC
P.O. Box 77010
San Francisco, CA 94107

10 9 8 7 6 5 4 3 2 1
First printing, August 2020

MEDIA
viz.com

shojobeat.com

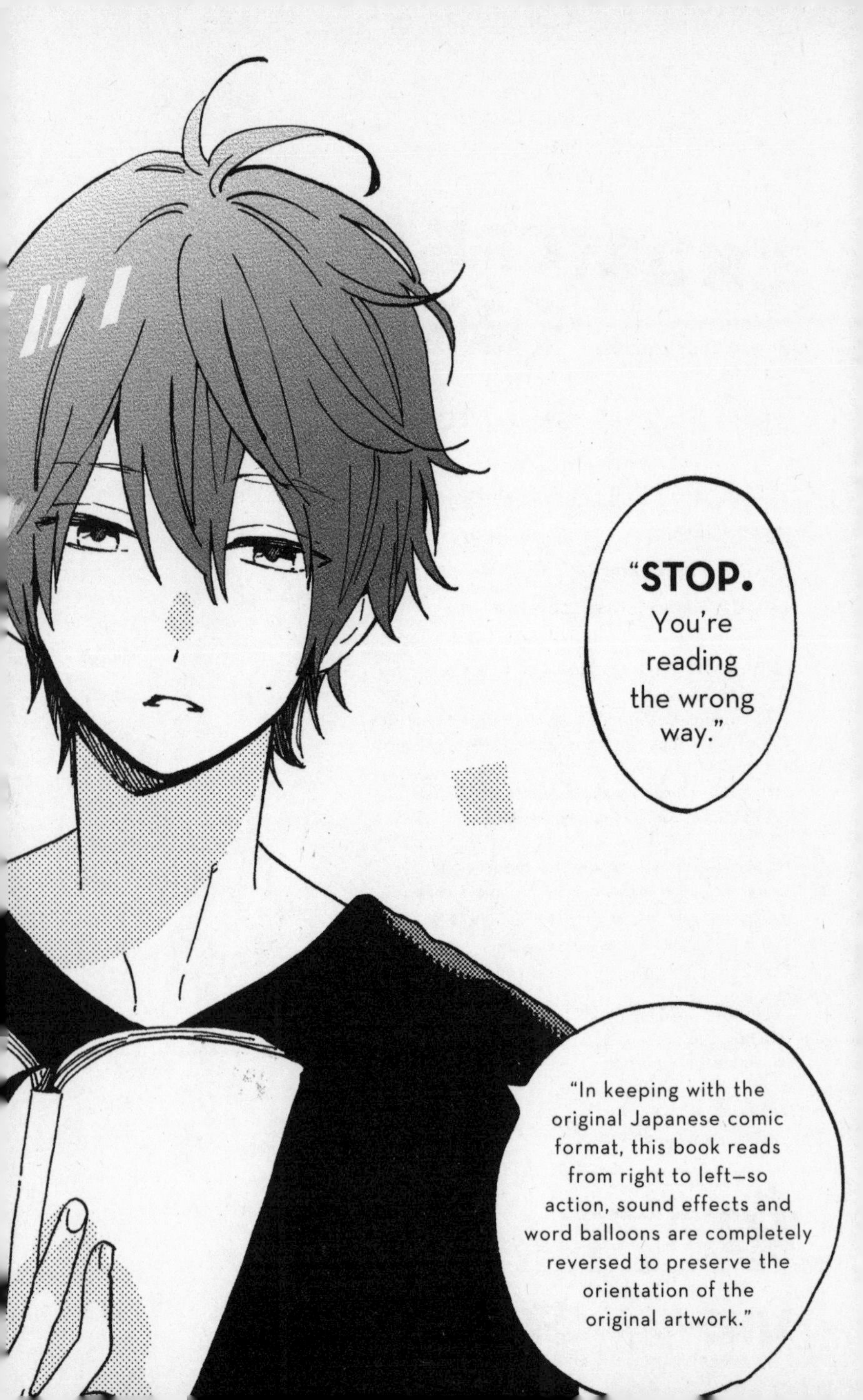
"STOP. You're reading the wrong way."
"In keeping with the original Japanese comic format, this book reads from right to left—so action, sound effects and word balloons are completely reversed to preserve the orientation of the original artwork."